British Government and Politics

Books in the Politics Study Guides series

British Government and Politics: A Comparative Guide (2nd edition)
Duncan Watts

US Government and Politics (2nd edition)
William Storey

International Politics: An Introductory Guide
Alasdair Blair and Steven Curtis

Devolution in the United Kingdom (2nd edition)
Russell Deacon

Political Parties in Britain
Matt Cole and Helen Deighan

Democracy in Britain
Matt Cole

The Changing Constitution
Kevin Harrison and Tony Boyd

The Judiciary, Civil Liberties and Human Rights
Steven Foster

The Prime Minister and Cabinet
Stephen Buckley

Britain and the European Union
Alistair Jones

Pressure Groups
Duncan Watts

The Politics of Northern Ireland
Joanne McEvoy

The UK Parliament
Moyra Grant

The American Presidency
Duncan Watts

Electoral Systems and Voting in Britain
Chris Robinson

Political Communication
Steven Foster

euppublishing.com/series/posg

British Government and Politics

A Comparative Guide

Second edition

Duncan Watts

EDINBURGH
University Press

First edition published 2006

Edinburgh University Press Ltd
22 George Square, Edinburgh EH8 9LF
www.euppublishing.com

Typeset in 11/13pt Monotype by
Servis Filmsetting Ltd, Stockport, Cheshire, and
printed and bound in Great Britain by
CPI Group (UK) Ltd, Croydon CR0 4YY

A CIP record for this book is available from the British Library

ISBN 978 0 7486 4494 0 (hardback)
ISBN 978 0 7486 4454 4 (paperback)
ISBN 978 0 7486 4455 1 (webready PDF)
ISBN 978 0 7486 5494 9 (epub)
ISBN 978 0 7486 5493 2 (Amazon ebook)

Contents

List of boxes   x
List of tables   xiii
Leaders of the two main parties in Britain since 1945   xv
Votes and seats in British general elections since 1945   xvi
US presidents since 1945   xviii

**1 The Setting of British Politics: British Society
   and the British People**   1
   Introduction   2
   The historical background   2
   British society and the British way of life   2
   Immigration and religion: their impact   6
   Political change   13
   Underlying British ideas and values   14

2 The Constitution and the Protection of Rights   24
   Part A   The Constitution
   Introduction   25
   The growth of interest in constitutional revision   26
   The characteristics of constitutions   27
   The Constitution of the United Kingdom   31
   The Blair government and the Constitution   35
   Part B   The Protection of Rights in Britain
   Introduction   44
   The protection of rights in Britain   44
   The case of South Africa   53
   The case of the USA   54

3 The Legislature   60
   Introduction   61
   What is the legislature?   61
   The structure of legislatures   62
   The British House of Lords   64
   The main functions of the House of Commons   74

The House as a watchdog over government   77
Elected representatives: the duties and responsibilities of
    British MPs   81
Parliamentary reform in recent years   90
The social composition of elected legislators   93
The pay and conditions of legislators   102
The case of Denmark   103
The case of the USA   104

4   **The Executive**   111
    Introduction   112
    The Executive in parliamentary and presidential
        systems of government   114
    The distribution of power within political executives:
        the trend towards first ministerial dominance   116
    The British Cabinet   118
    The role of Prime Minister   127
    The debate about prime ministerial power   128
    Constraints on the British Prime Minister   132
    A presidential prime minister?   134
    British ministers and their civil servants   139
    The conventions of ministerial responsibility   146
    The case of Holland   150
    The case of the USA   152

5   **The Judiciary**   157
    Introduction   158
    Judicial independence   158
    Judicial neutrality   162
    The growing importance of judicial review   173
    The developing trend towards judicial activism   175
    The politicisation of British judges: growing
        judicial power   177
    The case of the European Court of Human Rights   179
    The case of the USA   184

6   **Government Beyond the Centre**   189
    Introduction   190

The devolved United Kingdom   191
Devolution in Scotland   192
Devolution in Wales   202
Is Britain becoming a federal state?   204
English local government   211
The case of Spain   219
The case of the USA   220

7   **Political Parties**   225
Introduction   226
The role of political parties and the nature
    of party systems   227
The history of the two main parties since 1945   232
The attitudes and beliefs of political parties: the notions
    of Left and Right   236
The British Conservative Party   238
The Labour Party   244
Blairism in practice: 1994–2007   247
Third and minor parties in Britain and elsewhere   251
Party membership and finance   252
Party organisation: general trends   261
The organisation of British political parties   264
Party conferences in Britain   265
Party leaders: how the main British parties
    choose them   267
The powers and security of party leaders   270
The decline of political parties: do they still matter?   273
The case of Italy   275
The case of the USA   276

8   **Pressure Groups**   282
Introduction   283
Group activity in modern societies: pressure groups and
    movements   284
Pressure groups and political parties: their differences
    and similarities   285
Classifying pressure groups   287
The methods employed by pressure groups   291

The European dimension to British pressure-group
    activity   297
Pressure groups under recent governments   300
The benefits and disadvantages of pressure groups   306
The case of Scotland   308
The case of the USA   309

9   Voting and Elections   316
Introduction   317
Election campaigning   318
British election campaigns and campaigning   321
Electoral systems   328
Types of electoral system   333
British experience: the operation of FPTP in the general
    election of 2010   338
Some arguments surrounding the debate over
    FPTP versus PR   341
Voting behaviour   347
Voting in Britain   352
Turnout in elections   356
Turnout in the United Kingdom   358
Direct democracy: initiatives and referendums   360
The use of referendums in the United Kingdom   366
The case of France: the use of referendums   367
The case of the USA: election campaigning   368

10 Britain and the European Union   374
Introduction   375
The development and character of the EU   375
Democracy and the Union: the 'democratic deficit' in its
    workings   383
Britain and the EU: the intergovernmentalist approach
    in action   386
The impact of the EU on government and politics in the
    UK   388
Europe: a problem area in British politics   391
Britain, Europe and the future of the EU   397

11 Democracy in Theory and Practice   409
Introduction   410
The development of democracy   411
Democracy: its main forms   412
The characteristics of representative and liberal
    democracies   413
British democracy in practice   415

References   421
Index   433

Boxes

1.1 Recent immigration: asylum seekers, economic
      migrants and EU citizens   7
1.2 The non-white population of England and Wales, 2009   9
1.3 The diversity of Muslim attitudes   12
1.4 The debate about Britishness and being British   14
1.5 Trust in governments and politicians, 2010   18
1.6 Forces that have shaped British society and popular
      attitudes: a summary   19
2.1 Parliamentary sovereignty in the UK   30
2.2 Radical and moderate perspectives on constitutional
      reform   34
2.3 Progress on constitutional reform in the post-Blair era 41
2.4 The difference between liberties and rights   45
2.5 The European Convention on Human Rights   48
2.6 The fate of anti-terrorist legislation under the Human
      Rights Act   51
2.7 The European Union and the protection of rights   52
3.1 The Lords at work, 2008–9   68
3.2 Scrutinising European legislation   69
3.3 The method of appointment to second chambers in
      other countries   75
3.4 Types of bill   77
3.5 MPs and party loyalty   86
3.6 Levels of public confidence in the House of Commons
      and its members   89
3.7 The Coalition and reforms affecting the House of
      Commons   94
3.8 Are legislatures in decline across the world?   105
4.1 The leadership role: heads of state and chief executives 113
4.2 Some characterisations of the British Cabinet   118
4.3 The work of Cabinet committees   122
4.4 The Cabinet under Tony Blair and Gordon Brown   124
4.5 The character and importance of the Centre under
      Tony Blair and Gordon Brown   126

4.6   The Prime Minister and appointment to the Cabinet   129
4.7   The roles of Prime Minister and US President
        compared   137
4.8   The Home Office: the hierarchy of its ministers and
        their roles in early 2011   141
4.9   What sort of people became higher civil servants?   143
4.10   Perspectives on the relationship between ministers and
        their civil servants   145
5.1   The administration of justice in the UK   163
5.2   Judges as protectors of our liberties in Britain: some
        points to bear in mind   180
5.3   The UK, the European Court and prisoners' rights   182
6.1   The referendums in Scotland and Wales   193
6.2   The Scotland Act 1998   194
6.3   Scottish government in practice, since 1999: distinctive
        policies   197
6.4   Future action: the Calman Commission's plans for
        Scottish devolution   199
6.5   A note on devolution in Northern Ireland   205
6.6   Government in the English regions   207
6.7   Could federalism work in Britain?   210
6.8   A note on quangos   212
6.9   The structure of local government   217
7.1   Two-party systems in Britain and the United States   230
7.2   Consensus politics   233
7.3   Adversary politics   235
7.4   What is socialism? Differing perspectives   245
7.5   Tony Blair and the third way   249
7.6   British third and minor parties   253
7.7   State funding in Britain: for and against   262
8.1   A note on terminology   284
8.2   The types of relationship between groups and
        government   293
8.3   British pressure groups and the House of Lords   296
8.4   The use of direct action   298
8.5   Factors influencing the success of different groups   305
9.1   The importance of money in campaigning   320
9.2   Televised debates in British elections   326

9.3   Opinion polls: their uses, accuracy and value   329
9.4   The impact of the mass media on voting   350
9.5   Turnout: some international comparisons   357
9.6   Direct democracy: some definitions   361
10.1   The institutions of the European Union   378
10.2   Policies and policymaking in the EU   382
10.3   Political and popular reactions to Europe in Britain
           and other member states   392
10.4   Postscript: the crisis within the eurozone (2009–11)
           and its implications   401
11.1   Semi or façade democracies   414

Tables

1.1	The ethnic mix of the United Kingdom, 2001	6
1.2	The ethnic mix of England and Wales, 2009	8
1.3	The religious mix of the United Kingdom, 2001	11
3.1	The top five rebellions under the Blair/Brown governments, respectively	85
3.2	The working hours of the House of Commons	93
3.3	Regional averages in female representation, April 2011	96
3.4	Comparison of female representation in the 'top five' countries, the UK and the USA	99
3.5	The number of women elected in selected elections since 1945	100
4.1	Departed Cabinet ministers under the Brown and Cameron premierships	151
5.1	The recruitment of judges: a summary	161
5.2	The representation of women and ethnic minorities on the bench, April 2008	169
7.1	Party membership in European democracies	256
7.2	Membership trends of the three main British parties, 1951–2008	257
7.3	Incomes and spending of the main parties, 2010	260
7.4	The Conservative system in operation: the choice in 2005	268
7.5	The Labour system in operation: the choice in 2010	269
8.1	Examples of British protective (interest) and promotional (cause) groups	290
8.2	British groups: their characteristics summarised	291
8.3	Summary of access points available to British groups	299
8.4	The 'top five' lobbying organisations in April 2011, based on total spending	310
9.1	International voting systems	335
9.2	The outcome in 2010	339
9.3	Party majorities in recent elections	341
9.4	UK electoral systems currently in use	347
9.5	The relative importance of class voting	348

9.6   Average share of the vote for each party in post-war
          elections   352
9.7   Social class categorisations in common use by polling
          companies   354
9.8   Voting behaviour in the 2010 general election   355
9.9   Turnout in post-1945 general and European elections   359
9.10 UK experience of national referendums   367
10.1 An enlarging Union of twenty-seven states   380

Leaders of the two main parties in Britain since 1945

Conservatives	Period as Conservative leader	Labour	Period as Labour leader
Winston Churchill	1940–1955 *1940–1945; 1951–1955	Clement Attlee	1935–1955 *1945–1951
Anthony Eden	1955–1957 *1955–1957	Hugh Gaitskell	1955–1963
Harold Macmillan	1957–1963 *1957–1963	Harold Wilson	1963–1976 *1964–1970; 1974–1976
Alec Douglas Home	1963–1965 *1963–1964	James Callaghan	1976–1981 *1976–1979
Edward Heath	1965–1975 *1970–1974	Michael Foot	1981–1983
Margaret Thatcher	1975–1990 *1979–1990	Neil Kinnock	1983–1992
John Major	1990–1997 *1990–1997	John Smith	1992–1994
William Hague	1997–2001	Tony Blair	1994–2007 *1997–2007
Iain Duncan Smith	2001–2003	Gordon Brown	2007–2010 *2007–2010
Michael Howard	2003–2005	Ed Miliband	2010–
David Cameron	2005– *2010–		

* denotes period in office as Prime Minister

Votes and seats in British general elections since 1945

Year	Party	% votes	No. of seats	% seats
1945	Con	39.8	213	33.3
	Lib	9.0	12	1.9
	Lab	47.8	393	61.4
1950	Con	43.5	298	47.7
	Lib	9.1	9	1.4
	Lab	46.1	315	50.4
1951	Con	48.0	321	51.4
	Lib	2.5	6	1.0
	Lab	48.8	295	47.2
1955	Con	49.7	344	54.6
	Lib	2.7	6	1.0
	Lab	46.4	277	44.0
1959	Con	49.4	365	57.9
	Lib	5.9	6	1.0
	Lab	43.8	258	41.0
1964	Con	43.4	304	48.3
	Lib	11.2	9	1.4
	Lab	44.1	317	50.3
1966	Con	41.9	253	40.2
	Lib	8.5	12	1.9
	Lab	47.9	363	57.6
1970	Con	46.4	330	52.4
	Lib	7.5	6	1.0
	Lab	43.0	287	45.6
1974 (Feb)	Con	37.9	297	46.8
	Lib	19.3	14	2.2
	Lab	37.1	301	47.4

Year	Party	% votes	No. of seats	% seats
1974 (Oct)	Con	35.8	277	43.6
	Lib	18.3	13	2.1
	Lab	39.2	319	50.2
1979	Con	43.9	339	53.4
	Lib	13.8	11	1.7
	Lab	36.9	268	42.4
1983	Con	42.4	397	61.0
	All	25.4	23	3.5
	Lab	27.6	209	32.0
1987	Con	42.3	376	57.8
	All	22.6	22	3.4
	Lab	30.9	229	35.2
1992	Con	41.9	336	51.6
	Lib Dem	17.9	20	3.1
	Lab	34.3	271	41.6
1997	Con	30.7	165	25.0
	Lib Dem	16.8	46	7.0
	Lab	43.2	419	63.4
2001	Con	31.7	166	25.2
	Lib Dem	18.3	52	7.9
	Lab	40.7	412	62.5
2005	Con	32.4	198	30.7
	Lib Dem	22.0	62	9.6
	Lab	35.2	356	55.1
2010	Con	36.1	307	47.2
	Lib Dem	23.0	57	8.8
	Lab	29.0	258	39.7

US Presidents since 1945

President	Party	Term in White House
Franklin D. Roosevelt	Democrat	1945
Harry S. Truman	Democrat	1945–1953
Dwight Eisenhower	Republican	1953–1961
John F. Kennedy	Democrat	1961–1963
Lyndon Johnson	Democrat	1963–1969
Richard Nixon	Republican	1969–1974
Gerald Ford	Republican	1974–1977
James Carter	Democrat	1977–1981
Ronald Reagan	Republican	1981–1989
George H. Bush	Republican	1989–1993
William Clinton	Democrat	1993–2001
George W. Bush	Republican	2001–2009
Barack Obama	Democrat	2009–

CHAPTER 1

The Setting of British Politics: British Society and the British People

Contents

Introduction	2
The historical background	2
British society and the British way of life	2
Immigration and religion: their impact	6
Political change	13
Underlying British ideas and values	14

Overview

In this opening chapter, we examine the background against which the British political system operates. By understanding the nature of British political development and society, and the values shared by many of the island's peoples, we can better appreciate key institutions and practices in British politics, and the attitudes and behaviour of British citizens.

Key issues to be covered in this chapter

- Aspects of the historical development of Britain, in particular national unity and the preference for peaceful change
- The traditional cohesion of British society and the absence of divisions based on ethnicity, language or religion
- The forces that have contributed to its growing diversity, including the rise of nationalism in Scotland and Wales, immigration and the impact of growing support for Islamic religious beliefs
- The meaning of the term 'political culture'
- Characteristic British political attitudes and habits, and the changes affecting them in recent decades

Introduction

Our study of British politics is primarily concerned with the way in which our representative democracy functions. But political systems do not operate in a vacuum. They are shaped by the society in which we live and reflect the assumptions, habits and values of our people. This is as true of Britain as any other country, so that some analysis of the social basis of our political life and of the history and outlook of the British people, seems to be an appropriate place to begin our study of British government and politics.

The historical background

Most of the 196 countries in the world today are relatively recent creations, brought about by a struggle for independence in wars or revolutions from those powers which previously controlled their destiny. However, Britain has a very long tradition of independent nationhood, free from successful invasion for nearly a thousand years. Our institutions have evolved gradually over centuries, change usually coming about not as a result of civil upheaval or warfare, but by a process of adaptation. Generally speaking, they have maintained their name and much of their original form, but the way in which they operate has been modified in response to particular circumstances. For this reason, two writers were able to describe the situation as one of 'new wine in old bottles'.[1]

Our largely unbroken history of political independence has been matched by a long history of national unity. Wales was conquered in Tudor times and has since the Act of Union (1535), been governed via decisions taken at Westminster. Scotland, an independent country until the Act of Union (1707), was governed in the same way until it gained its parliament in 1999. Scots have long been aware of their sense of nationality and proud of their different administrative and legal systems, but over recent centuries the relationship between the two countries has generally been a good one, their fortunes interwoven.

Ireland is a different case. Relations with our neighbouring island have been turbulent and often unhappy. Twenty-six counties gained their independence from the rest of the UK in 1922, but the majority of inhabitants in the six counties of Northern Ireland have been keen to retain their allegiance to Great Britain. The province of Northern Ireland has had a troubled history. It had its own parliament until the era of prolonged disturbance and political violence that culminated in the imposition of Direct Rule from Westminster in 1969. As a result of the **Belfast ('Good Friday') Agreement** reached in 1998, it once again acquired an elected assembly.

There have at times been tensions between the component countries of the United Kingdom, but – leaving aside the substantial problems surrounding Ireland – for most of the time it has been a cohesive political unit, marked by a lack of serious conflict. As we shall see, such a portrayal of British political development may seem complacent and inaccurate in the light of some changes in recent decades. But if this book had been written thirty or forty years ago, few would have questioned the essential accuracy of the description.

The traditions of national independence and broad political unity owe much to the facts of geography. Britain is an island, the Channel offering protection from invasion and insulating the country from any revolutionary movements of the Continent. Indeed, one of the other important characteristics of British political development has been the preference for peaceful change.

Britain has evolved primarily by non-revolutionary means and has enjoyed a remarkable historical continuity. There has been no major break or upheaval, such as the American, French and Russian revolutions, nor much in the way of civil war or conflict. Certainly, riots and rebellions were common in both the sixteenth and seventeenth centuries. Moreover, the latter provided disruption to the traditional pattern of constitutional evolution, witnessing as it did 'a civil war, a royal decapitation, an abdication and an Interregnum generally regarded by our European neighbours as a radical horror, much as the Bolshevist regime in Russia was regarded by the other European powers in the 1920s and 1930s'.[2] But over the following centuries, the British reputation for peace and stability was restored. Although there has been violence at times in British history, there has been a degree of continuity that is unusual in comparison with most other countries. As a result, there has been institutional continuity. Britain has made fewer efforts than most countries to erase the political past and start again. The essential structure of our constitutional arrangements has been bent and bruised, but not broken.

Since the late 1960s, the picture of Britain as a united nation has been under threat as a result of the continuing troubles in Northern Ireland, and the developing strength of the nationalist movement in Scotland and Wales. In Scotland, the impetus to intensified national feeling has come from a variety of factors, including its distinctive historical traditions and institutions, the economic potential of 'Scotland's oil' and a feeling of remoteness from and neglect by Westminster. The resurgence of nationalism has led to strong support for the Scottish National Party that is committed to national independence from England. In Wales, the desire for separatism is much weaker and the growth of nationalism has a stronger cultural and linguistic dimension. Support for Plaid Cymru, the nationalist party, has been largely concentrated in five constituencies in rural mid-north Wales, although since the advent of devolution it has broken out of its rural Welsh-speaking heartland and captured traditionally strong Labour areas in industrial South Wales.

Today, the picture of national unity has to be qualified. Political diversity is now a feature of the United Kingdom. So too the **homogeneity** of British society has come under challenge. There is greater social diversity than in the Britain of fifty years ago.

British society and the British way of life

It was until a few decades ago a common-place in books relating to British society for writers to point out that Britain has been relatively free from much of the internal disorder that occurs when different sections of the community are pitted against each other. In a description of the social fabric of British politics, Blondel[3] described Britain as a relatively homogeneous society. Society was seen as cohesive, there being none of the important divisions of **ethnicity**, religion, language and culture to be found in other European states and the USA. We were portrayed as an integrated community in which values did not differ radically between different social groups.

In the absence of such distinctions, **social class** is the phenomenon that attracted particular attention. Continentals have long portrayed the British as unduly obsessed by social class and seen this as the explanation for an assortment of our economic and political problems. By comparison with countries such as Australia and the United States, considerations of class have been important and the British have been conscious of their social status in relation to others. But although at times this has led to feelings of envy and resentment, it has not usually provoked substantial tensions between different sections of the community of the type that threaten social harmony and cohesion.

Neither has that overall homogeneity been challenged by any town and country divide. Britain is a highly urbanised and industrialised country in which almost 40 per cent of the people live in seven large conurbations, rather more in towns of over 10,000 inhabitants and only 20 per cent living in the rural areas, in small towns and villages. There have never been the strong clashes of interest between town and country that characterise countries such as France with its powerful agrarian lobby.

The changing nature of British society in recent decades
Over the last four or five decades, British society has been transformed in several respects. Social class is less important and there is greater social mobility than in the early post-1945 years. Whereas in the 1960s, two thirds of the population were categorised as working class and a third middle class (based on such considerations as occupation, income, location, housing, accent, spending habits and general lifestyle), today the two categories are broadly equal. Education has been a great leveller, providing new opportunities for vast numbers of young people born into relatively poor circumstances, allowing them to acquire qualifications and improve their job prospects and earning capacity.

If divisions based on class have become less significant, in other respects Britain is now much more socially diverse. Britain has always had minority populations and successive bouts of immigration have modified the national character and shaped our national development. But until the 1950s, this did not significantly challenge broad social cohesion or ethnic unity. Since then, the situation has changed considerably. In spite of the introduction of controls, the onset of **New Commonwealth immigration** led to a substantial increase in numbers of Afro-Caribbean, Asian and other immigrants.

More recently, the entry of **refugees** and **asylum seekers** (whether as genuine seekers after political freedom or **economic migrants** in search of a better way of life) and the arrival of people from new member states of the European Union have further added to the diversity of the British population. The term 'super-diversity' is now sometimes used to describe the UK social composition.

Immigration and religion: their impact

The 2001 Census revealed that the UK was more culturally diverse than ever before. It showed that overall, the million or so non-white population of 1970 had become 4.6 million (7.9 per cent). Of those who belonged to other ethnic groups, Indians were the largest group, followed by Pakistanis, those of mixed ethnic backgrounds, black Caribbeans, black Africans and Bangladeshis. The remaining minority ethnic groups each individually accounted for less than 0.5 per cent of the UK population and together accounted for a further 1.4 per cent. More than half of the non-white inhabitants were born in Britain. Four out of five Afro-Caribbeans under thirty five had begun their life here and there were as many Afro-Caribbean Britons under thirty with a white parent as there were with two black parents.

Table 1.1 The ethnic mix of the United Kingdom, 2001

Nation	Total population	Asian and black	% Asian and black
England	49,138,931	4,459,470	9.1
Northern Ireland	1,685,167	12,569	0.7
Scotland	5,062,011	101,677	2.0
Wales	2,903,085	61,580	2.1
Total	58,789,194	4,635,296	7.9

Figures provided by the Office for National Statistics and based on the 2001 Census

NB The proportion of minority ethnic groups in England rose from 6% to 9% between 1991 and 2001, partly as a result of the addition of a new category, mixed ethnic groups.

Box 1.1 Recent immigration: asylum seekers, economic migrants and EU citizens

An estimated 567,000 people arrived to live in the UK in 2009, which was consistent with levels for the previous five years. Non-British citizens accounted for 83 per cent of all immigrants; a third were from EU countries. Immigration for formal study was the most common reason stated for entry (37 per cent), followed by work-related reasons (34 per cent).

Asylum seekers and non-EU economic migrants
As a signatory to the United Nations Convention Relating to the Status of Refugees, the UK has a responsibility not to return refugees to a country where they would face hunger and/or persecution. Some immigrants of the last decade or so have fled from war zones in which the British have been fighting, in particular Afghanistan, Iraq and the Balkans, following the particularly brutal wars after the break-up of Yugoslavia in the 1990s. Others claiming asylum include economic migrants seeking a better and perhaps freer way of life in Britain. They have come from countries such as Iran, Somalia, Sri Lanka and Turkey.

Immigration from 'new' EU countries of Central and Eastern Europe
Since the expansion of the EU from fifteen to twenty-five countries in May 2004, the UK has accepted immigrants from several new member states of Central and Eastern Europe. More than a million people from the eight **accession countries** in that region had arrived by April 2008. In particular, Poles (a majority of those who registered under the Worker Registration Scheme) have made a big impact on the composition of several towns and cities. Other groups have derived from Slovakia, Lithuania and (in smaller numbers) from the Czech Republic, Estonia, Hungary, Latvia and Slovenia.

Those who belong to the **ethnic minorities** are not evenly distributed across the country, tending to live in the large urban areas. The different groups share some characteristics, but there are often greater differences between the individual ethnic groups than between the minority ethnic population as a whole and the white British people.

Table 1.2 The ethnic mix of England and Wales, 2009

Ethnic group	% of population	% rate of annual growth
White	87.9	0.1
Mixed	1.3	4.7
Asian or Asian British	5.9	4.7
Black or black British	2.9	3.4
Chinese	0.4	3.8
Other ethnic group	1.6	13.7

Source: Office for National Statistics (ONS).

The distinctive feature of entrants from the New Commonwealth (and, more recently, of many asylum seekers from elsewhere) was that in many cases they were highly visible, because of a different skin colour. Migrants from Ireland or Central and Eastern Europe could blend in more easily with the way of life of the native population, whereas the negative attitudes and sometimes evident hostility experienced by new black immigrants made it more difficult for them to adapt to Britain's traditional culture.

Immigration has had a particular impact upon some towns and cities. Nearly half of Britain's non-white population lives in Greater London. The area of the country with the second largest proportion of the minority ethnic population is the West Midlands (nearly 14 per cent), followed by Yorkshire (8 per cent). **Multiculturalism** and **multiethnicity** have arrived and are here to stay. In fewer than thirty local authorities do ethnic minorities make up more than 15 per cent of the population. Leicester has the highest proportion of any city outside London, with 22.3 per cent (mainly Indian).

Tensions surrounding immigration

Immigration and race relations have been subjects of political controversy for several decades. At times there have been serious tensions between the white and non-white populations, on occasion disturbances and rioting. Immigration has provoked a sharp reaction

Box 1.2 The non-white population of England and Wales, 2009

The non-white population of England and Wales has grown from 6.6 million in 2001 to 9.1 million in 2009 nearly one-sixth of the population. There are in addition almost a million mixed-race people in the two countries. Data revealed by the ONS in 2011 reveal also that:

- The white British population has remained almost the same since the last census, an increase in births being broadly balanced by a similar number of people migrating.
- The white Irish population has declined by more than 70,000, because of falling birth rates and migration.
- The increase in the 'other white' population from 1.4 to 1.9 million is largely accounted for by immigration from Eastern Europe, but there have also been greater numbers arriving from Australia, Canada, New Zealand and South Africa.
- The non-white population has increased by more than 2.45 million, two thirds of the increase due to net migration, the rest mainly to higher birth rates among ethnic minority groups.
- The Chinese population has the highest growth rate of any of the ethnic groups, growing at an estimated 8.6 per cent per year.
- The increasing numbers of the four Asian groups has been in part due to immigration but also due to natural change – young age profiles result in a strong birth rate and a low number of deaths. The black African group has increased much more rapidly than the black Caribbean, largely because of Africans seeking asylum from the democratic Congo, Eritrea, Somalia and Zimbabwe.
- In 225/423 local authorities, the population comprises more than 90 per cent of white people, the 'whitest' being Blanaeu Gwent in Wales (96.5 per cent) and Copeland in Cumbria (96.3 per cent).
- The size of the non-British element has remained stable in London, but risen substantially in other areas, more than doubling in the North East and the South West. Brent, in London, is the most ethnically diverse borough, only just over a third of its population (38.1 per cent) qualifying as white British, the rest being predominantly mixed-race, Asian, black and Irish.

Source: 2001 census and ONS statistical bulletin, 'Population Estimates by Ethnic Group 2002–2009', 18 May 2011.

from the political **Far Right**, which has gained in electoral support in a number of northern towns and cities and itself been involved in civil conflict. The issues of asylum seekers and illegal immigrants arriving in substantial numbers arouses particular anxiety, when it seems that controls in place can be evaded.

Within ethnic minority groups, there are some more radical members who are alienated from the rest of society (see Box 1.3 on The diversity of Muslim attitudes). Others feel disaffected, perhaps conscious of the discrimination they still experience. But many have enriched the British culture and lifestyle, by the contributions they can make to the economy and society. When they can gain acceptance, they are contented with their lot and as integrated as they wish to be into the British way of life. They may well to different degrees wish to retain their heritage and identity, but still consider themselves as British.

At best, the relations between the different communities have been generally harmonious and problems that arise are ones that can be accommodated. Discrimination and sometimes intimidation do occur and such wrongs pose a challenge to white society. The majority of white people, particularly those whose routine brings them into contact with others of all ethnic backgrounds, have been tolerant and fairly comfortably embraced change. There has not been anything like the recurrent ethnic and racial problems that beset some other countries. Politicians – with a few prominent exceptions – are keen to promote good race relations and do or say nothing to endanger social cohesion.

Religious diversity
Religion has been a greater source of division than in the past. Religious rivalry has not been a traditional feature of the United Kingdom, except as part of the complex of problems associated with Northern Ireland. In countries ranging from Canada to France, religion has been an important factor in political life, but in Britain tolerance of religious differences – often based on indifference to the topic – has been the norm. But again, religion has been a cause of diversity in recent years.

In particular, immigration has been a key factor associated with religious diversity, leading to a rapid increase in support for Islamic beliefs

Table 1.3 The religious mix of the United Kingdom, 2001

Religion	England	Scotland	Wales	Northern Ireland	UK total	UK %
Buddhist	139,046	6,830	5,407	533	151,816	0.3
Christian	35,251,244	3,294,545	2,087,242	1,446,386	42,079,417	71.6
Hindu	546,982	5,564	5,439	825	558,810	1.0
Jewish	257,671	6,448	2,256	365	266,740	0.5
Muslim	1,524,887	42,557	21,739	1,943	1,591,126	2.7
Sikh	327,343	6,572	2,015	219	336,149	0.6
Other religions	143,811	26,974	6,909	1,143	178,837	0.3
Total all religions	38,190,984	3,389,490	2,131,007	1,451,414	45,162,895	76.8
No religion	7,171,332	1,394,460	537,935		9,103,727	15.5
Not stated	3,776,515	278,061	234,143		4,288,719	7.3
Total no. religion not stated	10,947,847	1,672,521	772,078	233,853	13,626,299	23.2

Figures provided by the Office for National Statistics and based on the 2001 Census. The no religion/not stated figures are not listed for N. Ireland and this accounts for the slight discrepancy in the final percentages.

Box 1.3 The diversity of Muslim attitudes

British Muslims derive from many different countries. They cannot be lumped together as a homogeneous group. They number some 1.6 million, many of whom were born in this country. Like everyone else, they have different personalities, different interests and different opinions. In religious matters, some are strict and devout, others less so.

Muslims have been in Britain since the 1950s. Specific Muslim groups originally settled in specific British cities. Those from Kashmir settled in Birmingham and Bradford, to be joined by others from the Punjab and North Western Pakistan. Indians Muslims from Gujarat settled in northern cities such as Huddersfield, Bangladeshis flocked to East London whilst North Africans and other Arabs went to live in West London. Many of these immigrants belonged to groups of Sunni Islam, but Britain also received small Shia groups from countries such as Iraq. In other words, Muslims from different places often had religious leanings that reflected different shades of Islamic belief.

The first generation of Muslims to arrive in Britain were often victims of racist attitudes and could do little but accept them. The second generation was more willing to challenge them and sometimes this led to fierce confrontations with the police and other authorities. But many members of Muslim communities still wanted to find and share a common set of values, hopes and aspirations that united whites and non-whites, and not to separate themselves from the rest of society. In the last decade, a more radical Islam has found a hearing in Britain.

(see Table 1.3 for an indication of the multi-faith society that Britain has become). This has had political repercussions. On the one hand, there have been demands from some Muslims for their own schools, raising issues about the desirability of allowing or encouraging separatist tendencies. On the other, the attack on the World Trade Center in 2001 (also known as 9/11) has had an impact, at the very least alerting us to changes that had already taken place in British society. A few months before, disturbances in the north of England had laid bare the grievances of British Muslims, forcing recognition of the fact that community relations were no longer just about race relations, but about faith as well. The post-Iraq War situation has led to developing antagonism among some Muslims for the actions taken by Britain and America against their fellow believers in that troubled country. In the 2005 election, some Muslim associations advised their followers not to support the Blair government that took Britain into war.

The position of Muslims in Britain has been the subject of much discussion since the outbreak of **terrorism** in London on 7 July 2005, better known as the London bombings. Fifty-six were killed and some 700 injured in the explosions. A fortnight later, further attacks again brought the capital to a halt, but this time they were bungled and no casualties resulted. The attacks were not the activities of foreign extremists brought up in oppressive states abroad and suffering from severe deprivation. They were the work of people brought up in multiracial Britain and thus posed a challenge not just for ministers, but for **civil society** too.

Political change

In recent years, diversity and tension have characterised aspects of the social scene. There has also been political change. We have seen that in response to growing national feeling the Scots have gained their own Parliament. So too has Wales gained a National Assembly. Such moves have been part of a developing interest in **devolution**, the decentralisation of power from Westminster. Some who opposed devolution feared a Balkanisation of the United Kingdom, believing that it would inevitably lead to eventual separatism. Devolution again raises the issue of what it means to be British, Scottish, Welsh or English.

The debate about identity has been given another twist by a further development of the last three decades or so, British membership of the European Community, now Union (see Chapter 10). Since the signing of the **Maastricht Treaty**, British people have become citizens of the European Union, although surveys suggest that the overwhelming majority do not consider themselves to be European in the way that inhabitants of France or Holland might do. The issue of Britain in Europe has posed challenges for politicians of all parties, for as yet there is little sign that the British feel enthusiastic about being part of the Union. They may perceive some advantages

Box 1.4 The debate about Britishness and being British

As a result of the issues surrounding ethnicity and to a lesser extent devolution there has been much discussion of national identity and the nature and values of Britishness in recent years. Today, the term 'Britishness' is used particularly in relation to the attempt to define what it means to be British. In a legal sense, people who were born in Britain or who are legally recognised as citizens can be described as British. According to this view, differences of ethnic background, language or religion are irrelevant. There are black Britons and white Britons, Hindu and Christian Britons. In a broader sense, Britishness is a term that refers to the common culture and national identity of the people of the United Kingdom, particularly those on the mainland.

In this wider sense, there is no prescribed list of qualities or characteristics that make up 'Britishness', but a recent CRE poll found that 86 per cent of those interviewed agreed that you do not have to be white to be British.[4] In June 2005, religious leaders debating 'Islam and Muslims in the World Today' at a London conference, discussed what they believed being British involved. Their views encompassed core values such as freedom of expression and religious practice, participation in the democratic system, valuing education and respect to and tolerance for others. But other speakers felt that Britain had a long way to go before all its communities could be united in a single purpose. One noted the lack of national cohesion in Britain, observing that 'people have more allegiance to football teams than they have to Great Britain' and went on to ask: 'Where is the glue that is going to hold society together?'

for the country in membership, but perhaps because of their proud traditions as an island race, and differences of language and culture, they are not yet convinced of the merits of closer involvement with our European partners.

Underlying British ideas and values

We use the term 'culture' in referring to the way of life that people experience, to describe the sum of their inherited and cherished ideas, knowledge and values. Their beliefs and values, and the things that they care about, are based on the experiences to which they are exposed throughout their lives. They may also derive from their class, ethnic group, language, gender or religion.

In assessing the attitudes and way of life of a people, it is easy to fall back on generalisations as a shorthand means of describing what they are like. Sometimes, these are related to ideas about national or group character. When in the 1960s the Beach Boys referred to 'California girls', the image they intended to convey was of a sun-tanned, lithe, fun-loving and easy-going category of young women. The term is a stereotype, but many members of their audience probably had a clear impression of what such girls were like. However, such generalisations have obvious limitations and are insufficient for those who want to analyse the culture of a country. They want a more reliable tool and turn to survey research. They find out the responses of a selected sample of the population to a series of questions about beliefs and actions, and then assess the overall findings.

Political culture refers to culture in its political aspect. It is the term given to those widely shared political beliefs, values and norms most citizens share concerning the relationship of citizens to government and to one another. Pye[5] describes it as 'the sum of the fundamental values, sentiments and knowledge that give form and substance to the political process'.

These long-term attitudes, ideas and traditions are passed on from one generation to the next. Usually, we think of the political culture of a country such as Britain, France or the United States, but it may be the citizens of an ethnic or religious community who are under consideration – perhaps the people living in a geographic community such as Londoners or Europeans, or those with a shared identity such as French Canadians or Sikhs in the subcontinent.

Political culture is different from public opinion. The term **public opinion** refers to the cluster of attitudes and beliefs held by people about a variety of issues, in our case those concerning politics and policy issues. It will vary on and across the issues of the day. By contrast, political culture – in Heywood's terminology[6] – 'is fashioned out of long-term values rather than simply people's reactions to specific policies and problems'.

In attempting to understand and categorise the political culture of any country or group, we often fall back upon references to national character and come out with generalised, impressionistic observations such as the observation that Italian politics are unstable, because of the volatile Mediterranean temperament of the Italian people. However, attempts have been made in several surveys to investigate the idea of political culture more closely. By taking a selected sample of the electorate and questioning those chosen about their political actions and beliefs, and then aggregating the findings, researchers have been able to search for patterns and produce a profile of the political culture of the sample. By inference, because the sample was a representative one, then the survey can inform us about the political culture of the entire population.

Research findings in a particularly country cannot be regarded as applicable for all of the people for all of the time. They inevitably focus on what the majority of the people appear to think and feel. However, some of the surveys carried out since the 1960s have pointed to the differences in the political beliefs of individuals within the same society. It has also shown that political culture is not an unchanging landscape, a fixed background against which the political process operates. Attitudes can evolve and change over time, for there are in society often a number of forces at work which serve to modify popular attitudes, among them migration and the emergence in a number of liberal democracies of a substantial underclass. Both can be a cause of greater diversity in popular attitudes, for immigrants and those alienated from majority lifestyles may have a looser attachment with prevailing cultural norms. In the words of one author, 'culture moves'.

Survey work is geared to improving our understanding of the political values of citizens in democratic countries. It enables us to make comparisons about the attitudes that characterise their inhabitants. Some surveys have pointed to the similarity of people's concerns across the globe. In 1965, an American, Hadley Cantril[7] found that they want a happy family life, a decent standard of living and good health and – in politics – they like conditions of stability and fear warfare.

More recently, Ron Inglehart[8] in research published in 1989 and 1997, has separately detected a shift of emphasis. Whereas older citizens emphasise materialist attitudes and values, preferring economic growth, a stable society based on respect for law and order and strong national defence, members of younger generations are more **post-materialist** in their thinking. They are concerned about the importance of ensuring a healthy environment, freedom of expression and more personal power in their social and political life. Writing in 2000, Russell Dalton[9] noted that whereas the proportion of citizens with post-materialist attitudes in Britain and the United States has been around 20 per cent over the last couple of decades, it has grown rapidly in other countries, notably Germany and the Netherlands where it is 36 and 39 per cent respectively.

Almond and Verba: The Civic Culture, 1963[10]

In writing of the British political culture, commentators have often pointed to long-standing features such as the commitment to the democratic process, majority rule and the **rule of law**. They note the preference for strong and effective government, which is equated in the minds of many voters with single party administrations. Yet alongside the importance attached to strong government based on a parliamentary majority, there is also a broad tolerance for the expression of alternative and minority opinions. There is in addition a deep attachment to personal liberty and the rights of the citizen, inroads into which are regarded with considerable mistrust. Excessive regulations, the use of speed cameras and the abandonment of trial by jury in some types of criminal cases make people uneasy, although at a time when the threat of terrorism is widely recognised inroads such as greater airport vigilance and more searches of personal possessions are widely accepted as inevitable and necessary.

Two American political scientists, Almond and Verba, attempted to probe more the attitudes and values that underpin the British political system in a landmark study published in 1963. They found that the British people were proud of and attached to their political institutions, were generally satisfied with what government did for them and combined deference (respect) towards the system with confidence and competence in participating and using it. As a result of the good fortune of historical development, they had reached an ideal mix of active and participant citizen and deferential and passive subject. This made Britain a distinctly manageable country to govern.

More recent survey evidence

In their 1980 update, Almond and Verba[11] noted that some of the attitudes and problems of the 1960s and 1970s had left their mark

Box 1.5 Trust in governments and politicians, 2010

The British Social Attitudes survey (2010)[13] collected data on trust in politicians and government. Following the **parliamentary expenses scandal** of 2009, this was an opportunity to assess the scale of the damage. It found that four in ten people no longer trusted politicians to put the national interest first and the majority of voters believed MPs never told the truth.

The study – charting social attitudes over the last three decades – found that mistrust in politics was now four times higher than it was in the mid '80s. Researchers insisted confidence in the political system had never been particularly high, but the MPs' expenses scandal appeared to have 'helped erode trust yet further'.

Trend data over the last twenty years shows that trust in MPs has remained at consistently low levels. In 1994 half of people (49 per cent) said they would almost never trust a politician to tell the truth when they were 'in a tight corner'. In 2007, this figure was exactly the same and has barely fluctuated.

Trust in government does, however, show decline. In 1987 between 37 per cent and 47 per cent of people trusted the government to put the interests of the country above their political party, but this figure had dropped off significantly by 1996 to just 22 per cent. The figure has only got above 30 per cent in one study since. Trust in politics has hit an all time low in the wake of the MPs expenses scandal as Britain adopts a 'straightforwardly cynical' attitude towards the workings of government.

on the political cultures. Britons had become less deferential and more sceptical of government, their trust in its essential benevolence having seriously declined. More recent research by Curtice and Jowell[12] suggested that the number of British people who trusted government to put the needs of the nation above the interests of party 'just about always/most of the time' fell steadily from 39 per cent in 1974 to 22 per cent in 1996, and 75 per cent trusted the government 'only some of the time/almost never'.

The original Almond and Verba view of British attitudes has been under challenge over recent decades. As we have seen, they themselves later detected signs of a growing distrust of government that has characterised recent decades. More seriously, the emphasis on the peaceful

Box 1.6 Forces that have shaped British society and popular attitudes: a summary

Traditional features pointing to a 'moderate' political culture

- The long history of national independence and unity
- The absence of successful invasion of the British Isles
- Broad historical continuity, the absence of upheaval, the preference for gradualism and peaceful change
- Traditional pride in and respect for governing institutions
- The absence of fundamental social divisions
- Strong attachment to democratic values, the rule of law and personal freedom

The challenge to traditional attitudes and modes of behaviour in recent years

- Increased dissatisfaction with governing institutions
- Decline of deference: less trust in government and of politicians
- Less commitment to peaceful change
- Greater willingness to resort to forms – including violence – of direct action to register protest
- Developing nationalism in parts of the UK
- Doubts about national identity, made more apparent by growing social diversity and EU involvement
- The development of a multiracial society, but increased tension between different communities

nature of British society and agreement about what needs to be done can no longer be taken for granted. There have been increasing levels of recorded crime, sectarian street violence in Northern Ireland, and urban rioting in several large towns and cities. The 'moderate' political culture, with its support of parliamentary government and preference for the rule of law does not command universal consent.

Public dissatisfaction with political institutions and the unwritten constitution has increased and more people seem willing to break the law when their consciences tell them that it is wrong. Support for unconventional forms of protest such as strikes, sit-ins and motorway protests has been on the increase. The activities of animal rights and fuel protesters and the support for countryside marches and anti-war demonstrations suggest a greater willingness to resort to **direct action**, made all the easier in today's society with its ease of communication via new means of technology such as mobile phones.

Broadly, there is still a preference for orderly, peaceful protest and little sympathy for methods that involve violence against people or property. But some of the long-held and generalised comments on British attitudes need to be updated as some traditional features have lost their former relevance. The portrayal of Britain in the early 1970s as a country based on homogeneity (sameness), consensus (broad agreement) and deference (respect for one's social superiors) now seems very outdated and complacent. Such features may have once been established features of British life, but all three characteristics have been under strain since the era when Blondel[14] and Punnett[15] first observed them.

· ·

 What you should have learnt from reading this chapter

- A description of British history, society and attitudes written a few decades ago would have probably read something like this. Continuity and tradition have been significant elements of British political development. Change has come about gradually, by evolutionary rather than revolutionary means. There has been a high degree of national unity in the United Kingdom. British society has been cohesive, not marked by conspicuous ethnic, linguistic or religious differences. It has been characterised by consensual attitudes, citizens generally showing a preference for agreement rather than division, and being willing to defer to and trust those who rule over them.

- Today, this picture seems unduly complacent and in some respects distinctly inaccurate. The preference for moderation and peaceful change has been challenged by some groups willing to resort to direct action to achieve their goals. Many people are much less trusting of government and more cynical about politicians, the more so in the light of the expenses scandal.

- The unity of the United Kingdom cannot be taken for granted, under pressure as it has been from the forces of nationalism in Scotland and Wales. British society has become markedly more diverse, as a result of the impact of Commonwealth and other immigration. This has had a profound impact on some communities, not least in terms of religious belief.

Glossary of key terms

Accession countries Accession is a term that strictly refers to those that join an organisation, but is usually employed in the context of the enlargement of the European Union. In this case, it refers to countries that joined in the Fifth Enlargement, namely eight Central and European countries, plus Cyprus and Malta that entered in May 2004.

Asylum seekers Refugees who seek asylum in a foreign country in order to escape famines, persecution, terrorism, war and other associated conditions that threaten their existence.

Belfast ('Good Friday') Agreement Signed in April 1998 by the British and Irish governments and the parties in Northern Ireland, the Agreement created the machinery for devolved government and a mechanism for resolving the troubles that had long beset the province.

Consensus Broad agreement about fundamental policies and goals.

Deference Respect: in this case, the willingness of many people to accept the views of their political and social superiors.

Devolution The process of transferring significant power from passing duties and powers from a higher authority to a lower one – e.g. from a central government to subordinate regional forms. The transfer stops short of any cession of sovereignty, so that powers devolved can always be taken back by the higher authority.

Direct action Political action outside the constitutional and legal framework, covering a huge variety of activities, many of which are militant but legal, although some of them are illegal or may be violent. It is essentially an attempt to coerce those in authority into doing something that otherwise they would not do.

Economic migrants Those who leave their own country in order to find a better standard of life in another one. Critics of immigration sometimes suggest that many asylum seekers are in reality economic migrants who want a better life in Britain.

Ethnic minorities All groups that have different national or cultural traditions from the main population; e.g. in British society, those who are not indigenous white people.

Ethnicity A mixture of different social characteristics that may include common origin, culture, geography, history, language and religion that give a social group a common consciousness and separates them from other social groups.

Far Right Far Right refers to the position occupied by individuals or groups on the political spectrum. Usually the term is used to imply support for extremist policies. Such individuals and groups tend to be xenophobic and believe in supremacist policies on racial issues – e.g. in Britain, a racist approach based on white supremacy.

Homogeneity Made up of similar elements, sameness.

Maastricht Treaty The Treaty on European Union which was negotiated at Maastricht (Holland) in December 1991, signed in February 1992 and operative since November 1993. It led to the creation of the EU in its present form, after agreement had been reached on issues such as steps towards further monetary and political union.

Multiculturalism Refers to the diverse range of ethnic groups and cultures that make up society. Multiculturalists argue that all people of goodwill – whatever their background – can live together, celebrate diversity, each community preserving its culture whilst respecting that of others.

Multiethnicity Refers to the diverse range of ethnic groups that make up society.

New Commonwealth immigration Immigration from members of the British Commonwealth that joined as a result of decolonisation (e.g. often poor, predominantly non-white countries in the developing world, in Asia, Africa and the Caribbean).

Parliamentary expenses scandal A major political scandal triggered by the publication by the *Telegraph* group in 2009 of expense claims made by MPs over several years. Public outrage was caused by disclosure of widespread abuse of the allowances and expenses system, following failed attempts by Parliament to prevent disclosure under Freedom of Information legislation.

Political culture The collective expression of the fundamental attitudes, beliefs, values and ideas that dispose people to react in a particular way in their approach to political issues. All societies have a political culture that gives form and substance to political processes.

Post-materialism A theory that explains the nature of political concerns and values in terms of levels of economic development. Whereas conditions of material scarcity mean that politics is dominated by economic issues, conditions of relative affluence and prosperity make people more concerned with the search for a better quality of life. This includes interest in issues such as animal rights, environmentalism, feminism, racial harmony and world peace.

Public opinion The opinion of the majority of the population on a particular issue, at a particular time and place. There can be no single public opinion. Rather, there are several opinions held by members of the public.

Refugees People who flee from some danger or problem, especially persecution. They leave their home without having a new home to go to.

Rule of law Government based on the idea of the supremacy of the law, which must be applied equally and through just procedures. The rule of law protects individuals from arbitrary government and requires that governments act in accordance with the law.

Social class The division of the population into categories on the basis of their economic and social status, determined by their background, occupation, income and other aspects of their lifestyle. The usual distinction is into manual (working class) and non-manual (middle and upper class) groups, although there are many sub-strata within these categories.

Likely examination questions

As this is essentially a background chapter, few questions are likely to be asked on the material here presented. But it is useful in informing your understanding of government and politics in Britain and elsewhere. A possible question might be:

What do you understand by the term 'political culture'? What are the characteristics of the British political culture?

Helpful websites

www.data-archive.ac.uk UK Data Archive (University of Essex). Evidence on British social attitudes and public opinion.

www.natcen.ac.uk National Centre for Social Research.

www.statistics.gov.uk Useful source of up-to-date information on economic and social features of British life.

Suggestions for further reading

The *British Social Attitudes* surveys, produced almost every year since 1983, provide valuable insights into the nature of national identity and analyses of changes in the British political culture. See especially J. Curtice and R. Jowell, 'The Sceptical Electorate', in R. Jowell, J. Curtice, A. Park, L. Brook and D. Ahrendt (eds), *British Social Attitudes: The 12th Report*, Dartmouth, 1995.

R. Inglehart, *Modernisation and Postmodernisation: Cultural, Economic and Social Change in 43 Societies*, Princeton University Press, 1997.

B. Jones (ed.), *Politics UK*, Prentice Hall, 2007. Chapters 2–4 provide introductory but useful coverage of the historical, social and economic contexts of British politics and chapter 5 covers political culture and political participation.

S. Vertovec, 'Super-diversity and its Implications', *Ethnic and Racial Studies*, 30:6, 2007.

CHAPTER 2

The Constitution and the Protection of Rights

Contents

PART A   THE CONSTITUTION
Introduction   25
The growth of interest in constitutional revision   26
The characteristics of constitutions   27
The Constitution of the United Kingdom   31
The Blair government and the Constitution   35

PART B   THE PROTECTION OF RIGHTS IN BRITAIN
Introduction   44
The protection of rights in Britain   44
The case of South Africa   53
The case of the USA   54

Overview

The constitution is at the heart of most political systems, describing the fundamental rules by which they operate. Usually, these rules are contained in a single written document, although in rare examples they may be located in major pronouncements, writings, statutes, precedents and legal decisions. Such constitutions may be an imperfect and incomplete guide to what actually happens in any country, but they help to shape the way in which they function, setting out the most important procedural rules, giving legitimacy to those who rule and providing individuals 'with a set of basic rights and freedoms.

In this chapter, we examine: the nature and characteristics of constitutions, noting in particular the distinctiveness of the British Constitution; the debate about constitutional reform in recent years and the changes introduced by the Blair and Cameron governments; the ways in which rights may be protected; and the early effectiveness or otherwise of the British Human Rights Act.

Key issues to be covered in this chapter

- General characteristics of constitutions
- The evolution and sources of the British Constitution
- Constitutional change under the Blair, Brown and Cameron governments
- The widespread existence of bills of rights around the world
- The protection of rights in Britain

PART A   THE CONSTITUTION

Introduction

Every country has a constitution of some kind. There are many definitions of the term, such as that provided by the *Oxford English Dictionary*: 'the system or body of fundamental principles according to which a nation state or body politic is constituted and governed'. When we think of constitutions, we normally have in mind the documents of countries such as France and the United States, which also embody a statement of the rights of the individual. But countries that do not possess such a single, authoritative statement still possess a constitution.

Constitutions declare the existence of the state and express the most important principles, rules and procedures of the political system. Specifically, they set out: the allocation of governmental activities; the power relationships between the various institutions; the constraints on the state's authority; and the freedoms of the individual citizen and the benefits to which he or she is entitled from the state. Article One of the 1948 Italian constitution clearly establishes some important information about the nature of the country and the way in which its system of government operates, by declaring:

> Italy is a democratic republic based on work. Sovereignty belongs to the people, who will exercise it in the forms and within the limits prescribed by the constitution.

A *constitutional regime* is one that operates within the rule of law and ensures that there are effective restraints on those who exercise power, as laid out in the constitution. Constitutional regimes are associated with the provision of a generally democratic and humane political order.

An *unconstitutional regime* operates on the basis of unchecked political power, so that the structural arrangements set out in the constitution are not put into practice. In such regimes, there is persistent neglect or non-enforcement of limitations upon rulers and the rights of the governed, as is the case in authoritarian states. In some countries, the rule of law is not upheld and there is a complete disregard of constitutional arrangements, perhaps because of a state of civil unrest (e.g. Somalia).

The importance of constitutions was recognised by the Spanish historian Julian Marais,[1] at the time when Spain acquired a new constitution: 'If the constitution does not inspire respect, admiration and enthusiasm, democracy is not assured'. In other words, the document acts as a kind of moral yardstick against which the performance of the political system can be judged. It acts as a reminder of the high ideals that inspired its creation.

Heywood[2] notes that 'there is an imperfect relationship between the content of a constitution and political practice'. Constitutions 'work' in certain conditions, 'notably when they correspond to, and are supported by, the political culture, when they are respected by rulers and accord with the interests and values of dominant groups, and when they are adaptable and can remain relevant in changing political circumstances'.

The growth of interest in constitutional revision

Constitutions tend to come about as a result of some major internal dissension or upheaval over a period of years, be it civil war, revolution or defeat in war. Following the dismantling of a governmental structure, those charged with writing a new one have to think about the way in which the political system should be organised. They are solemn and binding documents meant to last, having a certain timeless quality about them. Norway has the oldest single-document national constitution in Europe and is also distinctive in having its text written in another language (Danish, then the prevailing language). The constitution of San Marino is considerably older, having been enacted in 1600, but its contents are distributed over a number of legislative instruments. These examples are untypical. Most existing European constitutions are twentieth-century creations. Of those that are older, they have usually survived because – as with Norway – they have undergone several changes of a fundamental nature.

In recent decades, there has been a developing interest in constitutions and constitutional matters in many parts of the world; many constitutions have been rewritten, others revised. More than two thirds of those now in existence have been enacted since the end of the Second World War. In several cases, they were produced for states that gained their independence in the post-colonial period (India or Nigeria). In others (Portugal and Spain), they resulted from the collapse of fascist-type dictatorships in the 1970s. Eighty-five new constitutions were adopted between 1989 and 1999,[3] of which more than thirty were in central and southern Africa. Also, in that same period, it was necessary to write a constitution for each of the more than twenty states that were once part of the Soviet Union and its Central and Eastern European satellites, where peoples who once lived under communist tyranny were seeking to establish new institutions and principles for their political lives.

The purpose of this burst of writing and revising constitutions has been the same in most cases. Countries have seen a need to revamp their constitutions to bring their formal documents up-to-date and make them more in tune with the actuality of their governing arrangements. Andrew Heywood[4] makes the point that

> in general, it can be said that political conflicts assume a constitutional dimension only when those demanding change seek to redraw, and not merely re-adjust, the rules of the political game. Constitutional change is therefore about the re-apportionment of both power and political authority.

The characteristics of constitutions

Constitutions are often classified according to their characteristics. They may be:

Written or unwritten

The terms are unclear, for most of the British Constitution is written down somewhere, so that it is not technically unwritten. In 1963, Wheare[5] stressed that rather than having an unwritten constitution, Britain lacked a written one. Given the confusion of terms, it is probably more useful to distinguish between:

- *codified constitutions*, in which all the main provisions are brought together in a single document (India's constitution is the longest, containing 444 articles, twelve schedules and ninety-four amendments, with 117,369 words in its English version; the US Constitution is the briefest, its contents being conveyed in some

7,000 words, expressed in seven long articles and a mere ten pages) and

* *uncodified constitutions*, which exist where there are constitutional rules, many of which are written down, but have not been gathered together. (Apart from the United Kingdom, only Israel and New Zealand lack formal documents.)

Flexible or rigid

Flexible constitutions are rare. They can be altered via the law-making process (i.e. by a simple majority in the legislature) without much difficulty, as in New Zealand and the United Kingdom. In other words, no laws are regarded as fundamental and there is no formal process for constitutional amendment. In rigid constitutions, the principles and institutions assume the character of fundamental law. The procedure for amendment is deliberately made difficult, so that no change can be made without due consideration and discussion. Flexibility and rigidity are relative, not absolute terms. For instance, the American Constitution possesses a degree of flexibility that allows it to adapt to changing needs. Parties and pressure groups have developed, although they have no formal constitutional status. Moreover, all written constitutions depend upon interpretation and judges.

Unitary or federal constitutions

(See also Chapter 6.) Unitary systems are to be found in countries ranging from Britain to Israel, from France to Ireland. They tend to be especially suitable in smaller countries and in those where there are no significant ethnic, linguistic or religious differences. In unitary systems, all power is concentrated in the hands of the central government. As the constitution of the Fifth French Republic states: 'France is a Republic, indivisible'. Federal systems are characterised by a division between a federal (central) government and various regional units that may be called states (in the USA), *Länder* (in Germany) or provinces (as in Belgium) and have often developed in countries where the people are reluctant to surrender all power to a central government. In each case, the powers and functions of the central authority and the regional unit are clearly defined in a written constitution. Each authority is independent in its own sphere, although there may be concurrent powers shared between the two levels.

The distinction between the two forms can be exaggerated. In most democratic states, power is to some extent decentralised. Sometimes, as in Britain or Spain today, the degree of decentralisation to some areas may be extensive. When such autonomy has been granted to a regional authority, it is highly unlikely that it would in practice ever be taken away. Similarly, in countries that are federal, in recent decades there has often been a trend towards growing central power, so that back in the 1970s examiners could sometimes ask whether the United States was in reality becoming a centralised, unitary state. (In the recent phase of **devolutionary federalism**, the pendulum has swung back towards the states – see p. 220.)

Other characteristics of constitutions

Other characteristics that distinguish constitutions are:

- *some are monarchical, others republican.* This is not today a key distinction, for monarchy in democratic states takes the constitutional form. In Britain, Belgium, Denmark, Holland, Norway and Sweden, the monarch reigns by hereditary right; absolute monarchies are very rare. Republics have no hereditary head of state, but rather someone who is either elected by the people or their elected representatives.
- *some are presidential, others parliamentary*, a distinction that informs us about the relationship between the **executive** and **legislature**. In presidential constitutions, the two branches of government function independently on the basis of the **separation of powers** – e.g. in the US, the President is elected separately from Congress. In parliamentary systems, the executive is chosen from and accountable to the legislature.
- *some are based on the sovereignty of Parliament, others on the sovereignty of the people.* Britain provides an example of the former (see Box 2.1 on **Parliamentary sovereignty**), with Parliament formally possessing supreme power. America provides an example of the latter, its Constitution opening with the words: 'We the people of the United States . . . do ordain and establish this Constitution', an idea which echoes **Rousseau**'s belief that government should reflect the general will of the people.

Box 2.1 Parliamentary sovereignty in the UK

Parliamentary sovereignty has traditionally been viewed as a key element of the British Constitution. Constitutional experts such as A. V. Dicey[6] have proclaimed that Parliament has legal sovereignty (absolute and unlimited authority), in that it is the supreme law-making body in Great Britain. Only Parliament can make, amend and unmake law, and no other institution can override its decisions. No one Parliament can bind it successor.

In reality, the doctrine has been undermined in various ways over recent years, most notably by British adherence to the European Convention on Human Rights (see p. 56–7) and membership of the European Union. Both imply that any British government must modify its law to take account of European wishes. European law ultimately prevails over British law. Yet even before these European limitations, parliamentary sovereignty was a questionable notion. It implies that Parliament is supreme and all-powerful, yet in the twentieth century it is widely agreed that power has passed from Parliament to the Executive both because of the growing scale and complexity of government (and the consequent difficulties of achieving effective parliamentary control), and because of the extent of party discipline. Any government armed with a large majority has a good chance of pushing its programme through. Sceptics argue that though the doctrine implies that Parliament has real power, the truth is that it usually acts as a rubber-stamp for governmental action.

In reality, then, there are *political constraints* on Parliament's legal sovereignty. These include membership of the EU, the demands of the International Monetary Fund (where a government is seeking to borrow money from the IMF, it may impose stringent conditions on policy to be followed in the future), the activities of pressure groups, the City and other economic bodies, the powerful media and the electorate which has ultimate political sovereignty in that it can vote a government out of office. The need to gain and maintain public support is a crucial limitation on any group of ministers, especially in the run-up to an election.

Parliamentary sovereignty is in practice modified by the nature of the political system. In the last resort, the people are sovereign. In a democracy, their wishes must ultimately prevail. Government and Parliament need popular acquiescence and consent for their actions.

How the European Union impacts upon parliamentary sovereignty

When Britain joined the European Community as it then was, it accepted forty-three volumes of existing legislation, so that many directives and regulations passed before we became a member were suddenly binding upon us. Since then, in several areas, British law making has been influenced by the decisions of the European Court of Justice, most notably in the **Factortame** dispute concerning Spanish fishermen operating in British-registered vessels. The Conservatives passed the Merchant Shipping Act (1988) to define what was meant by a British-registered vessel. The statute was overturned by the Court, which found the legislation to be discriminatory, unfair and in breach of Community law. It was clear that in future national law could be made to bow to Community law, and that British courts had the right to review and suspend any British law which seemed to infringe that of the EC. This was not the first case to make this clear, for the supremacy of European law was recognised in earlier judgements concerning the need for equal treatment of men and women.

The Constitution of the United Kingdom

The UK does not have a written constitution in the sense of a single written document, though substantial elements of it are written in various places. It is largely because of its ancient origins that the British Constitution is so unsystematic. No attempt has been made to collate its contents together, and codify the various rules and **conventions** that are part of it. Yet those who work the Constitution generally understand the key issues involved.

If the UK seems to be at some disadvantage in not possessing a written constitution, the long constitutional history of the country does not point to any special urgency about creating one. Constitutions may be a safeguard against arbitrary seizures of power, but there is no history of dictatorships in our islands. Rights and liberties have developed organically, based not so much on law but on traditional freedoms and traditional practices.

The British Constitution has been a model followed by many other countries, and peoples in other countries who have long been denied their rights have seen Britain as an inspiration. As Wade and Phillips[7] put it, it 'embraces laws, customs and conventions hammered out, as it were, on the anvil of experience'. The British approach has been empirical, no attempt having been made to bring together the various constitutional laws and rulings. However, many of the basic principles and rules in Britain are recorded. As it has such a long history, much has been written about the British system of government.

Constitutional developments have come about gradually. Although many of the institutions have a long history, the role they play is constantly changing which is why Hanson and Walles[8] were able to refer to the British habit of placing 'new wine in old bottles'.

Sources of the British Constitution

Because of the way in which our political system has evolved over time, there are many sources that can be consulted in order to locate the elusive British Constitution. These include:

- *Major constitutional documents that express important constitutional principles*: e.g. Magna Carta (1215) asserted the view that a monarch could and should be controlled by his subjects.
- *Major texts and commentaries by eminent experts on the Constitution that have been so influential in their interpretation of the Constitution that they are seen as part of the Constitution itself*: e.g. Bagehot's *The English Constitution* (1867) and the introduction to it in its reproduced form (1963), which has come to be accepted as a major commentary on the state of the Constitution.
- *Major statutes that have an impact on the constitutional structure, in that they have changed the way we are governed or the relationships within the state*: e.g. the Parliament Acts (1911 and 1949), both of which trimmed the powers of the House of Lords.
- *The prerogative powers of the Crown*: the Royal Prerogative comprises a number of powers or privileges performed in the past by the monarch, but now performed in his or her name by ministers. Their authority derives from the Crown, rather than from Parliament, so that the Executive does not require parliamentary authority as it conducts these tasks. Ministers exercise prerogative powers individually or collectively. They include the rights to exercise mercy (a prerogative of the Home Secretary); declare

war and make treaties; give orders to the armed forces; appoint ministers; and dispense honours (all duties performed by the Prime Minister and his colleagues).

- *The law and customs of Parliament, the rules relating to the procedures of the House and the privileges of its members*: these are set out in the book consulted by the Speaker, Erskine May's *Law, Privileges, Proceedings and Usages of Parliament*, regarded as the authoritative commentary on the interpretation of parliamentary rules.

- *Common and case (judge-made) law*: common law is the immemorial law of the people (such as the claim to the right of free speech and free assembly), which in practice has been determined and implemented by judges. Judges have for centuries been an important source of rules on issues of constitutional significance. Their importance has been enhanced by the passage of the Human Rights Act (1998).

- *Constitutional conventions*: unwritten rules of constitutional behaviour, customs of political practice that are usually accepted and observed, e.g. that the choice of Prime Minister should be made from the House of Commons.

- *European Union law*: e.g. primary legislation as is to be found in the Treaty of Rome and the other treaties, and secondary law as is to be found in EU **regulations** and **directives**. European law takes precedence over UK law, is binding on the UK and applicable by UK courts.

The British Constitution in flux: the case for constitutional renewal

From the 1960s, many thinkers and writers began to urge the cause of 'constitutional reform', which became a fashionable topic for discussion among the chattering classes. It has been on the political agenda ever since. There were specific concerns such as the case for devolution of power to Scotland and Wales in the 1970s and 1980s, but subsequent concern was more wide-ranging.

Those who favoured constitutional change suggested that:

- whereas in the past the flexibility of the British Constitution had been regarded as an asset, the basis of good government, from the 1970s there were increasing doubts about the effectiveness of

Box 2.2 Radical and moderate perspectives on constitutional reform

Radical reformers took the view that fundamental surgery was required. In their view, the balance of the Constitution had been undermined in the long era of Conservative rule. Howard Elcock[9] felt that there were important issues of centralisation, accountability and human rights to address:

> Again and again, Mrs Thatcher swung her handbag and institutions which we fondly thought were part of the checks and balances of the British Constitution disappeared or were maimed beyond easy repair . . . [the problems] can only be satisfactorily resolved by Britain adopting a written constitution.

In *The Observer*, the academic and writer Andrew Adonis[10], later employed as a key adviser in 10 Downing Street, outlined the case for more moderate change:

> Ardent reformers claim that Britain is appallingly governed and barely democratic . . . In reality, Britain is seriously democratic and comparatively well governed. For all its shortcomings, I am hard put to name countries of a similar size or larger which on any long view have been better, more democratically governed. Germany is the only contender, though for less than fifty years . . . The case for reform is not that Britain's governance is chronically bad, but that it could be so much better. It could be so if Westminster revived its once proud tradition of incremental reform to adapt Britain's governing institutions to the times . . . since the First World War, inflexibility has been the rule.

Philip Norton[11] also adopted the moderate perspective. Conceding that there was a need for change, he argued for the strengthening of Parliament, the abolition or reduction of quangos and the devolving of more power to citizens at the local level. The emphasis was 'to strengthen the existing framework, not destroy it'. He rejected the alarmist Elcockian view that a dangerous centralisation of power had occurred and that checks and balances had been eroded. He accepted that in some areas there had been centralisation, as in other countries, but stressed that there had in some respects been a growing fragmentation of power, with power passing to bodies such as pressure groups.

some institutions. The political system seemed less successful in 'delivering the goods' than it had been and, in particular, there were serious problems at the periphery with the rise of nationalism in Scotland and Wales, serious disruption in Northern Ireland, a stagnant economy and poor industrial relations, and other signs of political discontent. Commentators began to wonder if constitutional malaise was at the root of many problems.

- Britain's Constitution was undergoing change. By signing up to the European Convention (especially by allowing individuals to appeal to the Strasbourg Court of Human Rights), ministers were acknowledging that European decisions could override those in British courts. Membership of the European Community/Union made this more of an issue, because it was seen as a threat to the traditional doctrine of the Sovereignty of Parliament.

- government in Britain was becoming increasingly centralised, powerful and undemocratic. There were too few checks and balances. Some pointed to the steady erosion of the functions and powers of local government, the increased number of **quangos** and the limitations on human rights. Given such dangers, if a fully-fledged written constitution was not a priority, we certainly needed measures to reform the second chamber, increase personal rights, bring in freedom of information legislation and other things which might shift power from Whitehall in favour of the citizen.

The Blair government and the Constitution

Labour was not always committed to constitutional reform. Prime Minister Callaghan once told Peter Hennessy[12] that the British political system really worked rather well: 'I think that's the answer, even if it's on the back of an envelope and doesn't have a written constitution with every comma and every semicolon in place. Because sometimes they can make for difficulties common sense can overcome.' Similar caution prevailed in the 1980s on some constitutional issues, though there was a growing acceptance of the need for reform in some areas. It was during the late Kinnock and Smith eras that Labour came to embrace the idea of substantial change, for several reasons:

- A genuine belief among some members of the case for constitutional reform, as being appropriate to a party committed to political and social change; they saw the Constitution as being archaic and in need of serious overhaul.
- A belief that the present system was not serving their party well (it seemed unable to win elections, have the opportunity to implement its own programme or effectively prevent aspects of the Conservative government's programme from being implemented).
- The need to win support from the Liberal Democrats who were long-standing advocates of constitutional renewal and whose support might be essential if Labour was to attain office in a **hung Parliament**.

Tony Blair had the opportunity to make the idea a reality. He signified his interest in constitutional renewal before the 1997 election, although some enthusiasts for the subject doubted the urgency of his commitment. He reminded such sceptics of the need to ensure that they did not get so far ahead of where the public was positioned, that 'you fail to take them along'. Yet he reaffirmed his belief that 'building a proper modern constitution for Britain is a very important part of what we are about'.[13]

In its 1997 manifesto, Labour criticised British government as 'centralised, inefficient and bureaucratic'. It wanted 'measured and sensible reform' to open up government, improve the quality of our democracy and decentralise power. To remedy this situation, it outlined a series of proposed reforms along the lines of a pre-election package agreed with the Liberal Democrats. The Conservatives saw little scope for substantial improvement in our constitutional arrangements and stressed the importance of the 'strength and stability of our Constitution – the institutions, laws and traditions that bind us together as a nation'. They feared that 'radical changes' might endanger 'the whole character of our constitutional balance' and 'unravel what generations of our predecessors have created'. In other words, the Constitution is a delicate flower and to tamper with something that has grown so organically could imperil the whole.

By 2001, the programme of constitutional renewal was well

underway. Among the initiatives undertaken during the lifetime of the Blair governments were:

- the incorporation of the European Convention into British law, via the Human Rights Act;
- the introduction of a new, proportional electoral system for European elections and – later – of a different one for Scottish local elections, under the terms of the Local Governance (Scotland) Act 2004 (the latter initiative was based on a report by the McIntosh Commission, set up by the then Scottish Office in 1997, but the details of the scheme were filled in by the newly created Scottish Executive);
- the establishment of the Jenkins Commission on the electoral system for Westminster (and an initially cautious welcome for its recommendations, although these were subsequently ignored);
- the near-abolition of the hereditary system in the second chamber (Phase One), the establishment of a Royal Commission, and then discussion of plans for a new body to replace the existing House of Lords;
- the introduction of devolution for Scotland and Wales (following the outcome of the referendums of September 1997), via the Scotland Act and the Wales Act;
- the passage of a Freedom of Information Act;
- the creation of a new authority for London, including an elected Mayor – along with provision for the adoption of elected mayors in other parts of the country;
- talks in Northern Ireland leading to the Good Friday Agreement, which, after some setbacks, led to the creation of an assembly and power-sharing executive;
- The wider use of referendums to establish support for constitutional change and the introduction of a new regulatory regime under which they should operate (the Electoral Commission, under the terms of the Political Parties, Elections and Referendums Act 2000);
- the Constitutional Reform Act (2005), which – among other things – provided for the establishment of a new **Supreme Court** to replace the judicial work of the House of Lords and a reduced role for the Lord Chancellor.

In defence of the Blair government's record on constitutional reform

The Blair government's performance on constitutional renewal can be defended in two ways. There is the general defence of the changes introduced, as well as a specific defence relating to individual reforms (see the appropriate section – e.g. the Human Rights Act on p. 46).

The general case is that the Constitution was in need of repair, the subject having been neglected over the years. What the government did to tackle the situation amounted to a major and unprecedented instalment of constitutional change. Several key measures were placed on the statute book, with few areas of the Constitution remaining untouched. The changes had been agreed with the Liberal Democrats and set out in the Labour manifesto. Much of their joint programme was achieved.

Of course, there were deficiencies in the package and things that might have been done differently, but nonetheless little or none of it would have been achieved if Labour had not been in power. No twentieth-century government had attempted so much in the constitutional arena, the package being– in the words of Tony Blair[14] – 'the biggest programme of change to democracy ever proposed'. This was in marked contrast to constitutional change in the past, which had always evolved slowly and over a long period of time. Moreover, the introduction of some reforms stimulated the creation of other changes. Experience of the use of **proportional representation** for elections to the Scottish Parliament opened the door to use of a proportional system in local government, just as the move to devolution in Scotland and Wales fuelled discussion of regional devolution in England and the case for an English Parliament.

A more interesting defence was offered by Lord Irvine,[15] the former Lord Chancellor. Having described the 'empirical genius' of the British nation as being its capacity to introduce piecemeal improvement by 'going step by step for change, through continuing consent', he pointed out that the Labour solutions were 'tailored to the particular needs of the British Constitution'. What did he mean by this?

1. The proposals in the package concerned specific issues on which the British Constitution needed updating, such as devolution and

Lords reform, among several others. Each reform dealt with a specific issue, as necessary. The essentially pragmatic changes were not part of an overall plan, as would have been the case if a new constitution was being written.

2. What was being introduced was important but gradual reform, in line with the very British evolutionary approach to change. Ours is an old constitution that has developed over centuries, the essence being retained but new developments being introduced from time to time.

3. The reforms were incremental, in the sense that an initially modest change could be developed, as became desirable or necessary. In several cases, the powers granted under new legislation were not extensive, as with the Welsh National Assembly and the Freedom of Information Act. But they could be expanded, according to experience and demand. For instance, the Human Rights Act, which was described on its introduction as being 'a floor, but not a ceiling'. In the same spirit, Ron Davies (in introducing the legislation for the Welsh devolved body), spoke of devolution as 'a process, but not an event'. So too Phase One of the Lords reform dealt with an important issue (removal of the hereditary peers), but there was scope for a Phase Two to develop the composition and powers of a second chamber in a more wide-ranging way.

The overall approach was distinctively British, an exercise in practical repair work. Changes came about without too much controversy, partly because of Labour's majority but also because Labour had learned from the difficulties of earlier administrations – e.g. it held referendums prior to the parliamentary passage of devolution, thereby allowing the public to already settle the substantive issue and Parliament to fill in the details. Similarly, over the House of Lords, it adopted a gradualist approach, getting rid of the hereditary peers before embarking upon discussion of the alternatives, a much more contentious matter. As we have seen, Tony Blair[16] had written of the need to carry people with him: 'there is a very great danger that groups like Charter 88 and other constitutional enthusiasts get so far ahead of where the public is that you fail to take them along.'

One side effect of the changes was to modify the Conservative approach to issues of constitutional reform. Whereas John Major had portrayed Labour as willing to 'tear up the Constitution', David Cameron was later to set up a Democracy Task Force. By then, the party had rethought its long-established views on constitutional change and come to see the case for creating a healthy and more accountable democracy.

Specifically, a case can be made in favour of the individual measures of the Blair government. For instance, in Scotland substantial political devolution was arguably necessary to take the sting out of nationalist demands for independence. In addition, following on the work of the previous administration, much was done to secure a settlement in Northern Ireland, resulting in new machinery being put in place, including a power-sharing executive and assembly. Even many of Tony Blair's strongest critics might concede that his efforts to resolve the long-standing problems in Northern Ireland were of profound historic significance.

An attack on the Labour record
Again, the case advanced can be both general and specific. From the political *Right*, the general attack was that a package of change was unnecessary, unwanted and undesirable. There was little interest among the public on constitutional matters, for it was a subject of concern only to political anoraks and groups like Charter 88. There were dangers in interfering with a structure that had evolved over the years, for tackling one problem might create others. Some Conservatives also pointed out that for all the talk of decentralisation, Tony Blair was busily acquiring more personal power, as was soon indicated by his dictatorial attitude over the issue of the Labour candidates for the leadership of the Welsh Assembly and his rejection (first time round) of Ken Livingstone as the Labour candidate for the London Mayoralty.

From the *Centre-Left*, the attack (or rather, the sense of disappointment) was twofold. Some writers criticised the programme for its overall lack of vision. Gillian Peele[17] took the view that the implications of individual reforms had not always been thought through and that they did not in some cases harmonise with each other: 'They are ill thought out, not joined up, with dissimilar patterns of solution introduced in the face of similar problems – different electoral

Box 2.3 Progress on constitutional reform in the post-Blair era

The Brown premiership

Prior to assuming the premiership in 2007, Gordon Brown trailed the idea of a constitutional reform bill. The emphasis was to be on change focused on Parliament, involving a rebalancing of the relationship between Parliament and the Executive and – among other things – giving MPs the right to vote before the country goes to war and to vet political appointments. There was talk of holding a 'constitutional convention', which would bring as many different views as possible into the process of reforming the Constitution, in order to claim a mandate for change.

Soon after taking office, the Ministry of Justice produced a Green Paper, based on a *Governance of Britain* agenda.[18] It outlined proposals to limit the powers of the Executive, make the Executive more accountable, reinvigorate our democracy and redefine the relationship between the individual and the state. A Constitutional Renewal Bill (later renamed the Constitutional Reform and Governance Bill) was published in 2008, which among other things included new provisions relating to the House of Lords. Suggestions followed for further development of devolution, consultation on the merits of a written constitution and debate on the possibility of electoral reform.

As the expenses scandal unfolded during the Brown premiership, the Prime Minister and other party leaders were involved in a fire-fighting exercise to allay mounting public alarm over the profligate behaviour of some MPs. This resulted in the **Parliamentary Standards Act (2009)**, which handed over the issue of MPs' expenses to an independent body. Little of the wider constitutional reform programme was accomplished, substantive change being left to the next Parliament. The Constitutional Reform and Governance Act (2010) was passed in the 'wash-up' period, in a limited form. It enshrined in statute the impartiality and integrity of the UK Civil Service and the principle of open and fair recruitment; required that treaties be laid before Parliament before they can be ratified; and made some amendments to the Parliamentary Standards Act (2009) in areas such as the tax status of MPs and peers, and resettlement grants for MEPs. More significant constitutional reform was sidelined, as the recession, the expenses scandal and the imminence of a general election came to dominate political discussion.

The Cameron premiership
In the Coalition agreement, a series of further constitutional reforms were agreed between the Conservatives and the Liberal Democrats. As a result the Parliamentary Voting System and Constituencies Bill received the Royal Assent in early 2011 and the passage into law of a Fixed-term Parliaments Bill was near to completion. The legislation will: reduce the number of MPs in the House of Commons from 650 to 600; change the way the country is divided into parliamentary constituencies; and take the power to dissolve Parliament away from the monarch.

The Coalition has also promised: to introduce legislation on the reform of the House of Lords; transfer more prerogative powers to Parliament; make provision for use of the **recall** to enable the public to get rid of unwanted MPs; decentralise power to local authorities; and provide for more locally elected mayors.

As with the initiatives taken by the Blair and Brown governments, the changes proposed by the Coalition relate to no wider constitutional agenda. In each case, the measures have been justified on their individual merits, rather than deriving from a clear view of the particular type of constitution required in the United Kingdom. As such, they are piecemeal reforms that are open to the criticism that they lack intellectual coherence. In the case of use of the **Alternative Vote** for future general elections, the referendum held in May 2011 registered a resounding victory for the 'no' side.

systems for the devolved assemblies and Europe, indeed different degrees of devolution within the United Kingdom.' Moreover, in her view some changes had not gone far enough. As Labour got nearer to power, so it became more timid. Ministers tend to be more so than shadow ministers, aware as they are that constitutional changes can create difficulties for themselves.

Others too have been underwhelmed by the package that Labour introduced and feel that an important opportunity to achieve radical reform was lost. They question Tony Blair's interest in the issue, noting that he rarely spoke about it. More seriously, they echo the Peele view above, noting the lack of an overall philosophy or coherent vision. As a result, the Constitution was tweaked by modest reforms, rather than fundamentally and methodically altered.

Again, this general view can be illustrated by reference to the limitations of individual changes such as the legislation on devolution and the House of Lords. For instance, the Conservatives pointed to the anomaly inherent in the devolution settlement, namely that Scottish MPs at Westminster could vote on purely English matters, whereas English MPs could no longer vote on matters affecting Scotland (for more on the so-called 'West Lothian Question', see pp. 200–2). They claimed that fuelling a sense of injustice, a sense of English nationalism would be encouraged that might lead to new constitutional demands. Many critics of the approach to Lords' reform were disappointed by the Blair government's reluctance to embrace the idea of an elected second chamber.

PART B   THE PROTECTION OF RIGHTS IN BRITAIN

Introduction

Bills of rights have been written into the majority of constitutions that have been created in recent decades. The French revolutionaries took up the ideas that inspired the **Founding Fathers** in the United States at the end of the eighteenth century. The principles they laid down in the *Declaration of the Rights of Man and Citizens* in 1789 were to inspire and divide the continent, and few European countries remained unaffected by them. Some states incorporated statements of human rights into their own constitutions, as did the Swedes in 1809 and Holland in 1815. In the twentieth century, and especially in the years since 1945, most constitutions have made some provision for the protection of basic rights, the South African constitution being a notable example (see pp. 53–4).

British ministers did not follow Continental example. However, some Dependent Territories and many newly independent Commonwealth countries had entrenched bills of rights in their constitutions. In several cases, these were based on the **European Convention** or the **International Covenant**. They conferred fundamental freedoms and provided for the protection of rights. In Canada, India and Zimbabwe, the Supreme Courts were given wide duties and powers in protecting human rights.

More recent statements of rights have been bold in their extension of rights into the social arena, with promised entitlements covering areas from employment to medical care. Hague and Harrop[19] note how several post-communist regimes have referred to the right to a healthy environment.

The protection of rights in Britain

Britain traditionally had a negative approach to rights. Few were guaranteed, even free speech which British citizens took for granted. The position was that they could do or say anything, provided that there was no specific law against it. Unlike the situation in other

Box 2.4 The difference between liberties and rights

Freedom of worship and freedom of expression are sometimes referred to as examples of *civil liberties or negative rights*, in that they mark out areas of social life which the constitution restricts or prohibits governmental intrusion on the free choice of individuals. They restrain the interference of government, marking out a sphere of governmental inactivity.

Social and economic rights are often described as *positive rights*. They extend the role and responsibilities of government into areas such as education, health provision and the right to work. They are more controversial because they expand the activities of government and are also dependent on the availability of resources.

Western democracies, there was no bill of rights or document setting out our basic entitlements.

In the late nineteenth century, A. V. Dicey[20] wrote of the 'three pillars of liberty' and the rule of law as our main protection. The pillars were Parliament, public opinion and the courts. The good sense and vigilance of the MP, the 'culture of liberty' which people had come to expect and the justice available in the courts would afford us protection, set against – as they were – a background in which there was equality before the law to which all were subjected.

Anxieties about freedoms and rights

Towards the end of the century, some academics, commentators and parliamentarians doubted if the means of protection for rights were adequate. They noted that Parliament, supposed to be our protector, had sometimes been the cause of lapses in our record on freedom. Bills pushed through by use of a governmental majority sometimes trampled on rights, as with the **Commonwealth Immigrants Act** (1968) or the **Criminal Justice and Public Order Act** (1994). Several laws introduced during the Thatcher years helped to persuade many people that traditional rights were in danger. Critics pointed to various areas of concern, including:

- police powers;
- the prevention of terrorism;
- obsessive secrecy and action against those who exposed it;
- restrictions on assembly and other rights connected with protest;
- discriminatory legislation on immigration and citizenship.

Klug, Starmer and Weir[21] used the International Covenant and the European Convention to develop a Human Rights Index, in a survey known as *The Democratic Audit*. The writers concluded that there was a 'weakness at the very heart of Britain's political and constitutional system'. They saw some merit in aggrieved individuals taking the journey to Strasbourg (see below) to gain their rights, but concluded by speaking of the 'grudging and unsystematic attitude' of ministers which means that 'the protection of political rights and freedoms in the UK generally moves forward in a slow, crab-like progression, by small increments, directed by the haphazard nature of individual applications and driven by the stick of Strasbourg.'

In 1966, British citizens had been given the right to take a grievance against those in authority to the European Court on Human Rights in Strasbourg, where British governments lost several cases. For many campaigners, this was not enough. There was no effective protection of liberties available in Britain. With this in mind, some called for the incorporation of the European Convention into British law. Others wanted a home-grown bill of rights. From the late 1960s onwards, lone voices had begun to speak of the merits of some such declaration. By the end of the century, several prominent judges and some MPs joined them.

Labour: the Human Rights Act

Labour accepted the case for incorporation in the early 1990s, under the Smith leadership. Along with many centre-left politicians, he and his successor, Tony Blair, recognised that the status of the Convention was anomalous. Britain was bound by it, but yet citizens had difficulty in using it. Moreover, ministers were tempted to play for time and not give way when infringements of rights were alleged. This was because they knew that Strasbourg justice was slow (five to six years to get a Court decision). Many people were tempted to give up the struggle, rather than wait for a European verdict.

In October 1997, New Labour produced a White Paper showing how, for the first time, a declaration of fundamental human rights would be enshrined into British law. The detail of the proposals showed that the courts were not being empowered to strike down offending Acts of Parliament, as happens in Canada. Instead, judges would be able to declare a particular law incompatible with the Convention, enabling government and Parliament to change it if they so wished, and providing a fast-track procedure for them to so do. In this way, the proposed Act would not pose a threat to the principle of parliamentary sovereignty.

The resulting Human Rights Act (passed in 1998) became operative from October 2000. It provides the first written statement of people's rights and obligations by enshrining most – but not all – of the European Convention on Human Rights into British law. It allows them to use the Convention as a means of securing justice in the British courts. Judges are now able to apply human rights law in their rulings. The Act also totally abolished the death penalty in UK law.

The effect of incorporation of the Convention was to introduce a new human rights culture into British politics. In general, decisions by Parliament, a local authority or other public body must not infringe the rights guaranteed under the Act. Where rights conflict, such as privacy versus freedom of information, the courts will decide where the balance should lie. Judges have the task of deciding cases as they come before them, in effect creating new law. If courts decide that a statute breaches the Act, they can declare it 'incompatible', but they cannot strike it down. They cannot overrule Parliament. It is for Parliament to amend the law, thus preserving the idea of parliamentary sovereignty. The ultimate decision in any conflict lies with Parliament, not the courts.

There were some initial concerns that the Act would clog up the courts (particularly in the early stages) and that the chief beneficiaries would be lawyers. It was expected that the courts would be deluged with all kinds of cases, some of them extreme. In Scotland, where the European Convention was already in force, 98 per cent of the cases in the first year failed. In the event, there was no legal free-for-all. Between 2000 and 2002, of 431 cases involving human rights heard in the high courts, the claims were upheld in ninety-four. Keir Starmer,[22] then a barrister much involved in such cases, has

Box 2.5 The European Convention on Human Rights

The European Convention was drawn up mainly by British lawyers in the Home Office. It began its work in 1953. Britain was an early signatory and its citizens had the right of access to the European machinery. This meant that although the Convention was not part of British law, citizens who felt that their rights had been infringed could take the long road to Strasbourg to gain redress and possibly compensation.

Via the broad phrases of the 66 Articles and several Protocols, the Convention sets out a list of basic freedoms such as:

Article 2:   The right to life
Article 3:   Prohibition of torture
Article 5:   Right to liberty and security
Article 6:   Right to a fair trial
Article 10:   Freedom of expression
Article 12:   Right to marry
Article 14:   Prohibition of discrimination
Protocol 1:   Article 1 – Protection of property
               Article 2 – Right to education
               Article 3 – Right to free elections

For each right, the basic statement is followed by a series of qualifications that list the exceptions to it. For example, although Article 10 guarantees freedom of expression, this is limited by considerations such as those 'necessary in a democratic society, in the interests of national security, for the prevention of disorder or crime, or for the protection of health or morals, for the protection of the rights of others'. The Strasbourg Court has the task of interpreting the Convention in a particular case. Now, with the incorporation of the Convention into British law via the Human Rights Act, British courts have similar scope.

There have always been some doubts about the content of the Convention, not surprisingly given that it is now more than fifty years old. Written in a very different climate of opinion, it has some contentious features, such as Article 5, which qualifies 'the right to liberty and security of person' by allowing 'the lawful detention of persons for the prevention of the spreading of infectious diseases, of persons of unsound mind, alcoholics or drug addicts or vagrants'. This may seem an arbitrary power in the hands of the authorities to detain people who have not committed a specific offence, but who have chosen to adopt an unconventional lifestyle.

concluded that 'hand on heart, the Human Rights Act has changed the outcome of only a very few cases'.

Life under the Human Rights Act

The Human Rights Act (HRA) makes it unlawful for any public body to act in a way which is incompatible with the Convention, unless the wording of an Act of Parliament means they have no other choice. It requires UK judges to take account of decisions of the Strasbourg court and to interpret legislation, as far as possible, in a manner compatible with the Convention.

From 2000, the British courts have had more power than ever before to hold the government and public bodies to account for their actions. Much of the discussion of the new Act has surrounded the question of the extent to which the judges will embrace their new opportunity with enthusiasm and flex their muscles at the expense of Parliament. Used to poring over the precise wording of British statutes, judges are now required to interpret what the law is in a particular situation when a citizen brings a case under the 'broad brush' phraseology of the European Convention. Many precedents (earlier cases) that previously influenced their legal judgements have lost some of their former relevance.

The HRA does appear to tilt the balance of the Constitution in favour of the judges. As Bogdanor[23] puts it, the measure 'considerably alters the balance between Parliament and the judiciary . . . for in effect the Human Rights Act makes the European Convention the fundamental law of the land'. Not all academics and commentators agree with his judgement. Morris[24] doubts that major social and political change will in future be driven by judges rather than legislators, noting that 'there is little evidence of this in those countries in which the Convention has long been domestically incorporated.'

British judges are unlikely to deliver judgements that involve a radically different interpretation of rights from that of the European Court, not least because British citizens retain a right of ultimate appeal to Strasbourg once domestic remedies have been exhausted. The likelihood is that over a period of time, British courts will establish substantial new protections for aggrieved individuals.

There have already been examples to illustrate how the HRA

has helped develop a law of privacy in the UK. Article 8 guarantees the right to respect for private and family life, one's home and correspondence. In 2002, the model Naomi Campbell successfully used the Act to make a complaint against a tabloid, which published details of her treatment for cocaine addiction at Narcotics Anonymous. In 2008, Max Mosley, the FIA president and motor-racing supremo, cited Article 8 in his vigorous denial of a report in the *News of the World* that there was a Nazi element in his sadomasochistic practices and won £60,000 in compensation.

Some Labour ministers were critical of the way in which the HRA has limited the power to tackle the terrorist threat (see Box 2.6 below). Wider fears about the Act have been expressed by a number of Conservatives. In 2005, Michael Howard[25] vowed to 'overhaul or scrap' the HRA, saying:

> The time has come to liberate the nation from the avalanche of political correctness, costly litigation, feeble justice, and culture of compensation running riot in Britain today . . . the regime ushered in by Labour's enthusiastic adoption of human rights legislation has turned the age-old principle of fairness on its head.

In the 2010 Conservative Manifesto, the party committed itself to David Cameron's earlier pledge to replace the HRA with a homegrown UK bill of rights. At the same time, the Liberal Democrats defended the HRA. In the Coalition agreement, the two parties committed themselves to establishing a commission to investigate the creation of a British bill of rights.

See Chapter 5 for further discussion of growing judicial power and consideration of whether judges are the best persons to decide issues of civil rights. Note how judicial review is being used to safeguard British liberties.

A home-grown bill of rights?

Advocates of a discrete, home-grown British bill are likely to take the ECHR and rights conferred in other international treaties as the starting point for any discussion of further development of the protection required. But some libertarian groups are dissatisfied with the Convention in its present form, as embodied in the Human Rights Act, and would like to see:

Box 2.6 The fate of anti-terrorist legislation under the Human Rights Act

Britain, alone in Europe, has withdrawn or derogated from Article 5 of the Convention. This guarantees the right to a fair trial and allows only limited circumstances under which a person may be deprived of liberty. Under part 4 of the Anti-Terrorism Crime and Security Act (2001), ministers were empowered to detain those considered a security threat, without trial. As a result, foreign nationals were held for three years in Britain's highest security prisons, Belmarsh and Woodhill.

In December 2004, the law lords decided that the detention of foreign terror suspects without trial was unlawful. There was no legal obligation for ministers to abide by the opinion of the senior judges, but the fact that they sat as a panel of nine rather than five was an indication of how seriously they viewed the threat to British liberties. In the words of Lord Scott: 'Indefinite imprisonment . . . on grounds not disclosed is the stuff of nightmares'. The punishment was considered disproportionate to the threat posed and discriminatory in that it applied only to foreign nationals.

Ministers tried to amend the original legislation, via their 'control orders' that applied to both UK and foreign nations suspected of involvement in terrorism. Human rights groups argued that these too were incompatible with both Article 5 (the right to liberty) and Article 6 (the right to a fair trial), a position again upheld by the courts in April 2006. A High Court judge issued a declaration that section 3 of the Act was incompatible with the right to a fair trial under Article 6 of the European Convention on Human Rights. Mr Justice Sullivan described the Act as an 'affront to justice'.

Judicial review and the European Convention

The development of the practice of **judicial review** by the higher courts since the late 1960s has become a recognised feature of our constitutional arrangements. The effect of the passage of the Human Rights Act was to systematise the process and to elevate the law lords in particular into a de facto constitutional court, charged with deciding whether particular legislative acts or executive actions were consistent with the obligations under the Convention, which the Act codified. (**NB** The law lords have now been replaced by the justices of the new Supreme Court, operative since 2009.)

The development of human rights law is becoming a feature of the work of all the higher courts, not merely the law lords. Around the same time as the Belmarsh judgement above, the high court ruled that human rights law applied to the actions of British troops in Iraq and the law lords ruled against the government on its **Roma** immigration control policies. Both cases involved human rights principles.

Box 2.7 The European Union and the protection of rights

The treaties involved in the development of the EU confer important rights. Certain categories of people benefit from aspects of Union policy, such as French agricultural workers whose standard of living has been protected by the Common Agricultural Policy. Again, the Treaty of Rome (1957) – many of the objectives of which are being fulfilled by the Single European Act (1986) – ensures freedom of movement and the transferability of professional qualifications throughout the EU. But many problems have arisen such as the non-recognition of qualifications, the unequal treatment of men and women, or disagreements over pensions and social security where the claimant has worked in more than one state. These and a multiplicity of similar issues can be brought to the attention of the Commission, the European Parliament or end up in the Court of Justice in Luxembourg.

Important gains affecting women's rights, especially in areas of equal pay, have derived from Court decisions. Other rights have been conferred by the Social Chapter, such as paternity rights, the maximum forty-eight-hour week for many workers and the right of workers to be represented in works councils.

Progress in the Lisbon Treaty (see p. 377)
Although signing the European Convention on Human Rights (ECHR) is a condition for EU membership, the EU could not itself accede to the Convention as it is not a state. Protocol 14 of the ECHR, which came into force in June 2010, allows for EU accession to the Convention and the Lisbon Treaty formally committed the Union to accession.

The EU's own Charter of Fundamental Rights was made legally binding in the Lisbon Treaty drawn up in 2000. Although originally not legally binding, the Charter was frequently cited by the EU's courts as encapsulating rights that they regarded as fundamental principles of EU law.

- the phraseology of some existing rights amended
- additional rights included
- and a statement of rights that was more attuned to the British situation today than one drawn up a half-century ago.

In 2009, the Prime Minister announced that he wanted to move forward on producing a new bill outlining the rights and responsibilities of British citizens, as an adjunct to the Human Rights Act. Such a bill could give people a clear idea of what we as citizens can expect from public authorities, and from each other, and a framework for giving practical effect to our common values.

At that time, the Conservatives were intent on repealing the Human Rights Act and seeing it replaced by a new document, better attuned to national needs. Their policy was implicitly criticised in the *Governance of Britain* document, which observed that:

> the effect of repealing the Human Rights Act would be to prevent British citizens from exercising their fundamental rights in British courts and lead to lengthy delays for British citizens who would need to appeal to Strasbourg to assert their rights. In addition, the European Court of Human Rights would be less likely to take into account the specific British context in making its decisions.

The Human Rights Act is unlikely to be the last word on the subject of rights. In the parliamentary debates surrounding the passage of the measure in 1997 and 1998, incorporation was described as the first step in a journey. Coalition ministers are considering how best to move forward on the matter.

The case of South Africa

After enduring years of systematic oppression of individual and group rights under the **apartheid** regime, the transformation in the position of the individual in South Africa has been remarkable. The Preamble to the 109-page 1996 constitution begins with a declaration of intent – to make a fresh start and build a more inclusive society:

> We, the people of South Africa,
> Recognise the injustices of our past;

Honour those who suffered for justice and freedom in our land;
Respect those who have worked to build and develop our country; and
Believe that South Africa belongs to all who live in it, united in
ourdiversity.

The Preamble later states that the object of the new constitution is
'to create a new order in which all South Africans will be entitled to a
common South African citizenship in a state in which there is equality between men and women of all races, so that all citizens shall be
able to enjoy and exercise their fundamental rights and freedoms'.
These rights are guarded by a Constitutional Court, which determines whether state actions are in accordance with constitutional
provisions.

Suspicion of parliamentary as well as executive power is reflected
in the constitution, for in the apartheid era both branches of government were involved in support for 'objectionable' measures. Not surprisingly, in view of past history, there is a strong emphasis in the new
version on anti-discriminatory provision, and an innovation is the
guarantee of rights in the area of sexual orientation. Under Article 9
(iii) on Equality, 'The state may not unfairly discriminate directly or
indirectly against anyone on one or more grounds, including race,
gender, sex, pregnancy, marital status, ethnic or social origin, colour,
sexual orientation, age, disability religion, conscience, belief, culture,
language and birth.' Specific social and economic rights are not spelt
out, but the inclusion of the wide-ranging Article 10 is potentially
significant in its implications: 'Everyone has inherent dignity and the
right to have their dignity respected and protected.'

The constitution has to date been amended on sixteen occasions.

The case of the USA

The American Constitution lays down a loose framework in which
government operates. It has stood the test of time, although it has
been subject to twenty-seven Amendments. Of these, the first ten
became a key issue in the ratification process following the conclusion of the Convention that devised the document. These form the
Bill of Rights that originally applied to the federal government only.
Today, most of them also apply at state and local level.

There is a difference between constitutional theory and everyday reality. In spite of the provisions of the 14th Amendment providing equal protection of the law and the 15th extending the right to vote to African-American males, there were constant denials of constitutional rights to black people. Such constitutional guarantees were not effected until the 1950s and 1960s, and in some respects are still open to evasion. This suggests that rights do not depend on the existence of a written constitution alone. The tradition of liberty in a country and the nature of its political culture are more important than any constitutional document.

Nonetheless, Americans view their Constitution with considerable awe and reverence, leading Louis Hartz[26] to write in 1955 of 'the cult of constitution worship'. The issue of constitutional reform rarely surfaces. Those who want to argue the case for change tend to talk in terms of restoring the original to its former glory, rather than of carrying out a radical overhaul. When innovations have been proposed – as with the suggestion of 'term limits' to curtail the length of time a congressmen may spend in office – they have failed to command the necessary support in the House of Representatives and the Senate.

· ·

 ## What you should have learnt from reading this chapter

- Constitutions are important, in that they proclaim the basic principles according to which people should be governed. In almost all cases, they exist in the form of single, authoritative documents that are often difficult to amend. Where there is no such constitutional statement, the country can still be regarded as having a constitution.

- The strength of a constitution is to be measured not by the text or format, but in the extent to which it operates successfully with reasonable stability, continuity and durability. Many 'written' ones do not prove to be long lasting, whatever the good intentions of those who draft them.

- The 'unwritten' British Constitution is flexible and has survived well, even if in recent years there have been regular calls for constitutional reform of the type introduced by the Blair government in its wide-ranging, if piecemeal, package. The issue remains on the political agenda, the Coalition having agreed to act on some measures and further investigate others.

- Most constitutions contain a declaration of rights, as in the case of the American and French ones. Early ones placed more emphasis on civil and political rights, but some of those devised in the last few decades, such as the South African document, have also included economic and social rights. The existence of a constitution and bill of rights is no guarantee that essential liberties and rights will be respected. Liberty ultimately depends more on the political culture of any country than on any written proclamation.

Glossary of key terms

Alternative Vote An electoral system – also known as 'instant run-off' – in which voters list the candidates in their constituency in order of preference. If no candidate obtains more than 50 per cent of first-preference votes, the votes for the bottom candidate are redistributed according to the voters' next preference. The intention is to ensure that any candidate elected has majority support and to provide a measure of justice for significant third parties.

Apartheid The governmental policy of strict racial segregation and political and economic discrimination against non-whites practised in South Africa until its official renunciation in 1992.

Bill of rights A formal statement of the rights and privileges to which citizens are entitled, usually embodied in a constitution.

Commonwealth Immigrants Act 1968 A controversial act that limited the number of Kenyan Asians who could enter the country to those who had a parent or grandparent who was born in or was a citizen of the UK. This meant that the right to British nationality promised at the time of Kenyan independence was cancelled.

Criminal Justice and Public Order Act 1994 An act that reduced existing rights and increased penalties for certain categories of 'anti-social' behaviour. Particularly controversial were sections covering the right to silence of an accused person (allowing for inferences to be drawn from their silence) and collective trespass and nuisance on land (including sections against 'raves').

Devolutionary federalism The devolving of responsibility for once federally run programmes to the states which – being closer to the people – are thought to be better placed to respond to local needs.

Directives A type of EU secondary law which is binding on member states as to the result to be achieved, but can be implemented as best suits the needs of the individual country.

European Convention on Human Rights (ECHR) The statement of basic liberties and rights devised by the Council of Europe in 1950 and enforced by the Strasbourg Court of Justice whose verdict is binding.

Britain has now incorporated the Convention into UK law, as have most other signatories.

Executive One of the three branches of government, along with the legislature and judiciary. The part of government concerned with making governmental decisions and policies, rather than passing laws. The Political Executive in Britain comprises the Prime Minister and the Cabinet.

Federal system A constitutionally defined structure in which a central (federal) authority shares power with smaller territorial areas, in the US known as states.

Founding Fathers The political leaders who attended the convention that drew up the US Constitution in 1787.

Hung Parliament A post-election situation in which no party possesses an overall majority in the House of Commons, such as the one that occurred in the general election of 2010 when no party reached the target of 326 seats.

International Covenant The International Covenant on Civil and Political Rights (ICCPR) agreed by members of the United Nations in 1966. In theory binding, it lacks effective enforcement machinery. Signatories have to report periodically on their record of compliance with its provisions to a Human Rights Committee.

Judicial review The constitutional function exercised by the judiciary of reviewing the laws, decrees and actions of the Executive and legislature, to ensure that they are compatible with the Constitution and established rights.

Judiciary The branch of government concerned with the administration of justice.

Legislature The branch of government that makes law through the formal enactment of legislation.

Parliamentary sovereignty The absolute and unlimited authority of Parliament to make, repeal or amend any law.

Parliamentary Standards Act 2009 An act hastily passed through Parliament, largely as a response to the expenses scandal. Its main provisions were to: create the Independent Parliamentary Standards Authority (IPSA), which would assume responsibility for the management of expenses and maintaining the Register of Members' Interests; and establish the office of the Commissioner of Parliamentary Investigations, who would, as part of the IPSA, oversee investigations into MPs thought to have been paid an expenses claim not within the rules as set out in the Act or who had failed to comply with the IPSA code of conduct relating to financial interests.

Quangos An acronym for quasi-autonomous non-governmental organisations that carry out public service functions. Although funded by government and having most of their members appointed by government, they are semi-public advisory bodies that do not operate under direct governmental control.

Recall The process by which elected officials may be 'recalled', deprived of office by popular vote.

Regulations A type of EU secondary law that is binding on all member states, without the need for any national legislation.

Roma Commonly known as gypsies, a traditionally nomadic people who originated in northern India but today are particularly concentrated in parts of Europe.

Rousseau Eighteenth-century French philosopher and writer who favoured the idea of democracy, but viewed majority rule as potentially unjust. He argued that government should be based on recognition of the collective will of the people, 'the general will'.

Separation of powers The principle that executive, legislative and judicial power should be separated through the creation of three independent branches of government.

Supreme Court The final court of appeal in all matters under English, Welsh and Northern Irish law, since 2009. In effect, it performs the judicial work previously undertaken by the role of the law lords in the House of Lords.

Theocracy A government ruled by or subject to the religious authority of a deity or priesthood.

Unitary system A structure in which there is a single sovereign body, central government, which does not share power with devolved or local institutions, although it may choose to grant power to them. Legal sovereignty lies entirely at the centre.

Likely examination questions

To what extent do constitutions shape political practice?

Discuss the merits and disadvantages of Britain's uncodified Constitution.

Discuss the view that Labour's programme of constitutional change (1997–2010) lacked any overall coherence or vision.

Is it true to say that constitutions are meaningless without recognition of basic civil liberties and rights?

Discuss the view that the passage of the Human Rights Act represents the first step towards the introduction of a written constitution in Britain.

 ## Helpful websites

For details of specific changes/proposals affecting particular areas of government see the appropriate chapter.

The following more general sites are likely to be of interest and value:

Charter 88 offers a pro-reform look at constitutional issues at www. charter88.org.uk

The Constitution Unit provides an academic analysis of the changes made and contemplated at www.ucl.ac.uk/constitution-unit

 ## Suggestions for further reading

M. Flinders, 'The Half-hearted Constitutional Revolution', in P. Dunleavy et al. (eds), *Developments in British Politics 8*, Palgrave, 2006.

R. Hazell and R. Rawlings (eds), *Devolution, Law Making and the Constitution*, University of Exeter Press, 2005.

R. Hazell (ed.), *The English Question*, Manchester University Press, 2006.

R. Hazell (ed.), *Constitutional Futures Revisited: the British Constitution in 2020*, Palgrave, 2008.

R. Hazell et al., *Does Freedom of Information Work? The Impact of FOI on Whitehall*, Palgrave, 2010.

CHAPTER 3

The Legislature

Contents

Introduction   61
What is the legislature?   61
The structure of legislatures   62
The British House of Lords   64
The main functions of the House of Commons   74
The House as a watchdog over government   77
Elected representatives: the duties and responsibilities of British MPs   81
Parliamentary reform in recent years   90
The social composition of elected legislators   93
The pay and conditions of legislators   102
The case of Denmark   103
The case of the USA   104

Overview

Legislatures are representative bodies that reflect the sentiments and opinions of the public. Their members consider public issues and pass laws on them. In Britain, there are various views of the role of Parliament within the political system. Some portray it mainly as a forum for the discussion of important issues and in which grievances are aired. Others believe that Parliament should be equipped with a range of powers in order that it can provide an effective check upon the Executive.

In this chapter, we examine the structure and composition of legislatures, and the power and influence of Parliament as a whole and of its individual members, asking what purposes Parliament serves and how effective it is in carrying out its tasks.

Key issues to be covered in this chapter

- The nature and functions of legislatures in general
- The role of the British House of Lords, its changing character and proposals for its future
- The work of the House of Commons
- The role and significance of MPs
- The backgrounds, pay and conditions of legislators
- The decline of legislatures and the need for parliamentary reform

Introduction

Almost all countries have a legislature as part of their institutions of government, although they function under a variety of different names. The term Congress is used in some countries; Parliament is employed in Britain and the Commonwealth; and on the Continent, it is more common to speak of the National Assembly (as in Afghanistan) or the States General (as in the Netherlands). The individual chambers are variously named, with titles ranging from the House of Representatives and Senate in the USA to the Knesset in Israel.

In the 1970s and early 1980s, some twenty to thirty legislatures (mainly in Africa and Latin America) were not allowed to function. Since then, the number of military regimes has diminished. In addition, new states have been established in parts of former communist-controlled Eastern Europe, again increasing the number. As a result of these changes, 189 are currently in existence.[1]

What is the legislature?

Legislatures are the governmental institutions in which policy issues are discussed and assessed. The roots of the name of the first modern legislature, the British Parliament, suggest this crucial function – 'parler', to talk. Most early legislatures were created to provide advice to the political executive, often a monarch, and to represent relevant political groups. Many legislatures have also been responsible for introducing public policies. The roots of the word 'legislature' are the Latin terms '*legis*' (law) and '*latio*' (bringing, carrying or proposing). Legislatures are, then, the branch of government empowered to make law. Whether known as assemblies or parliaments, they are forums for debate and deliberation.

The word 'assembly' is sometimes distinguished from 'parliament'. Its literal meaning is a gathering. Some writers portray an assembly as being a weaker body, more of a talking shop. In contrast, parliaments have law-making powers. Here, we are not making much of the distinction, for the labels employed vary according to countries and traditions. 'Assembly' can be used to describe either house and can be used interchangeably with 'legislature' and 'parliament'.

The structure of legislatures

The obvious distinction in the structural arrangements of different legislatures concerns whether they are unicameral or bicameral.

Unicameral legislatures

These have one chamber, examples ranging from Bulgaria to Hungary. **Unicameralism** has been on the increase in recent years and nearly two thirds of the world's legislatures now have only one chamber. Over time, some bicameral systems have evolved into unicameral ones. This has usually happened where: the problems of conflict and stalemate between the two houses have increased; there has been little need for extensive checks and balances; or representation in the popularly elected chamber has been thought adequate. Countries that have abolished the second chamber include Costa Rica, Denmark, Iceland, Sweden and New Zealand. Significantly, they have mostly been small in size and/or population. In such countries, the pressure of legislation is much less than in a country the size of Britain.

Lower houses range in size from the large (Britain 650 members, Italy 630 and India 545) to the very small (Iceland 63, Costa Rica 57 and Tuvalu 15). Unsurprisingly, size is related to population, though the proportions vary considerably in various states. India has on average one representative for every 2.1 million people; the USA one per 715,000; Germany one per 137,000; France one per 108,000; the UK one per 95,000; Norway one per 29,000; and Ireland one per 27,000.

From such figures it can be seen that countries with less inhabitants are at an advantage. The legislatures are smaller, giving members more chance to participate in the proceedings. Moreover, since they represent fewer constituents, the bonds between people and representatives are close. For these reasons, legislatures in smaller countries are more likely to function effectively than those in much larger ones.

Bicameral legislatures

These have two chambers, examples ranging from Australia to Great Britain; **bicameralism** now operates in just over sixty countries. Second chambers are more common in countries that are geographically extensive, where the size of the country, the need for regional representation and the sometimes sharp geographical cleavages make a second chamber seem desirable; in such circumstances, a single chamber might find itself overwhelmed by its legislative and other tasks. Federal countries are usually bicameral, the second chamber often being the more powerful one, as in Canada and Germany. In the USA, the two chambers are of formally equal status, but membership of the Senate carries greater esteem. It alone has the responsibility for confirming appointments and is particularly significant in the area of foreign policy.

Most non-federal second chambers are constitutionally and politically subordinate to first chambers, especially in parliamentary systems. Many have lost much of their power, so that in Britain and France they retain only the right to revise or delay (but not veto) legislation. Weaker versions of bicameralism (with one house much less powerful than the other) sometimes reflect the composition of the second chamber. The Canadian Senate is wholly nominated and the British House of Lords had a hereditary predominance until 1999.

Bicameralism has certain benefits. Second chambers:

- act as a check upon first chambers, the more important if one party has a landslide majority;
- more effectively check the executive;
- broaden the basis of representation, especially in federal states giving representation to the region;
- allow for thorough scrutiny of legislation, providing more time for careful examination of bills;
- act as a constitutional long stop, delaying the passage of bills and allowing time for debate.

Critics allege that second chambers:

- can be needlessly costly;
- perform no useful role not capable of being covered by a stream-lined lower house;
- slow down the task of government, sometimes delaying much-needed legislation;
- [sometimes] do not represent the electorate and are often of conservative leanings;

- are a recipe for constitutional stalemate or 'gridlock'. They institutionalise conflict.

The British House of Lords

For much of the nineteenth century, membership of the House of Lords was based on heredity and the chamber enjoyed equality of status with the House of Commons. However, its position became increasingly inappropriate when the franchise was extended and the lower house became more representative of the people. The Lords was able to survive the transition into a democratic age on the basis that its powers were trimmed and its membership modified.

In the twentieth century, there were several changes to the composition and powers of the second chamber. The main changes concerning *membership* were all introduced by the Macmillan (Conservative) government:

- *Payment of an attendance allowance* to peers to encourage a better turnout, 1957.
- The introduction of life peers by the *Life Peerages Act* 1958. This permitted men and women to be created as peers for the duration of their lives, on the advice of the Prime Minister (who usually consults with the Leader of the Opposition). The purpose was to diversify membership of the chamber, bringing in people from various walks of life who had something to contribute to the deliberations of the upper house. By being used to boost Labour membership, the Act could be seen as a skilful way of detracting criticism of the House of Lords as one-sided and unfair.
- *The Peerage Act 1963* allowed hereditary peers to renounce their title for the duration of their lifetime.

The main changes affecting the *powers* of the House of Lords were:

- *The Parliament Act 1911* (introduced by the pre-First World War Liberal government). This removed the power of absolute delay over legislation. In future, any bill that passed the Commons in three successive sessions would automatically become law. In other words, the House of Lords had lost its permanent veto.

- *The Parliament Act 1949* (introduced by the post-1945 Labour government). This further limited the delaying power of the Lords, so that any bill that passed in two successive sessions now became law. This effectively curtailed the delaying power to eight to nine months and made it harder for the upper house to frustrate the wishes of the elected one. It has been used on four occasions, most recently for the passage of the bill that abolished fox hunting.

It was difficult to achieve a fundamental reform of the second chamber that tackled functions, powers and composition. Party agreement was hard to establish and the subject was not viewed as a priority. The Conservatives lacked any real incentive to bring about major change, for the Lords had an overwhelmingly conservative membership and was generally more accommodating to Conservative ministers. Labour had no reason to approve of the Lords, disliking its overwhelmingly hereditary composition and finding it a bulwark that blocked any proposals for radical reform. But it was a convenient target for an easy attack on unfair privilege and could conveniently be blamed for any lack of decisive action by a Labour administration. As a result, major change was not forthcoming, although it had been envisaged in the Preamble to the 1911 Act:

> Whereas it is intended to substitute for the House of Lords as it at present exists, a Second Chamber constituted on a popular instead of an hereditary basis, but such substitution cannot be immediately be brought into operation . . .

Labour's 1998 changes: Phase One of Lords reform

The 1997 Labour manifesto committed the party to action to end by statute 'the right of hereditary peers to sit and vote in the House of Lords'. *Phase One* was to provide for the abolition of the hereditary peerage, which was carried out under the terms of the House of Lords Act (1999). All but ninety-two of the hereditaries were removed; those remaining in the revised chamber were to be elected by party groupings.

The House of Lords Act left the judicial and spiritual membership of the chamber untouched. The Lords spiritual comprise the two Archbishops (Canterbury and York), as well as the twenty-four next most-senior bishops. They retain their membership only for as long as they hold office within the Church. The law lords were members by virtue of their high judicial positions. They retained their seats until their death, so that there were at any one time more law lords than were necessary to enable the Lords to fulfil its judicial functions (see below). On the opening of the Supreme Court (2009), all sitting law lords became its first justices: they remained as members of the House of Lords, but were unable to sit and vote in the House.

Membership of the chamber now fluctuates. In March 2011, the 825* peers (of whom 180 were female) included:

720 life peers**
91 'elected hereditaries' under the 1999 Act
24 bishops

As a result of the 1998 changes, the overwhelming Conservative bias vanished. Of the 786 members referred to above, 217 were proclaimed Conservatives, 242 Labour and 91 Liberal Democrats. The votes of the 184 crossbenchers often determine the fate of ministerial policy.

The work performed by the House of Lords

Countries with second chambers have them for several reasons. Sometimes, their role is to provide continuity and stability in Parliament and law making; sometimes, to act as a constitutional long stop (preventing or delaying the passage of radical innovations); sometimes, to act as a revising body. (In federal states, the upper house can be used to provide for regional representation.) The House of Lords fulfils all three roles.

Back in 1918, Lord Bryce[2] distinguished four roles for the British second chamber:

• *The consideration and revision of bills from the House of Commons.* The House of Lords has the power to examine legislation in detail and may pass, amend or reject bills. Ministers may accept or

---

* Of these, only 786 are potential working members. Of the others, twenty are deemed to be on 'leave of absence', three are suspended, fifteen disqualified as senior members of the judiciary and one disqualified as an MEP.

** Including 687 created under the terms of the Life Peerages Act (1958) and twenty-three law lords created under the Appellate Jurisdiction Act (1876).

reject amendments, rejection leading to a process of negotiation between the two chambers. The Commons can use the 1949 Parliament Act to insist on getting its way.

• Revision is the key function today and the House spends just over half of its time on the scrutiny of public bills (see p. 77), some of which have been badly drafted or inadequately discussed in the lower house; many amendments are actually put down by the government.

• *The initiation of non-controversial legislation.* About a quarter of bills begin their parliamentary life in the upper house, although these are mainly those which are non-controversial and on which there is no strong party disagreement. Backbench peers can also introduce private peers bills. Few are passed, but they provide a chance to air topics ranging from social reform to a bill of rights.

• *The power of delay.* The Lords can hold up legislation under the Parliament Act, the extra time being designed to provide a pause for reflection and reconsideration. (In the past, this power has been used to frustrate the wishes of more radical governments; Labour has traditionally been wary of it.)

• *The holding of general debates.* Peers – under less pressure of time than MPs – can conduct useful discussions on matters such as leisure and the environment. There are many life peers who have expertise to contribute on issues ranging from education to race, health to policing. Such debates usually take up more than 25 per cent of the time of the Lords and are less rancorous than those in the Commons.

Finally, the Lords does valuable work in *scrutinising European legislation* (see Box 3.2), investigating some topics in great detail and producing authoritative, well-written reports. The scrutiny performed by the European Union Committee has been described by Bogdanor[3] as 'perhaps the most effective in the EU'.

Until 2009, the Lords also acted in a judicial capacity, as the *final court of appeal*. The role was transferred to the new Supreme Court in 2009.

Box 3.1 The Lords at work, 2008–9

- In 2008–9, the Lords sat for 134 days, on average just under 6.6 hours per day. It spent around 60 per cent of its time examining legislation (55 per cent on bills, 5 per cent on **statutory instruments**) and 40 per cent on scrutinising the work of government (28 per cent on debates, 7 per cent on questions and 5 per cent on statements).
- Of the Lords' 6,363 amendments on the 47 government bills, 1,824 were passed. For example, of 274 tabled amendments to the Borders, Citizenship and Immigration Bill (on strengthening border controls by combining customs and immigration powers and ensuring that newcomers to the UK earned their right to stay), 63 were passed but four resulted in defeats for the government.
- Eight government bills began life in the Lords, on issues ranging from Local Democracy, Economic Development and Construction to Marine and Coastal Access.
- General debates covered issues such as social networking (the impact of the practice on young minds and the importance of protection for child users); the role of offshore financial centres in facilitating tax evasion by British citizens and companies; and the 200th anniversary of the death of Charles Darwin and the impact and controversy surrounding his work.
- Short debates were held on issues including Gulf War illness and women in prison.
- The work of the Lords cost a total of £103.9 million, little more than £3 per taxpayer.

Source: Information provided by the House of Lords Information Office.

The case for the House of Lords

Defence of the House of Lords was, in the past, made more difficult because of its largely hereditary composition. This was widely regarded as inappropriate for a democratic age. Now that the hereditary element has gone, it is easier to concentrate on the merits of the House. Points often made for the defence are that:

- Most sizeable countries are bicameral rather than unicameral. Although countries such as Denmark, Israel and New Zealand manage well with one chamber, none of those countries has the

Box 3.2 Scrutinising European legislation

In 1974, the House of Lords established the Lords' Committee on the European Community, in order to scrutinise Commission proposals and to draw the attention of the House to those that raise important issues of policy or principle. Now known as the European Union Committee, it can suggest a debate on those matters it considers to be of sufficient significance.

The Committee examines the merits of proposals for legislation and undertakes wide-ranging investigations of EU policy. Its wide terms of reference even permit it to make freestanding enquiries into EU issues, in the absence of specific proposals. Its remit is much wider than that of its Commons' counterpart and its prestige is higher. Although some debates are held in the Lords, it is more common for reports to be communicated to ministers by letter.

The Committee has nineteen members and an elaborate system of seven sub-committees covering the principal areas of EU competence. There is a total working membership of around seventy-five to eighty peers. The main Committee reflects the broad political balance within the House, but the sub-committee members are chosen for their political expertise. The Committee examines proposals that are considered important by the Chairman.

In 2008–9, the Committee and its sub-committees considered some 800 EU documents, 360 of them in detail. Its reports covered topics such as: EU consumer rights; financial supervision and regulation; and money laundering and the financing of terrorism.

The Committee is widely acknowledged for performing a valuable role in scrutiny of EU legislation. Membership of the main and sub-committees is often very distinguished and the reports of high quality. They are useful as a source of information and of informed opinion. Although aimed in the first instance at the House and through the House at ministers, they are taken seriously by the institutions of the EU, including the European Parliament.

volume of work and particularly of legislation that characterise the British system. Unicameralism would be impossible without major streamlining of the House of Commons.

• Many writers still feel that a second chamber produces a valuable opportunity for careful scrutiny of government work. For all of its anomalies, past and present, the House actually performs this role rather well. As prime minister, John Major used to say: 'If it ain't broke, don't fix it.' It has been fixed to some extent, in a way that has lessened the anomaly of heredity that was an affront to many people in a democratic era. The removal of the hereditaries means that members now are mostly life peers, chosen because they have something special to contribute.

- The diversity of membership among the life peers means that there is normally someone who can speak with authority on even the most obscure subject. There is an impressive array of experience and talent. Many successful industrialists and businessmen become life peers, as do some trade unionists (especially after their retirement). So too, senior academics, people active in local government, the voluntary sector and the arts have also been given peerages. Relatively free from the constraints of time and able to speak in a less partisan atmosphere, debates do produce some interesting contributions from members with specialist knowledge and expertise, be it on education, the economy, welfare or a host of other topics.

- An appointed House provides an opportunity to bring in more women and members of minority groups, especially if appointment is placed in the hands of an independent appointments commission.

- The chamber has done useful work of revision and also shown a spirit of independence in the last couple of decades or so. The so-called resurgence of the Lords in that period has been attributed to: the large number of life peers and the specialisms they feed into debates; the arrival of television, which created a little more interest in its proceedings; and the greater willingness of party members to defy the whips and vote with the cross-benchers. Governments of both parties have been frequently defeated.

Tony Blair's first phase of reform has left a more justifiable House willing to assert itself. Whereas the Conservatives (1979–97) were defeated on 241 occasions, Labour (1997–2010) suffered 528 defeats. The issues covered ranged from proposals to modify the jury system to freedom of information, from privatisation of the National Air Traffic Service to fox hunting. During the passage of the Prevention of Terrorism Bill (2004–5) alone, the Lords inflicted eighteen defeats over the detention of terrorist suspects. The Coalition has suffered twenty defeats (as of 15.06.2011), four of them during the passage of the Parliamentary Voting System and Constituencies Bill in early 2011.

Two present peers have written interesting defences of the House of Lords. Melvyn Bragg,[4] the author, television presenter and one-time left-wing opponent of the House, was made a Labour peer, with the title of Lord Bragg of Wigton. Since his elevation, he has become aware of its virtues, in particular noting the quality of debate and the value of the work of revision:

> The debates on statements from the Commons – on Kosovo, for instance – are often of high quality, as are the Wednesday debates initiated by the different parties in rotation. But it is in the scrutinising of legislation that the House makes its true mark. In the first few years, I took several people to the place and often at night, say about 10, we would go into the debating chamber and find a score of mostly lawyers carefully clarifying Bills which had been whipped out hot and perhaps too hastily from the scrummage of the Commons . . .

The Conservative peer and constitutional specialist, Lord Norton,[5] has provided another insight. He argues that the existing second chamber adds value to the political process, in that it complements the work of the Commons and reduces the pressures upon it. In particular, Norton argues:

> The Lords fulfils well the functions of legislative revision, scrutiny, debate, and administrative scrutiny . . . It has the membership and the time to ensure that these functions are fulfilled effectively . . . [moreover] Legitimacy does not necessarily derive from election, but from recognition that people are properly qualified to fulfil a particular task and that the method by which they are selected is appropriate to that end.

In addition to these positive defences of the chamber, there is the negative case for broadly maintaining the present arrangements. This is based on a dislike of the main alternative, an elected or mainly elected alternative. In the eyes of its critics, such an option would not only duplicate the House of Commons but also become a rival to it, a danger that is increased in Britain if the upper body is elected by some scheme of proportional representation and can therefore claim to be highly representative of the people. Moreover, an elected body would be likely to press for greater powers than those enjoyed by the existing House; provides no obvious added value in terms of improving the quality of legislation; and might generate embarrassingly low voter turnouts.

The case against the present House of Lords

The major criticism still concerns the basis of membership. Phase One of the Blair package may have removed the hereditaries, but the House still lacks a democratic basis. Tony Benn has often remarked that when considering those who occupy positions of power, the key question is: 'Can they be removed?' In the present chamber, the answer is 'no'. Peers are there for a long period, be they bishops or life peers.

Specifically, it is argued that:

- (by many members of the Labour opposition) the task of Lords reform is unfinished. A Phase Two was always intended by the Labour government, for although the major anomaly of heredity has been removed, the present membership is still able to inflict damage on an elected Centre-Left government, by virtue of its Conservative dominance. On issues such as fox hunting, the Lords was between 1997 and 2010 only too willing to frustrate the wishes of the lower chamber. On three occasions, the Commons voted overwhelmingly to abolish blood sports, but the Lords proved obstructive. Hence the need to use the Parliament Act in 2004 to get the measure onto the statute book.
- (by critics) the present situation is not significantly better than it was previously. Heredity may be an unacceptable basis for membership of a legislature today, but so too is appointment. Given the basis of its present membership, the House of Lords does not have the legitimacy to flex its muscle, whereas with a democratic chamber, real power could be exercised. Those who oppose an elected House of Lords are said to fear a second chamber that could delay legislation, hold ministers to account, scrutinise treaties and public appointments. Yet these are powers exercised by second chambers in most liberal democracies.

- the current House of Lords should reflect Britain as it is today. As of March 2011, only 180 (21.8 per cent) were women and thirty-six (4.4 per cent) were from an ethnic minority. Continuing to appoint members would ensure an upper house of ageing white men, whereas an election – particularly one conducted under a 'fair voting' system – would yield an assembly that represents the people and in which women and minorities would have a chance of election.

Charter 88 has from its inception campaigned for a fully elected chamber. Its Director[6] complains of the failure to embrace fully the democratic idea:

> Only Britain could lay claim to be the mother of all parliamentary democracies, but refuse to allow voters to elect those that govern them. The only other wholly, or majority, appointed second chambers exist in small numbers in countries like Lesotho and Swaziland. It seems strange that we should wish to follow those examples rather than the elected chambers of Western Europe, the USA and Australia . . . ultimately only election confers legitimacy in modern government.

In a recent policy paper,[7] Charter 88 elaborated on the case against an appointed chamber:

> The Second Chamber should provide a counterweight to the House of Commons. It should also perform a broader constitutional role, reflecting the UK's evolving constitution. The current House of Lords does neither job effectively. Its powers are used sparingly, because it fears for its own legitimacy, and it is increasingly distanced from developments elsewhere in government.

The Constitution Unit has become increasingly alarmed at short-term Coalition plans to make the chamber reflective of the share of the vote secured by the parties in the 2010 election. These provide for an increase in the size of the Lords to 1062, making it 'bloated and dysfunctional'. UCL academic Meg Russell[8] has pointed out that whereas Tony Blair averaged a relatively high thirty-seven peer appointments per year during his time in office and Gordon Brown only twelve, David Cameron appointed 117 in under a year (an annual rate of 128).

The future of the House of Lords: differing ideas

Lords' reform has always been controversial and for this reason, it tends to lose its priority the longer a government remains in office. It wins few votes in a general election. Moreover, it has always been difficult to achieve agreement on the nature of the chamber that should emerge. Labour was unable to win sufficient backing in the House of Commons for any of the ideas it proposed. However, in the 2010 election all three parties were committed to change. The Conservatives and Liberal Democrats both expressed support for a democratic chamber and reaffirmed this in the Coalition agreement. Their detailed proposals for Lords reform were published in May 2011. They included:

- a 300-member hybrid house, of which 80 per cent were to be elected, 20 per cent appointed, and space set aside for some Anglican bishops;
- provision for members to serve a single non-renewable terms of fifteen years and for former MPs to stand for election.

Norton[9] has pointed out that such ideas amount not really to reform, but rather abolition and replacement.

The main functions of the House of Commons

The key roles of the lower chamber are:

- *Law-making.* The Commons has a significant role in the legislative process, not in the sense of 'making the law' but rather in reacting to the initiatives of government; about a third of parliamentary time is spent on making and amending legislation. Most public bills come from the government of the day, although some are introduced by backbench MPs (private members bills). Legislation takes up much of the time of the House; in 1999–2000, 560 hours were spent on government legislation and 83 more on that deriving from MPs. In Parliament, bills pass through eleven stages, five of which are in the lower house – First Reading, Second Reading (debate on principles), Third Reading (debate on details), Committee Stage (taken in **Standing Committees**) and finally the Report Stage (amended bill, reported back to whole House).

Box 3.3 The method of appointment to second chambers in other countries

The manner of determining membership of second chambers varies between countries. There are four main ways of choosing members of an upper house:

- *Direct election* is the most common and according to Hague and Harrop[10] is used in twenty-seven out of sixty-six chambers – e.g. Australia, the Czech Republic and the United States (see p. 104). Partial election is a possible variation, as considered for the British Phase Two. Election is widely used in federal countries, for there it can serve the purpose of safeguarding the individual states against encroachment by the federal government.
- *Indirect election* is the second most common (21/66). Sometimes, indirectly elected houses are selected by members of local authorities (the now non-existent Swedish body was composed entirely of members elected by local councillors), sometimes by members of the lower house (Norway). The French Senate is elected by electoral colleges of councillors and deputies in each department, so that it provides for a combination of election by local authorities and election by the lower house.
- *Appointment, usually by the government and sometimes for life* (16/66). Members are nominated for life by the government of the day. Canada has a second chamber, the Senate, whose members are nominated for life by the Governor-General in theory, but by the government of the day in practice. Nominations tend to be made on the basis of a candidate's support for the party in power. The Italian Senate has a handful of senators-for-life, in a powerful chamber that has equal status with the lower house. Those who wish to retain an appointed House of Lords sometimes argue for changing the means by which new members are appointed, with the introduction of a statutory appointments commission to replace prime ministerial appointment.
- *Vocational representation*. Ireland's unique Senate has members elected by graduates of Irish universities, others nominated by the Prime Minister and forty-three elected from five vocational panels (Cultural and Educational, Agricultural, Labour, Industrial and Commercial, and Administrative).

Governments normally get their way on legislation, because of their majority in the chamber. Just occasionally a bill may be withdrawn in response to Parliamentary pressure – i.e. the Post Office privatisation plans of the Major government were dropped before they reached the Commons. Very rarely is a government bill defeated, though the Shops Bill (to liberalise Sunday trading) was lost on a free vote in 1986 and the Blair government suffered four House of Commons defeats during its 10 years in office, all 2005–6. (In November 2005, an amendment to the Terrorism Bill to allow terrorist suspects to be held without charge for 90 days was defeated 291 to 322. Twice on the same day in January 2006 a motion to disagree with a Lords' amendment to the Racial and Religious Hatred Bill was lost.)

There is potential for amendment of legislation, but few changes are made against the wishes of ministers; around 90 per cent of those carried are introduced by ministers. In other words, even though it is the most time-consuming area of the work of the House, the impact of Parliament on legislation is modest. The conclusion is that Parliament is inefficient in its legislative role, a conclusion born out by a report of the Commons Liaison Committee,[11] which wanted more consultation and more pre-legislative study by Departmental Select Committees, among other things.

- *Raising and spending public money.* Parliament's permission is needed for raising and spending money, but this is virtually automatic. The government takes key decisions and although the House has the ultimate deterrent of rejecting proposals this did not happen in the twentieth century. The Commons plays a scrutinising role, mainly carried out in departmental Select Committees and via the Public Accounts Committee. But, as Graham Thomas[12] writes: 'Parliament has largely given up its role in financial matters to the executive'. This is indicated by the fact that only three days of parliamentary time per annum are devoted to consideration of the estimates of the money required by each government department.

- *Acting as a watchdog over the government.* Probably the most important function of the contemporary House of Commons is the scrutinising and influencing of government. This role is exercised

Box 3.4 Types of bill

Public bills alter the general law of the land and affect public policy. They concern the whole community. Most public bills are *government bills* and are brought in by the relevant departmental Minister who pilots them through the House. *Private members bills* are introduced by MPs and *private peers bills* by members of the upper house.

By contrast, *private bills* affect a section of the community or some particular interest such as a local authority or business. The procedure differs from that for public bills.

by MPs individually and by the House as a whole. The work of scrutiny and influence goes on all the time and finds expression in everything the House does. Parliamentary scrutiny is carried out in several ways, such as via questions, debates, committees and of course by the opposition parties – especially Her Majesty's Opposition. Often, the most significant criticism is that from government backbenchers, because ministers know that they need the votes of their MPs and so they may make concessions to them.

The House as a watchdog over government

Scrutiny via Her Majesty's Opposition

The existence of an official opposition party is regarded as one of the litmus tests of a democracy. In Britain, HM Opposition is the second largest party in the House. It is given special time and opportunities in the procedures of the Commons, and is traditionally consulted on issues where bipartisanship is desirable. Its importance is recognised by the payment of an official salary to the Leader of the Opposition and Opposition Chief Whip. The Opposition also gets a share of the '**Short Money**', the grant payable to opposition parties to help them carry out their parliamentary business, fund their travel and associated expenses and finance the running costs of the Leader of the Opposition's office.

*   The Opposition has three main functions:
*   *It opposes the government.* It stood at the previous election on the

basis of distinctive principles and policies, and naturally opposes ministers when they do things differently.

- *It supports the government where appropriate, not opposing for the sake of so doing.* This is the concept of responsible, constructive opposition. Careful scrutiny is given, but if ministers do things broadly seen to be in the national interest (e.g. over a foreign policy issue such as policy in Afghanistan), then the Opposition will try to be bipartisan. Sometimes, the Opposition will support the government when one of its policies is running into trouble from its own backbenchers, as when the Cameron-led Conservatives supported Tony Blair over the introduction of tuition fees.
- *The Opposition is also an alternative government.* If its criticisms are not responsible and well thought out, it will lack credibility and be seen as obstructive. The Opposition will need to review its policies as circumstances change and produce a coherent and convincing range of alternative courses for action.

Problems and opportunities for the Opposition

- The Opposition lacks the information available to the government. Ministers have civil servants/political advisers to brief them and are in a position to 'know the state of the books'. Oppositions lack 'official' help and detailed knowledge.
- Governments set the political agenda and the Opposition normally has to respond to it. Ministers can take over the best Opposition policies and the Prime Minister sets the election date to suit his party's advantage (or has done until 2010 – see pp. 94–5).
- There is pressure from dispirited activists to push the party back to an 'extreme' position with which they are more content – e.g. the Conservatives on Europe after 1997. Activists like to see clear water between themselves and ministerial policies, but shedding the middle of the road may put off more centrist voters.
- Morale can be low, especially after a massive election defeat – such as Labour in the early–mid-1980s and the Conservatives post 1997. There seems little point in turning up to be defeated by a massive majority. Division and in-fighting often set in, as some shadow ministers turn on the work of those who served as ministers in their party's previous spell in government.

- Prospects for re-election can seem dismal, when the majority is vast. It seems like a long heave, before the public forget the errors committed when they were in office.
- If they try to reverse party policy too quickly in order to expose governmental weakness, voters may ask why they didn't get things right when they were in government.

Whilst most days in the House of Commons are set aside for government business, twenty days in each session are set aside for opposition debates. Of these days, seventeen are at the disposal of the Leader of the Opposition and three can be used by the leader of the smaller, third party. Otherwise, the Opposition has no formal powers in setting the parliamentary agenda, although in reality they have a certain influence through a process known as the **usual channels**.

For ex-ministers, life in opposition requires a very different set of skills to life in government. It is about holding the government to account. Action in three areas is common to success: written parliamentary questions to wheedle out difficult detail and create material for media releases, parliamentary procedure (particularly devices like 'urgent questions', which force government ministers back to the floor of the House of Commons to explain their actions) and media work (via tight coordination through the central party press office).

Scrutiny via Question Time

Question Time is a very British practice, though Canada has a similar system. The practice of MPs asking questions of ministers in the House developed substantially in the twentieth century. Oral questions are asked to departments on a rota basis. Some are asked to find out information, but others are often vehicles for making a party point – perhaps by raising a constituency problem. Those not answered in the House get a written reply. In addition to those raised orally, some 35,000 written questions are asked.

Prime Minister's Question Time used to be held for fifteen minutes twice a week. Originally introduced by Harold Macmillan, it was modified by Tony Blair in 1997 to its present once weekly half-hour Wednesday session. He wanted a less confrontational system and – so critics alleged – to spare himself the extra session of an encounter for which he did not much care. For many politically interested television viewers, Question Time – as portrayed in news extracts or live on the Parliamentary Channel – is the high point of the parliamentary week, a regular joust between the party leaders.

The arrival of the television cameras and the use of extracts on news bulletins have served to personalise politics even more. Television likes Question Time, an entertaining spectacle that often generates little light but considerable drama. The institution began to degenerate in the Kinnock-Thatcher era and despite the changed format it is still a knockabout, rough contest. Though often viewed as an ordeal by the Prime Minister, he or she has the advantage of being well briefed and able to speak last.

Scrutiny via select committees

A system of departmental select committees began to function in 1980, after years of *ad hoc* committee arrangements. Fourteen committees were set up, each to monitor the work of one government department – e.g. one for Foreign Affairs, one for Home Affairs. Membership of the nineteen current committees varies from eleven to seventeen and reflects party strengths in the House. The Committee of Selection appoints members, for the lifetime of a Parliament. Often MPs are reappointed in the next Parliament, if they are re-elected – this longevity enables them to acquire a real expertise on their subject.

Select committees have powers to send for persons, papers and records, and receive evidence from ministers and civil servants. They can use the services of outside experts. They are each empowered to establish a sub-committee, two in the case of the departmental committees on the Environment, Food and Rural Affairs and the Transport, Local Government and the Regions.

The advantages claimed for select committees are that:

- members work in a less partisan way than is possible in the whole House; they try to produce an agreed report
- members are often well informed, developing a real specialism on the subjects within their orbit
- members can feed their knowledge back into House of Commons debates and so help to inform others
- they have made government more open, evidence being taken in public and ministers being examined in a thorough way.

But:

- in recent years, the Whips have tried to keep more independent MPs off committees and not reappoint those who are critical (the worst example occurred in 2001, when the Labour leadership made an abortive attempt to keep two committee chairpersons off the committees).
- on occasion, there have been other allegations of ministerial intervention. During the **Hutton Inquiry**, the Chairman of the Foreign Affairs committee declared that the Defence Secretary had made a request to his committee members, suggesting that they avoid asking awkward questions about the issue of Iraqi weapons of mass destruction.
- committees need more resources: they have too small a budget.
- they generate much paperwork, but their reports may or may not be debated – then they are put on a shelf and forgotten.
- they need more powers: ministers are sometimes evasive or decline to answer clearly.

Elected representatives: the duties and responsibilities of British MPs

The proper role of an MP has been much debated. The classic case for allowing an MP to act as an individual, once elected, was set out in 1774 by a well-known political theorist of the day, Edmund Burke, who had just been elected for Bristol. In a letter to his new constituents, he informed them that MPs should not be considered to be merely delegates or agents of the voters in the area for which they had been elected. Rather, they should be considered firstly as members of Parliament, representing the one interest of the nation. They must define this according to their own judgement of the issues to be decided by Parliament:

> Your representative owes you, not his industry only, but his judgement: and he betrays, instead of serving you, if he sacrifices it to your opinion.

Burke was of course writing before the advent of party and before the massive increase in constituency work of recent years. But many members would still argue that on issues of private morality, they have a duty to seek out information, listen to the speeches in the House and then make up their mind in the light of what they hear and not under the pressure of their constituency postbag.

Members of Parliament have several obligations that may on occasion conflict with each other. The four main spheres of responsibility are to:

- *Party*. It was because of the party label that the MP got elected. It is entitled to demand loyalty in return. Both parties well understand that lack of unity and discipline damaged Labour's position in the period 1979–87, just as they helped bring about the Conservative defeat in subsequent elections prior to 2010. MPs are expected to toe the party line in debates and votes, attend party committees and promote the party's outlook and policies – keeping the national leadership and local association satisfied with his performance. Austin Mitchell,[13] a long-serving Labour MP, has written disparagingly of the baleful influence of party, describing it as 'a career ladder to climb, a substitute for thought and a whirl of the obsessive. In Parliament, the party is a framework of control, ensuring that MPs tramp through the lobbies, feeding party points every day, providing yah-boo fun, and trundling them to every by-election as unpaid door knockers'.

- *Constituency*. MPs are careful to nurse their constituencies, by holding regular surgeries, promoting any constituency interests (such as fishing or the motor industry), attending political meetings and various social functions, and receiving any constituents who visit Westminster. Much of the work of MPs today is taken up with welfare-type work on behalf of constituents. They are expected to handle grievances and problems, and ensure that they are dealt with at the appropriate level – perhaps by asking a question, speaking in an **adjournment debate** in the House or seeing/writing to the relevant minister. The prospect of bad publicity in the media makes it likely that organisations will be responsive to MPs' activities.

- *Nation*. Each MP has an obligation to the whole country. He serves in the national legislature and can be expected to attend regularly and make a contribution by taking part in debates, asking questions, playing a part in select and standing committees, and scrutinising the Executive and making ministers accountable. He should inform himself about the various problems on which he is called to vote and ensure that he bears in mind the national interest as well as those above.

- *Conscience.* MPs have their own ideas and preferences. They may wish to introduce private members' legislation on some area of concern. They have their own conscience to consider and cannot be reasonably expected to speak and act in defiance of what they know is right or wrong.

Of course, there are *conflicting responsibilities* outlined above. An MP will be expected by his constituents to present the local viewpoint when there is a problem such as an industry in decline or the threat of closure of a car plant. But he needs to see the problem in its national setting. It may be that economic reality dictates that particular goods can no longer be economically manufactured locally.

Personal and party interests may conflict. A left-wing Labour MP may be unable to support his government's acceptance of a nuclear defence policy, just as a pro-European Conservative may feel he has to support positive involvement in the European Union in spite of the leadership's approach, which in opposition was often lukewarm. Personal and constituency interests may also differ. A pro-abortion MP may find himself out of step with his largely Roman Catholic constituents, just as a 'liberal' on capital punishment may find his views create local difficulties. So too might a pro-European member have difficulty in representing a fishing port where there is a backlash against the EU Common Fisheries Policy. (**NB** According to a survey in 2006,[14] in exercising their responsibilities, MPs on average work seventy-two hours a week, twelve more than in 1982. Of this, 40 per cent of their time is spent on constituency issues. Ninety per cent of them claim to be more interested in their constituency than they are in the party or national interest.)

Factors influencing the effectiveness of MPs

The ability of MPs to act effectively and independently as free agents has been restricted by the demands of party loyalty and by increasing domination of the House of Commons by the government of the day.

MPs know that their parties expect them to show support in the lobbies and that opportunities for independent thought and action are few. Those who have been dissidents have often fallen foul of the party, so that the number of mavericks is relatively small. For those MPs who have no hopes of future promotion or whose parliamentary career is coming to an end, party discipline may not be a problem and some on the Labour benches in the Blair/Brown years were prone to rebellion (see Table 3.1 below). For most, party is an obvious constraint.

An MP's ability to do his job well is also limited by:

- *inadequate facilities.* These may have improved over the last generation, but MPs who have had experience of the worlds of commerce and industry will probably find the lack of office space and equipment, and constituency help, a real impediment.
- *the immense amount and complexity of government business.* Government was probably always complex to those involved and there never was a 'golden age' in which MPs knew everything about every aspect of policy. In the twentieth century, the role of government has dramatically expanded and we now live in the age of the managed economy and welfare state. The voters expect more from their governments at home and the demands of global interests and responsibilities (such as involvement in the European Union) create additional areas of ministerial activity.
- *the growing burden of constituency work.* Constituents assume that their member will be active in taking up their problems, on anything from consumerism to welfarism – because these are the sorts of issue with which government is now concerned. Faced by this situation, the MPs find it best to specialise in selected areas, for it is unlikely that they can be informed about the whole range of policy issues. Their problem is not so much a lack of information but rather a lack of time in which to master it, not least because the responsibilities of constituency work have now become so much more demanding.

Table 3.1 The top five rebellions under the Blair/Brown governments, respectively

Prime Minister	Topic	Date	Size of rebellion
Tony Blair	Decision to invade Iraq	March 2003	138
	Decision to invade Iraq	February 2003	120
	Renewal of Trident missile	March 2007	94
	Renewal of Trident missile	March 2007	88
	Higher Education Bill: tuition fees	January 2004	72
Gordon Brown	Counter-terrorism Bill, re. 42 days	June 2008	36
	Energy Bill: treatment of renewable energy providers	April 2008	35
	Criminal Justice and Immigration Bill	January 2008	34
	Welfare Reform Bill: single parents with young children	March 2009	30
	Welfare Reform Bill: removal of JSA benefits for 18–25-year-olds	March 2009	29

NB In February 2011, Coalition MPs clocked up their hundredth rebellion. The largest of these was over tuition fees, in December 2010. Some twenty-one Liberal Democrats rebelled, while twenty-seven – including the party's ministers – backed the change, and eight abstained. Six Tory MPs voted against the motion and two abstained.

All MPs now have a very large postbag. Letters, faxes and emails are sent to them in ever-increasing numbers. Most MPs are dealing with correspondence for two or three hours daily. But they also have other representative duties, ranging from taking part in meetings

Box 3.5 MPs and party loyalty

Critics often lament the strength of party discipline and see MPs as 'lobby fodder', lacking in independent judgement. Michael Foot[15] once claimed that: 'two well-whipped forces confront one another in formal, pre-arranged combat. Speeches of Gladstonian power or Disraeli-ite wit are unlikely to shift a single vote'.

Unity is essential for any party, because:

- splits can mean the loss of the governing party's majority; the survival of both the Callaghan and Major governments was often in jeopardy.
- governments wish to legislate on programmes on which they have fought the election and need to count on translating ideas into action.
- divisions are harmful to parties, for they provide opportunities for other parties and journalists to expose and exploit their differences.
- parties which do face three ways in a division cause difficulty for the public and commentators who are unsure what party policy actually is.

Parties, then, like to avoid divisions, aware as they are that they can damage their credibility, in the way that the splits under John Major over Europe, taxation and other issues contributed to the Conservative defeat in 1997. They realise that there are inevitably internal differences, for parties are broad coalitions of sometimes quite widely differing viewpoints. But they expect that MPs will not often question party policy in public or be disloyal when crucial parliamentary votes are counted.

Most MPs can accept these constraints, even though occasionally a lone view such as Michael Foot's speaks out against excessive **whipping**. Why do MPs normally toe the party line?

- However much they doubt their own side's policy, the last thing they wish to do is to endanger the government's survival and see the Opposition occupy the ministerial seats.
- They know that in the privacy of a backbench meeting (in the 1922 Committee or in the Parliamentary Labour Party) they can argue for a concession from the Minister and – especially if its seems that their doubts are widely held – probably get one. The Minister may well be flexible in order to ensure that his bill gets safely through: several concessions were made during the

passage of the bill providing for tuition fees for students in higher education, 2003–4, in order to ensure that the government got the measure on the statute book.

- Finally, there is the 'carrot and the stick'. For some young MPs who hope to climb the ministerial ladder, the prospect of early promotion keeps them in line. Should there be persistent rebellion, then more formal sanctions may be applied such as loss of the whip – as happened to eight Eurosceptics under the Major government.

MPs were increasingly willing to rebel in Tony Blair's second term, in which the government had a very large majority. In 2003, the year when the invasion of Iraq was launched, its own members were in assertive mood. At the beginning of the year, the largest-ever rebellions were recorded over Iraq, but on fox hunting, foundation hospitals and hunting high levels of dissent were recorded. Furthermore, many members abstained rather than vote with the government. The habit of rebellion seemed to become well established, as many Labour MPs seemed keen to inflict a 'bloody nose' on a prime minister whose leadership style and policies they disliked. The Brown government, with a considerably smaller majority as a result of the 2005 election, suffered several smaller rebellions. Eleven of the Coalition rebellions have concerned Europe (predominantly by Conservative MPs). In early 2011, others covered issues such as fixed-term parliaments, reform of the postal service, taxation of the financial sector (mainly Conservatives) and the Educational Maintenance Allowance (mainly Liberal Democrats).

Free votes
In addition, of course, there are some free votes – primarily on sociomoral issues – in which MPs can choose to express their individual attitudes rather than act along party lines in the voting lobbies. In 2003, there was such a vote on fox hunting in which 329 Labour members rejected the preferred ministerial option of licensed hunts. The abolition of hunting is one issue on which MPs undoubtedly got their way, a total ban being achieved against the wishes of the Prime Minister who found himself using the Parliament Act to enforce a measure about which he had grave doubts.

In February 2010, there was a large all-party majority (234 to 21) against allowing prisoners to vote in UK elections, following a decision seven years previously by the European Court of Human Rights that banning convicted killer John Hirst from the polls had breached his right to participate in the democratic process.

with ministers and pressure groups to being available for interviews with journalists. The task is very time-consuming.

The significance of the average backbench MP

There never was a 'golden age' in which MPs were well informed about all aspects of government and were free to exercise judgement free of party pressures. But certainly 150 years ago, the demands upon members were much less than they are now and they additionally enjoyed much social standing within the community. Today, MPs are often derided by the voters, many of whom are cynical about their ideas, performance and integrity.

The capacity of individual MPs to influence national events is limited. They may ask questions, speak in debates, be active in standing or select committees and be well known as a crusader for good causes. Maybe a private members bill will be forever associated with their name. Most MPs do not have a high profile, but some are often seen on the media and can make an impact via broadcasting. Otherwise, much depends on what they regard as their primary tasks. There are different routes that they may follow, as described by Professor Richards some years ago in *Honourable Members*:[17]

- *Useful party members.* Such members tend to specialise in particular areas of policy and serve on the relevant committees and appear on the media to discuss issues on which they can contribute their expertise. They are useful to the party, often loyal in the lobbies and may become a Parliamentary Private Secretary or advance further.
- *Good constituency members.* Such MPs devote much of their time to constituency work, taking up personal cases and earning themselves a well-deserved reputation for diligence and effectiveness on behalf of those they seek to serve.
- *Individualists: independents within the system.* These MPs are sometimes members of the awkward squad, often colourful characters who are not easily contained within the party system. Genuine independents are few (e.g. ex-broadcaster Martin Bell, the member for Tatton, 1997–2001), but some MPs within the main parties often take a distinctive line and worry little about advancement. For example, Richard Shepherd (Con) has acquired a reputation

Box 3.6 Levels of public confidence in the House of Commons and its members

The expenses scandal

The parliamentary expenses scandal was triggered by the leak and subsequent publication by the *Telegraph* group in 2009 of expense claims made by MPs over several years. Public outrage was caused by disclosure of widespread actual and alleged misuse of the permitted allowances and expenses. The scandal aroused widespread popular anger against MPs and resulted in a large number of resignations, sackings, de-selections and retirement announcements, together with public apologies and the repayment of expenses. It also created pressure for political reform extending well beyond the issue of expenses. When three former Labour ministers were caught up in an 'MPs for hire' lobbying sting, it only served to intensify public feeling.

A loss of confidence in politics?

Every year, the Hansard Society does a form of 'health check' on public attitudes towards politics. Its 2010 Audit of Political Engagement[16] shows that while the MPs' expenses scandal has affected the public's satisfaction with and perception of MPs and the Westminster Parliament, there has not been a collapse of trust in politicians or politics:

- 26 per cent of respondents said that they trusted politicians generally (27 per cent in 2004), 73 per cent said they distrusted politicians (70 per cent in 2004). Because levels of trust were already low, the MPs' expenses scandal merely confirmed and hardened the public's widely held scepticism about politicians, rather than fundamentally changed their views.
- Public dissatisfaction with how MPs in general were doing their jobs rose by 8 per cent to 44 per cent in the same period, but dissatisfaction with how individual MPs were performing rose by only 3 per cent to 16 per cent. Twice as many people (38 per cent) were satisfied with the way that their own MP did his/her job than were dissatisfied.

Another significant finding was that there had been a big decline in the perceived impact of Parliament on people's lives, compared to other institutions like 'the media'. Only 19 per cent thought Parliament was one of the three influential institutions, an 11 per cent drop on 2004. But 60 per cent thought Parliament 'worthwhile', with only 14 per cent disagreeing.

> Moreover, while 71 per cent said they had discussed MPs'
> expenses in the last year, only 41 per cent said they have discussed
> politics or political news. Perhaps the gap between these figures
> suggests people may not regard MPs' expenses as a 'political'
> issue, which may help explain why the scandal has had such mixed
> results in terms of trust and satisfaction with MPs and Parliament.
> **NB** See also p. 18 for more on trust in politicians and trust in
> government.

as a persistent, diligent and courageous member, because of his willingness to act independently by pursuing causes of importance to him in the areas of freedom of information/state secrecy and abuse of executive power.

- *Part-timers.* Some MPs still seek to combine their parliamentary activity with an outside occupation, perhaps serving in journalism, the law or business. The number of part-timers has diminished in recent parliaments.

MPs can of course fit into more than one grouping. A hard-working part-timer can still be a good constituency MP. So too can an independent. Similarly, a long-term party loyalist can mature into a sturdy individualist.

Parliamentary reform in recent years

Parliamentary reformers argue that there is a growing imbalance between the government and Parliament. The trend of recent years has been towards the growth in executive power at the expense of legislatures, a trend not confined to Great Britain. Writers such as Philip Norton[18] feel that it can be overstressed and point out that in recent years Parliament has become more effective, with MPs becoming better informed and professional, and the House more effective. But even if they doubt some aspects of the diagnosis, they still see a need for further reforms to make Parliament work better.

Interest in the subject of parliamentary reform has increased in recent years as part of a general concern about the health and vitality of British political institutions. Surveys have shown that many people now question the way in which Parliament does its work. Some of the concern voiced by academic commentators and journalists is about the House of Commons as a collective entity, whilst at the popular level there is more scepticism about the conduct, performance and work of individual MPs. Such public disquiet has encouraged some people to seek to achieve their goals by extra-parliamentary action, rather than via traditional democratic channels.

Differing approaches to reform
There are differing approaches to the issue of Parliament's main role. For some writers, it is there mainly to sustain the government and provide a forum via which it can mobilise public opinion and in which the opposition parties can offer their criticisms of government policy. In other words, it is a debating chamber in which grievances are aired and the party struggle conducted day-to-day. If this view is taken, then it is unlikely that fundamental reform will be undertaken.

On the other hand, there are others who believe that Parliament must be a strong body, wielding power and influence. They think that it should hold the government of the day to account for its actions, acting as a vigilant watchdog. This is an idealistic view of what Parliament should be like, rather than a description of how it operates for much of the time. Those who want to see Parliament reformed in such a way that MPs have greater influence are talking the language of criticism. They lament the reduction of Parliament's influence in the twentieth century and want to see it act more effectively.

Academics and commentators advocate a range of ideas, some of which may be found in the following list:

- *More powerful select committees.* Critics say that more resources are needed, with a better budget, more staffing by experts, stronger powers to make ministers and officials answer, more attention to and debate of committee reports and less influence by the whips over selection of membership. The House did introduce payment for select committee chairs to come into force for the 2003–4 session, currently £14,581 on top of their standard MP's pay.
- *Better pay and facilities for MPs.* Pay and facilities are much better than they were a few decades ago, but many MPs still find that they cannot get all the secretarial and research help they need.

Many point to the need for more constituency help and better computer links with their local base.

- *Full-time MPs.* Many MPs regard membership of the House as a full-time occupation, though some MPs (traditionally mainly Conservatives) have second jobs. Critics say that no MP can do two jobs well and that the public are entitled to feel that they have the full commitment of their elected member. Pay and facilities need to be such that all MPs can be full-time; they can get experience of life outside Westminster in their holidays.
- *Less MPs.* In recent years, Philip Norton, Michael Howard and others have called for a cut in number to around 450. This would reduce the current payroll and by so doing enable more to be spent on better resourcing fewer MPs to enable them to operate effectively. As there are now more full-time MPs, pressure on the existing institution is considerable; for instance, MPs ask far more questions today, hoping that this will win them constituency approval. Norton wants a smaller, more professional house and makes the point that the present one is one of the largest elected chambers in the world (see Box 3.7 for details of current plans).
- *More free votes.* Strong party discipline seems to worry MPs much less than critics outside. They like free votes on social and moral topics, but accept that if governments are to push through their legislative programme then whipping is essential. Also, they know that there are other ways of influencing events.

Reforms have been introduced in recent years, including:

- *Changes to working hours.* In 2002, the House narrowly voted to end its antiquated sittings designed for a bygone age and work more family-friendly hours. Members decided that the House should not be remote and alien in its working practices. Rather, it should work hours that made it more accessible and intelligent to the voters who would receive a better explanation of key debates and divisions on the television. In 2005, following a revolt by a cross-party coalition of MPs and claims that the revised hours had 'sucked the very essence out of Commons debate', a compromise was reached, reverting to late sittings on Tuesdays.

Table 3.2 The working hours of the House of Commons

Monday	2.30 p.m.–10.00 p.m.
Tuesday	2.30 p.m.–10.00 p.m.
Wednesday	11.30 a.m.–7.00 p.m.
Thursday	11.30 a.m.–6.30 p.m.
Friday	9.30 a.m.–3.00 p.m.

NB The hours given show the usual finishing times, but on rare occasions the House may conclude its proceedings earlier or – more likely – continue beyond them. The Friday sessions only apply when private members' bills are being considered.

- *Improvements to the legislative process.* This has long been called for, to allow for more effective consultation and scrutiny. A Select Committee on Modernisation was set up after the 1997 election, and its first report – on the legislative process – urged more consultation on draft bills, more uses of pre-legislative scrutiny by select committees, better use of standing committees and that bills should be carried over from one session to the next, thus curtailing the use of the **guillotine**. (In October 2004, the House of Commons agreed to make temporary arrangements for carry-over permanent.)

Various changes have been introduced as a result of recent reports by the Commons Modernisation Committee, which considers the practices and procedures of the House. They have been cautious, but have potential for development. But procedural changes only go so far. Many critics feel that there needs to be a cultural change at Westminster about the role of the legislature in relation to the executive. This might involve changes such as electoral reform, an elected second chamber and fixed term parliaments (see also pp. 72–5, 340 and Box 3.7, respectively).

The social composition of elected legislators

In general, legislators tend to be overwhelmingly male, middle aged, middle class, and in North America and Europe, white; in fact,

Box 3.7 The Coalition and reforms affecting the House of Commons

Two flagship reforms of the Coalition were:

- *the Parliamentary Voting System and Constituencies Bill*. This provided for a referendum on the use of the alternative vote for general elections (as urged by the Liberal Democrats), and boundary changes to reduce the size of the House to 600 in time for the next election (as favoured by many Conservatives, who saw a redrawing of the political map as favourable to their electoral chances). This had a particularly sticky ride in the House of Lords, but was eventually received the Royal Assent early in 2011.

- *the Fixed Term Parliaments Bill*. This ends the Prime Minister's power to decide the date of the next election, thus ensuring that the next election takes place in May 2015; it also ends the Monarch's prerogative power to dissolve Parliament on the advice of the Prime Minister. It provides for five-yearly elections, thus making a rule of what has been the exception in recent electoral history in which elections have occurred in 1979, 1983, 1987, and again in 2001 and 2005; a four year interval is also the norm in European countries that have fixed terms. Mid-term dissolution would only be possible: if the government loses a confidence motion and no alternative government is confirmed by the House for fourteen days; or if more than two thirds of MPs (currently 434 out of a House of 650) vote for an early election. (In reality, Western European experience shows that only Norway succeeds in superglueing its electoral calendar. In Germany, post-war chancellors have thrice brought forward the election date, by engineering the requisite no confidence vote.) The bill is likely to be passed into law in mid 2011.

For and against fixed-term parliaments

Fixed-term parliaments are used in most elections in the UK, such as for the Scottish Parliament, National Assembly for Wales, the European Parliament and local elections. The French National Assembly operates on a five year cycle, the German Bundestag on a four year one. Both Australia and New Zealand have three year maximum terms.

Criticism of the current system centres on the fact that present arrangements give an advantage to the prime minister of the day, who can choose to call an election at the most advantageous time for him or her and thereby increase chances of re-election. It also means there is a period of uncertainty, before an election is called, which some say damages the conduct of politics. A recent example was the feverish speculation that Gordon Brown intended to call a snap election in 2007 to take advantage of a poll surge shortly after succeeding Tony Blair as prime minister. Opponents claim that knowing the date a long time in advance will lead to longer election campaigns, a lack of flexibility and the possibility of a 'lame duck' government limping on longer than it should. There is also the possibility that a government might still find a way of triggering an election when it wants one, by following German experience and engineering a vote of no confidence and deliberately trying to lose it.

European parliaments are notoriously unrepresentative of ethnic minorities. Berrington[19] has noted that 'almost every study of legislators in Western democracies shows that they come from more well-to-do backgrounds, are drawn from more prestigious and intellectually satisfying backgrounds and are much better educated than their electors'. As a general guide, right-wing parties have a heavy preponderance of legislators who have made their careers in business and commerce, whereas left-wing parties have a strong professional (particularly educational) representation. Law tends to be well represented in both parties, particularly in the United States. A growing number of people from the communications industry, newspapers, television and public relations, are now to be found in most legislatures.

The fate of women in national parliaments varies considerably across the world (see below). They have fared badly in the United States and in some European countries such as France, Greece, Ireland and Italy (all Catholic or Orthodox in religion) representation has traditionally been low. Scandinavia has high levels of female representation, often exceeding 40 per cent, its impressive record perhaps being explained by:

• a cultural and legal framework which is generally sympathetic to female advancement,
• a strong commitment on the part of political parties to promoting women as candidates and

Table 3.3 Regional averages in female representation, April 2011 (%)

Region	Female representation in lower chamber	Female representation in both houses combined
Nordic countries	42.1	n/a
Americas	22.3	22.5
Europe (excluding Nordic countries)	20.1	20.0
Asia	18.3	18.0
Sub-Saharan Africa	19.8	19.8
Pacific	12.4	14.7
Arab states	11.4	10.7

Figures based on those provided on the Inter-Parliamentary Union website, which is constantly updated (www.ipu.org)

NB Regions are classified by descending order of the percentage of women in the lower or single House; Nordic countries are all unicameral.

- the use of a proportional voting system, by which parties present lists of candidates to voters, rather than individual candidates.

Membership of Parliament in 2010, in particular the House of Commons

The House of Lords is unrepresentative of the nation. Few members belong to ethnic minorities or have a working-class background. There is a preponderance of middle-aged to elderly people, many peers having been appointed in middle age, having achieved distinction in their chosen field. The average age is currently around sixty-eight. Women are under-represented, although at 20.1 per cent of the membership in April 2011, little more so than in the lower chamber.

The House of Commons is overwhelmingly white. Of those elected up to and including the intake of 2001, all ethnic minority members belonged to the Labour Party. In 2010, of a record twenty-seven ethnic minority MPs, sixteen were Labour MPs, eleven

Conservatives. Eight MPs in the current House are Muslims, of whom for the first time there are three women, all Labour.

The Commons is also overwhelmingly middle class. Whereas Labour once saw it as its mission to bring 'workers' into Parliament, this is no longer the case. In 1918, 83 per cent of its MPs were working class; by 2010 the figure had dropped to 8.5 per cent. Many of its candidates are now drawn from the professions, a similar pattern to what has been happening with other social democratic and left-wing parties across much of Europe. The trend began in the 1960s, with an influx of Labour academics. Today, teachers in universities and schools are still strongly represented, as are other public sector professionals, political staffers and lawyers. The legal profession tends to be well represented in most legislatures, there being an obvious connection between lawyers who work in the law and parliaments that make it. Moreover, law provides a flexible work situation for candidates as they wage their campaign. They can also leave their job with relative ease and return to it, as they wish.

Other than the law, many Conservative MPs derive from business and city backgrounds, with a fair proportion of professionals who have worked in the media and public relations. Over half of them have been to public school (54 per cent), although far fewer have attended Eton (19 per cent) than was the case a few decades ago. Many MPs of all parties have a degree (more than 70 per cent), so that by occupation and education elected members are socially unrepresentative of those whom they serve.

MPs tend to be middle aged, because most people attain the position having made their mark in some other employment. This can be said to provide them with experience of life, but it also means that the voice of young people is neglected, causing some to feel alienated from the political system. In Britain, the average age of Conservatives at Westminster is forty-seven, of Liberal Democrats fifty and of Labour fifty-two. Fifteen MPs were under thirty at the time of the election.

Most people would probably be relieved to know that MPs are experienced and have levels of educational attainment higher than among the population at large, for members deal with complex issues of public policy. It is essential that they are literate and fluent, qualities not possessed by all UK inhabitants. Similarly, it is no bad thing that the small minority of persons in the community suffering from emotional disorders and various forms of inadequacy are not represented at Westminster. In other words, it is undesirable that the House of Commons should be an exact microcosm or mirror image of the whole population. Nor – in a chamber whose membership is elected – could that ever happen. Moreover, it is a fact that the people who come forward tend to be young to middle aged, highly educated, white and male.

Women in the House of Commons

In 1919, Nancy Astor became the first woman to sit in the House of Commons. However, progress on women's representation was slow, and did not increase to beyond 5 per cent of the membership until 1987. In 1997, the number of women elected to the Commons exactly doubled to 120, a record improved upon thirteen years later when 143 were returned. This still leaves Britain with a lower proportion of female representation than many countries not known for their democratic credentials, from Mozambique to Rwanda, from Argentina to Cuba.

Other than in 1970 and 1983, the bulk of female MPs have been on the Labour side and today the party is well ahead of the others in moving towards gender equality. There is a long way to go, but women make up nearly a third of the present Parliamentary Labour Party (81/258 MPs, 31.4 per cent).

Several factors contribute to the under-representation of women in Parliament:

- *child-bearing and home-making responsibilities*, which have traditionally prevented many women from seeking a parliamentary career until the children have become teenagers, the more so given the long and still often unsociable hours that MPs work. Members of selection committees, particularly in the Conservative Party, have tended to question women about their intentions and responsibilities with regard to their offspring.
- *the electoral system*. Whereas the use of proportional representation (see p. 334–46) encourages the adoption of a gender-balanced list of candidates, the use of single member constituencies makes their selection less likely.

Table 3.4 Comparison of female representation in the 'top five' countries, the UK and the USA

Country	Year of last election	% of women MPs	Electoral system
Rwanda	2008	56.3	List PR
Andorra	2011	53.6	List PR
Sweden	2010	45.0	List PR
South Africa	2009	44.5	List PR
Cuba	2008	43.2	Double ballot
UK = 50th	2010	22.0	FPTP
USA = 69th	2010	16.8	FPTP

[a] PR, proportional representation; FPTP, first past the post

Adapted from information provided by the Inter-Parliamentary Union (www.ipu. org), as calculated in April 2011 and based on lower houses in two chamber countries. The *world average*, calculated from the countries for which data was available, was 19.5 per cent. In the European Parliament elected in 2009, 257/736 (34.9%) MEPs were women; for the UK, the figure was 23/72 (31.9%).

• *the nature of parliamentary life*, which tends to be masculine and aggressive. Would-be female politicians may find themselves out of sympathy with the atmosphere of the House of Commons. The macho approach of some male members, obsessed as they are with point scoring and abuse, is unwelcoming to them. They may not feel confident about coping in such a traditionally male preserve.

The campaigning organisation, Fawcett, claims that there is active discrimination against women across the political parties, particularly in the candidate selection process. In addition, it suggests a neat summary of four other factors that can prevent women standing for Parliament – the four 'Cs' of culture, childcare, cash and confidence. Partly as a result of its persistent campaigning, the Sex Discrimination Act was amended in 2002 to allow parties to use positive measures such as all-women shortlists, to increase women's representation at all levels of politics.

Table 3.5 The number of women elected in selected elections since 1945				
Election	Conserv- ative	Labour	Liberal Democrat	Total number	% of members
1945	1	21	1	24	3.8
1964	11	17	0	28	4.4
1970	15	10	0	23	4.1
1983	13	10	0	23	3.5
1992	20	37	2	60	9.2
1997	13	102	3	120	18.2
2001	14	95	5	118	17.9
2005	17	98	10	128	19.8
2010	49	81	7	143	22.0

Does the under-representation of women and ethnic minorities matter?

Several points can be made in support of the proposition that it does matter, among them:

- It is dangerous in a democracy if groups with less wealth and power are under-represented, not just women and members of ethnic minorities, but also young people and members of the poorest section of the community. If they feel excluded, they may regard the legislature with some contempt and turn to other forms of political action to get their message across.
- Again, as long as certain groups are under-represented, there are likely to be fewer debates on issues affecting them, and the quality of debate may be poor, as many members do not take the matters under discussion seriously. As a result, full scrutiny by the media of the impact of government policy on such groups may be largely absent from the political process.
- Legislatures need the services of the most able people available, but at present much talent goes unrecognised. This is the more unfortunate, because the more women and members of ethnic

minorities that get elected, the more role models there are to encourage others of their own type to come forward and see politics as a realistic, attractive career option.

- All the mainstream parties talk of their aspiration to achieve a society in which people are able to progress on merit. They claim to dislike discrimination and to wish to encourage equal opportunities. It is therefore hypocritical for the legislature not to reflect these worthy principles in their composition.

Those who disagree might argue that:

- In a representative democracy, we select MPs broadly to reflect the interests of their constituents. To achieve this, it is not necessary for Parliament to be a mirror image of British society. The system is supposed to produce representation of people's political views. It is not essential or realistic to expect that membership will exactly be in proportion to the size of all the various groups within society.
- MPs should be able to represent the views of all their constituents, and it is not necessary to belong to a particular group or interest to put a case on their behalf. As long as they possess an ability to empathise with the needs of all sections of the population, they are capable of advancing its viewpoint. You don't have to inhabit a slum dwelling to appreciate that slums need to be cleared, even if your recognition of the full horrors might be more acute if you do so. Neither do you need to be a woman to understand that discrimination against women is hurtful, wrong and damaging to society.
- Women and other social groups are not homogeneous. They do not all possess the same needs and views. For instance, some women are pro-choice on abortion, some favour divorce and others are ardent feminists. Many take a contrary view. Class, employment, age, locality and lifestyle may be more important in determining political views than gender or race. For this reason, it is impossible to represent all women or minority peoples as a group, even if one wanted to do this.
- Above all, what we need are competent and caring people to represent us. The personal ability and party allegiance of any candidate should be the main determinants of who gets elected.

To draw attention to irrelevant factors such as gender in deciding on the selection of candidates may be unfair and result in reverse discrimination against the most suitable candidates for the job.

The pay and conditions of legislators

In terms of accommodation, equipment, staffing, library assistance and other amenities, American Congressmen are notably better placed than their British counterparts. Pay is markedly higher at $174,000 (February 2011), and perquisites are markedly more lavish. Perhaps the Commonwealth and Europe provide fairer allowances, for countries are generally less affluent in these areas than in the USA. Australia, Canada and New Zealand all provide superior office accommodation with separate rooms for the members and the staff who serve them.

MPs opted to forgo the 1 per cent rise for MPs in 2011–12 recommended by the independent Senior Salaries Review Body (SSRB), in the light of the imposition of a two-year pay freeze for public sector workers earning more than £21,000. They currently earn £65,738 (2011), on which they are subject to normal PAYE rates of taxation. They get help with the maintenance of an office and staff costs, including:

- an annual staffing allowance designed to pay for between two and three full-time equivalent staff
- certain IT equipment for offices
- training of staff
- exceptional expenses – e.g. for MPs who have constituencies with special problems.

Some members still voice criticism of the lack of constituency help they receive, whilst others feel that they could do with more research assistance at Westminster. The paucity of information technology services is frequently condemned, although there have been significant improvements in recent years. The new Incidental Expenses Provision is intended to help with expenses in running an office, such as office rents.

In recent years, there has been a developing trend to increased professionalism in the House of Commons. It has proved increasingly difficult to combine membership of Parliament with any outside activity, in part because of the growing constituency and other demands made upon MPs but also because other professions increasingly require full-time commitment from those who work for them. In both main parties, the tendency is to adopt relatively young candidates whose outside career experience has been in politically related occupations. Some would argue that such **career politicians** lack the sense of broad perspective that derives from having done another job; they have not inhabited the 'real' world and may not always possess the judgement that comes from knowing what goes on beyond Westminster.

The case of Denmark

Parliaments tend to be more effective in countries where minority or coalition governments are common. Ministers tend to seek more cross-party agreement to get their bills through and often seek to gain a broad consensus of opinion behind them. The average life of Danish administrations is around two and a half years, half the figure for Britain and Sweden. In order to survive, they are very reliant on parliamentary acquiescence. They build coalitions among MPs according to the issue under discussion. As Budge et al.[20] put it:

> [Danish] governments depend upon parliament rather than the other way round. But it is generally true that wherever coalitions are weak and quarrel internally, much more importance is attached to negotiations within parliament, than where governments are confident of winning legislative votes. Generally coalitions are weaker the more parties they include.

A country of only 4.5 million inhabitants, Denmark abolished its second chamber in 1953. Since then, special safeguards have been provided to prevent any legislation from being passed too hastily through the Folketing. For instance, one third of the members of that chamber can demand a referendum on a bill that has yet to receive royal approval. Again, the legislative procedure of the Folketing was revised, so that more time is given between the readings and to committee stages.

The case of the USA

The Founding Fathers devised a constitution based on the idea of the separation of powers, in which each component element could act as a check upon the influence of the other two. They expected that Congress would be able to dominate the federal government, and significantly dealt with it in Article 1.

Congress is a bicameral legislature, comprising the Senate and the House of Representatives. Both are law-making chambers directly elected by the people. They have broadly equal powers, making the Senate the most powerful upper house in the world.

In the federal USA, the Senate acts as a check on behalf of the states upon the House of Representatives, which is elected on the basis of population. The allotment of two senators to each state, irrespective of population, ensures that the voice of the states in all areas of the country is clearly expressed. Nevada, with less than half a million inhabitants, has as much representation as New York State with approaching 20 million.

In the nineteenth century, Congress was normally dominant and only three presidents were able to alter the balance of power in their favour. Thomas Jefferson, Andrew Jackson and Abraham Lincoln all had a Congress comprising a majority of supporters from their own party, but this was – and is – no guarantee of presidential power; yet they were people of great charisma and had evident leadership quality.

Writing in the 1880s, Woodrow Wilson[21] (later himself to be a 'strong' president) observed that 'in the practical conduct of the federal government . . . unquestionably, the predominant and controlling force, the centre and source of all motive and of all regulative power, is Congress'. With only a very few other exceptions, greater power resided on Capitol Hill than in the White House right down to 1933. Since the days of Franklin Delano Roosevelt, Americans have become used to a more assertive presidency. His assumption of office led to a massive extension of federal power as he sought to implement his New Deal proposals to lift the USA out of economic depression.

By the 1960s, commentators were beginning to write about the 'imperial presidency'. Some argued that presidents were acting too independently of Congress in both the domestic and foreign policy

Box 3.8 Are legislatures in decline across the world?

The constitutions of most countries describe the legislature, parliament or congress as the key decision-making body in the realm, or else accord it equal status with the executive. Yet in practice the reality is different, and over recent decades writers have often drawn attention to the alleged 'decline of legislatures'. In Britain, chapters have been written on the 'passing of Parliament', 'Parliament in decline' or 'the loss of parliamentary control'.

There is a wide spectrum of experience concerning national parliaments. In a minority of countries, legislatures are an essential part of the decision-making process; in many more (including most Western liberal democracies) they have been dominated by the executive branch; in several cases they are manipulated by an authoritarian government; and in a very few they are actually abolished or suspended, perhaps as a result of some form of military coup.

In the nineteenth century, the number of legislatures grew and their political significance increased and parliamentarianism was a feature of the period. In Britain, there are references to the years between 1832 and 1867 as the 'golden age of the private member'. Yet this situation was not to last. Many observers claim that in the twentieth century, in Britain and elsewhere, there was a general decline in the power and status of legislatures, relative to the power of executives and bureaucracies.

Evidence of the weakness of contemporary legislatures

- Increasingly, legislatures react to policy initiatives from the executive more than they create policy.
- Legislatures lack the support services (budgets, facilities and staffing) available to the executive.
- The technical expertise and knowledge resources available to legislatures are far less than available to those within the executive.
- Governments monopolise parliamentary time, often forcing bills through by procedural devices.
- Most legislation today emanates from the executive, not the legislature. In the middle of the nineteenth century, most social improvements were brought about on the initiative of private members.

But is the picture of legislative decline universal?
Some argue that the thesis of legislative decline overstates the picture. Legislatures may have declined as policy-shaping bodies, but – in Blondel's[22] words – they have become more important as 'communicating mechanisms'. As television cameras have been allowed into many chambers, members can directly address the public who – if only in snippets on the news – can see their legislators at work. This helps to raise the profile of MPs and emphasise the importance of the chamber as the central forum for national debate. Moreover, many assemblies have become more professional in recent years, improving the staffing and other resources available to members and adopting specialised committees to allow for more detailed scrutiny of the executive.

Norton[23] points out that in the new democracies legislatures have been created and in countries once under military rule, such as Brazil and Greece, they have been revived as soon as democracy was restored. In other words, the number of legislatures has greatly increased – 'they span the globe'. One reason for their adoption, he suggests, is that the public see them as important. Quoting Eurobarometer findings, he notes that 56 per cent of people in the UK saw Parliament as 'very important'. A majority of those surveyed in five countries examined similarly took this view.

Finally, in any case, the performance and power of legislatures varies. Not all assemblies are dying or impotent. Some are rather powerful structures, notably those of Denmark, Italy, Japan, Sweden and the United States – and the traditionally weak European Parliament has significantly developed since the introduction of direct elections for MEPs in 1979. In most other countries, legislatures can have significant impacts through their roles in enacting legislation, in representation and in oversight. At times, their power is shown to considerable effect, as in the case of the British Parliament in the Blair years. Faced with a huge government majority, the two houses were willing to challenge ministerial authority on issues such as Iraq, foundation hospitals, tuition fees and casinos. Members showed that they were not mere ciphers.

As a result of the trend towards growing executive power, some parliaments are rather compliant. Even so, Hague and Harrop[24] warn against generalisation, and conclude that:

> To speak of the decline of assemblies in an era of big government is too simple. In several ways, assemblies are growing in importance; as arenas of activity, as intermediaries in the transition from one political order to another, as raisers of grievances and as agencies of oversight. The televising of proceedings in many countries is making

assemblies more, not less central to political life . . . [Moreover] in the assemblies of Western Europe, backbench members are now more assertive; party leaders can no longer expect well-educated and well-researched backbenchers to be loyally deferential.

In any case, any tendency towards decline is certainly less true of presidential systems. Congress is strong in the USA, as are assemblies in some Latin American countries – though in the latter cases any display of assertiveness has sometimes provoked conflict with the administration and precipitated military coups. Even in the case of Congress, its main strength has usually depended more on blocking or delaying presidential initiatives, or scrutinising the performance and membership of the Administration, than in actually determining policy.

areas. It seemed that Congress could not act effectively in an age when federal activity had expanded so rapidly. In the early 1970s, it finally reasserted itself and streamlined its operations. Attempts were made to impose more control over the presidency (e.g. the **War Powers Act** of 1973), and changes made which were more to do with the internal organisation of Congress itself. As a result, Congress has been more willing and able to challenge presidential policy, and when – as now – the party in the White House lacks control of Capitol Hill the opportunities for conflict soon become apparent. President Clinton found his authority undermined, as his political opponents were more than willing to seize upon his sexual lapses as evidence of his unsuitability for the highest office – taking their opposition to the ultimate lengths of impeachment proceedings. He was only too aware that Congress was one national legislature that had become resurgent in recent decades. It remains the most influential legislature in the world.

· ·

 ## What you should have learnt from reading this chapter

- Like many legislatures, Parliament is effectively a reactive chamber. It can sometimes significantly modify, but not initiate, legislation. Its effectiveness has been enhanced by the greater use of select committees, improved facilities for members and greater independence and assertiveness of the second chamber. But it finds it difficult to challenge dominant, strong administrations.

- In Britain, the Executive dominates the legislature. The House of Commons is controlled by the government of the day, by means of its parliamentary majority. Such control is very evident when there is a landslide. The House has more influence when the majority is small. The unelected chamber has a relatively minor role, although it generally performs its tasks effectively. Reform of the second chamber remains on the political agenda.

- The membership of a country's parliament tends to be very unrepresentative of the national population as a whole, women often being very under-represented.

- In several legislatures, backbenchers have been active in seeking better resources to enable them to perform their role more effectively. Improved facilities, the use of specialist committees and the introduction of television cameras have all served to raise the profile of elected chambers.

- In recent decades, governments of many countries have often managed to muzzle legislatures. But they are not without influence. Indeed, in some cases their powers have been exercised more assertively in recent years. In more typical examples, they may have lost the power to initiate, lacking as they do the necessary technical competence. But they can play a part in starting up a great debate on policy issues that can be taken up elsewhere, particularly in the media. They can also exercise control over the Executive.

Glossary of key terms

Adjournment debate An opportunity for an MP to use a motion to adjourn the House of Commons to raise issues relating to his or her constituency or matters of public concern. There is a half-hour adjournment period at the end of the business of the day. Such debates are also held in Westminster Hall, in an attempt to give backbenchers more time to debate issues that cannot find space in the crowded schedule of the Chamber.

Bicameralism Refers to the existence of a two chamber legislature

Career politicians People committed to politics that they regard as their vocation. They know little else beyond the worlds of politics, policymaking and elections, perhaps having begun their career as a research assistant before working in the party organisation as a political staffer.

Guillotine An 'allocation of time motion' in the House of Commons to bring about the enforced closure of parliamentary debate either on the floor of the House or in committee. A guillotine was first used to manage debates in the House of Commons in 1881, when Irish MPs tried to obstruct the Coercion Bill.

Hutton Inquiry The Hutton Inquiry was a judicial inquiry in 2003 set up to investigate the circumstances surrounding the death of David Kelly, a biological warfare expert and former UN weapons inspector in Iraq, shortly after the decision to send troops into that country.

Short Money Short Money is the common name given to the annual payment to opposition parties in the United Kingdom House of Commons – introduced in 1975 by the then Leader of the House of Commons, Edward Short – to help them with their costs. Since April 2008, eligible parties have receive £14,015 for every seat won at the previous election, plus £27.99 for every 200 votes gained by the party.

Standing committees Committees of the House of Commons which examine bills in detail, clause by clause, to tidy them up and make them more acceptable; composed of MPs in proportion to party membership in the House.

Statutory instruments Statutory instruments are the principal form in which delegated or secondary legislation is made in Great Britain. *Affirmative instruments* – the most important type, comprising around 200 a year – must be approved by both Houses. The thousand or so *negative instruments* can become law without debate and are only debated if an MP specifically requests it.

Unicameralism Refers to the existence of a one-chamber legislature

Usual channels Usual channels refers to the way in which much parliamentary business is agreed on in private by the whips and senior MPs of the various parties, rather than in open debate. Essentially, this is to obtain cooperation between the two parties, in order to ensure as much business as possible can be dealt with in each parliamentary session.

War Powers Act 1973 Measure passed in US Congress to impose a sixty-day limit on the time for which a President can keep American troops abroad without congressional approval: treated with some disdain by subsequent presidents.

Whipping Whipping refers to the system of party discipline in the House of Commons, by which the Chief Whip and his/her assistants in a political party seeks to ensure that its MPs vote according to the official party line. The term derives from the hunting term, 'whipping in'.

? Likely examination questions

Can the House of Lords be made a more effective second chamber?

What is meant by parliamentary sovereignty? Is Parliament any longer sovereign?

How and with what success does Parliament control the Executive in Britain?

How effective is the individual MP? What changes might make MPs more effective?

To what extent does the experience of the British Parliament support the theory of 'legislative decline'?

Helpful websites

www.Parliament.uk Parliament site, with links to both chambers.

www.fawcettsociety.org.uk The Fawcett site, providing statistics and analysis of female representation in British politics at all levels.

www.europarl.eu.int The European Parliament.

www.ipu.org Inter-Parliamentary Union.

Suggestions for further reading

Useful articles

R. Kelly and I. White, 'All-women Shortlists', Parliament and the Constitution Centre, 2009.

P. Norton, 'Reforming the House of Lords: a View from the Parapets', *Representation*, 40:3, 2004.

P. Norton, 'Adding Value? The Role of Second Chambers', *Asia Pacific Law Review*, 15:1, 2007.

P. Norton, 'Making Sense of Opposition', *The Journal of Legislative Studies*, 14:1/2, March 2008.

Useful books

P. Cowley, 'Parliament', in A. Seldon (ed.), *Blair's Britain 1994–2007*, Cambridge University Press, 2007.

P. Cowley and M. Stuart, 'Ignored, Irresponsible and Irrelevant? Opposition MPs in the House of Commons', in N. Fletcher (ed.), *How to be in Opposition*, Biteback, 2011.

M. Grant, *The UK Parliament*, Edinburgh University Press, 2009.

P. Norton, *Parliament in British Politics*, Palgrave, 2005.

CHAPTER 4

The Executive

Contents

Introduction	112
The Executive in parliamentary and presidential systems of government	114
The distribution of power within political executives: the trend towards first ministerial dominance	116
The British Cabinet	118
The role of Prime Minister	127
The debate about prime ministerial power	128
Constraints on the British Prime Minister	132
A presidential prime minister?	134
British ministers and their civil servants	139
The conventions of ministerial responsibility	146
The case of Holland	150
The case of the USA	152

Overview

The Executive includes not only the chief executive but also the entire administrative system, for the civil service performs much of the actual work of policy implementation. We can therefore distinguish between politicians and civil servants. The Political Executive is the term used when we are referring to the government of the day, and the Official Executive is the term used when we are speaking of the bureaucracy whose task it is to administer the policies that ministers have laid down.

In this chapter, we are primarily concerned with the work and growing importance of the Political Executive, and the distribution of power within it. We are more concerned with the chief executive than the head of state, in cases where the two posts are separately held. At the end, we briefly examine the relationships between ministers and the civil servants who work in their departments.

Key issues to be covered in this chapter

- The nature, role and distribution of power within political executives
- The distribution of power within political executives
- The structure, work and importance of the British Cabinet and its committees
- The prime ministerial versus Cabinet government debate
- The description of modern prime ministers as 'presidential'
- The relationships of ministers and civil servants
- The ministerial responsibility of members of the Cabinet

Introduction

The term 'executive' derives from the Latin *ex sequi*, meaning to 'follow out' or 'carry out'. The role of the executive branch of government within the political system is then to carry out policies, laws or directives.

As long as there have been political systems, there have been individuals or small groups who assume the role of leadership. They have formulated and implemented public policy. At the apex of this executive structure, there is usually a single chief executive, be that person known as a president, prime minister, chief minister, first minister, supreme leader or monarch. On occasion, two offices may fulfil the executive role, as in France where the presidency and prime ministership both have significant powers. Rarely, there may be a ruling junta exercising shared leadership.

Rather than focusing on the debate of whether we have **prime ministerial** or **Cabinet government** in the UK, some political scientists prefer to think in terms of a '**core executive**'. The term refers to the complex network of institutions and people at the centre that between them are charged with the day-to-day government of the country, the making of policies and the implementation of laws. All of them are involved in a power relationship with other influential people and organisations in Whitehall and Westminster. This network represents the pinnacle of the decision-making process.

In Britain, the core comprises the first minister, the Cabinet and its committees, the offices that serve the first minister and Cabinet, and the departments headed as they are by senior ministers and including senior civil servants. In some listings, even the Chief Whip and those who chair backbench parliamentary committees maybe included. Membership of the core is liable to change and it is not always clear who should be included at any given moment. During the invasion and occupation of Iraq, it included the leaders among the military, but they would probably not normally be involved.

Box 4.1 The leadership role: heads of state and chief executives

Two distinctive roles can be distinguished, although the same person may in practice perform them:

- *The head of state* is an office of formal authority, but largely symbolic performance. The incumbent embodies the authority and power of the state, acting as its leading representative on ceremonial occasions. He or she is usually a president or monarch. Germany and Italy have non-executive presidencies of this type, whereas Britain, Belgium, Denmark, Holland, Norway, Sweden and Spain have constitutional monarchies in which the sovereign 'reigns, but does not rule'. Heads of state may have some residual political influence, but for the most part their task is to award honours, assent to legislation and receive/visit dignitaries of other countries. They are – or should be – non-partisan figureheads, who shun political controversy and maintain a position aloof from party strife. Their existence implies that beyond the cut and thrust of daily political life, something more eternal and solid endures. As such, they can be a rallying point in times of trouble.
- *The chief executive or head of the government* occupies a post carrying real political power and exercising a range of responsibilities connected with the performance of government.

On occasion, in the case of executive presidents, the same person performs the two posts. In France and the United States, the president wears 'two hats'. This may make the post demanding and time-consuming, but it also gives the holder a broad appeal as the focus for national unity and patriotism. The US president is in effect both in and beyond the political battleground.

The British Head of State: the monarchy
- The hereditary monarchy in Britain is the oldest of our national institutions. It is a constitutional monarchy, which means that it has lost its political role. In theory, it retains certain prerogative powers (see pp. 32–3 and 42), but these are largely exercised by the Prime Minister. In a constitutional monarchy, the monarch fulfils essentially ceremonial duties.
- When there is a clear outcome in the election, the monarch has no influence over the choice of Prime Minister. The parties make provision to elect their leaders. In the event of a party winning the election or being in government already, the elected leader automatically enters 10 Downing Street.

- When the outcome of a general election is uncertain (with no party winning an outright majority), some commentators have claimed that the monarch might be involved in calling the party leaders together to ensure that government could be carried on. However, this notion of a reserve discretionary power of the monarch to act as a broker between the party leaders in difficult situations is now considered by most commentators to be an archaic proposition, with no relevance for today. A note produced by the House of Lords Library Group in January 2011[1] stated that (in the light of the experience of May 2010): 'The Monarch would not expect to become involved in such discussions, although the political parties and the Cabinet Secretary would have a role in ensuring that the Palace is informed of progress.'
- The monarch has no real political power during the lifetime of a government and has not had any for well over a century. On rare occasions advice may be given, for as the political commentator Walter Bagehot wrote in *The English Constitution* (1867)[2] the monarch has 'the right to be consulted, the right to encourage, the right to warn' – in other words, the power of suggestion.
- The role of the monarch is largely symbolic. The incumbent is a figurehead who: receives visiting dignitaries; visits areas of the country to perform social functions (opening schools and civic centres); and tours abroad to represent Britain in the Commonwealth and elsewhere.
- Many people – especially the more elderly – find monarchy attractive, admiring the pomp, colour and splendour associated with royal occasions. For them, it seems to satisfy a popular need and evokes respect. It raises their morale and serves as a focus for their patriotic feeling.
- Others, members of younger generations often among them, are less enthusiastic. In their view, in a less deferential age, respect and loyalty have to be earned; heredity is no guarantee of capacity; the monarchy seems outdated, an emblem of privilege and costly to maintain; it represents the past, not the future, and it is time for it to be removed.

The Executive in parliamentary and presidential systems of government

In a situation of *parliamentary government*, the Executive is chosen from the legislature and is dependent for support upon it. Thus the British Cabinet is chosen from the House of Commons and responsible to it – as opposed to the situation in a presidential system, in which the Executive is separately elected and in theory equal to the legislature. Heywood[3] puts it well:

> A Parliamentary system of government is one in which the government governs in and through the assembly, thereby 'fusing' the legislative and executive branches. Although they are formally distinct, the assembly and the executive (usually seen as the government) are bound together in a way that violates the doctrine of the separation of powers, setting Parliamentary systems clearly apart from Presidential ones.

Most liberal democracies – ranging from Australia to Sweden, from India to New Zealand – have some kind of parliamentary government, often of a Westminster type. Historically, Britain had an era of legislative supremacy over the Executive. The situation evolved into one in which there was a relatively even balance between the two branches. The suggestion now made over several decades is that we have moved towards executive supremacy. The Executive tends to dominate the legislature, because the party and electoral systems usually produce a strong majority government, what Lord Hailsham[4] called an '**elective dictatorship**'.

Parliamentary government implies that government is checked by the power of Parliament, which monitors, examines and criticises its activities via such activities as Question Time and the use of select committees. Ministers are individually and collectively responsible to Parliament, and should resign if the administration has been defeated on a **vote of confidence** (as happened with the Callaghan government in 1979).

The United States and several other countries (particularly in Africa and Asia) have a system of *presidential government*. This does not refer to the fact that these countries have a president rather than a monarch as head of state. Both the Irish Republic and Germany have presidents in this role, yet both have parliamentary systems. As Heywood[5] explains: 'A presidential system is characterised by a constitutional and political separation of powers between the legislative and executive branches of government.' A presidential system is one in which the Executive is elected separately from the legislature, is outside of and in theory equal to it. The president is chosen by the people rather than from the legislative branch, and acts as head of the government as well as ceremonial head of state.

In a parliamentary system, the key politicians include the ministers headed by a prime or chief minister. In Britain, the Political Executive comprises the Prime Minister, the Cabinet with which he or she works, and other members of the government, usually a total of around one hundred. Almost all of these people are elected, although some members may be chosen from the House of Lords.

The distribution of power within political executives: the trend towards first ministerial dominance

The task of a political executive is to provide leadership. This involves taking the initiative in formulating, articulating and implementing goals. In most cases, the support of a Cabinet has traditionally been seen as crucial to the first minister. In Australia, Canada, India and New Zealand, first ministers operate through a system of collective Cabinet government. Cabinets may share in the making of public policy, as well as offering advice to the political leader and helping in the broader coordination of government policy. They form part of a collective leadership.

During the twentieth and twenty-first centuries, the power of political executives has been on the increase, for many of the reasons given for the decline of legislatures (see Chapter 3). Factors for this enhanced position include:

- *The growth of party government*, involving tight party discipline to ensure loyalty from elected representatives in the voting lobbies.
- *The expansion of governmental responsibilities*, in an age of interventionism in economic and social policy. This involves increased legislative tasks and has resulted in the growth of vast bureaucratic machinery to administer government programmes.
- *International action and globalisation*. In an age of speedy travel and communication, countries are today so closely bound up with each other, that first ministers and their Cabinets are increasingly involved in issues of foreign policy, handling crises, responding to disasters and providing global leadership.

Today, the Political Executive (the government) dominates the process of policy making. In many cases, it controls the agenda of the legislature and monopolises parliamentary time as it seeks to develop and implement its legislative programme. However, within the Political Executive, there has also been a shift in the balance of power. As Heywood[6] points out: 'By common consent, the main beneficiary of this process has been the chief executive'.

The increasing power of first ministers within Cabinets
The widespread increase in the personal power of first ministers at the expense of their Cabinet colleagues has been brought about by several factors: the centralisation of party machines, the growing importance of international diplomacy and the development of the mass media (especially television) among them. Few political leaders are now merely *primus inter pares* (first among equals). They are the focus of attention, to the extent that academics and commentators regularly refer to 'prime ministerial government'. However, the precise role and political importance of first ministers relative to their Cabinets varies from system to system and also varies over time, according to the circumstances and personalities involved.

Effective first ministers become the spokespersons for the aspirations of the people, can galvanise their support for the identified goals and develop strategies for their accomplishment. They operate under various labels. Germany has a chancellor, Ireland has a taoiseach and Britain has a prime minister. They are heads of government whose power derives from their leadership of the majority party – or coalition of parties – in the elected assembly. Governments need the support of a majority in parliament if they are to survive. In Britain and the Commonwealth, one-party government has been the norm; only rarely do ministers find themselves struggling to gain the backing of a majority in Parliament. In most Continental countries, three- or four-party coalitions are common.

In countries where coalition government is common, the trend to first minister dominance is less apparent than where there is a single-party administration. In coalition situations, leaders of the largest party need to bargain with other party leaders over the allocation of ministerial offices and once the government has been established, they need to ensure that their partners agree on actions to be taken. There is less scope for personal dominance, the more so as the current first minister may find that around the Cabinet table are seated others who have occupied his/her position. For instance, the Dutch Prime Minister is particularly constrained by a tradition of ministerial equality, as well as the existence of often closely worded coalition deals.

The British Cabinet

The Cabinet typically comprises twenty-three or twenty-four leading ministers. It is the central committee that directs the work of government and coordinates the activities of individual departments. It has in the past been described as 'the core of the British constitutional system'.[7] Its members assume responsibility for all decisions on behalf of the government. It was common to describe the British political system as it operated in the early-mid twentieth century as one of 'Cabinet government'. Today, it is common to see references to 'the passing of Cabinet government' or to 'prime ministerial dictatorship'.

Box 4.2 Some characterisations of the British Cabinet

. . . the unique source of authority . . . the highest political prize in the country.

Walker, 1970[8]

. . . the major instrument of government.

Hanson and Walles, 1980[9]

. . . the directing committee or board of management of British government.

Madgwick, 1984[10]

. . . at the pinnacle of government.

Norton, 1984[11]

Membership

Most Cabinet members are drawn from the House of Commons, the dominant, elected chamber, although a small number sit in the House of Lords. Most Cabinet members run a department such as Education and Employment, Health or the Home Office. Some are non-departmental ministers such as the Lord Privy Seal and Chancellor of the Duchy of Lancaster. Lacking departmental responsibilities, they have the opportunity to rove over the whole area of government and are available to take on particular tasks, as assigned by the Prime Minister.

There is a 'pecking order' within the Cabinet. In Cabinet meetings, the attitudes and preferences of more senior ministers normally carry more weight than those of others present. The Prime Minister is at the helm, followed by the Chancellor of the Exchequer, the Foreign Secretary and then the Home Secretary. There may be a Deputy Prime Minister, whose ranking is usually below that of the Chancellor. The relationship of the Prime Minister and Chancellor is crucial. If they are united in their stance on a particular issue, other ministers will find it hard to achieve any contrary objectives.

The Chief Whip will normally attend Cabinet meetings, although the office does not really carry full membership of the Cabinet. The Chief Whip is there to advise Cabinet ministers of the feeling on the backbenches of the party, in order to ensure that the leadership does not lose touch with other MPs. This will help prevent damaging revolts in the House of Commons.

The role of the Cabinet

The work of the Cabinet involves:

- *deciding on major policy to be followed at home and abroad.* Government policy has often been stated in the election manifesto and reflects prevailing party policy. But when in office, the priorities for action have to be decided and a legislative programme drawn up. Details of policy have to be filled in, in the light of prevailing circumstances such as the financial state of the country and the advice received from key pressure groups. In 2010, as the government formed was a coalition, it was necessary to set out the agreed policy that would be followed. The representatives of the two parties charted the way forward in a seven-page document, *The Conservative–Liberal Democrat Coalition Agreement,* also known as *The Coalition: Our Programme For Government.*

- *dealing with unforeseen major problems.* New problems arise from time to time. There may be a crisis in the European Union, a sudden invasion of a friendly state, an outbreak of violence in an area of strategic interest, a fuel crisis at home, the discovery of a major human or animal disease (e.g. Aids, BSE or foot-and-mouth), a hospital bed shortage in a winter outbreak of a vicious variety of influenza or a tsunami (underground earthquake) affecting many countries in the Far East. All of these issues require a response from government. They are liable to throw them 'off course', not least because they invariably require a substantial injection of funding.

- *coordinating the policies of different departments.* If government is to function well and policy is to be successfully carried out, there needs to be coordination between government departments. In some cases, disputes may have to be resolved between departmental ministers or policies pulled together to ensure what Tony Blair sometimes referred to as 'joined up government'. There is a natural tension between Treasury representatives and spending ministers who want more money for defence, education, health, transport and other issues. Within the Coalition, the perceived urgency of reducing the deficit has meant that the Chancellor and Chief Secretary to the Treasury have been demanding cuts in spending from almost all departments.

- *planning for the long term.* Ideally, this is a key area of policymaking, but governments are often preoccupied with the here-and-now. Moreover, ministers come and go, making it difficult to plan ahead with consistency of purpose. Yet some issues require long-term planning, such as those concerning the environment, defence and pension policy. Often this work is done in Cabinet committees.

How the Cabinet operates

In the years after the Second World War, there were often two Cabinet meetings a week. Whereas the Blair Cabinets met on Thursdays, the Brown and Cameron meetings usually take place on Tuesdays. The session begins at 10 a.m. and traditionally lasts for two or three hours, although under Tony Blair some meetings were much shorter, sometimes as brief as thirty minutes. The length of meetings varies according to the style of the Prime Minister and political conditions, but the relative brevity of some recent meetings suggests that they are increasingly used for the announcement or ratification of decisions taken elsewhere.

The agenda is circulated by the Cabinet Office a day or two before the meeting. Many items are routine, such as the Foreign Secretary's report on the world scene and the discussion of forthcoming business. In the Blair government, considerable time was spent on the presentation of policy. David Cameron's meetings have tended to be longer than those of his predecessors, for he has felt the need to work for broad agreement between the two partners in the Coalition on strategy and policy.

The number of topics discussed and the time spent on each of them is necessarily limited. The more time that is spent on individual items, the less opportunity there is to cover other matters. Those that have a low place on the agenda stand little chance of detailed attention. Prime ministers are able to manipulate the agenda, keeping off or giving low priority to those that may cause embarrassing disagreement.

Nigel Lawson,[13] a Chancellor under Margaret Thatcher, has written of the unsuitability of the Cabinet as a body for thrashing out problems and making long-term plans:

> A normal Cabinet meeting has no chance of becoming a grave forum of statesmanlike debate. Twenty two people attending a two-and-a-half hour meeting can speak for just over six and a half minutes each on average. If there are three items of business – and there are usually more – the ration of time just exceeds two minutes, if everyone is determined to have his say. Small wonder then that most ministers keep silent on most issues.

It is widely recognised that rather than providing a forum for detailed discussion of a wide range of policies, the main role of the Cabinet is to facilitate cohesion and coordination of governmental policies generally, and to provide or establish the parameters in which those policies are prepared and pursued. Many, if not most, government

Box 4.3 The work of Cabinet committees

Cabinet committees, small working groups of the whole Cabinet, have been used in many large democracies as key organs of decision-making. In many cases, their use developed during wartime and thereafter it was convenient to formalise their use. They focus on specific areas of policy or on overall strategy. In recent years, they have been increasingly involved at the point of decision-making, their decisions being notified to and ratified by the whole Cabinet. In Australia, decisions cannot be reopened without the consent of the Prime Minister.

In Britain, committees existed in an unsystematic form in the nineteenth century, but it was the impact of two world wars and the rapid expansion of governmental activity in the post-1945 era that created the present committee structure. Up until the 1970s, their existence was officially denied, but within a decade academics and journalists had probed to find out more. Ministers are now willing to identify them. There are two types of Cabinet committee:

1. *Standing committees* are named, permanent committees responsible for a particular policy area such as Northern Ireland, the European Union and local government. The most important is the Economic and Domestic Policy (EDP) Committee, chaired by the Prime Minister. It is, in effect, a kind of 'inner Cabinet' of senior government members.

2. *Ad hoc committees* vary in number according to the preferences and style of the Prime Minister. They are concerned with particular policy areas; it may be a sudden crisis (e.g. the Falklands invasion, 1982) or an issue such as the abolition by the Thatcher government of the Greater London Council; the Cameron government has a Banking Reform Committee and an Olympics subcommittee. Once the necessity has passed or the crisis or event ceases to be relevant, ad hoc committees are disbanded.

In the Coalition government, each Cabinet committee includes members of the two parties involved. Furthermore, each committee has a Chair and a Deputy Chair, one from each party. There is, in addition, a Coalition Committee, and an operational working group, to handle appeals over Coalition disputes and to plan future policy. David Cameron or Nick Clegg chair the Coalition Committee and the Prime Minister also chairs the National Security Council's sessions on Threats, Hazards, Resilience and Contingencies, and on Nuclear Deterrence and Security.

The value of committees

Important deliberative work is done in committees. They consider issues in more detail than does a Cabinet meeting. Often, as we made clear in the *Crossman Diaries*,[12] decisions are made in committees and not referred to the whole Cabinet, which only gets involved if there are major differences of opinion between ministers and departments. Decisions in committee are 'reported back' to the Cabinet, which can revise or veto committee proposals. But as the Prime Minister chairs several important committees, disagreement is not common.

Committees are today vitally important areas of governmental activity, with a major role in determining and resolving government policy. Crossman was worried about their constitutional impact. He saw them as one of the symptoms of the 'passing of Cabinet government'. He observed the way in which the point of decision was being 'permanently transferred either downwards to the powerful Cabinet committees or upwards to the Prime Minister himself'. Certainly, the creation and composition of committees has been a key element in strengthening prime ministerial power.

policies are developed in Cabinet committees (see Box 4.4), in informal groups such as **inner and kitchen Cabinets**, and in bilateral discussions between the Prime Minister and individual colleagues. They are then reported back to the full Cabinet for approval. In other words, the Cabinet tends to rubber-stamp decisions taken in other places. As Burch[14] points out:

> In essence, Cabinet tends to resolve those issues that cannot be resolved elsewhere. It may also . . . lay out broad strategy and take a very general oversight role in relation to policy-making. It is, however, misleading to suggest that the Cabinet collectively and consistently controls policy-making.

In assessing the importance of the Cabinet as a whole, it is important not to include these other areas of policymaking. The role of the Cabinet meeting under recent prime ministers has at times been significantly reduced. But if we use the term Cabinet in an 'umbrella sense' to cover this network of decision-making arenas, its importance is very considerable. In other words, power has been dispersed from the whole Cabinet to some of its component elements.

Box 4.4 The Cabinet under Tony Blair and Gordon Brown

Prime ministers vary in the use they make of their Cabinets. Some tend to be forceful and dominant, others more content to delegate to those around them. Attlee, the post-war Labour premier, saw his role essentially as chairman of the Cabinet. He led an able team and although he could be assertive, it was meaningful to write of 'Cabinet government' under his leadership.

Tony Blair used the Cabinet less and ad hoc committees more than his predecessor, John Major. On occasion, he attended its meetings for only a short time. He tended to lay down his preferred policy, as on the Dome, and expected agreement. Generally, he had Cabinet backing because the party was relieved to be firmly established in power and recognised that for several years he was an electoral asset. There were divisions, for he had some powerful figures around him. But his inclination was to act decisively and strongly, though he granted reasonable discretion to ministers to get on with their tasks as long as it was evident that they were in line with agreed policy. Peter Hennessy[15] delivered his verdict in 2001: 'The Cabinet is no longer a central organ of government. Cabinet Ministers still matter as heads of Departments, but Cabinet meetings no longer really count. The system is no longer collective. It is a centralised system directed by 10 Downing Street.'

In the later period of the Blair premiership, from the run-up to the Iraq War onwards, there was increasing criticism of the Blairite style of leadership and especially of his failure to hold meaningful Cabinet discussions and keep his ministers fully informed of his intentions. These criticisms were highlighted in the Butler Report,[16] which had some scathing things to say about the way government had been conducted in recent years – an informal style with too many sofa chats, too many occasions when minutes were not taken and a consequent lack of clarity about what was decided.

Gordon Brown employed a larger Cabinet than his predecessor. Indeed, after the mid-2009 reshuffle, thirty-one ministers were either members of his Cabinet or invited to attend its meetings. This inspired some criticism from academics, who felt that the Cabinet had become too large. George Jones[17] noted that: 'We have got the largest government that we have ever had. It is a huge body and unprecedented.' David Butler[18] pointed out that 'anyone who has sat on a committee knows that its efficiency diminishes with size.' Following the reshuffle, which brought more non-Cabinet ministers into Cabinet meetings, Brown established an eight-strong 'inner Cabinet' to plot strategy. Threats to his authority led to his 'war room' in 12 Downing Street attaining even greater prominence, as he sought stability among trusted key figures, both politicians and civil servants.

The work of the Cabinet Office and Secretariat

The Cabinet has a Secretariat of about forty senior civil servants whose job is to timetable meetings, prepare agendas and documents, and draft and circulate minutes. The Secretariat is so important that its head is the country's top civil servant, the Cabinet Secretary, who is in daily contact with the Prime Minister and Cabinet members. He attends Cabinet meetings, though not when party political items are being discussed, and some Cabinet committees. The relationship between the Premier and the Cabinet Secretary is a crucial one. Crossman revealed its importance, noting how the two men decided the Cabinet agenda and the order of the items on it, and agreed the minutes afterwards. Michael Heseltine subsequently commented on these two aspects in the **Westland** controversy (1986).[19]

The Secretariat is assisted by a Cabinet Office of some 1500 civil servants, who prepare the work for committees and follow up their decisions. The term 'Cabinet Office' is now generally used to cover the whole machinery that services Number Ten, the Cabinet and the departments; the word 'Secretariat' rarely features.

Apart from its traditional duties as outlined, there is within the Cabinet Office permanent machinery to cope with emergencies such as threats to fuel and water supplies, or terrorist activity. This is the Civil Contingencies Unit, which can, as the occasion demands, transform itself into a mixed committee of ministers, officials, the military, the policy and the security services, with the Home Secretary in the chair.

From an early stage as PM, Tony Blair and his team were keen to see a 'dynamic centre'. This involved more power for the Prime Minister's Office, which would work closely with the Cabinet Office. The Prime Minister[20] answered a parliamentary question on the future of the Cabinet Office back in 1998. He put it in this way:

Box 4.5 The character and importance of the Centre under Tony Blair and Gordon Brown

Tony Blair was concerned that 'the Centre' acted as a power-house that would ensure that his government operated effectively. He wanted to see effective control of its communications and a new emphasis on the delivery of services. For him, the Centre comprised: the Prime Minister's Office, based in 10 Downing Street; the Cabinet Office, which backs on to it; and the Treasury, the headquarters of which is next door. In his first term in office, there was indeed a remarkable assertion of prime ministerial control over relations with the media, which were under the firm grip of Alastair Campbell. This was less easy to achieve in regards to the delivery function, much to the Prime Minister's frustration.

In his second term, Blair appointed Sir Michael Barber to lead the Prime Minister's Delivery Unit and this gave the premier more effective control over the operations of government. However, it was difficult to establish a centre of unprecedented power and coherence, because at the Treasury Gordon Brown was a towering figure who was also interested in assuming control of the delivery agenda. The outcome was that whilst there was in effect a new 'prime minister's department' in all but name, involving a much closer bond between the Prime Minister's Office and the Cabinet Office; the Treasury, the third arm of operations, was prone to secrecy and was notably uncooperative in its dealings with its Downing Street neighbour.

When *Gordon Brown* assumed office in mid-2007, he recast the personnel, structures and physical lay-out of the Centre. In his final change, he seemed more concerned to make 12 Downing Street (the home of the Prime Minister's Information and Research Unit, Press Office, and Strategic Communications Unit) the war room for planning and fighting the Prime Minister's general election campaign. More preoccupied with this media-focused operation and less absorbed with progress-chasing delivery than his predecessor, he moved the Delivery Unit into the Treasury.

Source: information largely derived from John Rentoul, 'No. 10 from Blair to Brown', *The Hidden Wiring*, vol. 1, Mile End Group, Autumn 2009.

The role of the Cabinet Office has traditionally been to help the Prime Minister and the Government as a whole to reach collective decisions on Government policy. Since the election, the three principal parts of the centre – my own office, the Cabinet Office and the Treasury – have worked closely and effectively together, and with other Departments, to take forward the Government's comprehensive and ambitious policy agenda.

Under Tony Blair, there was a closer fusion than before between the Prime Minister's Office and the Cabinet Office.

The role of Prime Minister

The Prime Minister is head of the executive branch of government and chairman of the Cabinet. He has several responsibilities, ranging from oversight of the security services to liaising with the monarch in a weekly meeting, keeping her informed of what the government is doing and advising on matters such as the constitutional implications of a royal marriage or divorce. The key roles of the Prime Minister are:

- *Leader of the party in the country and in Parliament.* The Prime Minister owes his position to the party and in carrying out his duties cannot afford to forget that connection. He uses his powers of leadership to keep the party united, working out compromise solutions as necessary; managing the party is crucial to his prospects for survival. He cannot afford to grow out of touch with the people he leads. On several occasions, the Blair/Brown premierships found difficulty in retaining the support of MPs for particular policies, leading to major revolts in the voting lobbies (see p. 85).
- *Responsibility for the appointment and dismissal of members of the Cabinet, acting as it chairman; appointment of other members of the government.* In relation to the Cabinet, this also includes appointing members of Cabinet committees, many of which he also chairs. Chairmanship of the Cabinet involves drawing up its agenda – in partnership with the Cabinet Secretary – and agreeing the minutes after the weekly meeting. His role in regards to the Cabinet enables him to steer the political agenda in his chosen way.
- *Leader of the government at home and abroad.* The Prime Minister answers questions in the House at PM's Question Time on

Wednesday lunchtimes. He also acts as the country's voice on occasions such as the death of Princess Diana or some national disaster, and represents Britain in summit conferences in Europe, with the American president and at the UN. In this role of national leadership, he will sometimes appear on TV and address the nation directly. At other times, he will be seen glad-handing representatives of other bodies, national and international, as when David Cameron appeared alongside David Beckham and Lord Coe to give a personal face to the abortive 2018 World Cup campaign.

- *Responsibility for a wide range of appointments, exercising a considerable power of patronage.* Appointments once made by the monarch are now mostly made on the advice of the Prime Minister. He appoints people from bishops to members of the Privy Council.
- *Determining the date of the next general election, up to and including 2010* (see pp. 94–5).

The debate about prime ministerial power

'For a Prime Minister to dominate the whole business of governing, he or she needs a formidable equipment and some good fortune.'

P. J. Madgwick, *An Introduction to British Politics*[21]

R. H. S. Crossman,[22] a former Oxford don and then a Labour MP, was the first main exponent of the idea that Britain had acquired a system in which the Prime Minister had supreme power: 'The post-war epoch has seen the final transformation of Cabinet Government into Prime Ministerial Government', with the effect that 'the Cabinet now joins the dignified elements in the Constitution'. His observations were matched by those of another writer and politician, Professor John Mackintosh, who similarly discerned[23] the passing of Cabinet government: 'The country is governed by a Prime Minister, his colleagues, junior ministers and civil servants, with the Cabinet acting as a clearing house and court of appeal'.

Similar claims have been oft repeated since the early 1960s, observers suggesting that a prime minister presiding over a single-party government and equipped with the traditional prerogatives of the Crown, is immensely powerful. But it was the premiership

Box 4.6 The Prime Minister and appointment to the Cabinet

Central to prime ministerial power is the ability to appoint members of the government and in particular the twenty or so members of the Cabinet. The power of hiring, reshuffling and if necessary dismissing colleagues illustrates the strengths and limitations of the Prime Minister's position.

On forming an administration, the premier has to decide how large the Cabinet will be and what offices of state are to be included within it. Government departments can be combined, created and abolished, so that post-war Cabinets have varied in size from sixteen to twenty-four. Sometimes, a prime minister may create the post of Deputy Prime Minister. He may decide to have a combined Secretary of State for Health and Social Security, as opposed to separating the two roles as is currently the vogue. Transport may form a separate ministry or be part of the Department of the Environment.

Once the size and offices have been determined, the Prime Minister must then decide on its membership, who to include and who to leave out. He is constitutionally free to appoint whom he wishes to the Cabinet, but in practice he is politically limited. In making his decisions, he is likely to be influenced by several factors:

- *They will be members of the same party*, normally MPs. In the past, a very few non-political persons have been included, but they have normally been given a life peerage. The Prime Minister will need two or three Cabinet members drawn from the House of Lords, in order to pilot government legislation through the chamber.

- *'Big figures' of party standing are usually included*. In every administration, there are some figures who almost pick themselves and who have a substantial say over which office they would like to occupy. Tony Blair would have been ill advised to leave out Gordon Brown, Robin Cook and John Prescott after the 2001 election. They had been key members of his first administration and each had their own following and status in the party and country. Senior figures who resent their omission or who leave a government under duress can be strong critics once they have the freedom of the backbenches. Even with a large majority until 2005, Tony Blair never felt able to rid himself of a Chancellor with whom his relations were sometimes immensely difficult.

- *A balance of party opinion is ideal.* A prime minister normally wants to achieve a balance of Left/Right and pro/anti European opinion in the party, so that all of its component elements feel that they have a voice representing their interests at the top. On occasion, a strong incumbent may feel able to shed members of a different viewpoint, but to do so is risky. It was President Johnson in the United States who concluded that it was safer to have 'his opponents on the inside of the tent pissing out, than on the outside, pissing in'. By including persons not of the same persuasion, the danger to party unity is minimised.

- *The need to reward loyalty.* The Prime Minister may wish to offer due recognition for those who have backed his battle for the party leadership or who have stood by him in Cabinet discussions when the going was tough. Most prime ministers like to have some of their political – and sometimes personal – friends around them.

- *A blend of youth and experience is desirable.* There will come a time when figures of similar age to the Prime Minister – or perhaps older – have had their day. Wise prime ministers are likely to recognise and encourage new talent, to ensure that there is another generation likely to take over the reins of leadership.

- *The inclusion of members representing different groups in society.* The Prime Minister normally ensures that women are represented near the top and maybe – in the case of Labour – members of ethnic minority groups as well. Ideally, it is wise to choose a Scotsman as Secretary of State for Scotland, and similarly the same type of representation for Northern Ireland and Wales, as well.

- *Ability.* Hopefully, in having regard to the above factors, he will also bear in mind the need for personnel to have the relevant skills, experience and expertise. Prime ministers like to include some people 'with a safe pair of hands'. If they have good presentation skills and are persuasive on television, that is a bonus.

The first Cameron Cabinet, the only post-1945 one to be a coalition, draws on the membership of both parties, having eighteen Conservatives and five Liberal Democrats among its twenty-three regular attendees. At the time of its formation, the oldest member was sixty-nine (Ken Clarke), the youngest about to turn thirty-eight (Danny Alexander). Two were former presidents of the Oxford Union (William Hague, Michael Gove) and two edited the Oxford student magazine (George Osborne and Chris Huhne). Only four were female, several millionaires.

of Margaret Thatcher that provided the debate about whether Britain has 'government by prime minister' with a new impetus. She appeared to stretch the power of the office to its limits. So too Tony Blair was accused of operating via a system of personal rule or 'too presidentially' (see pp. 135–8).

Critics of this concentration of power have long pointed to its dangers. Former left-wing MP and ex-minister Tony Benn was specific in his challenge:[24]

> The wide range of powers . . . exercised by a British Prime Minister . . . are now so great as to encroach upon the legitimate rights of the electorate, undermine the essential role of Parliament, [and] usurp some of the functions of collective Cabinet decision-making . . . In short, the present centralisation of power into the hands of one person has gone too far and amounts to a system of personal rule in the very heart of our system of . . . parliamentary democracy.

The central elements in prime ministerial power today are well known but difficult to measure. They include:

- the power of appointment and dismissal of Cabinet and other ministerial offices
- power over the structure and membership of Cabinet committees, any of which the PM may chair
- the central, overseeing non-departmental nature of the office
- leadership of the party
- single-party government
- the distribution of patronage
- (for some) wartime leadership
- a high degree of public visibility.

These features have operated for much of the century, but in recent decades some have assumed a growing significance. For instance, the Prime Minister is now much more visible than ever before, because of the growing trend towards international summitry and a high degree of television exposure. No occupant of Number Ten since the last world war has been anything less than very powerful. Any prime minister today has a formidable display of powers at his or her disposal.

Constraints on the British Prime Minister

Yet the thesis of prime ministerial government can be overstated and suffers from the tendency to overgeneralisation. Power can be seriously circumscribed and dependent on the circumstances of the time. It is not merely that some prime ministers are more powerful than others, but that any single incumbent will be more powerful at certain times than at others in the course of the premiership. Even the strongest among them are not always able to sustain the same degree of performance throughout their term.

Individuals have made a greater or lesser impact upon the office. All have been subject to some constraints, among them:

- *The Cabinet.* On major issues, even a strong prime minister will wish to keep his Cabinet united behind him. It normally comprises some figures of public and party standing, potential rivals if they are ignored or antagonised. In the build-up to the invasion of Iraq, it was essential for Tony Blair that he could count upon the support of Gordon Brown, John Prescott and Jack Straw. The circumstances surrounding the formation of the Cameron Cabinet made it necessary from the beginning for the Prime Minister to keep the Liberal Democrats on board, in particular to ensure that leader Nick Clegg found policies sufficiently acceptable that he could sell them to his party.

  The way in which the Prime Minister and his colleagues work together will depend upon the mix of personalities involved, the relationships being complex and fluid. Much also depends on the issues and problems with which they are faced.

- *Party.* Strong premiers can be hard on party backbenchers, expecting loyalty in the voting lobbies even for policies they dislike. When ministers are going through a difficult period – and especially when party MPs fear for their seats in the next election – they may find that support melts away. Prime ministers who lose backbench backing may find that they cannot rely on continued consent to their leadership, as Margaret Thatcher found out in 1990. So too the Blair leadership came under increasing criticism from a number of backbenchers who were intent on terminating his premiership. In his autobiography, Peter Mandelson[25] claimed that Tom Watson, MP for West Bromwich East, was acting under orders from Gordon Brown when he led a rebellion against Tony Blair that succeeded in forcing the former Prime Minister to quit Downing Street early.

- *Parliament.* Prime ministers need to retain support in Parliament to get their policies through the chamber. Even a prime minister who makes only limited other appearances in the House, still has to appear every Wednesday to be grilled at Question Time, defend his policies to occasional select committee hearings and sell his policies on Iraq, tuition fees and other contentious issues. In March 2003, Tony Blair could not have gone ahead with his backing for President Bush if MPs had rejected his case for war. Primarily, getting parliamentary support means keeping government MPs happy, but over Iraq he wanted to ensure that there was sufficient agreement from the Opposition to his policy to help him defeat a Labour rebellion.

- *Events.* It was Harold Macmillan, the Conservative Prime Minister of the 1950s–60s who saw 'events, dear boy, events' as his greatest danger. No prime minister knows what hazards are around the corner, issues ranging from war in Iraq to an outbreak of foot-and-mouth disease that can derail or at least threaten the administration. The Brown government had to deal with the collapse in the banking sector and the subsequent impact of global recession. In the case of the Coalition, policy has been shaped by the need to bring public spending under tighter control.

- *Hostility in the media.* Even a telegenic incumbent can have a tougher ride when the novelty and shine wears off. A poor performer on television will soon find that the medium is a two-edged weapon, useful to charismatic politicians but a problem for the less articulate or persuasive. Whereas Tony Blair had a remarkable degree of Press support in 1997 and 2001, war and other issues inspired marked hostility in 2005 from sections of the Tory press, especially the *Daily Mail*.

The power of the Prime Minister considered

There has certainly been a remarkable growth in the power of the executive branch of government in the last 100 years, but the distribution of power within the Executive is liable to change at any time. The trend to prime ministerial dominance has been characterised by an ebb and flow of power, rather than a continuous increase. A much-quoted observation by Lord Oxford (formerly Liberal PM Asquith)[26] reflects the varying nature of political power. He judged that: 'The office of Prime Minister is what its holder chooses and is able to make of it.' His emphasis on the ability, character and preference of the incumbent is generally accepted, as is the role of particular circumstances.

Prime ministers do not have unlimited power. If they did, they would be behaving as dictators. It is one thing to have dictatorial tendencies, another to be a dictator. Dictators cannot be removed, other than by a military coup or similar event. Prime ministers can always be evicted from Number Ten at the next election. The electorate is the ultimate limitation on even the most powerful premier. If leaders are seen as too powerful, remote, out of touch or untrustworthy, voters can react against them and bring their party down.

The formation of a coalition government in May 2010 could well mean that Prime Minister Cameron has no choice but to operate in a more collegiate fashion than some of his recent predecessors. The terms of the agreement set out in 2010 provide for regular consultation with his coalition partners in the process of decision-making. Moreover, he may find it politically useful to bind the whole Cabinet, Conservative and Liberal Democrat members alike, into unpopular decisions about public-spending cuts, thereby sharing the blame.

A presidential prime minister?

Academics, commentators and critics have often made the comparison between the power of the Prime Minister and that of the US President. Whilst some write of 'prime ministerial government', others use the phrase 'presidential [or quasi-presidential] rule'. It is possible to argue the case that the Prime Minister increasingly dominates the British political system, whilst quibbling about whether we live under presidential rule.

The central assertion of those who see the premiership as having become increasingly presidential is that the forms and devices of presidential politics as practised in the USA bear a strong resemblance to the trends that have become discernible in the 'advanced and sophisticated politics of competitive leadership operating at the heart of the British system . . . the net effect has been one of placing a greater emphasis upon the brand name of leaders and their capacity to inject a personal appeal into a political resource on behalf of their respective organisations'.[27]

Those who detect presidential qualities in British prime ministers point to:

- the large apparatus in Downing Street with which modern premiers equip themselves. In particular, Tony Blair developed the Prime Minister's Office, which became a de facto if not formalised Prime Minister's Department. Presidents – lacking the degree of backing a prime minister derives from the Cabinet – rely heavily upon an array of advisers and consultants, many of whom are located in the Executive Office of the President.

- their pre-eminence in domestic and foreign policy, enabling them to assume much responsibility over substantial areas of governmental activity at any particular time, as the need or wish arises. After consultation with their political advisers, they decide what needs to be done and impose their inclinations upon Cabinet colleagues (as Tony Blair is often alleged to have done over the invasion of Iraq).

- the priority attached to the presentation of policy and the way in which prime ministers seek to manipulate the media, in order that they get their message across directly to the people. Tony Blair was criticised for making key policy announcements at staged and televised public events, rather than in the House of Commons, in which his record of attendance and voting were sometimes criticised.

- the attempts of prime ministers to engage in 'populist outreach', by speaking to the people not as leader of a political party but rather as a national leader addressing the concerns of the whole nation. Tony Blair assumed this manner when describing the late Princess Diana as the 'People's Princess'. In the same way, prime ministers visit troops in war zones to rally morale and identify with the military effort being made on our behalf, thereby seemingly acting as a head of state or indeed as the US President does in his role as Commander-in-Chief.

- the way in which elections have increasingly come to be seen as a duel between two leaders, in an age in which politics has become personalised. Television is a medium infatuated with personalities and has encouraged the emphasis upon personal characteristics.

- the quality of what Michael Foley[28] has called '**spatial leadership**', a technique whereby prime ministers such as Margaret Thatcher and Tony Blair liked to appear 'above the fray' of battle, sometimes talking about the government and what it must do, as though they were not the key force in shaping its direction and policies. This was a technique adopted by President Reagan who seemed able to escape from any difficulties in which his administration was mired. In his early years, Tony Blair was known as 'Teflon Tony', a reference to his ability to retain an aura of dignity and authority, unsullied by the events that happened to his ministers. (The label lost much of its relevance after his credibility and reputation were tarnished by the events surrounding the Iraq War.)

The Blair experience

Foley[29] has argued that the most obvious exponent of a more presidential style in the UK has been Tony Blair, whose leadership techniques ranged from the use of the traditional channels of news management and media cultivation to more innovative forms of direct communication. These included: a rapidly developed Number Ten website; the usage of soft format television outlets; local and regional news contacts; lifestyle and ethnic publications; and the adoption of prime ministerial 'town meetings' in which the Prime Minister would engage directly with public audiences. Foley notes that even towards the end of his premiership, at a time when his reputation was in evident decline, he still explored new means of keeping his channels open to the public. Among other things, these included 'the use of citizen petitions via the Number 10 website' personal approaches to organisations like *YouTube*; and continued efforts to promote a positive image through connections to popular culture, lifestyle issues and even celebrity outlets.

The disadvantages of such a style were apparent when Blair became more politically vulnerable. Such an approach to government tends to raise expectations to a level that leaders find difficult to satisfy. They find that high exposure, when combined with disproportionately low levels of political leverage, leaves them isolated

Box 4.7 The roles of Prime Minister and US President compared

There are several points that can be made in comparing the premiership and presidency:

- In Britain, we have separated 'pomp from power', having a chief executive and head of state. In the USA, the two roles are combined in one person, giving the incumbent enhanced prestige as he appears to be elevated above the daily political battleground.

- The President has greater security of tenure, having a fixed four-year term. Although the Prime Minister may serve five years if he chooses to delay dissolving Parliament, he is liable to be defeated in the House (very infrequent) or to find difficulty in managing with a knife-edge majority (again, unusual). Arguably, the fact of being able to determine the date of the election and to engineer a situation in which the electorate 'feels good' (because of a thriving economy) tips the balance towards the Prime Minister, although the move to fixed-term elections destroys this advantage.

- Britain has a plural executive, the Prime Minister and his Cabinet being collectively responsible to the House of Commons. The US Cabinet meets less regularly, its members having less political standing in their own right. They are not rival contenders for the party leadership, as they may be in Britain.

- Prime ministers are accountable to the legislature, from which their governments are derived. They have to attend the House weekly at Question Time and sell/defend their policies in debates and before committees. Whereas Tony Blair felt it necessary to put the proposal to wage war against Iraq to a vote – which might have gone against him – the President did not have to struggle to achieve congressional approval. Prime ministers are always liable to defeat in the chamber, however unlikely the scenario. Presidents are not answerable in the same way, their administrations not being formed from the legislature. They answer directly to the people in the next presidential election.

- Prime ministers derive much of their authority from their leadership of disciplined political parties. This enables them – especially if they have a sizeable majority – to pass the bulk of the programme outlined in the Queen's Speech. Presidents can find it difficult to achieve their legislative programme, even when they have a majority in both chambers of Congress. Whereas Margaret Thatcher was able to reform the system of health service provision in the way that she and her ministers favoured, Bill Clinton

> was unable to do so a few years later. The strength that comes from party leadership gives the Prime Minister the edge in terms of domestic policy, in which the President is more constrained. In Mayhew's[30] words: 'to suppose that an American party winning Congress and the presidency thereby wins the leeway of a British governing party is to be deluded by the election returns'.
>
> - On foreign policy, the President has a clear advantage, not merely by virtue of America's pre-eminent global role. Post-war presidential power has depended heavily upon the incumbent's ability to act decisively at times of crisis. He can consult whom he wishes and then decide how to act. The Prime Minister may take key decisions in a Cabinet committee with a small group of ministers, but on a matter of major international policy would ultimately need to carry his Foreign Secretary and Cabinet colleagues with him. Usually, the Prime Minister gets his way, but he does not dominate the process of making and conducting foreign policy to the extent that the President is able to do.

and regarded as blameworthy for all that goes wrong. Criticisms emerged over issues of personal trust and the use of executive power, with reference made to his 'overreach and governmental detachment from the public; neglect of Parliament, Cabinet prerogatives, party traditions, constitutional practices and collective decision-making precedents'.

The Prime Minister as president: an appropriate comparison?

The notion of the British presidency has been criticised on several counts. Primarily, critics point to the differences in the roles and powers of the Prime Minister and US President, as outlined (see Box 4.7) Moreover, if some premiers seem to have behaved in a presidential manner, then the description fits less easily in the cases of John Major and Gordon Brown. Even in the cases of Margaret Thatcher and Tony Blair, their 'presidential' leanings can be viewed as more a matter of style than of substance, because of differences in the systems of government. But of course Professor Foley did not argue that the UK premiership was evolving into a US-style presidency; his book was entitled '*The British Presidency*'.

Foley concludes his original study by observing that the Prime

Minister has become presidential, but in a uniquely British way. He is not a head of state, nor does he derive power directly from the people. He cannot ignore the Cabinet, even if it is sometimes by-passed on individual policy matters. The constitutional position in the two countries does not make for real convergence. There is a fundamental difference between presidential and parliamentary government.

British ministers and their civil servants

As we have seen at the beginning of the chapter, the Executive in Britain comprises a political element (the elected politicians) and a non-political, administrative element (the unelected officials or civil servants). Theoretically, the position is that ministers make the policy decisions and civil servants administer them. Constitutionally, ministers are responsible to Parliament for the policies and administration of the departments they head.

The underlying rationale for this division of responsibilities is that politicians are elected on the basis of promises made at the last election. These priorities should determine their aims and approach to policy issues when in office. Civil servants, permanent appointees, are expected to be anonymous, neither receiving the credit nor blame for the success or otherwise of these policies. They provide advice to ministers to enable them to formulate and supervise the administration of policy decisions.

In practice, such a distinction is difficult to maintain. Not surprisingly, there have over many decades been suggestions that civil servants frustrate the will of ministers and governments. Some ministers of either party seem unable to impose their will on the departments they lead, whilst others have conflictual relationships with their higher civil servants.

Government ministers

By ministers, we are referring to around eighty to ninety senior government members, including Cabinet ministers, ministers of state and parliamentary under-secretaries, who work in departments of state or ministries. These include the Treasury, the Home Office, the Department of Health and the Foreign Office.

Such is the volume of work in departments run by a Cabinet minister that other layers of ministers have been created. The thirty or so ministers of state and the same number of parliamentary undersecretaries are collectively known as 'junior ministers'. Below them, are the forty to fifty private parliamentary secretaries (PPS) who are the general assistants of ministers and really act as 'dogsbodies'. They are unpaid for their work. Broadly, the more important the government department, the more ministers and junior ministers it will have. At the Treasury, there are two Cabinet ministers and more than fifteen junior ministers (see Box 4.8 on the hierarchy of ministers and their roles within the Home Office).

Below these ministers there is a hierarchy of civil servants. The Cabinet minister usually deals with them via his private secretary (normally a bright, up-and-coming civil servant charged with the responsibility for organising the minister's busy schedule) or through his Permanent Secretary.

A minister is very reliant on the performance of the civil servants who work in his department. They are the people who organise his day, arrange his appointments, write letters on his behalf, draft replies to parliamentary questions, arrange meetings and offer advice on how to deal with political issues as they arise. Yet the minister does not choose his civil servants. Ministers work with the people who are there when they come to office. For personal support in his dealings with officials, a minister relies on his junior ministers and political advisers.

The minister at work

The minister has two main roles. He is an MP, an elected politician with duties in Cabinet and Parliament. He is also the administrator of a large Whitehall Department consisting of civil servants (officials).

As a politician, he has his normal constituency duties as an MP, but as a minister this will involve him also in speaking in the House of Commons in debates, appearing before the relevant select committee, taking his turn at the despatch box in Question Time and piloting any legislation through the House concerning the department. Of course, also as a politician, he is in the Cabinet if he is a senior party figure. Here, he will argue the case for his department in any issues that arise and take part in more general discussions of government policy.

Box 4.8 The Home Office: the hierarchy of its ministers and their roles in early 2011

The Home Office is the lead government department for immigration and passports, drugs policy, crime, counter-terrorism and police. Its organisation includes agencies, independent public bodies and inspectorates. The Home Secretary and five other ministers head the department.

Home Secretary (Theresa May) Cabinet member
Three Ministers of State for:
   Security and counter-terrorism (Pauline Neville-Jones)
   Immigration (Damian Green)
   Policing and criminal justice (Nick Herbert)
Two Under-Secretaries of State for:
   Equalities and criminal information (Lynne Featherstone)
   Crime prevention (James Brokenshire)
Three Parliamentary Private Secretaries, Ed Timpson, David Rutley and Mary Macleod, who serve respectively under the Home Secretary, the Minister of State for Immigration and the Minister of State for Policing and Criminal Justice.

Three agencies provide frontline services from within the Home Office, the UK Border Agency, the Identity and Passport Service and the Criminal Records Bureau.

In addition, *the department sponsors twenty-one non-departmental public bodies (NDPBs) and other bodies*, which carry out operations on behalf of the government but are operationally independent of the department that sponsors them. Of these, seven have an executive role (e.g. the National Policing Improvement Agency), the others having advisory (e.g. the Advisory Council on the Misuse of Drugs), inspection (e.g. HM Inspectorate of Constabulary) or tribunal (e.g. Office of the Surveillance Commissioners) roles.

As a head of a Whitehall department, his role is to supervise and take a keen interest in the work being done – the manager who takes responsibility and who takes the key decisions. In theory, he listens to the advice put before him and uses his judgement – in practice, in a large department such as the Home Office, he perhaps decides only 10–15 per cent of the vast array of issues that come up. But he needs to ensure that he runs a smooth, well-oiled machine, has competent people on whom he can rely and be vigilant to see that he is getting the best advice.

Since the creation of new agencies under the **Next Steps programme** in the 1990s, the areas of policymaking and implementation in government departments have been separated in the cause of efficiency. This has reduced the minister's direct responsibility for what happens in whole areas of government work. Although he answers in the Commons on matters covered by an agency, the day-to-day management of such enterprises is left to chief executives who take a share of responsibility for what happens.

The senior civil servant at work

The senior civil servants, often known as higher civil servants, comprise around 800 leading officials. Only this group will really be involved in working with ministers on policy, and the number likely to have much direct contact with him on a typical day will be considerably smaller than that figure.

At the head of the civil servants in each department is the *Permanent Secretary*, below whom will be the deputy and assistant secretaries (of course, some senior civil servants will now be working in agencies; these are said to be detached from the process of policymaking, although some senior officials are involved in offering guidance to the Chief Executive on advice which should be given to ministers).

The role of those core higher civil servants who work in Whitehall is concerned with:

- Preparing legislation, drawing up answers to parliamentary questions and briefing the minister.
- Administration – overseeing and carrying out the day-day work of the department or some part of it. This may involve meeting up with representatives of pressure groups or dealing with difficult, non-routine casework.
- Helping to develop the department's attitudes and work, looking at alternative lines of policy, surveying the advantages and difficulties of these, foreseeing practical problems.

It is the Permanent Secretary whose role is crucial. He or she is a member of the highest grade of the civil service and is the leading official in the department. He is responsible to the minister for what

Box 4.9 What sort of people become higher civil servants?

Civil servants have been recruited on merit (by passing competitive examinations) since the middle of the nineteenth century. Often, those who were selected for entry were among the brightest and best graduates, with first-class degrees from older and more prestigious universities. However, by the 1960s, academics and commentators increasingly lamented their lack of relevant training and skills, and the narrow and unrepresentative social background from which they emerged. Their ability was not doubted, but the sort of studies (History, the Classics, etc.) seemed to be of doubtful relevance to the work they would be doing in Whitehall. Moreover, they lacked experience of the outside world, having gone into the civil service on completion of their academic courses. The Fulton Report (1968) called for changes, so that there might be a movement away from this 'cult of the amateur' in favour of greater professionalism.

Over the last two decades or so, more has been done to ensure that there are more temporary secondments between commerce, industry and Whitehall, and far more recruitment from the private sector. Under the Blair government, an attempt was made to ensure that there were more, shorter and flexible secondments from the civil service into industry, especially civil servants at the junior level who operate outside of London.

The persistent bias in favour of public school students who become Oxbridge (Oxford or Cambridge University) graduates has been more difficult to address, although since the early 1990s the issue has been taken more seriously. There has been a broadening of the basis of recruitment with:

- more recruitment from non-Oxbridge universities
- a movement away from the arts subjects
- greater scope for women and members of ethnic minorities.

It is increasingly considered important to ensure that those who advise ministers and influence policymaking should be more representative of the community, although there is still a long way to go before this can be achieved. Changes have occurred, as the comment by a Permanent Secretary in the Department for Children, Schools and Families in January 2010 indicates[31]

If you go back to the 1940s and 50s, only one in seven of the most senior civil servants had gone to a state school . . . By the 1960s this figure had increased to one in four and it has been getting better ever since. But, over the decades, one thing hasn't changed – the myths and common misconceptions about what kind of people get to the top of the Civil Service. New research published this week reveals it is not what you might think.

The first survey into the socio-economic background of the top 200 members shows that the vast majority of people – about two thirds – went to a state school. If you just look at those who were educated in the UK, the figure rises to almost three quarters. That's a higher number than in many other influential professions; higher than journalists, judges and medics. Put these figures together with research that already exists about gender, such as the fact that women now hold the majority of all Civil Service jobs and more than a quarter of top management posts, and they show that the Civil Service is far more diverse than is often reported.

goes on and given the minister's involvement in political work, the Permanent Secretary has to direct and supervise most of the department's normal work, perhaps 85–90 per cent of it.

The minister–civil servant relationship

'Ministers decide, civil servants advise'. This is the classic statement of the relationship, the civil servants being 'on tap, but not on top'. Officials are supposed to be non-partisan and impartial. They are there to serve any government, offering advice and suggestions but allowing the minister – who after all takes responsibility for what goes wrong – to make decisions. It is the minister who is the elected politician, responsible to the House of Commons; he has to be able to justify what has been done.

Ministers are of course transient. They come and go, perhaps serving for a full administration or maybe being moved after a couple of years. By contrast, their officials may have been in the department for a long time and have developed considerable expertise. They become familiar with the realistic range of policy choices available and know the advantages or otherwise of various lines of policy. Their views will reflect a 'departmental view', but this may conflict with the government's or minister's priorities. In this situation there is scope for conflict between them.

Much has been written about 'mandarin power', mandarins being the very senior officials who have close and regular contact with min-

Box 4.10 Perspectives on the relationships between ministers and their senior civil servants

For many years, academics, journalists, politicians and top offi-cials have engaged in discussion about where power lies in British government, with the politicians or with the bureaucrats who serve them. Much depends on the perspective of those who analyse the relationship.

For our purposes, three views of the relationship can be categorised:

1. *The traditional view*, namely that ministers decide issues in the light of the advice they are given by their civil servants. The offi-cials loyally set out to serve their ministers' wishes, implementing the decisions made. The minister takes the praise or blame for what has been done, for good or ill.
2. *The radical perspective* adopted by critics on the Left, which con-centrates on the social background and attitudes of powerful civil servants who use their establishment connections and their wiles to frustrate left-wing ministers who want to change the direction of policy in a way that sharply challenges the status quo.
3. *The New Right approach* that stresses the way in which estab-lishment civil servants with a vested interest in the expansion of public services, are successful in pursuing their own interests and are immune from the market pressures that influence people in business and commerce.

Although they have a different vision and different objectives, non-consensus politicians of the Left and Right are liable to be frustrated by the way in which the civil service operates and may wish to see changes in Whitehall.

isters. It is suggested that often, because of their ability, experience and expertise, they exert a powerful influence over what happens in a department, especially over the policies that emerge. Radical com-mentators and MPs (and prime ministers such as Margaret Thatcher who wanted to 'get things done') are wary of mandarins, seeing them as a conservative force hostile to necessary innovation. At worst, they may frustrate the minister and be obstructive, concealing informa-tion. The suspicion is the greater because of their rather privileged public school, Oxbridge background; some are to be seen in the best gentleman's clubs in London.

Strong ministers will insist on their policy. It is often said that the first forty-eight hours will reveal whether a minister will assert his individuality and strength, or whether he will be a pushover, excessively dependent on his officials. At best, there is a constructive relationship between both sides.

The conventions of ministerial responsibility

Ministerial accountability to Parliament has two aspects:

- The collective responsibility of ministers for the work of the government.
- The individual responsibility for the work of the department they head.

Both forms of responsibility are embodied in conventions that cannot be legally enforced. They developed in the nineteenth century and have been widely recognised as important elements of the Constitution ever since. However, in recent decades, they have been much modified in practice, leading some commentators to question whether or not they have the same significance once accorded to them.

Collective responsibility

The convention means that ministers are collectively responsible to the House of Commons for governmental policy. In public, they are required to stick to the agreed Cabinet line and stay united. As a nineteenth-century prime minister, Lord Melbourne, once cynically remarked: 'It doesn't matter what we say, as long as we all tell the same story'.

The convention obliges ministers publicly to support decisions made in Cabinet, or resign. It has three aspects: unanimity, confidence and confidentiality.

- *Unanimity.* Ministers are expected publicly to support Cabinet decisions, because unity and cohesiveness is vital to government.
- *Confidence.* The Cabinet is expected to maintain the confidence of the House, its decisions being accepted by a majority of all MPs voting in the House of Commons. If they do not, the Cabinet is expected to resign.

- *Confidentiality.* What is said in Cabinet remains in Cabinet. This ensures an environment in which ministers can freely speak their minds, but also reinforces unanimity.

In practice, these three tenets are occasionally broken without incurring any penalty. Ministers have on occasion 'agreed to disagree' with their colleagues, and yet have remained in Cabinet.

There will be times when Cabinet members feel uneasy about what is being proposed and there may be sharp controversy behind closed doors. They have the opportunity to voice their discontent. But when the policy is decided, they either resign because they cannot go along with it, or else they decide they can live with it and agree to stay silent about any reservations. The position was laid down clearly by Lord Salisbury,[32] more than a hundred years ago: 'For all that passes in Cabinet, every member of it who does not resign if absolutely and irretrievably responsible, and has no right afterwards to say that he agreed in one case to a compromise, while in another he was persuaded by his colleagues'.

In recent decades, the policy has been extended downwards, well below Cabinet level. All members of the government are bound to back official policy, even though only Cabinet members will have been present at the time of decision. Today, even the lowest rank in the administration, the unpaid PPSs, are expected to 'toe the line'.

The doctrine still has its uses, for it:

- ensures that ministers 'sing from the same hymn sheet', helping to ensure that policy is clear and coherent;
- avoids the confusion that can arise when different members of an administration say different things, as happens sometimes under US administrations.

Yet today, collective responsibility lacks the force it once had and is applied in a way that suits the government of the day. For instance:

- some ministers get round the obligation by leaking their views, perhaps in coded language;
- others make speeches containing thinly veiled criticisms of government policy (Michael Portillo, under John Major) or express personal views (Peter Mandelson on Europe, under Tony Blair);
- in 1975 Harold Wilson and in 1977 James Callaghan actually

allowed ministers to agree to differ on divisive aspects of European policy, in the face of evident disunity.

The convention is liable to be waived when it suits the Prime Minister, which is why some commentators regard it as a 'constitutional myth'. The doctrine purports to make the government responsible to the House of Commons, the implication being that if a serious blunder is committed then the government as a whole is liable to be defeated. Yet governments have survived countless crises from Westland to Iraq and no mass resignation of ministers has occurred. Party discipline ensures that MPs stay loyal in the voting lobbies, so that crises sometimes provide impressive demonstrations of unity (Westland, 1986).

Individual ministerial responsibility

Individual responsibility refers to the responsibility of each government minister for the work of his department. He or she is answerable to the House of Commons for all that happens within it. The positive aspect of this is that MPs know that there is someone to whom they can direct their questions and anxieties about policy, at Question Time, in committees, in debates and privately to MPs. The negative aspect is that thereby civil servants are kept out of the political arena and shielded from controversy, making it possible for any future administration to have confidence in civil service neutrality.

'Responsible' means on the one hand that ministers are required to inform Parliament about the work and conduct of their departments, explaining and if necessary making amends for their own and their officials' actions. They take the praise for what is well done and the blame for what goes wrong. In this sense, answerability and accountability still apply. But 'responsibility' goes further and implies liability to lose office, if the fault is sufficiently serious.

In this second sense, resignations for political or administrative misjudgements and mistakes have in recent decades become extremely unusual. There never was a 'golden age' in which ministers fell on their swords whenever the performance of their departments was found wanting, although in the nineteenth century resignation was not uncommon. Since the end of the Second World War, they have been rare.

Many political blunders and misjudgements and departmental administrative failings are committed, but they go unpunished by the ultimate sanction. In almost all cases, ministers try very hard to avoid resignation. They generally stay in their jobs at least until the next reshuffle, almost regardless of how badly they have performed their tasks. A number of high-profile cases highlight the failure to step down when a policy failure has been revealed. For instance, Norman Lamont failed to resign as Chancellor in 1992, when Britain was forced ignominiously to leave the Exchange Rate Mechanism after a day of financial chaos. He survived until forced out in a reshuffle.

In practice, then, the convention does not normally apply. Its application has been watered down, for often MPs on the government side rally behind the beleaguered minister. Many commentators are sympathetic to ministers who find themselves in political trouble over an episode in which they had no direct involvement. In the Home Office, which deals with controversial issues that create much public anxiety, the volume of mail received every day is massive. It would be unreasonable to assume that ministers can read it all or know the details of every response sent out in their name. Finally, the creation of Next Step agencies has blurred responsibility. They have a degree of autonomy, so that when a problem occurs – perhaps a mass prison break-out – there is an issue of who is to be held responsible, the head of the Prison Agency (responsible for administration) or the Home Secretary (responsible for the broad lines of policy). In the case of the Parkhurst gaol-break (1995), neither Michael Howard nor Sir Derek Lewis were willing to accept responsibility, each blaming each other.

Today, whether or not a minister resigns under the convention will depend on his support from the party, Prime Minister and Cabinet colleagues. If there is prolonged adverse publicity that may be damaging to the government, a resignation is more likely to occur.

In spite of the absence of resignation in most cases, the doctrine nevertheless has its uses. It ensures that someone is accountable, in that there is a minister to answer questions. In this way, it facilitates the work of MPs to investigate the grievances and press the claims of their constituents. Secondly, civil servants are not normally named when any error has occurred, but the knowledge that if they make a misjudgement then their minister will be answerable in the House, helps to ensure that they act with care in handling departmental issues. Finally, it facilitates the work of opposition, in that it ensures someone has to justify what has been done to those who wish to expose departmental or policy failings.

Why do ministers resign?

Over the last two decades, calls for ministerial resignations have grown significantly. They were infrequent in the 1940s and 1950s, but particularly since 1990 the number of serious calls for resignation has noticeably increased, only in small part because of the increase in the number of ministers on the payroll. This does not necessarily mean that there has been a substantial change in the way in which ministers behave, nor that there has been a deterioration of standards in public life. More likely, it reflects the fact that the media now routinely attack government ministers on issues on which they mostly used to refrain from comment.

Most ministerial resignations have had little to do with ministers taking responsibility for the work of their department, under the principle of ministerial responsibility. They fall into other categories, mainly personal misconduct (often financial or sexual), misjudgements and mistakes, and ideological and/or policy differences with the government. There were twenty-five under the Major administration and thirty-six under Tony Blair.

The case of Holland

Holland employs a very proportional method of voting which results in the representation of several small parties. Not surprisingly, governments tend to be coalitions, so that the distribution of ministerial offices by the Prime Minister ('Minister-President') is limited by the often-lengthy bargaining that precedes the formation of a new administration. Once such an administration is formed, leaders are reluctant to conduct any reshuffle for fear of offending a partner in the government, a situation which, in the words of Hague and Harrop,[33] makes for 'skilful conciliators, not dashing heroes'.

The style of Dutch government tends to be collegial rather than hierarchical. The fourteen or so members of the Cabinet are given

Table 4.1 Departed Cabinet ministers under the Brown and Cameron premierships

Minister	Year of resignation	Reason for departure
Peter Hain, Secretary of State for Work and Pensions/Wales	2008	Finance: funding of his bid for Labour's deputy leadership, wish to fight to clear his name
Hazel Blears, Secretary of State for Communities and Local Government	2009	Ideology/policy and finance: as a Blairite, disillusioned with direction and approach of Brown government, but also involved in controversy over MPs' expenses and a possible candidate for reshuffle
Jacqui Smith, Home Secretary	2009	Finance: damaged by expenses row and revelations about dubious claims, perhaps anticipating loss of position in reshuffle
James Purnell, Secretary of State for Work and Pensions	2009	Ideology/policy and finance: having been mentioned in expenses row, keen to leave because of his doubts about Brown's ability to lead party in next election
John Hutton, Secretary of State for Defence	2009	Ideology and policy: as a Blairite, uneasy about direction of Brown leadership
Geoff Hoon, Secretary of State for Transport	2009	Personal and financial/policy: wish to 'spend more time with family', but involved in expenses row and uneasy about Brown leadership
Caroline Flint, Minister of State for Europe (Cabinet rank)	2009	Policy/financial: as a Blairite, uneasy about direction of policy and Brown's treatment of women; mentioned in expenses row
David Laws, Chief Secretary to the Treasury	2010	Finance/personal: the financial misdemeanour involved expenses claimed for a room rented from his gay partner
Liam Fox, Secretary of State for Defence	2011	Personal/financial: following speculation about relationship with friend/adviser and concerns of a conflict of interest

considerable freedom to recruit their own departmental staff and group of personal advisers, rather than have to work with people imposed upon them. This further weakens the Prime Minister's power of appointment, so that he is not free to appoint, reshuffle or dismiss colleagues as he pleases, nor to take a hand in official appointments.

The result is that 'ministers serve *with* Prime Ministers, rather than *under* them'. In the age of television, in which 'media visibility grows apace', the Dutch Prime Minister is 'more than a chairperson, but remains far less than a chieftain'.

The case of the USA

Presidential power in the United States has waxed and waned, reflecting considerations of personality and style, circumstances and the limitations and opportunities presented by the office. Historically, Americans have swung back and forth in their views about the sort of president they favour. At times, they demand strong, assertive leadership and admire those incumbents who can provide it. Indeed, most of the presidents rated highly by academics and the rest of the population have been active presidents. Yet within a short period of being on the receiving end of such activism and vigour, there can be a reaction against it. In the words of one writer, Gary Wasserman,[34] presidents have walked a thin line between too much and too little power in the White House.

Overall, the presidency has irregularly but vastly grown in power and significance from the limited role accorded it in the Constitution. The key roles that a president fulfils, covering as they do that of chief of state, chief diplomat, commander-in-chief, chief executive, chief legislator and party leader show how broad that power can be, particularly when exercised by a president who wishes to give a strong lead. By the 1960s, Americans seemed willing to accept a vigorous use of presidential power, as activists such as Kennedy and Johnson were willing to introduce a range of presidential initiatives at home and abroad.

Yet the experience of the 1970s illustrates the dilemma to which Wasserman has drawn attention. Following the resignation of Richard Nixon, there was a reaction against the powerful presidency of the previous decade, as many Americans came to believe that the institution no longer seemed to be subject to adequate constitutional checks and balances. Since then, there has been more talk of the weakness rather than the strength of presidents, who are restrained by a variety of historical, legal and political limitations. Recent commentators have describe the office in such terms as the 'tethered' or the 'constrained' presidency. Back in the early 1960s, Richard Neustadt[35] had noted that presidential power amounted to 'the power to persuade'. The ability of individual presidents to gain acceptance for their policies is dependent on their skill in selling these policies to other political players in Washington, their use of the media and their ability to control the bureaucracy. By 'going Washington' and 'going public', they have a chance of turning their programmes into political action.

There is an ambivalence about the presidency, to which President Kennedy[36] drew attention: 'The President is rightly described as a man of extraordinary powers. Yet it is also true that he must wield those powers under extraordinary limitations'.

- -

 ## What you should have learnt from reading this chapter

- Executives have a key role in political life for it is members of the government who devise policies in the light of information and advice that they receive, and get them on the statute book. The Official Executive has the task of implementing the policies devised by the Political Executive.

- Because of the expansion of governmental activity in the twentieth century, the powers of the Executive have grown; the chief executive is today far more powerful than one hundred years ago.

- Various circumstances, ranging from television to the new importance of international summitry and overseas visits, have provided political leaders with a new pre-eminence, and they are no longer national leaders alone but also world statesmen.

- Because of these trends, many writers have discerned a trend towards prime ministerial government in Britain and commented on the extent of 'presidential power'. The Prime Minister is indeed very powerful today, but the extent of that power and influence can vary according to the incumbent and the circumstances of the time.

A glossary of key terms

Cabinet government The theory that the Cabinet forms a collective political executive in which each member in theory has an equal influence. All power is vested in the Cabinet, which acts as a constraint upon the power of the Prime Minister. The principle of collective responsibility ensures that the Cabinet either makes or is consulted about all important political decisions. Some commentators claim that Britain has moved away from Cabinet government towards a system of 'government by prime minister.

Core executive The complex network of people and institutions that circles around the Prime Minister and Cabinet, including the Cabinet Office, the Prime Minister's Office and the leading civil servants in Whitehall.

Elective dictatorship The term coined by Lord Hailsham to describe the constitutional imbalance in which executive power has increased, only to be curtailed by the peoples' votes at the next election. In between, a government armed with a strong majority can drive its legislative programme through the House of Commons, helped by strong party discipline.

Inner and kitchen Cabinets Inner Cabinets comprise an informal group of the most senior members of the Cabinet, who under some prime ministers may meet with the Prime Minister and discuss/decide policy away from the rest of the Cabinet. For David Cameron, key figures include George Osborne and Michael Gove.

Kitchen Cabinets are the small coteries of advisers and confidantes with which prime ministers like to surround themselves and talk over issues at the end of the day. They usually include some members of the Cabinet, although under Tony Blair more importance was attached to the views of key personnel such as Alastair Campbell, Philip Gould, Peter Mandelson, Jonathan Powell and others.

Next Steps programme Named after the short title of the Ibbs Report, 1988, which saw the creation of executive agencies as a remedy for management failings and inefficiency within the civil service. The agencies have some managerial autonomy over the service for which they are responsible – e.g. Benefits Agency.

Prime ministerial government The theory that the office of Prime Minister has become so powerful that he or she now forms a political executive similar to a president. According to Crossman, one of the original advocates of the thesis, Cabinet government had passed away, the Cabinet being relegated to becoming only a 'dignified part' of the Constitution. In contrast, the office of Prime Minister had become a powerhouse, 'the efficient secret of government'. Executive power is therefore concentrated in the hands of the Prime Minister.

Spatial leadership A reference to the way in which some recent US presidents and British prime ministers have tried to remain above the political fray and the problems in which ministers are mired, seeking to detach themselves from the fortunes of the government.

Vote of confidence A procedure used by members of a legislative body to remove a government from office. To be successful, the procedure typically requires a majority of legislators to disapprove of the government's actions – e.g. to issue a vote of 'no confidence' or a motion of censure. A motion of no confidence is a motion traditionally put before a parliament by the opposition, in the hope of defeating or weakening the government.

Westland A government crisis in 1986 brought about by the failure of the Westland helicopter company. An American bid was lined up to take over Westland, but Michael Heseltine wanted the Thatcher government to show its support for European initiatives by backing a bid from a European consortium. He felt his views were sidelined, if not ignored. He dramatically walked out of the Cabinet over the failure of the Prime Minister to listen to his viewpoint, feeling that the Cabinet was not being fully consulted.

Likely examination questions

How does the British Prime Minister seek to control his Cabinet?

Discuss the view that 'Cabinet government' in Britain has been replaced by 'government by Prime Minister'.

What are the main constraints upon the power of the British Prime Minister?

Discuss the view that modern prime ministers have too much power.

'The power to persuade.' Is this the only real power possessed by a chief executive in a liberal democracy?

Is the principle of the collective responsibility of the Cabinet worth preserving?

'The idea that the British Prime Minister has become a presidential figure like the American incumbent ignores the substantial differences between the two roles.' Discuss.

Helpful websites

www.number-10.gov.uk The Downing Street site.

www.cabinet-office.gov.uk/ The Cabinet Office site.

www.whitehouse.gov/ The White House site.

Suggestions for further reading

Useful articles

D. Bell, 'A tale of two civil servants', *The Guardian*, 20 January 2010.

M. Bennister and R. Heffernan, 'How Does the Cameron-Clegg Relationship Affect the Role of Prime Minister?', draft paper for PSA Conference, 2011.

R. Heffernan, 'Prime Ministerial Predominance? Core Executive Politics in the UK', *British Journal of Politics and International Relations* 5:3, 2003.

R. Heffernan, 'Why the Prime Minister cannot be a President: Comparing Institutional Imperatives in Britain and America', *Parliamentary Affairs*, 58:1, 2005.

N. Jackson, 'The Blair Style: Presidential, Bilateral or Trilateral Government', *Talking Politics*, January 2003.

G. Jones, 'Cabinet too big to make decisions', *Daily Telegraph*, 29 June 2009.

Useful books

S. Berlinsky et al., 'Choosing, Moving and Resigning at Westminster, UK', in K. Dowding and P. Dumont (eds), *The Selection of Ministers in Europe*, Routledge, 2009.

S. Buckley, *The Prime Minister and Cabinet*, Edinburgh University Press, 2006.

P. Hennessy, *The Prime Ministers: The Office and its Holders since 1945*, Allen Lane, 2000.

CHAPTER 5

The Judiciary

Contents

Introduction   158
Judicial independence   158
Judicial neutrality   162
The growing importance of judicial review   173
The developing trend towards judicial activism   175
The politicisation of British judges: growing judicial power   177
The case of the European Court of Human Rights   179
The case of the USA   184

Overview

The independence of the judiciary is an essential feature of democratic regimes. Because it is autonomous, it has often been regarded as having only peripheral interest for those who study politics. But in recent years, the dividing line between politics and the law has become blurred. Judges have become increasingly significant actors in the political system. Their greater willingness to concern themselves with issues affecting public policy has aroused disquiet among some elected politicians, who see their policymaking role as being under threat.

In this chapter, we examine the political significance of the courts and the role and appropriateness of judges in commenting on and resolving political issues.

Key issues to be covered in this chapter

- The independence of the judiciary
- The independence of judges in practice
- The notion of judicial neutrality
- The functions of the judiciary
- The impact of judicial review on the political process
- The effectiveness of judges in protecting civil liberties
- The increasingly political role of judges in politics
- Disquiet about the background and outlook of judges

Introduction

The judiciary is the branch of government responsible for the authoritative interpretation and adjudication of law, and the arbitration between parties in any legal dispute. The term includes those individuals and bodies (primarily judges and the courts) that administer and interpret the meaning of laws. In democratic countries, it is expected that the judicial system will be able to function freely, without any interference from the government of the day.

Functions of judiciaries

As the key figures in the judiciary, judges perform several functions:

- They peacefully resolve disputes between individuals, adjudicating in controversies within the limits of the prescribed law.
- They interpret the law, determining what its means and how it applies in changing circumstances.
- They uphold the will of the legislature, acting as guardians of the law, taking responsibility for applying its rules without fear or favour, as well as securing the liberties of the person and ensuring that governments and peoples comply with the 'spirit' of the constitution.
- (particularly in states with a codified constitution) They have responsibility for **judicial review** of particular laws and administrative actions.
- (of senior judges) They may be asked to chair enquiries.
- (if they are law lords) They sit in Parliament, contributing to its debates on public policy and sharing in the various tasks performed by the House of Lords.

Judicial independence

In many states, the constitution provides for an independent judiciary. Its existence is a fundamental characteristic of **liberal democracies**. **Judicial independence** implies that there should be a strict separation between the judiciary and other branches of government. It is expected that the judicial system will be autonomous, able to function freely and without any interference from the government of the day. It is in regard to the independence of the judiciary that the key differences between authoritarian and liberal states become clear. The degree of independence of judges from political interference varies from country to country, and even within a single country's history. In some parts of the non-Western world, there is a strong independent judiciary. India has generally retained the high standards of a judicial system put in place in the days of the colonial era. In Turkey, the constitutions of 1968 and 1982 'provided entrenched security of tenure for judges and prosecutors'. However, in several other states the judiciary is under constant pressure to deliver verdicts acceptable to the regime, making life difficult for those who exhibit a commitment to justice for all.

Judicial independence in Britain
Lord Denning[1] described the independence of the judiciary as 'the keystone of the rule of law in England'. For politicians to interfere in issues before the courts would be seen as an affront to the idea of the rule of law. Yet in the way that judges have traditionally been appointed, there is room for doubt.

The independence of the British judiciary is supposed to be protected in three ways:

• the way in which judges are selected
• their security of tenure
• their political neutrality.

In Britain, there is other protection. Judges receive fixed salaries that are not subject to parliamentary approval. There is also a tradition that the remarks and sentences of judges in court cases should not be subject to parliamentary debate or criticism. In the words of a former Lord Chancellor, Lord Hailsham,[2] parliamentary criticism was 'subversive of the independence of the judiciary'. This tradition is on occasion breached. In the miners' strike (1984–5), a Labour MP was suspended from the House, on account of his reference to 'tame Tory judges'. Subsequently, some right-wing politicians, particularly in the Thatcher and Major eras, were much irked by the observations of certain judges and especially by the allegedly lenient sentences they imposed. They made their views known in the House of Commons.

The principle of judicial independence is now officially enshrined in British law. The Constitutional Reform Act (2005) provides for the separation of the judiciary (legal system) from the legislature (Parliament) and the executive (government). Its key changes included:

- limitations on the judicial role of Lord Chancellor
- the establishment of a new Supreme Court separate from the House of Lords and the removal of law lords from the legislature
- the creation of a new independent **Judicial Appointments Commission**.

The selection of judges

The recruitment of judges should not be influenced by political considerations or personal views. It should be done on the basis of merit or by popular choice. In practice, there are three main methods of selection: appointment, co-option by other judges and popular election.

The appointment of judges in Britain

At the beginning of the twentieth century, judges were appointed by the Lord Chancellor as a means of rewarding those who had provided political services. But since the days of Lord Haldane (Lord Chancellor), political allegiance has been relatively unimportant and merit (appropriate legal and professional qualities) has been paramount. Until recently, the most senior judges were appointed by the Prime Minister, following consultations with the Lord Chancellor. Today, however, the Judicial Appointments Commission (JAC), established under the terms of the 2005 legislation, makes judicial appointments. Its brief is to select candidates for judicial office on merit, through fair and open competition, from the widest range of eligible candidates. In support of the change, the relevant minister, Lord Falconer,[3] argued that:

> In a modern democratic society, it is no longer acceptable for judicial appointments to be entirely in the hands of a government minister. For example, the judiciary is often involved in adjudicating on the lawfulness of actions of the executive. And so the appointments system must be, and must be seen to be, independent of government.

Table 5.1 The recruitment of judges: a summary

Method	Examples	Merits or otherwise
Appoint-ment	Practised in most countries, especially for senior judges – e.g. in Britain and in appoint-ments to the American Supreme Court.	Provides opportunity to choose people on basis of merit. Many of those selected have, at some time, had to pass examinations in order to demonstrate their abilities, before they can be considered for service. At best, it is possible to appoint judges from a wide variety of backgrounds. The dangers are that appointment becomes a means of rewarding relatives and friends (nepotism) and that people are chosen not according to their judicial merit but rather for their political leanings and known views on matters of public life, such as the appropriate scope of state intervention in economic and social life (partisanship).
Co-option by judges already in post	Italy, Turkey	Good means of ensuring judicial inde-pendence, but may produce a judiciary out of touch with popular opinion – especially given the backgrounds and outlooks of many judges. Also, it can lead to a self-perpetuating elite, if the existing members seek recruits who share their own outlook.
Popular election	Some US states, such as Georgia	Judges are more responsive to the prevailing state of public opinion, and – in some cases – are liable to use of the **recall**. There is no guarantee that able, competent justices will be chosen. As Lord Taylor[3] observed some years ago: 'You wouldn't want the election of someone who was going to operate on our brain; you would want someone chosen because he knows what he's doing.' Moreover, those elected may feel unduly beholden to those who nominated them as candidates or to the majority of voters who favoured them. Minorities may not get a fair deal in states dominated by one party.

In the case of appointments to the new Supreme Court, a selection commission will be formed as and when vacancies arise. It will comprise the President and Deputy President of the Court and a member from each of the JAC of England and Wales, the Judicial Appointments Board for Scotland and the Northern Ireland Judicial Appointments Commission. It will put forward only one name for the Minister of Justice/Lord Chancellor to consider (see Box 5.1, which clarifies the roles of key figures within the judiciary).

The security of tenure of judges

Once installed in office, judges should hold their office for a reasonable period, subject to their good conduct. Their promotion or otherwise may be determined by members of the government of the day, but they should be allowed to continue to serve even if they are unable to advance. They should not be liable to removal on the whim of particular governments or individuals. In some cases, they may serve a fixed term of office. They usually remain in position for many years. US Supreme Court judges normally serve for a very long period, although theoretically they may be removed by impeachment before Congress if they commit serious offences.

In Britain, a judge once appointed can serve until retirement age, which is at least seventy. They are very hard to remove. Those who function in superior courts are liable to dismissal on grounds of misbehaviour, but in the rare cases where this may have been an option they have generally been allowed to retire quietly. Neither are lower judges normally dismissed. Dismissal only applies in cases of dishonesty, incompetence or misbehaviour. In 1983, one judge was dismissed for whisky smuggling! Under the 2005 Act, the power to remove judges remains with the Lord Chancellor, although the Lord Chief Justice has acquired some disciplinary powers.

Judicial neutrality

Judicial independence and judicial neutrality are linked but distinct concepts. They combine to ensure justice, in the sense that disputes are settled in a fair and impartial manner. This implies, among other things, that the judiciary is able to uphold the rule of law and to protect individual rights and liberties, by avoiding becoming the

Box 5.1 The administration of justice in the UK

For many years, some constitutional writers were unhappy about the role fulfilled by the Lord Chancellor in British government. They:

- noted the overlap between the Lord Chancellor's political and judicial roles and argued for a clearer distinction between government, Parliament and the judiciary;
- pointed to the difficulties in obtaining information in the House of Commons because of the division of legal functions between the Lord Chancellor and Home Secretary;
- wanted to see a single 'Minister of Justice' at the head of a department with undivided responsibility for the administrative aspects of the judicial system.

The situation was clarified by the passage of the Constitutional Reform Act, operative since 2007. Under its terms:

- the *Home Secretary* retains responsibility for the police and the security service, as well as oversight of crime reduction, counter-terrorism and other crime-related areas.
- the *Lord Chancellor* is no longer the head of the judiciary and there is no longer any requirement for him to be a judge or a member of the House of Lords. He becomes the Secretary of State for Justice, with responsibility for courts, prisons, probation and constitutional affairs and a focus on reducing re-offending. He retains some functions previously exercised by the Lord Chancellor. For example, jointly with the Lord Chief Justice, he or she still exercises disciplinary authority over the judges and has responsibility for the Office for Judicial Complaints, the body that investigates complaints made against judicial office-holders. The current Secretary of State for Justice and Lord Chancellor, Kenneth Clarke, sits in the House of Commons.
- the *Lord Chief Justice*, currently Lord Judge, takes over much of the previous judicial work of the Lord Chancellor, having responsibility for the system of courts and judges. Among other things, he: represents the views of the judiciary of England and Wales to Parliament and government; oversees the welfare, training and guidance of the judiciary of England and Wales; discusses with government the provision of resources for the judiciary, which are allotted by the Lord Chancellor of judges; and deals with the allocation of work in courts in England and Wales.

The hierarchy of judges
The head of the judiciary, the Lord Chief Justice, is also Head of Criminal Justice and President of the Courts of England and Wales. He is the leading judge, sitting on important criminal, civil and family cases. He gives judgments and lays down practice directions in many of the most important appeal cases. The Master of the Rolls (i.e. the roll of solicitors) heads the Civil Division of the Court of Appeal. He is the second most senior judge in England and Wales, after the Lord Chief Justice.

Lord Phillips is the first President of the Supreme Court. The Court contains several of the country's most senior judges – ten of whom were previously the Lords of Appeal in Ordinary (law lords). In addition to the President, it has a Deputy President and ten other Justices.

The other group included within the ranks of the senior judges are those who sit in the High Court. All of the senior judges are chosen from barristers of at least ten years' experience.

Below them are circuit judges who sit in the Crown Courts, then the recorders (part-time judges) and at the bottom of the hierarchy are the magistrates (Justices of the Peace), lay people rather than trained lawyers.

creature of government or a legal defence for privileged and propertied groups.

Judicial neutrality is a necessary condition of judicial independence. It assumes equality before the law, that all persons can expect equal consideration of their case and be treated in the same way unless there are specific circumstances that mean they should be treated differently. Judges set aside any personal bias and issues of social background as they interpret the law. In this way, decisions can be taken objectively and disputes settled fairly and impartially, on solely legal grounds.

Judicial neutrality in Britain is ensured in several ways, notably that:

- judges are not expected to take any active, public role in party politics
- Supreme Court justices are not expected to join the fray in debating contentious party political issues
- (in court) judges should follow points of law and confine themselves to the detail of the case

- if there are reasons to doubt the validity of judgements delivered, they can be challenged under the rules of appeal
- in some cases, there are other courts to which a person can go to seek redress – e.g. a decision in a case involving civil liberties may go to the Court of Appeal and then the Supreme Court: it could ultimately end up in the Court of Human Rights, Strasbourg
- the watchful eye of the media: in the case of the extradition hearing of General Pinochet by the law lords, one of the five judges (Lord Hoffman) was revealed to be prominently involved with Amnesty International. The hearing had to be held again, with a replacement for him.

Are judges neutral? By convention, judges are above and beyond politics, apolitical beings who interpret but do not make the law. As such, their discretion is limited. But such a view is naive and a series of distinguished British judges from Denning to Devlin, from Radcliffe to Reid, have acknowledged that their role is much more creative than mere interpretation. This is because, apart from their work in relation to sentencing criminals, judges are involved in passing judgement in numerous cases relating to areas such as governmental secrecy, industrial relations, police powers, political protest, race relations and sexual behaviour. They are not simply administering the law in a passive way, there is much potential for them to make law as they interpret it.

In fulfilling their role, judges are expected to be impartial, and not vulnerable to political influence and pressure. They are expected to refrain from partisan activity and generally have refrained from commenting on matters of public policy. The 1955 *Kilmuir Guidelines* urged them to silence since 'every utterance which [they] make in public, except in the actual performance of [their] judicial duties, must necessarily bring [them] within the focus of criticism'. The *Guidelines* were later relaxed, but Lord Hailsham as Lord Chancellor in the early Thatcher years was keen to see their spirit observed. His Conservative successor, Lord Mackay, was sympathetic to a more relaxed approach, allowing judges to give interviews. More recently, in a greater spirit of openness, senior judges have been willing to express their views on public policy, although this is not to ally themselves with backing for one party.

The separation of judges from the political process is not quite as clear-cut as the concept of an independent judiciary might suggest. Some holders of judicial office also have a political role, among them the Lord Chancellor (now, of course, with much-reduced judicial responsibility), the Attorney General and the Solicitor General. Although they are supposed to act in a non-partisan manner in their judicial capacity, at times this can be difficult. The legal advice given to the Blair government by the Solicitor-General over the legality of the decision to send troops into Iraq concerned a sensitive issue that has become more controversial in the light of subsequent revelations, with suggestions that he leaned over backwards to support the ministerial case for intervention.

In other ways too, judges may find themselves caught up in political controversy. They may be asked by the Prime Minister to chair important enquiries and make recommendations for future action. Lord Hutton was asked to enquire into the death of David Kelly, the former weapons inspector who committed suicide in 2003 after suggestions that the 'September dossier' arguing the case for military action against Iraq had been sexed-up. Sometimes, the findings of such enquiries are contentious and inspire criticism of the judge involved. Hutton was accused of producing a report that 'whitewashed' the Blair administration whilst heaping blame upon the journalist Andrew Gilligan and the BBC.

The reason why judges should remain politically neutral is clear. If they make a partisan utterance, it is felt that this would undermine public confidence in their impartiality. They need to be beyond party politics and committed to the pursuit of justice. Yet in practice there are real doubts as to whether judges can ever be completely neutral, for all members of the bench have their own leanings and preferences. Because of such considerations, the issue of judicial neutrality has aroused much academic and political controversy.

By the nature of the role they perform, judges are expected to be somewhat detached from society. By virtue of their calling and training, they are likely to possess an innate caution and a preference for order. Not surprisingly, they are often seen as conservative and out-of-touch in their approach. There have been many examples when this has been the case, particularly in the United States in the 1930s. The nine elderly Supreme Court justices disliked legislation that was intended to broaden the scope of federal action. They struck down key parts of the New Deal programme that had been enthusiastically endorsed by the electorate.

Critics of the judiciary go further and allege that the social background of judges present a subtle threat to the notion of judicial independence. In many liberal democracies the type of person appointed to judicial office tends to be middle class and affluent. As such, they are not representative of the society in which they operate. It is quite possible that their attitudes are unlikely to reflect those prevalent in society.

On the whole, judges do behave in as neutral a manner as can reasonably be expected. Whatever the fears of the Left about its treatment in some past cases and the views expressed by Griffiths and others, in the developing climate of **judicial activism** there is a greater willingness to take on government ministers. Indeed, it could even be argued that the situation has changed from one in which judges were seen as anti-Left to one in which they are seen as anti those in authority, challenging their decisions in several important areas. The issue of judicial review (see pp. 173–5) and the public statements made by senior law officers are important evidence of this trend.

The background of judges in Britain

Many judges reach their eminence having practised at the **Bar**, the membership of which has long been held to be elitist and unrepresentative. As a result of the manner of selection and the choice available, judges in the past were usually born into the professional middle classes, and often educated at public school and then Oxbridge. They tended to be wealthy, conservative in their thinking, middle aged when first appointed (in their sixties before they attain a really powerful position on the Supreme Court or Court of Appeal) and – like so many people in 'top' positions in British life – vulnerable to the accusation of being out of touch with the lives of people from different backgrounds. Observers sometimes complained that they were unable to understand the habits and terminology of everyday life, reflecting instead the social mores of thirty or forty years ago. They questioned the appropriateness of such persons to operate at a time of highly politicised argument on issues of human rights and civil liberties.

In an update of his original study, *Anatomy of Britain*, Anthony Sampson[4] concluded that the social background of judges 'has changed less than that of senior civil servants or even diplomats'. He recognised that officially no regard was paid to gender, race, religion, sexual orientation or political affiliation in appointing judges, but claimed that the choice when making a senior judicial appointment was in practice extremely limited, often to a handful of candidates. His research illustrated the exclusiveness of the judiciary:

- 100 per cent of judges were white
- 95 per cent were men
- 90 per cent had attended public school/Oxford or Cambridge educated
- their average age was 60.

With regard to the law lords, at the time when Sampson was writing his revised edition, all were male, educated at Oxford or Cambridge, half of them coming from three colleges that had a traditional reputation as 'nurseries for lawyers'. Only one of those educated in England had not attended a public school. Sampson acknowledged that they were persons of 'mostly original thinking, more liberal-minded and thoughtful than most earlier Law Lords, with a strong instinct for independence . . . But [they] could not claim to represent, or know about, a wide section of the British population and most of them were candidates from a similar background to their predecessors of forty years ago'. Their average age when he wrote was around 68.5 years.

Since then, there has been a breakthrough in one respect. One of the last all-male bastions of the British establishment admitted a woman for the first time. The UK's first woman law lord, Lady Brenda Hale, was previously a judge in the Court of Appeal. A former academic and specialist in divorce and the law on children, she has long argued that a more diverse and reflective judiciary would make a difference to how judging is carried out. As a result of her appointment, Britain has belatedly followed the example of Australia, Canada, New Zealand and the United States, all of whom have had women judges in their highest courts. However, critics of the composition of the judiciary can continue to point to the lack of female and ethnic-minority judges in the Appeal or High Court, and their serious under-representation on the Circuit bench, as Table 5.2 highlights.

Table 5.2 The representation of women and ethnic minorities on the bench, April 2008

Rank	Overall number	No. of women	% of women	No. of ethnic minority	% of ethnic minority
Lords of Appeal in Ordinary	12	1	8.3	0	0
Heads of Division	5	0	0	0	0
Lord Justices of Appeal	37	3	8.1	0	0
High Court judges	110	16	14.5	3	2.7
Circuit judges	653	87	13.3	20	3.1
Recorders	1,305	194	14.9	61	4.7
Judge Advocates	9	0	0	0	0
Deputy Judge Advocates	12	2	16.7	0	0
District judges	438	98	22.4	20	4.6
Deputy District judges	773	213	27.6	31	4.0
District judges in magistrates court	136	30	22.1	3	2.2
Deputy District judges in magistrates court	167	42	25.1	12	7.2
Masters, Registrars, Costs judges and DJ (PRFD)	48	11	22.9	1	2.1
Deputy Masters, Registrars, Costs judges and Deputy District judges (PRFD)	115	39	33.9	5	4.3
Overall total	3,820	736	19.3	156	4.1

Source: A. Home, Judicial Appointments, House of Commons Library, 3 September 2009.

The Left in Britain has long been critical of judges and wary of the power they exercise. Throughout much of its history, many in the Labour movement have felt that their party has suffered from the decisions made by those on the bench, particularly in the area of industrial relations. The most famous example of such treatment was the Taff Vale case at the turn of the twentieth century, in which the right of the unions to take strike action was seriously restricted. In the 1980s, a number of **sequestration** cases were heard, in which union funds were taken away as a result of judicial decisions. But the suspicion has not arisen solely as a result of the unfavourable verdicts that judges have often delivered to the Labour Movement. It derives from a feeling that their judgements in court are influenced by their backgrounds, attitudes and methods of selection. In other words, they are biased.

Sampson quotes a Labour document *Manifesto*,[5] produced in the 1980s, which proclaimed (of judges): 'Their attitude to the political and social problems of our time is shaped and determined by their class, their upbringing and their professional life – their attitude is strongly conservative, respectful of property rights and highly authoritarian'. Other left-wing writers have suggested that in cases involving official secrecy, the performance of Labour councils and trade unions, the partiality of judges is evident. In their view, the nature of judicial backgrounds and the conservatism of their attitudes undermine the idea of judicial neutrality.

The most frequently quoted attack on the characteristics of judges was made by John Griffiths.[6] In his words, judges 'by their education and training and the pursuit of their profession as barristers, acquire a strikingly homogeneous collection of attitudes, beliefs and principles which to them represent the public interest'. He complains that, in exercising their discretion, judges rather assume that the public interest favours law and order and the upholding of the interests of the state, over any other considerations. His critique suggests that judges are more willing to defend property rights than wider human rights or personal liberties:

> They cannot be politically neutral because . . . their interpretation of what is in the public interest and therefore politically desirable is determined by the kind of people they are and the position they hold in our society: [and because] their position is part of established authority and so is necessarily conservative, not liberal.

According to this view, the backgrounds and attitudes of judges make them unsympathetic to – indeed, biased against – minorities, especially strident ones, and hostile to ideas of social progress. Militant demonstrators have often received harsh words and stiff punishments from judges who dislike the causes and methods with which strikers and others are associated.

The allegations of gender and social exclusivity, if not so much those of political bias, made by Griffiths have been taken up by many commentators and also by government ministers.

Is the attack on the background and character of British judges fair?

By virtue of their training, notions of restraint, caution, restriction, respect for property and family, and obedience for law come naturally to judges. They have often revealed a leaning towards conventional moral values, ones that are congenial to many members of the Conservative Party – and probably to many Labour supporters as well. In this sense, if the decision is not strictly determined by the legal/factual material available to them, they decide cases on the basis of values that are generally conservative, and their decisions may have ideological overtones. There is no such thing as an absolutely neutral decision.

The nature of their social backgrounds and professional training are likely to incline them in a particular way. But it does not follow that because people come from a certain type of social background they must all be biased in a particular direction. It is easy to make sweeping generalisations about judges and their behaviour. They are not a homogeneous group. There is a range of judges operating in different courts and at different levels, and if the Griffiths critique stresses their homogeneity so too the writings of Drewry[7] and Lee[8] have emphasised their diversity.

In any case, a generally privileged background does not necessarily render a judge biased in outlook or open to the allegation of possessing conservative opinions. Lee has suggested that an examination of the actual record of judges at work indicates that the attack on judicial neutrality is an unfair one. He makes the point that if historically judges have decided against trade unionists, it may not be because of their alleged conservatism but rather because, on the occasions concerned, the unions were behaving wrongly according to the law as laid down at the time.

Moreover, judges develop their outlook after their appointment. Whatever their background, their views are likely to evolve in the light of their experience. After some years of service, the tenor of their decisions cannot always be predicted on the basis of their class, education and training. Budge et al.[9] quote the example of a decision delivered by the late Lord Hailsham in the House of Lords in 1997. Here was an 'unambiguously political' judge who on occasion was more than willing to go against the grain. In giving a judgement in a case in which a woman was being prosecuted for breaking regulations governing overcrowding in boarding houses (though actually she was running a refuge for battered wives), he observed that:

> This appellant . . . is providing a service for people in urgent and tragic need. It is a service which in fact is provided by no other organ or our much vaunted system of public welfare . . . When people come to her door, not seldom accompanied by young children in desperate states and at all hours, because, being in danger, they cannot go home . . . the appellant does not turn them away . . . And what happens when she does? She finds herself the defendant in criminal proceedings . . . because she has allowed the inmates of her house to exceed the permitted maximum, and to that charge, I believe, she has no defence in law.

Hailsham then cast his vote against the side he undoubtedly favoured, because he felt constrained by precedent or duty. In this case, the law was clear. Often it is not and here judges do have a wider variety of discretion. As we have seen, in a sense, the judiciary as an institution in every society, whatever the background of its members, is bound to be conservative, since its task is to maintain order and the stability of the state. This implies respect for precedents, history and the established way of doing things.

There has been in recent years a new breed of judges who are in no way anti-Left, but much more willing to challenge government power. As we examine below (see the following section), they are more willing to take on ministers and criticise their attitudes and approach. As Lord Taylor[10] (the Lord Chief Justice who found himself in open disagreement with Conservative Home Secretary, Michael Howard) has written: 'The suggestion that judges are biased towards the Establishment does not stand up to examination'. It is true that in the Blair era, Labour again found itself under attack from the judges, but this was in part because they were often arguing the civil libertarian case on issues such as jury reform, official secrecy and sentencing policy, among other things. In 2002, Lord Woolf[11] argued that in the light of recent asylum cases, the judiciary had an important role in defending individual rights, given a tendency by government to override them.

There has been an attempt to widen the professional and social background of the judiciary in recent years. The Department of Justice is seeking to identify the barriers that deter able candidates from wishing to become judges and to find ways of solving or minimising these problems in order to widen the pool of applicants for judicial appointment. Until now, if they do get appointed, 'women and minorities have been most likely to attain office in less prestigious courts . . . women gain ground quicker in the judiciary than do ethnic minorities, [so] that the door has to be pushed much harder to open the judiciary to greater minority representation in comparison to greater gender equality'.[12]

The growing importance of judicial review

Judicial review is a key function of the courts. It refers to the power of the courts to interpret the constitution and to declare void actions of other branches of government if they are deemed to be in conflict with its requirements. Some countries have a very strong system of judicial review, Canada, Germany, India, Italy, Norway and Switzerland among them. The doctrine is common in Latin American states and is particularly important in federal systems. In the United States, it is the job of the Supreme Court to ensure that each layer of government keeps to its respective sphere and to settle any dispute that arises between them. It rules on constitutional matters in the same way that it has the final say on other legal issues.

Judicial review in Britain

In Britain, there is no equivalent to the American Supreme Court that can strike down legislation as unconstitutional. The task of judicial review has not until relatively recently been viewed as a feature of the courts. No court has declared unconstitutional any act lawfully passed by the British Parliament, the sovereign law-making body.

Yet particularly since the 1980s, statistics indicate that there has been an increasing resort to the process of judicial review. The number of annual applications for permission to seek judicial review increased rapidly from the 1980s onwards, rising from around 500 in the early 1980s to over 4000 in the early twenty-first century. (Many more applications for judicial review are initiated, but difficulties in obtaining legal aid and the High Court's refusal to grant leave for review, rule them out of consideration.) About a third of these cases refer to actions taken by local authorities, around a quarter by government departments. Lord Woolf[13] has noted that many of those involving a department fail, perhaps some ten for every one that is won. What makes the news is because those that succeed are high-profile cases of political significance. They get the headlines.

The scale of increase has been made to appear more dramatic than it is, because of its concentration in two particular areas: immigration especially, and homelessness. Beyond these two areas, the rate of growth has been much less apparent which is in some ways surprising. Figures for cases involving the two contentious area of the treatment of prisoners and entitlement to social welfare provision have remained low, perhaps because the victims of mistreatment have other means of remedy such as tribunals which they find successful, or more likely because they are unfamiliar with the processes of going to law, cannot afford to seek the advice of lawyers and lack the vigour to see a complex case through to a conclusion.

The Home Office is the department that has been most challenged in the British courts, attracting as it does some three quarters of all challenges to government decisions. In the 1990s under the Major government, there were several cases involving the then Home Secretary, Michael Howard, who was found to have acted unlawfully in a number of cases. It was judged that he had wrongly delayed referring the cases of IRA prisoners to the parole boards and had failed to give a cult leader, the Reverend Moon, a chance to make representations before his exclusion from Britain. Under the Labour governments (1997–2010) there were many more cases in which the verdict went against the minister. Often, they involved issues of immigration and the rights of asylum seekers. Some Labour ministers felt impelled to lament in public their concern about the activities of the courts in scrutinising government actions and striking them down with the regularity with which they do. Paul Boateng[14] pointed out that 'the judges' job is to judge, the government's job is to govern'. At various times, then Home Secretary David Blunkett accused judges of routinely rewriting the laws that Parliament had passed and bluntly made it clear that he did not agree with their findings.

Judicial review in Britain is a weaker doctrine than in the more usual Continental and American experience. There is no written constitution against which the constitutionality of actions and decisions can be judged. Whereas, elsewhere, the principle enables the judiciary to review and strike down decrees, laws and actions of government that are incompatible with the constitution, in Britain it means the right to determine whether the Executive has acted beyond its powers. It enables judges to assess the constitutionality of executive actions in the light of ordinary laws, using the doctrine of **ultra vires**. This is a much narrower and more limited version of judicial review, enabling the courts to declare the actions of ministers unlawful, but not allowing them to question the validity of the law itself.

The upsurge in cases involving this modest doctrine of judicial review has been striking. It reflects the growing human rights culture in Britain, with many lawyers willing to take up cases to challenge what they regard as the misuse of executive power. Attracting as it does much attention from the media, it has caused embarrassment to a succession of ministers and on occasion resulted in public confrontations between the courts and the politicians. It is an indication of the increasingly political role played by justices. Some politicians view this increase in judicial activism (see below for further elaboration) with considerable anxiety.

The developing trend towards judicial activism

Judicial activism refers to the willingness of judges to venture beyond narrow legal decisions, in order to influence public policy. Its advocates take the view that the courts should be active partners in shaping government policy, especially in sensitive cases such as those affecting asylum, immigration and the rights of detainees in police custody. They argue that they are more interested in justice, in 'doing the right thing', than in observing the exact letter of the text and see a role for the courts in looking after the groups denied political influence, notably the poor and minorities.

Judicial activism has been a feature of recent decades in many parts of the Western world, as judges have become more willing to enter into the political arena. In some cases, judges have discovered hitherto undetected 'implied' rights in a careful reading of the constitution. In the Netherlands, Hague and Harrop[15] point out that although the constitution does not allow for judicial review, the Dutch Supreme Court has developed case law on issues on which parliament has not legislated, especially in authorising euthanasia. The same writers have noted how the degree of judicial activism varies from country to country. On a least active–most active spectrum, there is a continuum ranging from the United Kingdom, Sweden, France, at the least active end to Australia, Canada and the United States at the other.

In the United States, there has long been a conflict between those who subscribe to judicial activism and those whose preference is for the more conservative doctrine of **judicial restraint**. The latter believe that the task of judges is to apply the law and not to wander into wider, interpretative territory. They argue that the courts should limit themselves to adopt a passive approach and implement legislative and executive intentions rather than impose their views on other branches of government.

Judicial activism has been on the increase in many countries, because of:

- the increasing tendency of governments to regulate over new and broader territory, such as laying down new restrictive regulations on asylum seekers and deciding whether or not gay partners should have the same rights as married heterosexual couples. Such moves are contentious and open to challenge in a way that many of the decisions of government a half century ago were not.
- the greater willingness of people on the political Left to use the courts, a reflection of the decline of traditional socialist attitudes according to which judges were seen as defenders of the status quo, deserving of mistrust and suspicion.

- the post-war development of international agreements and conventions that have proclaimed more rights and encouraged the view that state decisions are open to challenge – the European Convention on Human Rights (1950) is an obvious example.
- the response of campaigning activists and media commentators to what they recognise as the growing confidence of judges in proclaiming on wider policy issues. The process is self-reinforcing. The more judges become involved in political decision-making, so too the more rights-conscious groups see scope for use of the courts as a means of redress.

The politicisation of British judges: growing judicial power

The general political role of British courts has been increasing in recent years. Particularly from the 1980s onwards, judges have become involved in many areas from which they were previously excluded, most notably local-national government relations and industrial relations. In the former, the growth of centralisation under the Thatcher governments left many Labour-controlled local authorities seeking clarification and redress or defending their position in the courts, as their traditional rights were overridden. In the latter, the new corpus of law imposing restraints upon trade union action meant that judges were involved in making decisions on issues such as ballots prior to strike action, secondary picketing and sequestration of assets. If they did not act to extend their interpretative role, they nonetheless were regularly in the business of delivering judgements in accordance with the letter of the law. The print workers' union, SOGAT 82, found itself on the receiving end of financial penalties for a technical breach of the law, without in its view sufficient allowance being made for the special circumstances of the case. Other unions too felt displeased with the treatment they received in the courts.

Yet if the growing political involvement of judges in these cases worked in favour of the Conservative government, this was not to be the case in the following decade. We have seen that the increasing use of judicial review involved judges in conflict with ministers, as did the greater willingness of more European-minded judges to speak out in favour of the incorporation of the European Convention into British law and against ministerial policy on issues such as the sentencing of convicted criminals. The decisions of the Court of Human Rights in Strasbourg against the British government only added to ministerial misgivings during the Major administration, so that by the middle of the decade there was clear hostility between the politicians and the judges. Conservative spokespersons frequently denounced the trend towards increased judicial involvement in political controversies of the day.

Under the Labour government, it might have been anticipated that relations between the Blair administrations and the judges would have been better, given the promising start made by ministers by incorporating the European Convention into British law – in line with much judicial opinion. Yet the passage of the Human Rights Act itself offered the prospect of further politicisation of the judiciary, which could become more embroiled in the political arena as judges seek to decide on the interpretation and/or validity of a particular piece of legislation. Furthermore, as we have seen, in several cases of judicial review decisions went against ministers and judges at the highest level have been willing to confront publicly the policies pursued on issues such as freedom of information and trial by jury.

There are many politicians and some academics who regret the trend to politicisation of the judiciary. They feel uneasy about unelected judges stepping so boldly into the political arena. They stress that under the British constitutional arrangements, Parliament is the main protector of our liberties. It is a sovereign body and its members alone should make decisions. Because they are elected, politicians need to remain sensitive to the wishes of the voters, whereas judges lack accountability and are seen as a group remote from present-day reality. Ewing and Gearty[16] have asked whether it is

> legitimate or justifiable to have the final political decision, on say a woman's right to abortion, to be determined by a group of men appointed by the Prime Minister from a small and unrepresentative pool . . . Difficult ethical, social and political questions would be subject to judicial preference, rather than the shared or compromise community morality.

In other words, according to this view, the solution to inappropriate behaviour by the government of the day should be in the polling booth, rather than in the courtroom. Politicians should not rely on judges to make difficult decisions and they are inappropriate persons to do so, given their narrow backgrounds and preference towards defending established interests in society.

On the other hand, the division of power between the three branches of government is a means of protecting people from arbitrary government, an antidote to potential tyranny. An independent judiciary is well suited to deciding difficult issues of the day, and if they are not elected then at least – in the words of one American source – 'they read the returns too'. They are not immune from what goes on in society and can offer a view that commands respect, because of the broad esteem in which judges are held – a greater esteem than that currently enjoyed by politicians as a whole.

On issues relating to the liberties of the people in particular, judges have a role to play. Of necessity, it is a secondary role, in that the Executive has the initiative and introduces law, whereas judges react to them, reviewing them once they are in place. But it is an important role in any modern democracy and an independent judiciary is an appropriate body to exercise it.

The case of the European Court of Human Rights

The European Court in Strasbourg – not to be confused with the Court of Justice which meets in Luxembourg and is part of the machinery of the European Union – comprises as many judges as there are member states of the **Council of Europe**, currently forty-seven. A country can nominate a representative of a non-European state, as did Liechtenstein in 1990 when it selected a Canadian as its choice.

Before the Court considers a case, the country involved must have accepted its compulsory jurisdiction, as almost every signatory has. Written and oral evidence is heard at the hearing, and the judges decide whether a violation of the European Convention has occurred, on the basis of a majority vote. They can award 'just compensation'.

The British record in Strasbourg was for many years a poor one, especially prior to incorporation of the European Convention via the Human Rights Act. Among many other cases involving

Box 5.2 Judges as protectors of our liberties in Britain: some points to bear in mind

Judges protect our liberties well

- Judges always have had a role in interpreting Common Law and for centuries have been willing to defend the rights of freeborn Englishmen to speak freely.
- Some judges have long shown an interest in the idea of a British bill of rights. For several years before the introduction of the Human Rights Act, more European-minded judges such as Lord Scarman were calling for its incorporation into British law. Judges in the Strasbourg Court (the European Court of Human Rights) issued several judgements from the 1970s onwards which enhanced the rights of sections of the British people, be they prisoners, victims of corporal punishment, those caught up in immigration appeals or detained in the Maze prison. In early 2011, they criticised governmental policy over several years in denying any prisoners in the UK the right to vote.
- More recently, a limited concept of judicial review has been developed in which, if not the policy at least the lawfulness of governmental actions have been found wanting. See the example described on pp. 51–2.
- A number of judges have been willing to criticise aspects of government policy that seem detrimental to civil liberties – for instance, Labour ran into difficulties with its Freedom of Information Bill when it was going through the Lords, and in its attempts to make inroads into the principle of trial by jury. The law lords in the House of Lords ruled against the Home Secretary's right to set minimum tariffs for prisoners serving long-term sentences (November 2002).
- Above all, it is judges who are charged with interpreting the Human Rights Act, now that the European Convention has been incorporated into British law. The Act offers a new weapon for aggrieved individuals and much depends upon how judges react to cases brought under its terms. Controversially, in 2011 under the terms of the Act, they have criticised the denial to paedophiles by British governments of any right of appeal against their names being on a registered list of offenders.

Judges cannot be trusted to protect civil liberties

- Some groups in the community have always found judges intolerant on issues of civil liberties, because of their background and legal training, as well as their preference for the status quo. They tend to be intolerant of minorities, especially young protesters, minority activists and others prepared to question existing ideas and values.
- On the Left, many would claim that over the last two centuries judges have used their discretion against trade unionists, individually or collectively. The right to strike has sometimes been put at risk by judicial decisions, as over the Tolpuddle Martyrs and Taff Vale.
- Other critics of the judges as protectors of civil liberties claim that they should not be so involved in the task anyway. It is Parliament's task to protect individuals, for MPs are elected to look after their constituents.
- Judges are not as socially representative as many would wish. There ought to be more members of ethnic minorities on the bench, and more women and younger judges.

The judiciary has seemed increasingly concerned to uphold civil liberties in recent years, with the arrival on the scene of a new and perhaps more progressive body of senior judges in action. Although they have no home-grown British bill of rights upon which to base their decisions, the Human Rights Act has equipped them with a new weapon with which to defend the rights of individual citizens. However, it is still the case that a broadening of the recruitment and training of the judges would do much to improve people's faith in their suitability for the task.

Britain in the 1980s and 1990s, the Court criticised treatment of suspected terrorists interned in Northern Ireland, allowed prisoners to correspond with their lawyers and others, upheld the rights of workers not to join a trade union, declared immigration rules to be discriminatory against women and restricted the power of the Home Secretary to lock up under-age killers. Some of the Court's judgements have aroused the irritation – indeed anger – of sections of the Conservative Right, whose members have been prepared to contemplate British withdrawal from the Convention. The Labour administration (1997–2010) that had incorporated the Convention also found some of its rulings unpalatable. Over the matter of prisoners'

Box 5.3 The UK, the European Court and prisoners' rights

In 2001, convicted killer John Hirst went to the High Court to claim that the government's denial of his right to vote was a breach of his right to participate in the democratic process. It ruled against him, the judgement pointing out that within the Council of Europe there was a broad spectrum of approaches to the question of prisoners voting and that Britain fell into the middle: 'In the course of time, this position may move, either by way of fine tuning, as was done recently in relation to remand prisoners and others, or more radically, but its position in the spectrum is plainly a matter for Parliament, not the courts.' Hirst subsequently took the case to the European Court of Human Rights in March 2004. It ruled the British government – with its blanket ban on prisoner voting – was in breach of the European Convention on Human Rights. The British government appealed to the European Court's grand chamber, but in October 2005 it upheld the ruling.

Following that decision, Labour ministers launched a two-stage consultation. The first, completed in 2007, considered the principles of prisoner enfranchisement, and the second, completed in 2009, looked at the practicalities of any such move. However, by the time of the general election in May 2010, the government had not responded to the results of the consultation. In November 2010, the Council finally demanded that the UK 'put an end to the practice of delaying full implementation of Strasbourg Court judgements' and gave the government six months to put its house in order. In February 2011 MPs voted overwhelmingly in favour of maintaining the blanket ban, thereby seeming to strengthen the Cameron government's hand as it sought to water down the European ruling. The motion called for the retention of the status quo, in which all prisoners, except those on remand or imprisoned for contempt or default, are barred from voting.

The Cameron government accepted the need to allow some prisoners the vote. Unless it met the August deadline to introduce legislation remedying the situation, then European judges would start to award damages in more than 2,500 outstanding claims from prisoners excluded from European and general elections, a bill estimated to be at least £70 million – with the prospect that the average compensation could increase, the longer the defiance continued.

Ministers had to act and under one option they considered, judges would be given discretion to determine which prisoners could vote. Eventually, having initially said prisoners serving up to four years would get the vote, ministers decided to limit the concession to only those prisoners sentenced to serve a year or less. However, this policy is at some point likely to be tested in the courts and there is the possibility of defeat. Recent case law lacks clarity. It is possible that a measure of judicial discretion in each prisoner's case, combined with restrictions on certain narrow categories of prisoner, might be sufficient to fulfill the Court's requirements.

For Prime Minister David Cameron, the dilemma was intense. He claimed to be 'absolutely horrified' by the idea of changing the law but reluctantly accepted that there was no alternative. He knew full well it was a policy almost certain to attract bruising headlines and enrage many traditional Tory supporters, some of whom would like to see ministers make a stand against rulings of the European Court.

Overseas experience
European experience varies greatly. Other than the UK, the only other European countries with an outright ban on prisoners voting are Russia, Armenia, Bulgaria, Czech Republic, Estonia, Hungary, Luxembourg and Romania; until a legal challenge is brought in those countries, the Council is unlikely to seek to force a change in their domestic legislation. In thirteen European countries, electoral disqualification depends on the crime committed or the length of the sentence. Italy, Malta and Poland, for example, ban those deemed to have committed serious crimes. In Greece, anyone sentenced to life receives a permanent voting ban. Many nations, including Denmark, Sweden and Switzerland, have no form of electoral ban for imprisoned offenders. In some of them, however, severe restrictions make it very difficult in practice for offenders to vote. In Cyprus, for example, an inmate must happen to be out of prison on the day of the elections and in Slovakia, prisoners can legally vote but no provision is made to allow them to do so. The Republic of Ireland lifted its ban in 2006, passing legislation enabling all prisoners to vote by post in the constituency where they would ordinarily live. Germany's law actually urges prisons to encourage their inmates to vote, although it does ban those whose crimes undermine 'democratic order', such as political insurgents.

rights, it delayed taking action and the issue was left for the Coalition to contemplate (see above).

Although since incorporation most cases under the Convention can be handled in the British courts, there remains the ultimate right of redress in Strasbourg where many controversial cases are finally resolved.

The case of the USA

In America, the highest judicial body, the Supreme Court, is clearly a political as well as a judicial institution. In applying the Constitution and laws to the cases that come before it, the nine justices are involved in making political choices on controversial aspects of national policy. The procedures are legal, and the decisions are phrased in language appropriate for legal experts. But to view the Court solely as a legal institution would be to ignore its key political role. As Chief Justice Hughes[17] once wrote: 'We are under the Constitution, but the Constitution is what the judges say it is.'

In interpreting the Constitution, the justices must operate within the prevailing political climate. They are aware of popular feelings as expressed in elements of the media and in election results. They know that their judgements need to command consent and that their influence ultimately rests on acceptance by people and politicians. This means that the opinions expressed on the bench tend to be in line with the thinking of key players in the executive and legislative branches, over a period of time. Rulings in one age can be overturned by judgements delivered at another time. This was true of **segregation**. 'Separate but equal' was acceptable in 1896 in the *Plessy* v. *Ferguson* case, but by 1954 it was deemed 'inherently unequal'.

The question of how to use its judicial power has long exercised the Court and those who preside over it have held different opinions. Some have urged an activist Court that enhances individual rights. They believe that the Court should be a key player in shaping policy, an active partner working alongside the other branches of government. Such a conception means that the justices move beyond acting as umpires in the political game, and become creative participants. Chief Justice **Earl Warren** was an exponent of the philosophy. His court was known for a series of liberal judgements on matters ranging from school desegregation to the rights of criminals. Decisions were made which boldly and broadly changed national policy.

The broadly progressive approach of the Supreme Court in the Warren and – to a lesser extent – Burger eras changed under the leadership of Chief Justices William Rehnquist and John Roberts. More conservative in its membership and tone, his court made inroads into past liberal decisions, notably on abortion and **affirmative action**. The nine judges did not view it as their task to act as the guardian of individual liberties and civil rights for minority groups. As Biskupic[18] puts it: 'Gone is the self-consciously loud voice the Court once spoke with, boldly stating its position and calling upon the people and other institutions of government to follow'. Yet for all the lip service paid to greater judicial restraint, 'most of the current justices appear entirely comfortable intervening in all manner of issues, challenging state as well as national power, and underscoring the Court's role as final arbiter of constitutional issues.' [19]

 What you should have learnt from this chapter

- Courts of law are part of the political process, for governmental decisions and acts passed by the legislative body may require judicial decisions to be implemented. Courts need to be independent to be respected, but this is difficult to achieve in practice. There is never full independence as far as appointment is concerned. Moreover, as Blondel[20] warns, judges cannot be expected 'to go outside the norms of the society'.

- As a broad trend, the role of judges in the political system has increased in liberal democracies but also even in authoritarian societies. Some fear that this political involvement has gone too far and talk of a 'judicialisation' of political life.

- In Britain, senior judges have been more vocal in venting their views on issues of public policy. Recent pronouncements show that they are more than willing to challenge governmental decisions. Well before the passage of the Human Rights Act (a major development in enhancing judicial power), Lord Bingham[21] felt able to write: 'Slowly, the constitutional balance is tilting towards the judiciary. The courts have reacted to the increase in the powers claimed by government by being more active themselves.'

- Several commentators and politicians have voiced anxiety about the nature and politicisation of the judiciary. Lord Lloyd[22] is less concerned than many critics about the backgrounds from which judges are chosen, their competence or their capriciousness in adjudication. For him, Parliament – comprising the elected MPs – should decide on whether abortion or capital punishment is permissible, and what the age of consent should be: 'The fact of the matter . . . is that the law cannot be a substitute for politics. The political decisions must be taken by politicians. In a society like ours, that means by people who are removable'.

- Others emphasise their fear of judicial power. They are concerned that judges are unrepresentative and argue for a reformed and more diverse judiciary.

Glossary of key terms

Affirmative action Policies and actions designed to compensate for the effects of past discrimination, by giving preferences to specified ethnic and gender groups

Bar The Bar comprises lawyers who are qualified as barristers. They are collectively known as 'members of the Bar'.

Council of Europe An international body established in 1949 to achieve a greater unity between its members in order 'to safeguard and realise the ideals and principles that are their common heritage'. Open to any democratic European country, it was given a key task, namely to work for the 'maintenance and further realisation of human rights and fundamental freedoms'.

Judicial activism The idea that the courts should be active partners in shaping public policy. Supporters see the courts as having a role in looking after the groups denied political clout, such as the poor and ethnic minorities, and in protecting individual freedoms.

Judicial Appointments Commission (JAC) The JAC is an independent commission that selects candidates for judicial office in courts and tribunals in England and Wales, and for some tribunals whose jurisdiction extends to Scotland or Northern Ireland.

Judicial independence The constitutional principle that there should be a strict separation of powers, in which there is a clear distinction between the judiciary and other branches of government.

Judicial restraint The idea that the courts should not seek to impose their views on other branches of government. They want a passive role for the courts and feel that they should confine themselves to implementing legislative and executive intentions

Judicial review The power of any court – strong in North America and Scandinavia – to refuse to enforce a law or official act based on law, because in the view of the judges it conflicts with the constitution. In much of Europe (including Britain), a weaker version applies, in which the courts cannot rule acts of Parliament as being unconstitutional but can review and squash ministerial actions based upon them that are deemed as being beyond their powers. The British rejection of a strong version is based on the idea that ultimate power rests with the democratically elected representatives of the people, not appointed judges.

Liberal democracies Representative democracies in which there is limited government, respect for rights and a free media, among other characteristics

Segregation The separation of facilities for people on the basis of their racial group, as was commonly practised in the American Deep South until the late 1960s. In 1968, all forms of segregation were declared unconstitutional by the Supreme Court.

Sequestration The removal of (financial) assets from their owner, until the individual or owner complies with a court order.

Ultra vires Beyond the legal powers (of a person or organisation).

Warren Earl The controversial fourteenth Chief Justice in the United States, a judicial activist best known for the sweeping decisions of the Court over which he presided (1953–69), which ended school segregation and transformed many areas of American law – e.g. regarding the rights of the accused and ending school prayer.

Likely examination questions

Distinguish between judicial independence and judicial neutrality. To what extent and how effectively are they enforced in Britain?

Does it matter that the social composition of the judiciary is not a microcosm (mirror-image) of society at large?

Are judges biased?

'Judges make law.' Discuss.

How adequately do British judges protect civil liberties?

Why has the Labour Party been traditionally suspicious of the judiciary? Has it any reason to be suspicious today?

Helpful websites

www.justice.gov.uk/ Ministry of Justice.

www.judiciary.gov.uk/ The Judiciary.

www.echr.coe.int European Court of Human Rights (Council of Europe machinery).

Suggestions for further reading

Useful articles

M. Garnett, 'Judges versus Politicians', *Politics Review*, September 2004.

Baroness B. Hale, 'The Appointment and Removal of Judges: Independence and Diversity', paper delivered to the International Association of Women Judges, Sydney, May 2006.

A. Horne, Judicial Appointments, www.parliament.uk, 3 September 2009.

L. Jeffries, 'The Judiciary', *Talking Politics*, January 2003.

T. McNally, 'The judiciary is becoming more diverse, but too slowly', *The Guardian*, 9 May 2011.

P. Norton, 'Judges in British Politics', *Talking Politics*, January 2004.

G. Peele, 'The Human Rights Act', *Talking Politics*, September 2001.

M. Ryan, 'A Supreme Court for the United Kingdom', *Talking Politics*, September 2004.

C. Thomas et al., 'Judicial Diversity and the Appointment of Deputy District Judges', Initial Research Findings undertaken for the Commission for Judicial Appointments, March 2006.

Useful books

G. Drewry, 'Judicial Independence in Britain: Challenges Real and Threats Imagined', in P. Norton (ed.), *New Directions in British Politics?*, Elgar, 1991.

J. Griffiths, *The Politics of the Judiciary*, Fontana, 6th edn 1997.

A. Le Seuer (ed.), *Building the UK's New Supreme Court*, Oxford University Press, 2004.

A. Sampson, *Who Runs This Place? The Anatomy of Britain in the 21st Century*, Murray, 2004.

CHAPTER 6

Government Beyond the Centre

Contents

Introduction   190
The devolved United Kingdom   191
Devolution in Scotland   192
Devolution in Wales   202
Is Britain becoming a federal state?   204
English local government   211
The case of Spain   219
The case of the USA   220

Overview

In almost all countries, governments recognise the need to allow some scope for regional or local initiative. It would be impractical for them to involve themselves in the minutiae of detail and govern entirely from the centre.

In this chapter, we distinguish between unitary and federal states, noting the characteristics of the two types of governmental system and their benefits and disadvantages. We then examine movement towards decentralisation in British politics and assess the 'areal distribution of power', the way in which functions and powers are allocated across the levels of government, in an era of devolution.

Key issues to be covered in this chapter

- The distinction between unitary, federal and confederal states
- The extent of federalism throughout the world, its merits and demerits
- Why power has historically tended to shift towards the centre in liberal democracies
- More recent moves towards decentralisation of power and decision-making
- British experience of devolution in Scotland, Wales and Northern Ireland
- Developments in British local government
- The nature of federal devolution in the UK

Introduction

Most political systems have found it necessary to create governmental structures below central administration, but their distribution and power vary from country to country. However, broadly there are three types of governmental system: unitary states, federations and confederations.

Unitary, federal and confederal states

Bullman[1] has classified European states into four categories. He distinguishes:

1. *classic unitary*, in which there is no regional structure other than for centrally controlled administrative purposes, although there is likely to be a system of local government. Examples include Greece and Luxembourg.
2. *devolving unitary*, in which there is some elected regional machinery possessing a (not necessarily uniform) degree of **autonomy**, with also a tier of local government. Examples include France and the United Kingdom.
3. *regionalised*, where the directly elected regional governments are equipped with significant legislative powers. Examples include Italy and Spain.
4. *federal*, where responsibilities and powers are shared between the centre and the regional or state units according to a written constitution and there is no possibility of central government abolishing the other tier. Sub-national government enjoys constitutionally guaranteed autonomy. Twenty-four of the world's 193 countries are federal, their citizens including 40 per cent of the world's population. Examples include Germany and the United States.

In *unitary states* of either type, all legitimate power is concentrated at the centre. Central government has indivisible **sovereignty**. It may decide to delegate power or functional responsibilities to territorial units, known variously as departments, prefectures, regions or states. But such peripheral governments exist only at the behest of central government that can revoke the functions and powers at its convenience.

Unitary states have certain advantages. Because power is concentrated at the centre, there is little likelihood of tension between the centre and the periphery. Also, there is a clear focus of national loyalty. Citizens identify with the country as a whole, rather than with their state or region. On the other hand, government can become over-centralised, with too little scope for local initiative and there may be inadequate recognition of diversity, be it ethnic, geographical, linguistic or religious.

In *federal states*, political authority is diffused; functions and powers are shared between a federal (central) government and regional governments, set out in a written constitution and – if necessary – arbitrated upon by a supreme court. The two tiers have guaranteed spheres of responsibility, the states enjoying autonomy within their sphere of responsibility and the central government conducting those functions of major importance, which require policy to be made for the whole country.

Confederacies are a looser form of federalism, in which central control is modest and the component elements retain primary power. Confederations allow for cooperation between states as circumstances demand, but leave the initiative firmly in the hands of individual states. Switzerland is often described as a confederation. Its twenty-six cantons exercise substantial power and the Berne government exerts relatively little influence over key aspects of Swiss life. The Commonwealth of Independent States (CIS) formed out of the old Soviet Union in 1991 is a more recently created example of the genre, which facilitates economic or military cooperation.

The devolved United Kingdom

The United Kingdom is a unitary state. Other institutions exist, but their powers are subordinate to Westminster. The process of **centralisation** of power peaked in the Thatcher years, in which important elements of local government were abolished (e.g. the Greater London Council) and the remaining authorities were brought under tighter control from London.

The debate about devolution of power to Scotland and Wales did not begin with the election of the Blair government in 1997. Against a background of rising nationalism in Scotland – and to a lesser extent in Wales – the previous Labour government (1974–9) had spent a considerable amount of time on the issue. Its proposals for elected Scottish and Welsh assemblies were not implemented, having failed to achieve the required majorities in separate referendums in Scotland and Wales in 1979.

On coming to power in 1997, Labour quickly moved to announce referendums in Scotland and Wales on the principle of establishing new devolved machinery. In Scotland the outcome was an overwhelming 'yes' vote on two questions (see Box 6.1), but in Wales the majority in favour was remarkably narrow. As a result of these votes, ministers proceeded to establish devolved government in the two countries via the Scotland Act and the Wales Act of 1998, respectively. The legislation devolved power on a substantial scale, particularly in Scotland. The statutes laid down the composition, functions and powers of the new devolved machinery.

Devolution involves the ceding of power by Parliament to new elected bodies. Bogdanor[2] defines it as 'the transfer to a subordinate elected body, on a geographical basis, of functions at present exercised by ministers and Parliament'. As such, it differs from federalism which

> would divide, not devolve, supreme power from Westminster and various regional or provincial parliaments. In a federal state, the authority of the central or federal government and the provincial governments is co-ordinate and shared, the respective scope of the federal and provincial governments being defined by an enacted constitution . . . Devolution, by contrast, does not require the introduction of an enacted constitution.

Devolution in Scotland

Many Scots had long been dissatisfied with Westminster rule. They felt that remote London ministers did not attach priority to Scottish needs. Their failure to understand the situation north of the border was often given as an explanation for Scotland's higher than average levels of unemployment and the gravity of its industrial decline. More positively, Scots saw themselves as a nation. Scotland had always retained distinctive traditions and institutions, most notably its own coinage, educational and legal systems, and religion. There was in the late twentieth century a growing sense of **national conscious-**

Box 6.1 The referendums in Scotland and Wales

Scotland

In 1979, as a result of a proposal from a Labour MP, a Scotsman who represented an English constituency, a clause in the devolution bill required that 40 per cent of the registered electorate in each country must support the proposals. The 'Yes' vote amounted to only 32.9 per cent of the registered electorate.

In 1997, Scottish voters were asked two questions:

Do you support a Scottish Parliament?
Should a Scottish Parliament have tax-raising powers?

74.3 per cent backed a Scottish Parliament and 63.5 per cent favoured one with tax-raising powers. The result was uniform across the country, with every one of the thirty-two voting regions opting for a Parliament and thirty of them also wanting the tax powers as well. The turnout of 60.1 per cent was higher than many pro-devolutionists had expected.

The outcome shows the unreality of the earlier 40 per cent rule, for even though there was substantial support in Scotland for both propositions by those who voted, it remains the fact that barely 45 per cent of the registered electorate voted for the Parliament and only some 38 per cent for the tax-varying powers.

Wales

In Wales, the 'Yes' campaigners won by the narrowest of margins, 0.6 per cent of the vote, on a fractionally higher than 50 per cent turnout. Almost three in four voters either did not bother to vote or said 'No'.

ness that exceeded the strength of regional feeling felt by Geordies in the Northeast of England or Tykes in Yorkshire. It was nurtured by a Scottish culture and by Scottish sport. It was expressed in surveys that showed that many Scots felt Scottish rather than British.

Scotland had experienced **administrative devolution** from 1885, the year of the establishment of the Scottish Office. In 1939, the Office moved from Whitehall to Edinburgh, its existence being an acknowledgement of the political need to bring Scottish government closer to the people for whom it made decisions. Prior to devolution,

Box 6.2 The Scotland Act 1998

Following the successful referendum, a Scotland Act was passed in 1998. Effectively, the first Parliament in 292 years was to assume the responsibilities previously exercised by the Scottish Office. This meant that it had primary legislative powers over:

Health	Law and home affairs
Education and training	Sport and the arts
Local government, social work and housing	Agriculture, fishing and forestry
	The environment
Economic development and transport	Other matters

In all, there are forty-seven devolved issues grouped under these headings, so that the Parliament and the Executive chosen from it have a wide range of responsibilities. There are, however, a series of 'reserved matters' on which power resides in London, for it is considered that they can be more effectively handled on a United Kingdom basis. These include:

The Constitution	Employment
Defence and national security	Social security
Foreign affairs	Transport safety and regulation
Major economic policy and fiscal affairs	

The machinery provided for in the legislation includes a Parliament of 129 Members of the Scottish Parliament (MSAs), seventy-three of whom are elected by first past the post (FPTP) as constituency representatives and fifty-six additional members chosen via a party list. An executive is selected from and accountable to the Assembly. The Executive is led by a First Minister nominated by the majority party in the Parliament and appointed by the monarch. The First Minister chooses other members of the Executive, in the same way that the UK Prime Minister chooses the members of the Cabinet.

therefore, decisions were taken at Westminster and implemented in St Andrew's House. There was a Secretary of State for Scotland who had an input into Cabinet decisions and an overall responsibility for the activities of the Scottish Office.

Pro-devolutionists wanted to see decisions taken in Scotland by a Scottish parliament, subject to democratic control. They wanted **legislative devolution**, with laws made and implemented by representatives of the Scottish people. Although the SNP wanted full **independence**, it campaigned for devolution in the run-up to the 1997 referendums. It was the best option on offer and in the view of many supporters might provide a basis for future separation. Its backing meant that all parties in Scotland – other than the Conservatives – were in favour of the establishment of the Edinburgh Parliament.

The merits of Scottish devolution

As a result of the passage of the Scotland Act (see Box 6.2), a Scottish Parliament met in Edinburgh in May 1999 for the first time since the Act of Union was signed in 1707. More than a decade later, it is possible to provide some initial assessment of the case for devolution and how it is working in practice.

Devolution is widely seen as democratic, in that it allows people to express their distinctive identity and have a say in the development of the life of their own particular regions. In the words of Donald Dewar, then Secretary of State and later to become Scotland's first First Minister, the new system would 'strengthen democratic control' and 'make government more accountable'.

Many decisions are now taken by the Scottish Executive and Parliament in Scotland. Ministers have to defend their decisions and policies before the elected representatives of the people, MSPs who are elected under a highly proportional and therefore 'fair' voting system. This means that the Executive can also claim 'legitimacy'. Whereas in general elections, no post-war British government has based its support on more than 50 per cent of the popular vote, in Scotland the 1999 Executive (a Labour-Liberal Democrat coalition) had 56.6 per cent backing from the electorate; in 2011, the single party administration of Alex Salmond was not far short with 53.5 per cent support. This compares favourably with the 43 per cent and 35 per cent achieved by Labour at Westminster in the 1997 and 2005 elections. (The 59 per cent achieved in the 2010 general election was untypical, because the government comprised two coalition partners.)

Another virtue deriving from the electoral system is that – able to vote in multimember constituencies – the voters have been able to make a choice between candidates and vote in greater numbers for minority parties and groups such as women and ethnic minorities who otherwise might fare badly under FPTP. The social composition of the Scottish Parliament has a more impressive gender balance than the House of Commons. Of the 129 MSPs elected in 2011, fifty-one (34.9 per cent) were women; in Labour's case, the number constituted nearly half (17/37) of its intake. (While the number of non-whites has increased since 1999 to 2.9 per cent of all candidates, only two, 1.6 per cent, were elected.)

Devolution also has the merit of countering the dangers of an over-powerful, excessively centralised state. Indeed, in celebrating the referendum victory that preceded the passage of the bill, Tony Blair observed that 'the era of big centralised government is over'.

Finally, devolution may be judged according to the results it has produced, in terms of distinctively Scottish policies (see Box 6.3).

Supporters can claim that the Parliament has made a difference and that when problems have arisen at least they have been debated in a genuinely Scottish forum. A poll in the *The Scotsman*[4] indicated that whatever reservations Scots had about their new Parliament, there was a rising sense of Scottish patriotism, and that 'a confident, modern and exciting' country was emerging. People were proud to call themselves Scots, 80 per cent of them seeing themselves as more Scottish than British and were optimistic about their country's future.

Potential problems surrounding devolution

At the time when it was first introduced and subsequently, opponents portrayed devolution as fraught with danger. They claimed that although in the United Kingdom the sources of unity are much greater than the sources of diversity, once parts of the whole are allowed to enjoy a measure of self-government then there is a danger of the whole edifice splintering apart, a kind of 'Balkanisation' of the UK. Such fears were strongly expressed by the Conservatives, who resisted the Blairite proposals in the 1997 election and referendum. They feared the ultimate disintegration of the United Kingdom if parts were able to go their separate ways, because the Scottish Nationalists would not be satisfied with devolution, a halfway house between unity and independence.

Box 6.3 Scottish government in practice, since 1999: distinctive policies

The Labour-dominated Executive, tempered by the need to placate its Liberal Democrat allies, introduced a range of measures that differed from those introduced by Labour ministers at Westminster. Political leaders in London were forced to accept that it was an inevitable consequence of devolution that policies in Edinburgh and London could diverge, even when the same party was in control in both capitals. Most notably:

- student tuition fees have been rejected in Scotland
- Clause 28 (on the teaching of homosexuality in schools), fox hunting and smoking in public places have been abolished before the rest of the UK followed suit
- foundation hospitals have not been introduced
- elderly people have received entirely free care in nursing and residential homes
- teachers' pay and conditions have improved
- a cull in the number of unselected quangos has been gradually undertaken.

The Scottish National Party formed a minority administration in 2007, led by Alex Salmond as First Minister and governing with Green backing on a 'policy-by-policy' basis. As Cairney[3] has pointed out, 'minority government quickly [became] the norm in Scotland in the sense that while the . . . Government [was] challenged regularly on its policies or governing record, its right to govern [was] not.'

It soon became apparent that a non-Labour administration would diverge in its policies and approach from the government at Westminster. This was evident in the change of name adopted by the post-2007 Executive. In September 2007, without seeking Westminster approval, ministers announced that the Executive was to be rebranded as the Scottish government.

Since Salmond took office, a number of distinctive policies have been introduced, including:

- cutting NHS prescription charges;
- freezing council tax;
- handing older people free personal and nursing care payments;
- a £73 million small business bonus;
- and, most controversially, the decision of Justice Secretary Kenny MacAskill to free Lockerbie bomber Abdelbaset al-Megrahi on compassionate grounds.

Indeed, the SNP – whilst extracting what has been possible out of devolution – has from the beginning sought to expose flaws in its operation, in the hope that this will fuel pressure for separation. It is a separatist party, its long-term goal being national independence for Scotland. It views with envy the experiences of the Baltic states that have in recent years gained their independence and argues that – given its resources – Scotland too has the potential to exist as a viable state.

Since 2007, Alex Salmond has tried not only to show voters that an SNP-led government is different in character from its predecessor, but also – by pragmatic means – to pave the way for the eventual achievement of the party's ultimate goal of independence. The arrival of a Conservative-dominated coalition administration in Westminster at a time of severe cuts in public spending may make this more likely. In 2011, the fortunes of the SNP dramatically increased in the build-up to the election, enabling the party to win an outright majority in the Parliament

The ingredients exist for future Edinburgh-London conflict. Many Scots still retain a deep-seated loathing of Thatcherism, which Cameron and the Scottish Conservatives have as yet failed to expunge from the Scottish psyche. The SNP administration may seek to exploit this sentiment and point out that with only one Scottish MP the Conservatives certainly have no mandate to govern Scotland; the Coalition in total has only twelve of the fifty-nine Scottish seats. Moreover, Labour, the party that did best in Scotland with 42 per cent of the votes (up 2.5 per cent) and its forty-one seats (no change), will be as powerless to protect Scotland from spending cuts as it was at preventing the dismantling of Scottish industry in the Thatcher era.

This combination of very different parties in power north of the border and at Westminster represents uncharted territory. The French call such a situation cohabitation. It is premature to assess how it might work in practice.

With the Calman Commission (see Box 6.4) proposing the next steps in devolution, the greatest steps towards greater powers for Scotland appear to be taking place regardless of the SNP dreams of independence. For the while, Salmond seems content to extract as much power for the Holyrood assembly as he can and adopt a

Box 6.4 Future action: the Calman Commission's plans for Scottish devolution

The Calman Commission was established as a result of a successful opposition Labour motion (supported by the Conservatives and Liberal Democrats, and opposed by the SNP) in the Scottish Parliament. Its task was to provide an independent review of the experience of Scottish devolution since its inception. The Commission published its Final Report,[5] *Serving Scotland Better: Scotland and the United Kingdom in the 21st Century*, in June 2009.

The Commission declared devolution to be a success, claiming that – especially in economic matters – the Union works to Scotland's advantage. Among its twenty-four recommendations was a 'radical' plan for Holyrood to take charge of half the income tax raised in Scotland. The Parliament has always had the power to vary the standard rate of income tax – the so-called Tartan Tax – by three pence in the pound, but this has as yet never been used. The Commission also recommended that:

- control over air passenger duty, land tax and landfill tax, and stamp duty could be devolved to the Scottish Parliament from Westminster. This would be balanced by a relative cut in the Scottish block grant. (It rejected the devolution or assignment of oil and gas tax receipts to the Scottish Parliament.)
- a number of other powers should be devolved to Scotland from Westminster. Holyrood should have control over air gun legislation, powers over drink driving and speed limits and the running of the Scottish elections, issues on which the Scottish government had previously clashed with UK ministers.

Responding to the findings of the review, the UK government announced in November 2009 that new powers would be devolved to the Scottish government, notably on how it can raise tax and carry out capital borrowing, and the running of Scottish Parliament elections. These proposals were detailed in a White Paper[6] in advance of a new Scotland Bill, with the intention that they become operative before the 2015 Holyrood elections. Following the formation of the Coalition, the Westminster government renewed the Labour pledge to implement the findings of the Commission. The Liberal Democrats in Scotland would like to go further and introduce **devolution-plus**.

gradualist approach on the contentious issue of Scotland's future in the United Kingdom. However, he is committed to holding a referendum on independence later in the parliamentary session.

One other difficulty of devolution often mentioned by its critics is the West Lothian (now more usually referred to as the English) question: 'Why should Scottish MPs at Westminster be allowed to have a say on purely English matters while English MPs will no longer have a say on Scottish matters?'

The English question

Such a dilemma would not arise under a federal system, for under federalism the division of functions is clear-cut. If England had a system of regional councils, then each region (and Scotland and Wales) could have similar devolved powers, leaving the United Kingdom Parliament to deal with the residue of issues, those key ones affecting the four countries collectively. But as yet there is no public demand for legislative devolution across the UK (see pp. 205–6), and even if this were ever introduced it is doubtful whether the powers granted to regional bodies would ever be equal to those of the Scottish Parliament, so that statutory responsibility for English devolution would probably remain at Westminster.

The so-called English question was never a source of contention when, prior to Direct Rule, Northern Ireland had its own Parliament at Stormont while the province sent members to the House of Commons. (The situation arises again under the Good Friday Agreement, which provides for an assembly and an executive body; see p. 205.) However, logic does not always apply in these matters, and there is some evidence that English people feel disadvantaged under current arrangements. They resent the fact that an issue primarily relevant to England can be decided on the basis of Scottish votes in the House of Commons. Such commentators drew attention to the way in which during the Blair years the Scottish Labour contingent at Westminster helped ministers push through contentious policies on tuition fees and foundation hospitals.

Bogdanor[7] points out that the difficulties inherent in the West Lothian question have been resolved – or at least accommodated – elsewhere without much difficulty. Devolution has proved perfectly feasible in countries such as France, Italy, Portugal and Spain. For instance, in Italy fifteen of twenty regions have no exclusive legislative powers, but the other five have wide responsibilities in economic and social affairs; in Spain, seven of seventeen have greater autonomy than the others. But 'there is no West Sardinian Question nor any West Catalonian Question'.

Be that as it may, the West Lothian question does raise the issue of whether in a unitary state it is possible to devolve substantial powers that are denied to other regions. Many commentators might argue that in Britain there was little choice. It would have been politically unrealistic to deny recognition to the Scots whose wish for a change in their constitutional status had been so clearly stated in the elections of 1987–97. If the price of meeting their aspirations was the creation of an anomaly, then this was a price that had to be paid. However, Bogdanor does go on to observe that:

> devolution will alter the role of Westminster very radically, by introducing the spirit of federalism into its deliberations. Before devolution, every Member of Parliament was responsible for scrutinising both the domestic and the non-domestic affairs of every part of the United Kingdom. After devolution, by contrast MPs will normally play no role at all in legislating for the domestic affairs of Northern Ireland or Scotland, nor in scrutinising secondary legislation for Wales . . . Westminster, from being a parliament for both the domestic and the non-domestic affairs of the whole of the United Kingdom, is transformed into a domestic parliament for England, part of a domestic parliament for Wales, and a federal parliament for Northern Ireland and Scotland. The West Lothian Question, then, draws attention to the fact that devolution will transform Westminster into the quasi-federal parliament of a quasi-federal state.

As part of the Coalition agreement, the Conservatives and Liberal Democrats agreed to establish a commission to consider the 'West Lothian' or 'English' question. A typical Conservative attitude had been expressed some years earlier by William Hague,[8] who observed that: 'English MPs should have exclusive say over English laws . . . People will become increasingly resentful that decisions are being made in England by people from other parts of the UK on matters that English people did not have a say on elsewhere . . . I think it is a dangerous thing to allow resentment to build up in a country. We have got to make the rules fair now.'

One solution sometimes offered is the creation of an English parliament with full legislative powers akin to those of the Scottish body, with full legislative powers also being conferred on the existing Welsh Assembly at the same time. The Westminster (United Kingdom) Parliament would continue to meet and legislate on matters of UK-wide competence such as defence, foreign affairs and economic matters, with the parliaments of England, Wales, Scotland and Northern Ireland legislating in their respective territories. Opponents dislike the addition of another layer of government and argue that, by virtue of its size, an English parliament would dwarf all other institutions.

Devolution in Wales

Wales has been a relatively neglected part of the constitutional reform argument. Politicians and commentators who have spent much time in consideration of the West Lothian question and associated issues have rarely given much thought to the important features of the devolution debate distinctive to Wales.

It was not self-evident to many Welsh people why in 1997 they were offered a different form of devolution from Scotland. Welsh supporters of devolution pointed out that their country too has a distinctive identity and that even if their country lacked the distinctive institutions characteristic of the Scottish tradition, nonetheless they had something that Scotland lacked – a distinctive language. Ministers took a different view, arguing that Wales is less of a nation than Scotland, not least because of its smaller size and different history as a conquered territory. They were aware that nationalism in Wales was always more about preserving the Welsh culture and language than it was about self-government and pointed to the overwhelming rejection of devolution in 1979 as evidence that there was less demand for devolution in the province.

In the 1997 referendum, Wales was offered an assembly without legislative and revenue-raising powers of the kind given to Scotland. The modest nature of the proposals may in part have accounted for the lack of enthusiasm shown by the Welsh for devolution. They did not reject Labour's solution, but neither did they offer strong backing.

Under the terms of the Wales Act (1998) a National Assembly of sixty members was established, with Members of the Welsh Assembly (MWAs) to be elected in the same way as the MSAs (forty constituency and twenty additional members). The Assembly was not given the power to introduce primary legislation. It was responsible for secondary legislation, fleshing out bills already passed at Westminster and it could act as a pressure group on the London government for greater consideration of Welsh interests. From the Assembly, an executive was to be formed. Initially, a Labour minority administration assumed office, but this gave way to a series of Labour-led coalitions under the leadership of the First Minister, Rhodri Morgan, who stepped down in 2009. The office of Secretary of State for Wales (with a seat in the Cabinet) remains.

Welsh devolution in practice

Critics dismiss the devolved machinery as a 'talking shop', pointing to its lack of effective power. It is true that the powers are limited, but this did not stop Wales from embarking on some policy initiatives that distinguished Welsh arrangements from those in England. SATs tests for seven year olds and prescription charges were abolished and the first Children's Commissioner established in the UK. In addition, the **quangocracy** in Wales (much disliked by many Welsh people) was tackled. Even before the new machinery was established, the Wales Act had provided for the removal of nine quangos and more were due to be abolished at a later date (see also pp. 213–14).

In the light of early experience, some Labour MWAs – including the First Minister – were keen to see more legislative power located in Cardiff. The former Secretary of State for Wales, Ron Davies, always claimed that devolution 'was a process, not an event'. This was true, and a review of current arrangements took place against a background of increasing support for the idea of strengthened devolution, as revealed in several opinion surveys.

The arrangements made in the 1998 Act were developed in the Government of Wales Act (2006), which created an executive body, the Welsh Assembly government, legally separate from the National Assembly for Wales. The National Assembly's functions, including those of making subordinate legislation, were transferred to the Welsh ministers, a move that clarified the respective roles of the legislature and the Executive. The result now mirrors much more closely the relationship between the UK government and the UK Parliament, and that between the Scottish government and the Scottish Parliament.

In 2010, according to a poll[9] on St David's Day, only 18 per cent were satisfied with the limited powers conferred on the assembly. Most Welsh people favoured more devolution; by 56 per cent to 35 per cent, they said they would vote for an assembly with full legislative powers in a referendum scheduled for 2011. This increased support for more powerful devolution coexisted with a decline in support for Welsh independence. In the March referendum, on a 35.2 per cent turnout, 63.5 per cent voted 'yes', and 36.5 per cent voted 'no', in response to the question: 'Do you want the Assembly now to be able to make laws on all matters in the 20 subject areas it has powers for?'; twenty-one of twenty-two local authorities voted 'yes', the exception being Monmouthshire. (The result of the referendum does not mean that the Assembly can make laws in more areas than before.)

Overall, the way services are provided in Wales and England has diverged increasingly over the past decade, although to some extent that has more to do with radical changes in England than anything that has happened in Wales. While the government in Westminster has pressed ahead with radical reforms such as private sector involvement in the public services, foundation hospitals and city academies, the Assembly government has retained more traditional models. Again, like Scotland, but unlike England, the Assembly government has attempted wherever possible to reopen disused railways such as the Vale of Glamorgan and Ebbw Valley lines.

Is Britain becoming a federal state?

As we have established, Britain is a unitary state. But there have been important changes in recent years to the pattern of government, some of which seem to indicate a move in a more federal direction. Devolution has been the British route to decentralisation, Northern Ireland, Scotland and Wales all having devolved administrations with power remaining theoretically in Westminster's hands.

Box 6.5 A note on devolution in Northern Ireland

Northern Ireland is the least integrated part of the United Kingdom. It is often viewed as 'a place apart', for the province has a distinctive history and political culture. The nature of its government has long been a contentious issue, for the province faces a unique constitutional problem. The Protestant majority conclude that the province should be governed as part of the United Kingdom, whilst a large, predominantly Catholic minority would prefer to see the island united as one Irish republic, or claim so to do. Protestant Loyalists are proud to be British, Catholic Republicans prefer to be considered Irish. Reaching any accommodation between the two groups has been very difficult, despite the continued efforts of British and Irish governments of the last two decades to bring about a resolution of the problems.

Under the terms of the Good Friday Agreement (1998), as ratified by the people on either side of the border, there was to be, among other terms:

- a devolved assembly with law-making powers in the province, elected on the basis of proportional representation;
- an executive of ten ministers who would operate on the basis of power sharing between the leaders of the two communities.

Following conclusion of the Agreement, there was still conflict over the decommissioning of IRA weapons, the reform of the police service, the continued presence of British troops and several other issues. As a result, although the Assembly and Executive were established, they were suspended on four occasions during which time government continued to operate via direct rule.

Devolution was renewed in May 2007, when control of Northern Ireland was transferred from the Northern Ireland Office to the Executive, which currently continues to be dominated by the DUP and Sinn Fein, following the 2011 elections. The last piece of Northern Ireland devolution was slotted into place in Belfast in March 2010, when the Assembly voted for the transfer of policing and justice powers from London to Belfast. The breakthrough was the culmination of years of effort by the British government, Dublin, Washington and local parties to bring full devolution to fruition.

The degree of devolution granted to Northern Ireland is somewhere in between that originally granted to the Scots and the Welsh. Like the Scottish Parliament, the Northern Ireland Assembly has legislative powers, but unlike the former, the latter has no tax-varying powers. The members of the Assembly decide on many matters affecting the province that continues to send seventeen MPs to Westminster. As in the case of Scottish MPs, they can vote on English issues, whereas English MPs cannot vote on issues affecting the six counties. But little is heard of the Belfast question in British politics.

England remains the odd one out in the devolution settlement. There have been no equivalent plans for an English Parliament. Moreover, the Labour government's commitment to regional devolution in England was killed off by the November 2004 referendum in the North East (see Box 6.6).

The only devolved institution introduced in England has been the Greater London Authority (GLA), under the leadership of an elected mayor. The new machinery was approved by an overwhelming 72 per cent to 28 per cent in the 1998 referendum. It is now well established. Some of this may be down to the fact that the two mayors (Ken Livingstone and Boris Johnson) have been maverick persons with strong public personas, who can provide clear leadership. Livingstone, running initially as an independent, was able to use the office to build a personal political following and achieve a major policy innovation, the introduction of congestion charging.

Unlike the North East, 'London' is a coherent community with a general interest that needs to be addressed through its own institutions of government, as it had been before the (unpopular) abolition of the Greater London Council by the Thatcher administration in 1985. It is that sense of general interest that the North East (and maybe even more so the other English regions) lacks. There was no underpinning of regional identity and region-focused civic understanding to support elected regional assemblies. Against that background, and no matter how much northerners felt disadvantaged by Westminster centralism, regional government was not judged to be a credible and desirable alternative.

The London experience and the passage of the Local Government Act (2000) have led to the development of another innovation, the creation of elected mayors in other authorities. The Act set out a range of options as to how a local council could be constituted, install-

Box 6.6 Government in the English regions

The case for a system of elected regional government

The arguments in favour of regional government have been effectively summarised by Stoker et al.:[10]

- The *political case* stresses the way in which a system of regional government could serve to revitalise British democracy, which – excessively centralised – fails to cater adequately for the differing interests, needs and values of the various regions.
- The *economic development* case is based on the need for effective governmental capacity at the regional level. Regionalism is an 'economic imperative', for policies are needed to provide physical infrastructure and investment incentives, and to provide a platform and voice for regional issues and concerns.
- The *European case* argues that developments in the EU – including the development of a 'Europe of the regions' – point to the need for regional government. In several EU countries, it has been recognised that the best way of maximising influence in Brussels and ensuring a flow of EU aid is for regions to make their own bids.
- The *technocratic case* is based on the complexity of British social, ecological and economic problems, which require tailormade solutions that will not emerge from a top-down approach, especially in areas such as land-use, planning, transport and economic development.

Developments under Labour, 1997–2010

In 1997, Labour was committed to establishing powerful regional machinery. In 1998, it established eight *Regional Development Agencies* (RDAs) appointed by and directly accountable to ministers in Whitehall. Their brief was to further the economic development and regeneration of the regions, and promote a regional strategy. Labour also set up indirectly elected *Regional Chambers*, later to be known as Regional Assemblies, in each RDA region. These were to advise the RDAs and provide a modicum of democratic oversight and accountability, their membership being drawn from serving councillors in local government. The intention was that the chambers might evolve into elected regional assemblies.

In May 2002, the government published a White Paper, *Your Region, Your Choice*,[11] outlining future plans for its assemblies. It promised that referendums would be held in areas where there seemed to be 'sufficient public interest', to see whether an elected assembly was wanted. Initially, three such referendums were planned, for the North East, the North West and Yorkshire and the Humber. The first occurred in September 2004 in the North East, where voters overwhelmingly rejected the proposal by 77.9 per cent to 22.1 per cent. If the scheme had gone ahead, there was the possibility of a rolling programme of regional government in England, with some areas obtaining new machinery in advance of others. In the light of the lack of public support, no more referendums took place and the idea of elected regional government was indefinitely shelved. Labour announced that the existing regional assemblies were to be abolished in 2010 with their executive functions transferring to the RDAs.

Coalition policy

In July 2010, Business Secretary Vince Cable[12] announced the abolition of the RDAs, which he denounced as 'centrally led', 'unaccountable' and 'costly'. Moreover, 'they had left the economy still as regionally unbalanced as before, if not more'. In a move that flies the flag for small-scale localism, they are to be replaced by twenty-four Local Enterprise Partnerships (LEPs) to attract investors and promote businesses across England.

The only devolved institution introduced in England has been the Greater London Authority (GLA), under the leadership of an elected mayor. The new machinery was approved by an overwhelming 72 per cent to 28 per cent in the 1998 referendum. It is now well established. Some of this may be down to the fact that the two mayors (Ken Livingstone and Boris Johnson) have been maverick persons with strong public personas, who can provide clear leadership. Livingstone, running initially as an independent, was able to use the office to build a personal political following and achieve a major policy innovation, the introduction of congestion charging.

Unlike the North East, 'London' is a coherent community with a general interest that needs to be addressed through its own institutions of government, as it had been before the (unpopular) abolition of the Greater London Council by the Thatcher administration in 1985. It is that sense of general interest that the North East (and maybe even more so the other English regions) lacks. There was no underpinning of regional identity and region-focused civic understanding to support elected regional assemblies. Against that background, and no matter how much northerners felt disadvantaged by Westminster centralism, regional government was not judged to be a credible and desirable alternative.

The London experience and the passage of the Local Government Act (2000) have led to the development of another innovation, the creation of elected mayors in other authorities. The Act set out a range of options as to how a local council could be constituted, installing a directly elected mayor being one of them. Only eleven have chosen to go down this route, although in December 2010 Leicester City Council decided to establish the position with effect from May 2011. Elected mayors of this type are to be found in American cities such as Washington and New York, and in European capitals such as Barcelona and Paris. However, in the UK there has already been some backlash about their perceived excessive powers and in Stoke-on-Trent the office has already been abolished.

Yet if the introduction of mayors becomes the pattern of the future outside London, then we will perhaps experience what Coxall and Robins envisage:[13]

ing a directly elected mayor being one of them. Only eleven have chosen to go down this route, although in December 2010 Leicester City Council decided to establish the position with effect from May 2011. Elected mayors of this type are to be found in American cities such as Washington and New York, and in European capitals such as Barcelona and Paris. However, in the UK there has already been some backlash about their perceived excessive powers and in Stoke-on-Trent the office has already been abolished.

Yet if the introduction of mayors becomes the pattern of the future outside London, then we will perhaps experience what Coxall and Robins envisage:[13]

[the development from] a unitary state to a mosaic of federal, devolved and joint authority relationships between core and periphery, with the English core becoming more decentralised as regional and urban identities find political expression.

When commentators speculate on moves towards a federal structure in Britain, they do not usually imply a uniform division of power between Westminster and provincial units formally set out in a written document. Rather, they envisage a situation in which the policy of devolution is gradually applied to all parts of the United Kingdom, just as it is now applied to Scotland and Wales. Such a pattern is more akin to the model proposed by some Liberals in the late nineteenth century, a pattern then labelled as 'Home Rule All

Box 6.7 Could federalism work in Britain?

The attraction of federalism is that it offers such a clear-cut division of responsibility that would be neatly applied all-round in the United Kingdom. There need be no jealousies between component parts, because all would have the same powers and be represented in the same way in the Westminster Parliament. A federal UK could be applied in two ways:

1. We could have parliaments or assemblies for England, Northern Ireland, Scotland and Wales, with these bodies looking after the main 'internal' policies such as education, welfare and transport. The Campaign for an English Parliament favours such a devolved parliament and would like to see it granted the same powers as the Scottish body: 'An English parliament would be full devolution for England as England, constituting the most radical, genuine and progressive decentralisation of power in the history of the UK' (www.thecep.org. uk). In such a scenario, there would also be a UK Parliament still at Westminster.

    The trouble here is that England would predominate in the UK Parliament, for if representation was worked out on a population basis, England would need about 83 per cent of the seats. English representatives would be able to force any policy through, in spite of the opposition of the other countries. It would be unreal to expect England to accept that they should be over-represented or have a blocking mechanism.

2. The alternative solution would be to recast England on the basis of eight to ten regions, similar to the ones used for Labour's Regional Assemblies. Each region would have its own budget to provide its own educational, transport and other services, just as would the three countries that currently have devolved machinery. Given a blank sheet of paper, this might be a logical way of dividing up the United Kingdom. It is certainly a very decentralist approach and would provide a clearer, neater division of responsibility between the centre and the nations and regions. But given the outcome in the North East referendum, there is no evidence of sufficient regional consciousness to make regional government of this type a likely possibility.

Round'. Bogdanor[14] seeks to distinguish this from a strictly federal system and refers to it instead as 'federal devolution'.

The European dimension

Of course, another line of possible development is to imagine a more federal Britain in a federal Europe. The pioneers of post-war Europe always envisaged that their attempts at cooperation would take Europe towards some kind of 'United States of Europe'. British Conservatives have long feared the idea of a federal Europe seeing this as a form of centralisation, involving the creation of some giant Euro super-state. The formal creation of such a 'monster' may be as yet a long way off, but they see moves to integration (e.g. the single currency) as steps in that direction.

The British take a different view of federalism to most Europeans who see federalism as decentralisation in practice. Whereas John Major was keen to insist on the notion of **subsidiarity** being written into the Maastricht Treaty and sought to sell the agreement as a decentralising measure to halt the drift of power to Brussels, several other European leaders were bemused for they could also endorse subsidiarity. They view it as the very essence of federalism, for it involves the idea that decisions should be taken at the lowest level of government possible. As the Treaty puts it in article 3b:

> In areas which do not fall within its exclusive competence, the Community shall take action, in accordance with the principle of subsidiarity, only if and in so far as the objectives for the proposed action cannot be sufficiently achieved by the Member states and can therefore, by reason of the scale or effects of the proposed action, be better achieved by the Community.

English local government

The need for a network of local councils

Given the size and population of Britain, it would be impossible to devise and operate all services from Westminster and Whitehall. Some intermediate system of administration is required to deliver services. Britain has traditionally operated several services on a regional basis, without there being any way in which the decision-making bodies are

Box 6.8 A note on quangos

Quasi Autonomous Non-Governmental Organisations (Quangos) have been established by ministers and funded from the public purse, but yet have an independence of action usually denied to officials in the bureaucracy. This is because they are not controlled directly by national elected politicians.

Quangos are officially known by bodies such as the Cabinet Office and the Treasury as non-departmental public bodies (NDPBs). In their categorisation, the term includes four types of organisation (executive, advisory, tribunal and independent monitoring boards), but excludes public corporations, National Health Service (NHS) bodies and public broadcasting authorities (BBC and S4C). Technically, there is a difference in meaning between quangos and NDPBs. The term quango originally referred to bodies that are, at least ostensibly, non-governmental organisations, but nonetheless perform governmental functions. NDPBs differ from **Executive Agencies** as they are not created to carry out ministerial orders or policy, and enjoy greater independence.

In making their claims and counter-claims about the range of bodies discussed, politicians generally refer to 'quangos', whatever their particular type. Their number grew rapidly in the late twentieth century. Although the Conservatives had committed themselves to curbing the growth of such non-elected bodies in 1979, their numbers increased. If the count includes the executive agencies, Health Service Trusts, opted-out schools and hospitals and Training and Enterprise Councils, then the opposition attacks based on 'the number's game' were justified.

There were other reasons for criticism of quangos in addition to the frequency of their use. Critics targeted the twin issues of patronage and accountability. They disliked the way in which those appointed to serve on these public bodies were usually men connected with or sympathetic to the Conservative Party, or – in some cases – wives of Conservative MPs. They saw them as being unaccountable to the general public. Moreover, ministerial accountability to Parliament is blurred, when problems develop for which an agency is responsible. When there is a jailbreak, the Home Secretary can avoid taking responsibility by saying that this is an operational matter – the responsibility of the Director-General of the Prisons Agency – rather than an issue of policy for which the minister must accept the blame.

Tackling quangos, 1997–2010

After 1997, there was no substantial attack on the quangocracy, some older bodies being replaced by newer ones and most others being retained. In 2005, Lewis[15] claimed that at least 111 appointed bodies had been set up after Labour came to power, in 1997. Otherwise, Labour's distinctive contribution was to create organisations with a broad remit, crosscutting bodies such as the New Deal Taskforce and the Social Exclusion Unit. These were seen as 'filling in the gaps' between other agencies, to ensure the more effective delivery of policies.

In its 2009 report on *Public Bodies*, the Cabinet Office[16] – using its narrower interpretation of the term – counted 679 NDPBs, as compared with 1,128 in 1997, a reduction of nearly 40 per cent. However, the figure is misleading, because before 2002, the Cabinet Office counted bodies attached to each of the devolved assemblies, which after 2002 were no longer included in the figures. The 2009 report is clear: 'Since 1997, the total number of NDPBs has fallen by 91 – over 10 per cent.' Moreover, the associated costs of running them increased from £18 billion in 1997 to £38.4 billion in 2009. **NB** Such costs had been rising at an even faster rate in the Thatcher/Major years than during the Blair and Brown premierships.

The experience of Wales and the Coalition approach

In Wales, the new Welsh Assembly government (WGA) had been intent on tackling the issue of quangos, although it found that this could not be done quickly. In 2004, the three largest (the Welsh Development Agency; the training and education body, Elwa; and the Wales Tourist Board) were scrapped and their powers taken 'in-house' by the Welsh Assembly. In addition, three more lost power, the Wales-wide councils for arts, sport and the countryside.

In 2010, the new Coalition government was intent on shrinking the state and its ancillary organisations. It wanted to make savings, and ensure improved governance and accountability. According to McAllister,[17] there were some lessons to learn from Welsh experience. She has drawn attention to the need:

- to be clear on the rationale for change before making grand announcements and to determine the core objective – efficiency, improved accountability or political point scoring? If one of the first two, savings can be made through skilful rationalisation although doubts have been cast on the real savings in terms of staffing levels and efficiency in duties discharged.
- to consider the governance map in the round, the best configuration of government and arms-length bodies. Some duties might

remain best discharged by specialist bodies removed from government. Yet the specific benefits of arms-length bodies have scarcely featured in current discussions. McAllister refers to the 'risks for effective administration and capacity for good scrutiny [of] dumping more on an already overloaded state' and the potential advantages of having 'an effective source of external expertise [in] policy-making and strategy'.

• to show 'devolutionary sensitivity' in making announcements about abolitions and mergers, as in coalition talk of merging UK Sport and Sport England. 'Fine . . . if sport were not a devolved matter and if there had been proper consultation and agreement from the home nations. UK Sport has shown itself to be an effective coordinator of provision for high-performance athletes from the four nations in the UK, especially at Olympic and Paralympic level.'

In Autumn 2010, ministers announced a huge cull of quangos as part of their bid to improve accountability and cut costs. Having reviewed 901 bodies – 679 quangos and 222 other statutory bodies – it threatened to axe 192 public bodies such as British Nuclear Fuels, British Shipbuilders, the Audit Commission, the Film Council, the General Teaching Council for England, the Human Fertilisation and Embryology Authority and the Regional Development Agencies, and to merge a further 118. The future of some bodies is still under consideration, but 380 will definitely be kept. The quangos whose functions are being returned to Whitehall departments include the Disability Living Allowance/Attendance Allowance Advisory Board and the Appointments Commission. The Olympic Park Legacy Company will have its functions transferred to the London Mayor. 'Committees of experts' will replace others, such as the Zoos Forum, the Herbal Medicines Advisory Committee and the Air Quality Expert Group.

subject to democratic control. At the local level, the role of councils has gone far beyond merely administering services on behalf of the centre. Rather, it has played an important role in shaping and directing key aspects of public policy, although that role has been reduced in recent decades.

Local government is a creature of central government, working within a framework of parliamentary legislation. It can only act in those areas specifically laid down by Parliament. By contrast, French local government has a broad competence, which allows it to act except in areas specifically ruled out by national legislation.

The case for local government is based on two interrelated themes: democracy and policy effectiveness. Local government is based on the principle that public policy decisions should be taken as close to the people as is practicable. The rationale for this is that whereas centrally imposed solutions may prove inappropriate to many areas, local councils can provide the most appropriate local response to a particular situation based on their local knowledge. Councils are more accessible to local people who can more easily seek redress for any problems they face. Such an approach has the additional benefits of diversity and flexibility, matching services to particular local needs. Individual councils can be used to experiment with new ideas and policy innovations.

In addition, because local government is closer to the people than central government, it is therefore more accountable. Elected local councils help to strengthen the democratic process, encouraging as they do the participation of citizens, by voting or standing for office. Moreover, the network of councils means that there are multiple centres of power, acting therefore as an important safeguard against an over-powerful central state.

Central–local relations: the growth of central control

Although the British system of local councils operates under a framework of controls from Westminster and Whitehall, it was for many years an active and vibrant one. Most obviously, in the period after 1945, it reached its heyday, in what now seems to have been in some respects a golden period for local government. The growth in local spending coincided with the creation and expansion of the Welfare State. Councils assumed additional responsibilities particularly in areas such as social services, spending a growing share of the national income, employing more people and enjoying a considerable degree of freedom to determine local policy responses.

The situation began to alter in the mid to late 1970s, when the expansionist phase of provision came to an end. Labour began to curb spending by councils as part of its programme of cuts in 1976. However, most noticeably, it was the impact of Thatcherism that began to change the political agenda as far as local councils were concerned. The arrangements for local government finance and the balance of national and local influence in policymaking were areas that became more sharply politicised after 1979. In addition, profound changes affected the structure of local government and led to the more rapid creation of quangos.

Ministers wanted a greater role for the private sector in the delivery of local services, stressing the enabling rather than the direct service provision role of local government. In the field of public housing, in addition to the policy of selling council houses, active encouragement was given to the involvement of non-governmental agencies such as housing associations. In education too, previously an area of local autonomy, central control was increased in several ways, most obviously by the introduction of the national curriculum. The government placed the emphasis on consistency and efficiency, rather than diversity and choice.

Overall, during the Conservative era, more than 100 separate Acts of Parliament included provisions that made changes to local government in the UK. Broadly, they fell into three categories:

- Those concerned with finance, particularly how local authorities raised or received their income and the rules and legislation concerned with how they spent their money.
- Those concerning the activities in which local government was engaged.
- Those related to the framework of local government, affecting its structure. These included the abolition of the six existing Metropolitan councils and the Greater London Council in 1986, as well as the creation of a number of entirely new authorities. The present structure of local government was laid down in the Major years (see below). In addition to structural changes, there were other developments, most notably the development of the concept of local councils as enabling authorities which did not provide services directly (instead, they allocated contracts for service delivery to competing providers) and a raft of policy changes that tightened control just in the areas in which councils had previously had much discretion – namely education and housing.

As a result of the changes made, there was after 1979 increased central control over local councils, involving a substantial reduction

Box 6.9 The structure of local government

During the twentieth century, the structure of local government was reformed and rationalised. By 2000, there were fewer local government areas than in 1900 and they were larger in size. In the patchwork system of English local government, there is a combination of one-tier and two-tier authorities:

- *One-tier councils*, usually referred to as unitary bodies, include thirty-six metropolitan authorities based in six large urban areas (e.g. Birmingham, Coventry and Walsall in the West Midlands conurbation) and fifty-six in the rest of the country (e.g. Bristol, Milton Keynes and Reading). They are all-purpose authorities that provide the whole range of local government services.
- *Two-tier councils* operate in the other parts of England. There are twenty-seven county councils, below which are 201 district councils (DCs). In a shire county such as Staffordshire, the county council provides services such as education, waste management and strategic planning. The district councils (e.g. Cannock Chase DC and Lichfield DC) have responsibility for issues such as housing, waste collection and local planning. (**NB** London has had a two-tier system since 2000, with responsibility for the provision of services divided between the GLA and thirty-two borough councils.)

There are in addition more than 10,000 elected parish and town councils. Town councils generally represent larger populations than parish councils. Not all parishes have councils. These deal with activities such as allotments, bus shelters, cemeteries, litter bins, parish lighting, parks and playgrounds; they also have a consultative role in planning. The county of East Sussex has ten town councils and eighty-two parish councils.

Councils such as counties, districts and unitaries are known as principal local authorities in order to differentiate them in their legal status from parish and town councils, which are not uniform in their existence. Local councils tend not to exist in metropolitan areas but there is nothing to stop their establishment.

in the degree of local autonomy. In 1997, the new Blair government was committed to giving councils a higher profile and restoring life and vigour into the way they function. The Prime Minister[18] was keen to revive this ailing area of British democracy. It would be 'modernised . . . re-invigorated . . . reborn and energised' under Labour rule. New Labour's plans for the reviving of local democracy included a proposal for a directly elected Mayor of London and a new assembly, and gave councils throughout England the chance to consult the people in their vicinity about how they would operate in future.

For the most part, Labour in office did not show much interest in major structural reform. It preferred to concentrate on democratic renewal, internal management and service delivery. In particular, under the terms of the Local Government Act (2000), it gave councils throughout England the chance to consult the people in their vicinity about how they would wish to see their local authority operate in future. It wanted to see reform of the internal structure of councils, placing much emphasis on the nature and quality of local leadership. By 2003, the local consultations had taken place and of the options available, inhabitants in 316 areas chose a leader and Cabinet, ten an elected mayor or Cabinet, one an elected mayor and council manager and fifty-two have made alternative arrangements based on the older system.

The impact of Europe upon local government

A further development over the past two decades has been the growing impact of Europe upon British local government. For a number of reasons, British local authorities began to develop direct relations with the institutions of the European Union and with partner local authorities on the Continent. In the main, these circumvented British central government, indicating that a new dimension was emerging in central-local relations. The developing relationship between local authorities and the European Union took two principal forms:

1. The provision of EU funding through programmes such as the European regional and social funds. Some authorities such as Birmingham were notably effective in attracting European money to finance major construction projects.
2. Local authorities began to participate in European networks, working with councils in other countries in the search for common solutions and in a bid to influence the direction of Union policy.

This European dimension has assumed an ever-increasing significance in recent years, as councils have seen the EU as a potential means of protecting and fostering their autonomy. This is in line with the doctrine of subsidiarity laid down at Maastricht, notably that wherever possible governmental activities should be carried out at the most local level of provision.

The case of Spain

In Spain, seventeen autonomous regions – each with an elected assembly and government – were established under the 1978 constitution. The extensive devolution of power to the regions was largely a way of enabling the new democracy to accommodate militant Basque and Catalan demands. The amount of devolution varies, 'ordinary' regions having less power, whereas the two regions above and areas such as Galicia and the Balearic Islands have more extensive competences. Issues other than defence and foreign affairs, social security and the direction of broad economic policy have been passed to the autonomous communities, but it is up to each one to decide how they exercise their new powers, the proviso being that they must do so in a way not in conflict with the Spanish constitution. Some regions have been unwilling or unable to assert their autonomy to any considerable degree.

The Spanish form of devolution has been labelled as one of 'differentiated' or 'asymmetrical federalism'.[19] Spain operates as a devolved unitary state over much of the country, yet there are parts of the country that function in a way akin to regions in a federal system. This is why Spain is sometimes referred to as a de facto federation, in that it allows more self-government in some of its autonomous communities than most federations allow their constituent parts. The central government in Madrid insists that Spain is an indissoluble state and would resist any attempt at secession. But if it is true that sovereignty legally remains at the centre, no government would contemplate any resumption of central control over the Basques and Catalans; to revoke their autonomy would politically be a near impossibility.

The experience of Catalonia was used by Scottish supporters of Home Rule in their campaign for effective devolution. They noted that devolution has not led to the break-up of Spain, but rather that it has weakened separatist demands. More extreme parties seeking national independence have lost much of their appeal and the peaceful nationalist parties in Catalonia and the Basque Country have concentrated on making devolution work and getting the best possible deal for their region. However, there are in both regions many politicians who continue to work for some scheme of 'shared sovereignty' and a strong Basque terrorist opposition, ETA, which is not reconciled to the present constitutional arrangements.

The case of the USA

By British or French standards, the USA is a very decentralised country. Federalism has been beneficial in many ways, its advantages to Americans including the following:

- It recognises the distinctive history, traditions and size of each state, allowing for national unity but not uniformity.
- It provides opportunities for political involvement to many citizens at state and local level.
- States are still a powerful reference point in American culture, and many citizens identify strongly with their state as well as with their country.
- States provide opportunities for innovation, and act as a testing-ground for experiments which others can follow in areas such as clean air and health care.

Key developments since the 1980s

As president between 1981 and 1989, *Ronald Reagan* presided over a 'devolution revolution'. After his eight years in office, the states were funding more of their own programmes and the number run by the federal government in Washington was markedly curtailed. *President Clinton* (1993–2001) stressed the importance of cooperation between the federal and state/local governments and offered support for state experimentation and was encouraged by the new found vitality of state capitals. As a result of such approaches, the last two decades or so have been categorised by Singh[20] as an era of 'devolutionary federalism'.

Like his predecessors, *George W. Bush* (2001–9) portrayed himself as 'a faithful friend of federalism'. Particularly in his early days in office, he leaned on the advice of leading state officials. But later developments worked against such a pro-devolution policy, noticeably:

- the dislike of the Religious Right for some state laws, such as same sex marriages in Massachusetts and euthanasia in Oregon;
- the fears of the business community about excessive state regulation; and
- the attack on the twin towers which focused attention on Washington, as Americans looked to the White House for a lead in combating terrorism.

In the early days of the presidency of *Barack Obama*,[21] the most significant developments for federal-state relations were the presidential election and economic recession. In the 2008 election campaign, there was no indication that Obama had a guiding approach to the issue, so that after his election he had no clear mandate to implement any changes in the distribution of federal and state power. Nonetheless, his election and the accompanying Democratic gains in Congress had some implications for federalism:

- Federal power was used to promote different policy priorities, for instance the use of federal regulation in areas such as regulation of greenhouse gas emissions.
- State experimentation was encouraged on a different range of issues than had been apparent during the Bush administration, particularly by permitting state auto emission standards that exceeded federal requirements as well as state expansion of coverage through the Children's Health Insurance Program (CHIP).
- There was a greater willingness on the part of the White House and Capitol Hill to respond to state pleas for additional funding, whether for particular programmes such as Medicaid or for general emergency stabilisation assistance.

. . . .

✔ What you should have learnt from this chapter

- In several democracies that have long exhibited a high degree of central control, there has been a move in recent years towards some decentralisation. Since the 1980s, there has been a new mood of state renewal in the United States. Elsewhere, greater decentralisation has been introduced, in response to the difficulties experienced by some countries in managing the process of decision-making. Blondel[22] concludes:

> one could argue that the regionalism that has been introduced in these countries constitutes an imitation of federalism – indeed, is federalism in all but name. Such a conclusion would not be valid for the French or Italian cases up to the mid-1990s, but where it was valid, as it might be in the Spanish case, it would mean that the difference between federal and unitary states is becoming smaller, not only in practice but formally as well.

- The devolution of greater and lesser power to Scotland and Wales respectively, matches what has been happening in other EU states. In Spain, the peoples of some areas of the country have more control over their future than their fellow Spaniards elsewhere. It is as yet unclear whether, in the long term, the use of devolution as a means of defusing tensions and frustrations proves to be the antidote to separatism or a first step on the road to federalism.

- In the United Kingdom, the pattern is similarly confused, leading Ward[23] to conclude that: 'one's overall impression of Labour's constitutional design is how different the pattern of devolution in each country has been. Each of the assemblies has a different size and composition, a different system of government, and a very different set of powers'.

Glossary of key terms

Administrative devolution The transfer of administrative offices and responsibilities from central government (in Whitehall) to outlets around the country: decentralisation of the government machine.

Autonomy The right to or state of self-government: literally self-rule, a situation allowing peoples to be governed according to their own preferences and laws.

Centralisation The concentration of political power or governmental authority at the national level. Centralised governments are therefore those where all the major political decisions are made at the centre, in the case of the UK at Westminster and in Whitehall.

Devolution-plus A step that goes beyond the recommendations of the Calman Commission to deepen Scottish devolution, devolution-plus would see the Scottish Parliament solely responsible for raising the money it spends. This would still not be full fiscal autonomy ('devo-max'), which would give Scotland complete control over taxation. Devolution-plus could be an option in the referendum due later in the current parliament.

Direct Rule The imposition in 1969 of rule from Whitehall/Westminster over the six provinces of Northern Ireland that had previously elected members to a devolved parliament at Stormont. Initially intended to be a temporary suspension of devolution whilst alternative arrangements were worked out, direct rule only came to an end when the Good Friday Agreement was implemented.

Independence Separatism.

Legislative devolution The transfer of the power to legislate in certain areas from the national parliament (at Westminster) to subordinate elected bodies (Scottish Parliament).

National consciousness The belief of members of a national community that they share common aspirations, culture and values: nationalism refers to the desire of such people to have their own separate, sovereign state.

Quangocracy A label – usually employed by critics – for a system in which quangos abound. Those who dislike them refer to their use as an indication of a serious 'democratic deficit' and bemoan what they sometimes call 'the appointed state'.

Sovereignty Supreme or unlimited power: in politics, the ultimate source of legal authority, which – in the United Kingdom – is the Westminster Parliament.

Subsidiarity The notion that decisions should be taken at the lowest possible level, consistent with the demands of efficiency, as is written into the Maastricht Treaty: the idea is that each level of government has its most appropriate geographical area.

? Likely examination questions

Examine the respective benefits and disadvantages of unitary and federal forms of government.

Explain the differences between devolution and federalism.

Has devolution worked for Scotland?

Can devolution work in the United Kingdom?

To what extent is the United Kingdom still a unitary state?

🖥 Helpful websites

Materials are produced and queries answered by staff associated with the Scottish and Welsh devolved bodies:

www.scottish.parliament.uk

www.wales.gov.uk

The Constitutional Centre produces regular updates on matters affecting the government of the United Kingdom.

The Scottish National Party and Plaid Cymru sites offer a different insight into the governance of the two countries:

www.sup.gov.uk

www.plaidcymru.org

Two general local government sites are:

www.local.gov.uk and www.local.detr.gov.uk

 Suggestions for further reading

Useful articles

V. Bogdanor, 'The English Question', *Politics Review*, 17:2, November 2007.

V. Bogdanor, 'Sovereignty and Devolution: Quasi-federalism?, *Politics Review*, 19:3, February 2010.

A. Trench, 'Devolution since 2007', *Politics Review*, 20:2, November 2010.

Useful books

B. Hadfield, 'Devolution in the United Kingdom and the English and Welsh Questions', and B. Winetrobe, 'Scottish Devolution: Developing Practice in Multi-Layer Governance', both in J. Jowell and D. Oliver (eds), *The Changing Constitution,* Oxford University Press, 2007.

R. Hazell and R. Rawlings (eds), *Devolution, Law Making and the Constitution*, The Constitution Unit, 2005.

A. Trench (ed.), *Has Devolution Made a Difference? The State of the Nation*, The Constitutional Unit, 2004.

CHAPTER 7

Political Parties

Contents

Introduction	226
The role of political parties and the nature of party systems	227
The history of the two main parties since 1945	232
The attitudes and beliefs of political parties: the notions of Left and Right	236
The British Conservative Party	238
The Labour Party	244
Blairism in practice: 1994–2007	247
Third and minor parties in Britain and elsewhere	251
Party membership and finance	252
Party organisation: general trends	261
The organisation of British political parties	264
Party conferences in Britain	265
Party leaders: how the main British parties choose them	267
The powers and security of party leaders	270
The decline of political parties: do they still matter?	273
The case of Italy	275
The case of the USA	276

Overview

Mass political parties were the key agency in mobilising the voters for much of the twentieth century. Unlike pressure groups, they sought to secure the levers of power and carry out programmes devised by people who shared a common identity and a broadly similar outlook. By the new millennium, there was some evidence that the Western European pattern was in decline.

In this chapter, we primarily examine the British party system and assess to what extent it still retains its traditional characteristics. We ask whether the parties any longer offer radically different visions of society and retain the allegiance of their traditional supporters.

Key issues to be covered in this chapter

- The role and importance of political parties
- The variety of party systems and the British two-party system
- The attitudes and policy approaches of the Labour and Conservative parties
- Third and minor parties
- Features of party finance, membership and organisation
- The alleged decline of parties: do they matter?
- Parties in Italy and the United States

Introduction

Modern democracy is unthinkable without competition between political parties. They are ubiquitous, existing in different forms under different political systems. They bring together a variety of different interests in any society, and by so doing 'overcome geographical distances, and provide coherence to sometimes divisive government structures'.[1] Via the electoral process, they determine the shape of governments. European, American and other democracies are party democracies.

The primary purpose of political parties is to win elections. This is the main feature that distinguishes them from pressure groups, which may try to influence elections but do not usually put up candidates for office. Parties are, then, organisations of broadly like-minded men and women that seek to win power in elections in order that they can then assume responsibility for controlling the apparatus of government.

Parties articulate the needs of those sectors of society that have created them and look to them to advance their interests. But they must go further, for to win an election they need wider support. If they wish to be in government – either in a single-party administration or some form of coalition – then they cannot afford to follow a narrow doctrinal programme for this would alienate important groups in the community and make it difficult for other parties to contemplate cooperation with them. In the words of the old examination quotation: 'Pressure groups articulate and political parties aggregate the various interests in society'.

In the last two or three decades, there has been a noticeable decline in the fortunes of once-strong parties, several of which have lost members and voters in large numbers. They function in an era of **partisan dealignment**, which has led to a far greater volatility in voting behaviour than ever before. Voting is no longer 'habitual and ingrained', as Punnett[2] described it back in the 1970s. Parties can no longer count on the degree of support they once could almost take for granted.

The role of political parties and the nature of party systems

As we have seen, parties are defined by their central task of seeking office with a view to exercising political power. However, their impact on the political system is wider than this. They have several broad functions in most countries. They:

- *serve as brokers for ideas and organise opinion.* They take on board the ideas of individuals and groups and aggregate and simplify these demands into a package of policies. In this way, they clarify the political process for the voter who is confronted with a choice of alternative proposals, programmes and leaders. The voter is then able to choose the party that most resembles his or her own policy preferences. That choice can be made from a range of ideological parties deeply committed to particular goals (the German Greens) and pragmatic parties whose programme is flexible, moderate and incrementalist in approach (the American Democrats).

- *are a source of political knowledge.* Even for voters who lack any strong party ties, their ideas and outlook are likely to be influenced by the information that parties offer and by their perception of what the parties support. In this way, parties socialise people into the political culture.

- *act as a link between the individual and the political system.* Most people rely on various political interests to represent their concerns and demands. Parties formulate, aggregate and communicate a package of such demands and if they win power attempt to implement them. In this way, parties facilitate the individual's integration into the political process. They act as bridge organisations, mediators between the conflicting interests of government and the electorate.

- *mobilise and recruit activists.* Parties offer a structure into which an individual can channel his interests. They provide contact with other individuals and groups and an opportunity to become political foot soldiers or local or national politicians. In many democracies, the recruitment, selection and training of parliamentary candidates is a key task. Parties offer candidates support during election campaigns and in many countries are responsible for the campaigning itself, both locally and nationally.

- *provide an organisational structure via which to coordinate the actions of government, encouraging those who belong to them to work towards shared objectives.* Leaders and their colleagues (including party whips) seek to persuade members of the legislature to vote for their policies and where necessary do coalition deals to secure a majority for particular programmes.
- *serve as a source of opposition.* The parties not in government provide explicit, organised opposition. In Britain there is a fully institutionalised party designated as Her Majesty's Loyal Opposition, with is own shadow ministerial team.

Types of party systems

The term 'party system' refers to the network of relationships between parties that determines how the political system functions. The most usual means of distinguishing between different types of party system is by reference to the number of parties involved. In a classic study, Duverger[3] referred to particular variations such as 'one-party', 'two-party' and 'multi-party' systems. However, in addition to the number of parties is the issue of their electoral and legislative strength – whether or not parties have the prospect of winning or sharing political power. Some are 'major', others 'third', 'minor' or 'small' parties.

There are four categories of party systems:

1. *One-party systems.* There are several variants of this type, but they are mostly associated with authoritarian governments in which a single party enjoys a monopoly of power – e.g. in remaining communist regimes such as China, there is no permitted effective opposition.
2. *Two-party systems.* In these systems, as in Britain, New Zealand and the United States, there are two major parties, each of which has a chance of obtaining a majority of seats in the legislature and capturing political power. There will be other parties – some sizeable – but they have not in the past meaningfully competed for office. They are never likely to win outright.
3. *Dominant-party systems.* These exist in a country where there is free competition between parties, but only one party is likely to achieve an absolute majority of the votes cast and dominate

governmental office. There may on occasion be a sharing of power with another party, but the likelihood is that one party will enjoy a long period of continuous rule. Before majority rule, the Nationalist Party in South Africa was in this position. So too was the Liberal Democrat Party in Japan until the 1990s. In the 1980s, commentators noted that Britain had one-party dominance in a traditionally two-party system. Within a country, there may be a dominant-party system operating at a regional level. In the rural Midwest of the USA, the electorate is overwhelmingly Republican.

4. *Multi-party systems*. These are common in European countries, such as Belgium, Italy and Switzerland. Government tends to be based on coalitions of more than one party, maybe three or four. Under this type of party system, there is not usually a clear distinction between government and opposition, for many of the broadly centrist parties tend to be members of the administration. Such systems are common where **proportional representation** is employed.

The British two-party system

Historically, Britain has had a two party system, Labour and the Conservatives being the dominant parties since the 1930s. In only two elections since 1945 has one of the major parties failed to win an outright majority. The high peak of the two-party system was in 1951 when between them Labour and the Conservatives won 98.6 per cent of the votes and 96.8 per cent of the seats.

The two-party system has generally been resilient, although the rise in third party support since the mid 1970s has made the picture more confused. The two main parties have lost electoral support and their overwhelming dominance in parliamentary seats. Indeed, between 1979 and 1997 only one party (the Conservatives) secured victories at the polls, leading to suggestions that we had a dominant-party system, or a two-party system with one-party dominance.

The election of 2010 cast further doubt on whether we still have a two-party system. The two main parties won less than two thirds of the popular vote (the lowest figure post-war). Between them, they gained 565 seats at Westminster, although their joint share of the parliamentary seats was the lowest in any post-war election (86.9 per

Box 7.1 Two party systems in Britain and the United States: their causes, advantages and disadvantages

Conditions favourable to the development of two-party systems

- *The natural tendency for opinion on issues to divide into a 'for' and 'against' position* which often follows the basic division between those who generally favour the status quo (Conservatives in the UK and Republicans in the USA) and those who wish to see innovation and a faster rate of change (Labour in the UK and Democrats in the USA).
- *The electoral system.* The simple majority system used in Britain and the United States means that the candidate with the most votes wins, whether or not he or she actually obtained a majority of all the votes cast. This discourages parties from splintering and restricts the growth of new parties. Duverger[4] noted that: 'The simple majority, single ballot system favours the two party system; the simple majority system with second ballot and pro-portional representation favours multi-partyism'.
- *The existence of broad broker parties that aim to win backing from all sections of the electorate.* The two main parties in Britain and America accommodate their aims to the general feeling of the people, which keeps them moderate and middle-of-the-road. As such, there is little scope for a third party to establish itself on a popular basis.
- *The tendency of a two-party system to perpetuate itself.* Once established, the parties do all that they can to keep it that way and prevent a fractious section of the population from breaking away. If necessary, they modify their policies to cater for any new cause.
- *The absence (in Britain) of deep ethnic, linguistic, religious and sectional differences within the population.* In the USA, there is a much less homogeneous population, but many of the diverse elements within the population are accommodated within the melting pot of American life. The American Dream is widely shared, the belief that there is an opportunity for anyone to move from 'log cabin to White House'. There is a similarly common commitment to shared values of individualism and enterprise, which partly explains the failure of any left-wing socialist party from establishing itself.
- *The problems faced by third or other parties.* Lack of finance and other resources, the difficulty of establishing a distinct identity

and the danger of being squeezed out by the two main rivals all make life hard for a new party trying to break through. In the United States, there are in addition several legal and other barriers to third party advancement.

The advantages of two-party systems

- *They promote effective, stable and strong government.* The success of the British political system has often been attributed to the fact that there have been two strong parties, either of which is usually capable of forming a government on its own. Stability is promoted because a government can carry out its policies relieved of the possible fear that it will be suddenly overthrown by a coalition of the minority parties.
- *The system simplifies voter choice*, because only two parties are viable as governing bodies. Accordingly, the people can vote directly for or against an outgoing government, not merely for a party.
- *Government is clearly accountable to the electorate.* The voters know who to praise or blame for the policies in operation, whereas in a coalition situation responsibility is less clear-cut. Governments can govern, but there is another one in waiting, should they fail.
- *Moderation is encouraged.* If an opposition party knows that its turn will come, this encourages it to be constructive and pose as an alternative government, and not to lapse into extremism, which will probably alienate the large number of people in the political centre.

The disadvantages of two-party systems

- *Voter choice is restricted.* This matters less when the main parties are popular and command majority support, but is more serious when many voters feel alienated.
- *Two party systems, far from promoting moderation, can be characterised by adversary politics*, with an emphasis on conflict and argument rather than consensus and compromise. Governments sometimes come in and undo the work of their predecessors.
- *There is a growing dissatisfaction with the performance of the main parties.* Especially in Britain in recent years, all has not been well with the adversarial two-party system. Governments have not always delivered the goods and neither has the main Opposition party necessarily been appealing. In the UK support for third parties (Liberal Democrats and Nationalists) has been growing in recent decades and the share of the popular vote

obtained by the two main parties has been significantly reduced in recent elections (see p. 352). In the United States a low turnout suggests that some people are unimpressed by the presidential challengers – in 1992, they showed a willingness to opt for a third candidate, Ross Perot.

cent) other than 2005. The third party (the Liberal Democrats) won fifty-seven seats, sufficient to make them a viable coalition partner for the Conservatives. No fewer than six parties won seats in Great Britain and another four (plus an Independent) did so in Northern Ireland. Moreover, in recent elections, there have been national and regional variations, that make the two-party system primarily an English phenomenon. Leaving aside Northern Ireland, which has a distinctive political system, Scotland and Wales both have a strong nationalist party, creating a situation in which there are four main parties competing for power. Labour is the largest of the four in both countries, so that in effect there is a one-party dominant, four-party system for Westminster elections.

The history of the two main parties since 1945

1951–79

In spite of fierce electoral competition and strong theoretical disagreements over the role of the state, private or public ownership of industry and the pursuit of greater social equality, there was between 1945 and 1979 a broad range of agreement between the parties over key economic and social policies, so that the period was often termed 'the era of **consensus politics**'. In those years, whatever was said by the party that was in opposition, once it assumed office it tended to follow broadly similar lines of policy to its predecessor. Governments of either party displayed broad support for:

- a **mixed economy** that included retention of some nationalised public utilities
- the welfare state
- full employment
- the maintenance of strong national defences.

Box 7.2 Consensus politics

Consensus implies a wide measure of agreement. In political life, it refers to a circumstance where a large proportion of the population and of the political community are broadly agreed upon certain values, even if there is some disagreement on matters of emphasis or detail.

The period 1951–79 is often described as an 'era of consensus politics', for there seemed to be general agreement about the policies to be pursued. Governments did seem to accept much of what their predecessors had done and found themselves adopting similar solutions to the problems that arose. Peace, prosperity and welfare were widely accepted goals. Some commentators portrayed elections as a contest to decide 'which team of politicians would administer the policies on which everyone was substantially agreed'.[5] Disputes were often more about the degree, the method and the timing of change, rather than representing fundamental conflicts. Even nationalisation, a hot potato of the late forties, had ceased to be an area of major controversy. Hence Robert McKenzie[6] could portray a situation in which the two parties conducted 'furious arguments about the comparatively minor issues that separate them'.

Not all observers have seen the era of consensus politics in the same light. Reviewing the era, Ben Pimlott[7] saw the consensus as 'a mirage, an illusion that rapidly fades the closer one gets to it'. Other critics pointed out that there has always been a considerable level of agreement about fundamentals in British politics, such as support for key institutions and the commitment to peaceful change. Kavanagh and Morris[8] claim that 'the ideas and some of the practices of consensus existed before the Second World War', and state the extension of state ownership and intervention of the interwar years as evidence.

The 'era of consensus' was in no way an era of all-pervasive sweet reason and compromise and at times there were bitter party clashes. It was, after all, in the 1970s that Samuel Finer[9] first put forward the theory of '**adversary politics**' (see Box 7.3). Pimlott noted that the word consensus was little used before the 1980s and that it was then used to distinguish **Thatcherism** from the period that preceded it. His point was that it was much easier to detect consensus in retrospect than it had been at the time.

On the Continent, where proportional electoral systems are common, policies do tend to be more consensual. Many governments are coalitions in which representatives of the various parties involved do work together and hammer out policies acceptable to all of them. Commentators have often pointed to the example of West Germany, where stable coalition governments and economic prosperity were seen as going hand in hand. Of course, the semi-circular shape of Continental parliaments, in which deputies sit according to how far right or left they are, encourages cooperation among them. By contrast, the design of the House of Commons forces MPs to choose whether they are on the government side or on that of the Opposition.

1979–present day

This period of so-called consensus came under threat in the mid to late 1970s, as the Conservatives under the leadership of Margaret Thatcher began to embark upon a radical overhaul of their post-war thinking and approach. Instead of following traditional evolutionary and conservative policies, her governments took a more radical, neo-liberal stance quite distinctive from that of Conservative administrations in the 1950s–1970s. Labour initially responded to its defeat in 1979 by moving sharply to the Left, so that in 1983 there was a polarised contest between a right-wing Tory administration and a left-wing Labour opposition. However, in response to successive further defeats between 1983 and 1992, Labour moved back towards the centre ground. By 1997, this process had gone so far that Labour had become New Labour and jettisoned many of its traditional policies (see pp. 246 and 247–8 for Blairite Labour attitudes and policies).

Under John Major and his successors (see pp. 240–3 for the attitudes and policies of the Conservatives in recent years), the modern Conservative Party has continued to espouse more right-wing policies than in the years of consensus. These have included support for privatisation and pro-market economic policies; lower direct taxation; reduced governmental expenditure; a tough stance on immigration and asylum seeking; greater emphasis on law and order; and a more hostile attitude to the European Union and the issue of closer integration among its members.

Box 7.3 Adversary politics

Adversarial politics are characterised by ideological antagonism and an ongoing electoral battle between the major parties. The term is used to refer to a period in which there is fundamental disagreement between the parties on the political issues of the day. British politics are essentially adversarial in nature. In a two-party system, in which one main party is in office and the other is in opposition, the one defends its policies whilst the other attacks them. The opposite end of the spectrum would be the consensus model, by which policies are adopted only if there is widespread agreement as to their desirability.

The term 'adversary politics' was coined by Finer,[10] to describe the British political system. He felt that the FPTP electoral system produced a regular swing of the pendulum, in which there was little continuity of policy. One party came in and undid what its predecessor had done, so that policies lurched from Left to Right. The electoral system was therefore based for polarising opinion. By contrast, the comparison was made with West Germany, where stable coalition governments and economic prosperity were seen as going hand in hand.

Adversarial politics provide the public with a clear examination of the government's policies and of the alternatives posed by the opposition parties. Defenders of the adversarial approach would say that it serves democracy well, because ministers are forced to justify their performance and their policies in the face of a concerted onslaught. On the other hand, adversarialism means that parliamentary business is often conducted in a hostile manner, in which there is much point-scoring on both sides and there is opposition seemingly almost for the sake of it. The shape of the House of Commons encourages such conflict across the floor of the House, pitting as it does one side versus the other.

It was in some ways surprising that Finer should have written his description in the early 1970s, at a time when Britain was experiencing what other writers would describe as an era of consensus politics. As we have seen, in the preceding couple of decades, ministers had often accepted what their predecessors had done and the differences between Labour and the Conservatives in office often seemed to be not very great.

The attitudes and beliefs of political parties: the notions of Left and Right

Parties are created around broad principles. Although most of their members are not strict ideologues, these broad ideologies provide recognition and mean something to many people. Budge et al.[11] describe ideology as 'a theory about the world and about society, and of the place of you and your group within it'. These ideologies are important 'not only in telling leaders what to do but in telling their supporters who they are and thus making them receptive to leaders' diagnoses of the political situation'.

Parties in many countries tend to employ similar names, so that across the Continent words such as Christian, Conservative, Democrat, Green, Labour, Liberal and Socialist are in regular use. This suggests that they have assumptions and ideas that are similar. These common values and beliefs enable us to interpret events and policies more clearly.

Many voters still subscribe in some degree to causes such as **socialism**, in its various forms. However, even those parties within the socialist family can differ sharply over their vision of end goals and the tactics to be pursued in attaining them. **Marxian socialism** is probably the most developed and influential ideology, for many groups have been formed to argue for it, debate what it means or even react against it. Some socialists are fundamentalists who wish to stick to the ideas of Marx as they see them. Others are revisionists who wish to place them in the context of society today, which has changed dramatically from the time in which he wrote. A small minority of adherents are willing to countenance violence and upheaval to achieve their aims, whereas the overwhelming majority pursue the democratic route to socialism. In practice, old-style socialism has gone out of favour, the breakdown of Soviet control in Eastern Europe being widely hailed as a triumph for free-market societies in which capitalism can flourish and individuals lead freer and fuller lives, as well as become more prosperous.

Parties can be classified according to their place on the political spectrum. The terms 'left' and 'right' were originally used to describe the attitudes adopted by different groups in the French Estates-General in 1789. They are still employed today.

Very generally:

- *A left-wing person* challenges traditional attitudes and practices and wants to see reform. This involves a more active role for government in bringing about desirable change. He or she may also believe in higher levels of taxation to pay for improvements, some redistribution of wealth from the better-off to the least well-off and movement towards a more equal and less class-bound society. Some left-wingers are keen to see more state control over basic industries, believing that private ownership is unsuitable as a means of running the railways and other essential services.

  People on the Left tend to believe in the ideas of 'liberty, equality and fraternity (brotherhood)', which was a popular cry in the French Revolution of the late eighteenth century. They also talk in terms of progress, reform and rights, and are more likely to be internationalists. (In other words, they see issues affecting Britain in world terms.)

- *A right-wing person* is more likely to support the status quo, keeping things as they are unless there is a very strong case for change. He or she is unlikely to favour too much government regulation, favours private enterprise over state ownership and likes to think that people are left in freedom to run their own lives. He will probably favour lower levels of taxation, good rewards for effort and enterprise, and freedom more than equality. An unequal society is accepted as inevitable, even desirable. Right-wingers tend to emphasise a belief in authority, duties, order and tradition, as well as seeing issues from a national rather than an international point of view.

People in the centre of the political spectrum tend to support:

- a mixed economy
- acceptance of the marketplace as the best means of running the economy
- the duty of the government to take action to ensure that vulnerable members of society are not exploited
- tolerance towards ethnic and other minorities
- constitutional change, including a statement of personal rights.

Left and Right in British politics

The terms 'left', 'right' and 'centre' are still commonly used to describe parties and their leading members in discussion of the British political scene. Yet these labels can be misleading and confusing. People who seem left-wing on one issue may adopt a right-wing approach on another. More seriously, the division of Left and Right has become somewhat blurred, for in the **New Labour** era many enthusiasts employed terminology and adopted approaches more traditionally associated with the Conservative Party. The party shed its nominal socialism and positioned itself firmly in the political centre, seeking to maximise its appeal to moderates of the Left and Right. As the Liberal Democrats inhabited similar territory, it meant that the middle ground became very crowded.

Even if many members of the Labour and Conservative parties still portray themselves as belonging to the Left or the Right, the leaderships are aware of the need to attract and maintain support from a wide variety of interests and from people with a wide range of political beliefs. As in most two-party systems, the two main parties are **catch-all parties**, in both cases having their own left and right whose members advance a range of views on the issues of the day.

The terms Left and Right remain as a convenient shorthand by which to summarise different attitudes on important political, economic and social questions. Members and supporters of both main parties share a number of distinctive ideas and philosophies, to which we will now turn.

The British Conservative Party

British Conservatism has a long history. It embraces a broad spectrum of ideas about the nature of man, society and political change. It is a right-wing creed that emphasises preserving the best of the past (including the traditions and institutions of the country) and allowing society to develop gradually, adapting only where change is proved to be necessary. At different times the party has placed more or less emphasis on conserving the past and on reform.

The party was astonishingly successful in elections in the twentieth century. In part, its success was brought about by a willingness to adjust to changing circumstances. Unlike some Continental right-wing parties primarily representing the middle and upper classes, the Conservatives never allowed themselves to be in the position of opposing all progress in order to preserve their self-interest. Under more progressive leaders, the party reached out to working-class voters and was of appeal to many of them. Without working-class support, it would never have won as many elections as it has, in an age of mass franchise.

The party has always been concerned about electoral success. In the words of Glyn Parry,[12] 'the primary and abiding aim of the [Conservative] Party is the achievement of power'. In the consensus years, this mattered more than being too preoccupied with ideas. Indeed, an excess of ideological baggage was seen as a barrier to success. In matters of ideology, the wise Conservative 'travels light'.[13]

Ideas and policies

The Conservative Party constitution describes the leader as 'the main fountain and interpreter of policy'. Leaders are therefore able to lead the party in accordance with their own ideas, values and preferences. However, there are certain abiding themes to which all Conservatives would subscribe:

- A cautious approach to change
- Distrust of the role of 'big government'
- An emphasis upon law and order
- An emphasis upon 'Britishness' (patriotism, defending institutions)
- A preference for freedom over equality, and private over state enterprise.

In the post-war era, the Conservatives generally stuck to **One Nation policies** that were seen as pragmatic (practical, realistic). Most came to accept the Welfare State and the need for more governmental intervention and regulation. However, under Margaret Thatcher in the 1980s, the emphasis was rather different. She was committed to traditional party policies such as a firm stand on law and order, and promoting the idea of 'Great Britain'. But she scorned the timid 'wets' of the post-war era and wanted clearer, more distinctive Tory policies. Her approach was markedly more ideological, strongly favouring free enterprise, market forces, lower taxes and more consumer choice, and hostile to trade union power.

She stressed individual effort, wanted people to solve their own problems and admired perseverance and self-reliance, which she wished to see rewarded.

This more right-wing Conservatism endured after her retirement, during the leadership of John Major in which Conservatives continued to support less government and place emphasis on individual rather than collective values. He fully embraced her free market principles, but his rhetoric was milder and more consensual. His was a more emollient style, as was indicated by his preference for 'a nation at ease with itself', in which there were more opportunities for all, irrespective of background or colour. He was also by instinct more sympathetic to Britain's place being firmly planted 'at the heart of Europe', although events were to make this a position difficult to maintain and to divide the party into its **pro-European** and **Eurosceptic** or even **Europhobic** wings.

By 1997, the battle to achieve free market economic policies had been won. Conservatives of all shades (and New Labour too) were converts. In subsequent years, the potency of the European issue declined, as the party adopted an increasingly sceptical approach to the European Union expressed by the slogan 'in Europe, but not run by Europe'. There has, however, been a distinction among Conservatives between social liberals and more traditional Tories. Social liberals want to see the party become more inclusive, broaden its appeal and make itself more attractive to ethnic minorities, gays and others. Traditionalists are wary of social liberalism and feel more at home with traditional Tory attitudes, especially on such issues as support for authority, religion and family values.

The opposition years, 1997–2010

Conservative leaders in the post-Major era usually began their term in office by claiming to be 'modernisers', stressing their appreciation of the need to widen the party's basis of support and their support for greater social tolerance. When this did not shift the opinion polls in their favour and defeat loomed in an election, they tended to retreat to their comfort zones, the so-called core-vote strategy.

William Hague (1997–2001) was more right-wing and anti-European than Major. Yet he was also more libertarian than many Conservatives. Following the resounding defeat in 1997, Hague initially saw the need to widen the party's appeal. He used inclusive language and made it clear that he wanted the Conservatives to embrace the cause of those who were unfortunate or disadvantaged. However, as the next election drew near, there was an increasing tendency to populism on issues such as law and order, asylum seekers and the Euro. In the 2001 campaign, he had little to say on the state of the public services, the issue that mattered to many voters.

After the second successive electoral debacle in 2001, the new leader *Iain Duncan Smith* (2001–3) was successful in uniting the party around a Eurosceptic position, which carried conviction as he had a past record as a **Maastricht rebel** and had at one time contemplated a British exit from the European Union. He recognised the need to emphasise issues of more direct concern to the public and in particular to reform the public services. However, he was distracted by the conflict between social liberals and traditional Conservatives. In particular, on gay issues he found himself leading a parliamentary party that was seriously divided. His leadership came under sustained pressure, as the party continued to make headway in the polls. He resigned after defeat in a vote of confidence in his leadership.

A barrister by background, *Michael Howard* (2003–5) – a right-wing member of the Thatcher and Major Cabinets – brought experience to the leadership. He also seemed a more heavyweight figure than his predecessors and was a more able performer in the House of Commons, with a lawyer's forensic ability to question and a natural and sometimes biting sarcasm. Conservatives hoped he could score points off Tony Blair, but despite an increase in the number of Conservative MPs the party was again defeated in 2005.

In much of the twentieth century, the Conservatives had been seen as the natural pattern of government. Their leaders had managed to convey the idea that the party was uniquely capable of governing, whereas their opponents were derided as divided, ineffective, extreme or even un-British. By the early twenty-first century, they had shed that reputation and were no longer widely seen as competent, united or well led. There was a need for fresh faces and a major rethink about the sort of party that the Conservatives wished to be, for they were popularly viewed as too elderly, too out of touch and (surprisingly, in view of their historical record) too ideological.

The Cameron approach

Following the 2005 defeat, the new leader David Cameron labelled himself a 'modern **compassionate conservative**'. He claimed to be 'certainly a big Thatcher fan', but was unsure whether that made him a Thatcherite. He also described himself as a 'liberal Conservative' and 'not a deeply ideological person'. Indeed, some journalists claim that he initially spoke of himself to journalists at a dinner during the leadership contest as the natural 'heir to Blair'.

In his early years as leader, Cameron showed himself to be in many ways distinctive from his predecessors. He consciously tried to reposition his party, distancing his leadership from some of the attitudes and policies that its members previously expressed. He was socially liberal on gay issues, exhibited a concern for minority groups in general, did not adopt tough/harsh language when speaking of asylum seekers and stressed the need to think about the causes of crime as well as the manifestations of criminal behaviour. He focused on 'quality of life' issues such as the work-life balance and the environment. He also emphasised the improvement of government services (most prominently the National Health Service and the Home Office), schools, and international development – issues not recently seen as priorities for the post-Thatcher Conservative Party.

Some critics were unhappy with this attempted rebranding and repositioning of the party, and with the leader's interest in presentation. They saw it as too reminiscent of the political style of the early years of the Blair leadership. Others saw it as a necessary part of the bid to move the party back into the centre ground, whilst the party developed a set of credible alternative policies to Labour.

The policy review launched in 2006 with the publication of *Built to Last* was part of the long-standing tradition of reviews that had been conducted prior to the 1950, 1970 and 1979 general elections. However, its six themes – economic competitiveness, public service reform, quality of life, social justice, national and international security and overseas aid – struck a different tone from those covered in earlier exercises in rethinking party approaches. As they began their work, Cameron distanced himself from policies set out in the 2005 manifesto that he had helped to write. He did not talk about Europe, immigration and tax cuts and began to elaborate on his ideas of what the modern Conservative Party was all about. He emphasised the need to work with voluntary organisations to foster social well-being, a new approach to poverty and social justice, and a softer, greener form of Conservatism.

Cameron seized upon a phrase used by the Duncan Smith Commission on Social Justice and began to speak of the importance of repairing 'broken Britain'. He stressed the importance of personal responsibility and community, and began to develop his **Big Society** theme. This was to become the party's new 'big idea'. People were invited to take control over their own lives and join in the crusade. Many voters did not readily understand the idea – not carefully market-tested – but it did at least provide a unifying theme for the election campaign in 2010.

Cameron led the Conservatives to their best performance since the 1992 election, the party winning the largest number of seats (306) though still twenty seats short of an overall majority. The outcome was a hung Parliament that resulted in the formation of a Conservative/Liberal Democrat coalition and the installation of a Conservative Prime Minister in Downing Street. The fate of the Cameron government remains to be seen. When he became premier, David Cameron claimed that the priorities were 'the huge deficit, deep social problems and a political system in need of reform'.

Party prospects
The result in 2010 was disappointing to many Conservatives who felt that they had been presented with an open goal, given Labour's huge election handicaps and in particular the loss of its reputation for economic competence. It suggested that there was still a residual distrust among many voters of the Conservative brand. They feared that the party would not govern in the interests of ordinary people, for underneath – in spite of the rebranding – the party comprised 'the same old Tories'. Whatever their doubts about the incumbent government and their recognition of the need for change, this did not translate into a willingness to switch to the Conservatives.

In opposition, the Conservatives had experienced considerable difficulty in developing a set of attitudes and policies of broad appeal to the electorate. Although their 'victory' in 2010 was a modest one, it nonetheless suggested that the Cameron leadership had achieved some success in removing the party's 'nasty' image and making it electable once more. This was in line with the long-term tradition of the Conservatives. In the past, as in the last election, their ability to transform themselves and update their organisation and policies to meet the challenges of the day has stood them in good stead. The party has often pulled itself together under leaders able to rejuvenate its image and platform, as the experience of Peel, Disraeli and the post-1945 Conservatives indicates. Other parties come and go, but whatever the difficulties it is likely that in some form the Conservative Party will always survive, for conservatism is an abiding element of the political scene.

The Labour Party

In its 1918 Constitution, Labour committed itself to socialism. Socialism is an economic theory or system in which the means of production, distribution and exchange are owned by the community collectively, usually through the state. It is characterised by production for use rather than profit; by equality of individual wealth; by the absence of competitive economic activity; and usually, by government determination of investment, prices and production levels.

Socialism is not a precise term and different party thinkers and leaders have given it their own slant. However, many early socialists in the party saw the creed in terms of the original Clause Four of their Constitution:

> To secure for the workers by hand or by brain the full fruits of their industry and the most equitable distribution thereof that may be possible upon the basis of the common ownership of the means of production, distribution and exchange . . .

Clause Four was for several years a 'sacred cow' of the Labour movement and the Left of the party acted as its guardian. Traditionalists wanted to preserve it intact and continued to see socialism in terms of public ownership of key industries, known as the policy of nationalisation.

After the Second World War, some leaders such as Gaitskell tried to get Clause Four rewritten. He and most moderate, right-of-centre Labour MPs saw socialism more in terms of the pursuit of greater equality, a more just and fair society. Socialism was about 'a set of

Box 7.4 What is socialism? Differing perceptions

'[Of socialism] Its fundamental dogma is the dignity of man; its fundamental criticism of capitalism is, not merely that it impoverishes the mass of mankind - poverty is an ancient evil – but that it makes riches a god, and treats common men as less than men. Socialism accepts, therefore, the principles which are the cornerstones of democracy, that authority, to justify its title, must rest on consent; that power is tolerable only so far as it is accountable to the public; and that differences of character and capacity between human beings, however unportant on their own plane, are of minor significance compared with the capital fact of their common humanity.'

R. H. Tawney, *Equality*, 1931

'[Of equality, "the central socialist ideal"] By this, I do not mean identical incomes or uniform habits and tastes. But I do mean a classless society – one in which the relations between all people are similar to those hitherto existing between one social class; one in which although there are differences between individuals, there are no feelings of superiority or inferiority between groups . . . one in which, although people develop differently, there is equal opportunity for all to develop.'

Hugh Gaitskell, right-wing Labour leader of the 1950s-early 1960s

'[Detected in socialism] a set of values, of aspirations, of principles, which socialists wish to see embodied in the organisation of society.'

Anthony Crosland, *Socialism Now*, a revisionist work of the 1970s

Clause Four: key elements of the revised version, adopted in 1995

- The Labour Party is a democratic socialist party. It believes that by the strength of our common endeavour we achieve more than we achieve alone so as to create for each of us the means to realise our true potential and for all of us a community in which power, wealth and opportunity are in the hands of the many not the few, where the rights we enjoy reflect the duties we owe, and where we live together freely, in a spirit of solidarity, tolerance and respect.
- To these ends we work for: a dynamic economy . . .

- a just society . . .
- an open democracy . . . a healthy enviromnent . . . Labour is committed to the defence and security of the British people . . .
- Labour will work in pursuit of these aims with trade unions . . .
- On the basis of these principles, Labour seeks the trust of the people to govern.

Blairism
Two features of the new clause reflected the Blairite outlook:

1. The prominence given to enterprise, competition and the free market
2. The moral dimension, with references to personal responsibility, the family and our duty to care for each other.

These reflected two broad streams of influence on Blair's thinking. The first of these was Thatcherism – Tony Blair has been prepared to acknowledge that Margaret Thatcher got some things right, including the pursuit of economic realism and the need for Britain to compete in a global economy without the old protections afforded by state intervention.

The second was a mixture of old and new, and was responsible for the moral side of the Prime Minister's thinking. On the one hand, there were the old traditions of ethical and Christian socialism; on the other, there were the more recent developments in political ideas, known as **Communitarianism** (Etzioni) and the **stakeholder** society as elaborated by Will Hutton.[15]

The Blair approach was a long way from traditional socialism. Some on the Left of the party saw it as little more than Thatcherism with a human face. Even some formerly on the right of the party such as Lord Hattersley lamented that the previous importance attached to equality of outcome had been downgraded to equality of opportunity. But others – including many outside the party – were initially attracted by what Tony Blair called the **Third Way** (see pp. 249–50), a mid-way position between pure capitalism and excessive state control. As he put it:[16] '[Labour] has a social conscience . . . [but] it recognises that we also need economic efficiency, trade unions given their place in our democracy but not confused with government . . . Labour believes in good business as well as a good society.'

values, of aspirations, of principles' (Anthony Crosland,[14] one-time MP and minister). Like Gaitskell, he stressed that there should be equal opportunity for everyone to develop their potential. The Welfare State that the party did much to create embraced many Labour ideas about the importance of society, brotherhood and care for one another.

Following a series of electoral defeats in 1979 and after, Tony Blair set out to reinvent the party as New Labour. He boldly tackled the party's Constitution, rewriting Clause Four so that it now stresses community values such as equality of power, tolerance and respect, rights and duties, the emphasis being on society. He modernised the party, along similar lines to the way in which Bill Clinton had modernised the American Democrats. Its new values were tougher in some areas and on some groups who had traditionally looked to Labour to protect them (such as trade unions and the poor, whom he wished to give 'a hand-up rather than a hand-out').

Blairism in practice: 1994–2007

In opposition before the 1997 election and subsequently, Tony Blair adopted some terminology more usually associated with the Conservatives. He employed terms such as 'the market', 'achievement', 'opportunity' and 'aspirations', his whole approach representing an attempt to broaden Labour's appeal. In the process, his ideas and policies upset many traditional Labour voters who claimed that New Labour was too pro-business and excessively concerned about pleasing Middle England.

A conscious aim of the Blair leadership was to gather many of the moderates in British politics into 'Tony's big tent'. In the process, critics alleged that he had transformed the Labour Party, shifting it not just from a socialist into a social democratic party, but abandoning even social democracy as well. They portrayed him as a modern-day New Liberal of the early twentieth century, the spiritual heir to Lloyd George and Asquith rather than a descendant of the previous post-war Labour prime ministers, Attlee, Wilson and Callaghan.

There was some truth in the analysis, but much of the language of Tony Blair still echoed traditional Labour vocabulary. He talked of community, cooperation, fairness, partnership, society and solidarity.

Some of the actions of his government – constitutional reform, devolution, the introduction of a minimum wage, signature of the Social Chapter, the New Deal work programme and the injection of funding into education and the National Health Service – were very much in the Labour tradition and were policies that Conservatives – even many moderate ones – at the time opposed. In truth, Blair was non-doctrinaire, borrowing from several traditions, socialist, social democratic, New Liberal, pragmatic One Nation Conservative and even Thatcherite, as the circumstances seemed to make appropriate. There was no clear Blairite philosophy; rather, Blairism represented a retreat from ideology.

The decline and defeat of New Labour: what next?

Labour fought the 2005 election on a New Labour manifesto. Although the party won a historic third successive victory, the success was gained on relatively flimsy popular backing. Its share of the vote had declined to 35.2 per cent, only 21.6 per cent of the whole electorate. The result highlighted dissatisfaction with particular policies pursued by New Labour in office. Several measures had alienated sections of the electorate, notably top-up tuition fees; the willingness to use the private sector to support state provision in education and health; and above all the Iraq War. Its coalition of support was fraying, suggesting a need for the party to show greater sensitivity to the views of some people naturally inclined to support Labour.

Blair's successor, *Gordon Brown*, had been a central figure in the New Labour project and there were clear lines of continuity in some of his early statements and the policies of his predecessor. But he tried to dissociate himself from some more unpopular aspects of the Blair premiership. Moreover, his roots belonged to a more traditional Labour background and, if nothing else, the language by which he expressed his progressive views was different.

After initial rises in opinion polls following Gordon Brown's selection as leader, Labour performed poorly in local and European elections in 2009 and in the general election of 2010 suffered its biggest loss of seats (ninety-one) in any election since 1931. Brown was succeeded as Labour leader by Ed Miliband, a left-of-centre social democrat politician who was keen to distance himself from some of the thinking and policies of the New Labour era, but who shared

Box 7.5 Tony Blair and the third way

In Britain, the concept of the third way was most closely associated in academic circles with Anthony Giddens.[17] But the idea of a 'third way' was not entirely new. Harold Macmillan adopted a middle way for the Conservative Party in the 1930s. Essentially the third way was an attempt to find a middle route between Left and Right, between state socialist planning and free market capitalism. It appealed to centre-left progressives and moderate social democrats. Giddens used the term to refer to social democratic renewal. In his view, renewal was necessary in the late 1990s if the Left was to adapt to the probably irreversible transformation of Britain by Thatcherism, the revival of free market capitalism and the realities of globalisation.

The aim of the third way was basically to reject the old left and the new right. Its adherents sought to combine a market economy with a decent society, social justice with economic efficiency. Both markets and state should be disciplined by a public interest test. Legislation should provide redress for consumers and monitor the quality of state services.

Equality was defined as 'inclusion' and inequality as 'exclusion'. Social inclusion referred in its broadest sense to citizenship, with its civil and political rights, its obligations, and its opportunities for self-fulfilment and for all to make a contribution to society. It involved everyone having access to the requirements for a decent life, including education, healthcare, work and income. Measures needed to be put in place to reduce the involuntary exclusion of the disadvantaged. The old social democracy was likely to provide rights unconditionally. In the third way, rights of citizens were accompanied by reciprocal duties and it was vital that there was mutual responsibility between individuals and institutions. For example, parents had the right to send their children to school but they also had a responsibility for encouraging their children and supporting their school.

The third way provided the theoretical basis of the Blair government's thinking and vision for the reshaping of British politics and society. It was also a strategy for creating a new left-of-centre progressive consensus in Britain and elsewhere. Its exponents shared a commitment to practical social democracy. Shunning an excess of ideology, they proclaimed that 'what matters is what works'.

Fate of the third way
The concept of a third way was criticised by many conservatives and libertarians who continued to advocate laissez-faire capitalism.

It was also regaraded with disfavour by many social democrats, democratic socialists and other supporters of state ownership. Many of them saw it as a betrayal of traditional left-wing values. After the Blair premiership had come to an end, even some of his supporters were beginning to question its value as a future guide to policy.

When Tony Blair left office, Anthony Giddens[18] claimed that 'Gordon Brown will be a Third-Wayer – as in fact all successful left-of-centre leaders are today across the world. It doesn't mean he won't look for new policies and make changes. He will have to. As he has said, "mistakes have been made" – not only a catastrophic one in foreign policy [Iraq], but many in domestic policies too. For example, Labour has not made a sufficient impact upon inequality; and Brown will need to look again at the civil liberties question. But he won't abandon the core ideas that have shifted the political complexion of the country.'

A year later, Charles Clarke MP (a prominent ex-minister)[19] saw the need 'to discard the techniques of **"triangulation"** . . . which lead[s] to the not entirely unjustified charge that we simply follow proposals from the Conservatives or the right-wing media, to minimise differences and remove lines of attack against us'.

Others question whether the third way can ever resolve society's problems, for a reason advanced by Clive Hamilton,[20] an Australian analyst of public policy: 'Advocates of the Third Way have searched for a means of grafting traditional concerns for equality and social justice onto an economic system based on free markets. Yet they fail to consider whether attempts at reform are neutralised by the nature of consumer capitalism. The implicit philosophy of the Third Way is not based on any critical analysis of modern capitalism. In particular, it assiduously avoids any discussion of the sources and exercise of power, preferring to focus on "lifestyle choices". The belief that inequality and exclusion can be resolved by education ignores structural disadvantage and emphasises the failings of individuals.'

Hamilton goes further and suggests that there is a good reason why 'the triumph of neo-liberalism and the new right' have led to a widely perceived loss of interest in politics: 'The political ideologies of conservative parties and their social democatic opponents have converged.'

recent Labour commitment to adopting a form of 'capitalism that works for the people'.[21]

David Miliband,[22] the defeated candidate in Labour's internal leadership election and widely seen as a Blairite, said in the campaign: 'New Labour isn't new any more. What I'm interested in is next Labour'. He and the other candidates were desperate to break free from the destructive labels 'Blairite' and 'Brownite', and to move on from New Labour. Ed Miliband, the new Labour leader, said that he wanted to take the party on the path back to his form of socialism. Both Tony Blair and Gordon Brown rarely referred to 'socialism' amid fears it would alienate voters fearful of the left-wing Labour agenda of the early 1980s. However, Miliband insisted that he favours his 'form of socialism, which is a fairer, more just, more equal society. And that is the path that I will want to take our party on.'

The challenges facing Labour are similar to those facing social democratic parties elsewhere. The leadership is grappling with the task of achieving some fusion of the New Labour emphasis on maintaining a broad appeal and an acknowledgement of the need to regain their traditional '**blue Labour**' support. Though some in the Labour movement acknowledge the need to win back middle-ground voters who moved away, many traditionalists are much more interested in remotivating the party's core.

Third and minor parties in Britain and elsewhere

By a *third party*, we usually mean one that is capable of gathering a sizeable percentage of popular support and regularly gains seats in the legislature (e.g. the British Liberal Democrats). On occasion, it may win – or threaten to win – sufficient support to influence the outcome of an election.

By a *minor party*, we mean one that gains only a tiny percentage of popular support and rarely, if ever, gains any representation in the legislature – e.g. the British National Party.

The value of third and minor parties

- *They take up particular causes neglected by the other parties*, such as Prohibition in America or abortion (**Pro-Life Alliance in**

Britain in 1997 and 2001). Similarly, the Greens in many countries give special emphasis to environmental policies.

- *They ventilate certain grievances not being taken up by traditional parties* – as in the case of Plaid Cymru and the SNP, both of which have long argued for more attention to be paid to Welsh and Scottish needs, respectively. The same could be said of far right parties such as the British National Party, which thrives on unease over immigration and race relations. Arguably, it is better that even parties regarded by many people as 'beyond the pale' should be allowed to articulate their cause via the normal political process, for otherwise they might be more tempted by anti-democratic methods.

- *They can act as a haven for protest voters.* The Liberals and their successors have often fulfilled this role in British politics. Such protest can act as a spur to the traditional parties, saving them from apathy and indifference.

- *At times, they may affect the outcome of elections,* perhaps even exercise a balance of power. On rare occasions, a third party has maintained a government in power – e.g. the Liberals in the late 1970s. Liberal Democrat support was necessary for the Conservatives to form a coalition in 2010.

On occasion, third and minor parties have made a major breakthrough. In twentieth-century Britain, Labour came to replace the Liberals as the second party, in the inter-war years. But more often, small parties are doomed to a peripheral role. It may be part of the definition of a party that it seeks political office in order to implement its programme. For most, the hope is illusory. In Britain and America the many minor parties are unlikely ever to gain more than 1 or 2 per cent of the votes in any election.

Party membership and finance

Party membership has been declining in Europe over the last few decades. There are exceptions to the trend such as Greece, Portugal and Spain, but as their peoples were living under or recovering from authoritarian regimes early in this period the comparison is made more complicated. Now living in more open societies, citizens of

Box 7.6 British third and minor parties

The 2010 election confirmed the long-term decline in support for the two main parties and the increasing importance of third and minor parties. More people than ever before (34.9 per cent) voted for a party other than Labour or Conservative. However, the success of the 'other' parties in the European elections and the devolved parliaments was not replicated. A Green was elected, but there was no seat for Respect, the BNP or UKIP and the two independents were defeated.

The Liberal Democrats were the main beneficiaries of the erosion of Conservative and Labour support, winning more than 6.8 million votes. Other parties collectively won 2.8 million.

The Liberal Democrats

The Liberal Democrats were formed as a result of a merger between the old British Liberal Party and the Social Democrats, a breakaway, element from the Labour right. The new party soon established its own identity, but the past commitment to pro-Europeanism, racial justice and tolerance was preserved. Under Paddy Ashdown's leadership, the party moved nearer to the opposition Labour Party, abandoning its former equidistance. Under the leadership of his successor, Charles Kennedy, the Liberal Democrats distanced themselves from ministerial policies, especially as Labour ran into stormy waters. He and other Liberal Democrats criticised the timidity of the Prime Minister in not giving a clear lead in favour of Britain's early membership of the Euro. They reserved their most profound criticism for the conduct of events leading to the Iraq War, deeply uneasy as they were about the decision to embark on hostilities.

In electoral terms, the party has fared well in recent elections. In 2005, it won nearly 6 million votes (22 per cent), its sixty-two MPs being a higher total than at any time since 1923. In spite of losing five seats in 2010, it found itself in government, its leader Nick Clegg becoming Deputy Prime Minister. Political commentators have identified Clegg's leadership as promoting a shift to the radical centre in the Liberal Democrat Party, placing more emphasis on economic than on social liberalism.

Other parties

Whereas the Liberal Democrats are a third force to be reckoned with, having substantial parliamentary representation, the other

UK-wide parties have much less popular support and rarely gain any representation. Yet they do articulate the thinking of a section of the voters. The *British National Party* attracts much of its support from poor whites, who see their position threatened by the post-war influx of Commonwealth immigrants and asylum-seekers. It tends to do well in areas with relatively large Asian or Muslim populations, such as the East End of London, the West Midlands and some of the northern towns such as Oldham. In 2010, it put up significantly more candidates than in 2005 and won 1.9 per cent of the popular vote. This represented an average of 3.8 per cent of the share of the vote in the seats it actually fought, down on the 4.3 per cent achieved five years earlier.

One of the fast-growing parties in Britain is the *UK Independence Party*, committed to outright withdrawal from the European Union. From 1994, it has put up a candidate in every parliamentary by-election and gained a strong result in the 2004 Euro-elections. It put up 558 candidates in 2010, the largest minor party challenge ever to be mounted in the UK. At 3.2 per cent, it also scored the strongest percentage of the overall vote achieved by any minor party, but it failed to get any representation in the House.

On the Left, the *Socialist Labour Party* (SLP) comprises many ex-Labour members who came to find Blairism unpalatable. Members of *Respect*, a far-left coalition of the Trotskyite Socialist Workers Party, some Muslim groups and remnants of Old Labour, echo such distaste for the direction followed by New Labour. All of these groups strongly disapproved of Western military involvement in Iraq, a cause that had lost much of its resonance by 2010. Neither the SLP nor Respect made any significant headway in 2010, fielding only three and eleven candidates, respectively, and each winning around 0.1 per cent of the total votes cast.

The *Greens*, primarily an ecological party, have tried to broaden their appeal by taking up other policy themes in recent years. Following their success in getting two MEPs elected in 2009, they succeeded in winning their first parliamentary seat a year later. However, in spite of the increased number of candidates (335), the party's share of the popular vote dropped by 0.1 per cent to 1 per cent compared to five years earlier.

Of the other parties, the nationalists are by far the most important. The *Scottish Nationalist Party* is a separatist party, wanting independence from Great Britain. It is now the second largest party in Scotland, after Labour. It does not emphasise the usual cultural nationalism of parties of the nationalist type. By contrast, *Plaid Cymru* has always been a more traditional nationalist party, speaking up for the culture and language of Wales. This has tended to limit its appeal to Welsh-speaking areas, although there are signs in the Welsh National Assembly elections that the party is now extending its support into the southern valleys.

Both the SNP and Plaid Cymru are pro-European and have contested European elections keenly. They have done relatively well in these and the devolved elections, helped by the use of proportional voting systems. In the 2010 general election, they won six and three seats respectively.

these countries have taken the opportunity to benefit from their newly won freedom.

The UK now has one of the lowest rates of party membership among established and more recently established European democracies, as the figures in Table 7.1 indicate. Among EU countries, only Latvia and Poland have a lower percentage membership.

Some writers see declining membership as an indication of a lessening of enthusiasm for and interest in political parties. They point to the loss of members by established parties and adversely compare it to the growth in pressure group activity. Membership figures of leading pressure groups, particularly those in the environmental sector, have been impressive in comparison with those for political parties. (The RSPCA claims more than one million members.)

The low figures quoted for party membership may also reflect the fact that parties today spend less time on recruiting than in the past, for they once needed activists to engage in voluntary work and rally the local voters to turn out in support of their candidate. Nowadays, the 'nationalisation' of election campaigning has placed more emphasis on the whereabouts of party leaders and their senior colleagues. Finally, there may be too many other things that people can do with their time; for many, politics is a lower priority than once it was, perhaps because many of the 'big issues' of world peace and hunger have lost much of their impact on the European continent.

In explaining membership trends, Pattie et al.[23] point out that they have not been consistently downwards since the 1980s. Parties can boost their membership, particularly if they offer sufficient incentives. In Scandinavia the social democratic parties engaged in a drive for recruitment in the early 1990s. New Labour enthusiasts,

Table 7.1 Party membership in European democracies

2008: membership as percentage of electorate

Austria	17.3
Greece	6.6
Slovenia	6.3
Italy	5.6
Belgium	5.5
Norway	5.0
Portugal	3.8
Lithuania	2.7
Ireland	2.0
United Kingdom	1.2

Adapted from I. Van Biezen, P. Mair and T. Poguntke, 'Declining party membership in Europe', *European Journal of Political Research*, www.eui.eu/ Projects/, 2011.

under the leadership of a young, telegenic figure, initially saw it as essential to create a mass membership, at a time when its trade union links were being downplayed. However, in the case of New Labour, the growth in membership was an impressive blip in a broadly downward trend. It was short-lived, for within a year or two of Labour being elected the decline resumed.

Leiprakobsup[24] distinguishes two sets of explanations for membership decline, those based on sociological factors and those based on individual choice (rational-individual decisions). He stresses the importance of broad societal trends. He makes the point that parties and party systems in Western Europe derive from historically ideological and cultural conflict based on social cleavages and that parties have traditionally mobilised citizens along the demographic or social cleavage line. With the decline of these cleavages (e.g. social class in the UK), a factor beyond the parties' control, it is perhaps inevitable that people feel less allegiance with the party that traditionally represents their grouping.

Table 7.2 Membership trends of the three main British parties, 1951–2008

Year	Conservative	Labour	Liberal Democrat
1950–1	2,900,000	876,000	
1970–1	1,340,000	680,000	
1980–1	1,200,000	348,000	
1990–1	1,000,000	261,000	91,000
2000–1	311,000	272,000	73,000
2008	250,000	166,000	60,000

Source: J. Marshall, *Membership of UK political parties*, House of Commons Library, 2009.

NB The figures for the Conservatives are in most cases 'best estimates'. In *The Conservative Party from Thatcher to Cameron*, Polity Press, 2011, Bale estimates combined party membership in 2010 at a little over 400,000. Figures declared on their websites by the SNP and Plaid Cymru for 2008 were 15,100 and 10,000, respectively.

Finance

The role of money in political life is an issue of daily debate in old and new democracies alike. It is the driving force for modern competitive political systems, a point recognised some decades ago by a Californian politician, Jesse Unruh, who described it as 'the mother's milk of politics'. Party financing is a vital aspect of modern party politics. The ways in which parties get access to money can influence the outcome of elections, determine the relationship between party leaders and members, affect the number of women elected and condition the level of public trust as a whole. Parties everywhere are finding difficultly in raising sufficient income to meet increased costs.

The widespread fall in figures for party membership has implications for party finances. In many European countries, the decline in income from membership has been compensated for by the establishment of some form of state funding of party activity. Such aid is normally unconditional, being dependent upon the support achieved in the previous election. German parties receive generous subsidies that often constitute well over a quarter of their income.

Among Anglo-Saxon countries, Australia, Canada and the United States have seen state funding as a necessity to bridge the gap between the expenditure that is necessary for political purposes and the funds raised from voluntary donations to parties and candidates. America has a scheme of federal funding for candidates willing to accept strict limits upon raising and spending corporate money. It is conditional aid, the amount being triggered by the decisions of private individuals. Political finance is almost completely candidate-oriented, whereas in Canada and the UK in particular, campaigns are run predominantly by parties.

Parties receive funding from three main sources, other than by public subsidy:

- Subscriptions from individual party members
- Donations, either from companies or from individuals (sometimes these are one-off sums from generous benefactors or take the form of bequests)
- Contributions from associated bodies, such as affiliated trade unions.

Many people feel uneasy about huge contributions from wealthy businessmen, particularly those who reside outside the country concerned. However, it is the income from business organisations and trade unions that generates the greatest anxiety. There is a common perception that 'he who pays the piper calls the tune'; money may be given not just because an organisation shares the broad outlook of the party it is backing, but in the hope and anticipation that decisions taken by ministers will be favourable to it.

The finance of British parties

Operating a political party is an expensive enterprise. British parties need funding for four main categories of expenditure:

- *Maintaining headquarters* – day-to-day running costs and an administrative machine to deal with relations with branches who need back-up support. In particular, as far as the public is concerned, the educational work of the parties is important. They conduct research and produce pamphlets, contributing to broader political understanding.

- *Reserve funds* – to deal with any emergency that may arise, such as repairs to central headquarters.
- *Campaign costs* – fighting general and other elections requires heavy spending on propaganda, speaking tours and the services of sophisticated agencies and political consultants, to help get the message across. With the advent of European, devolved and mayoral elections, the campaigning costs have significantly increased in recent years.
- *Local constituencies* – these have their own expenses, again maintaining headquarters, printing leaflets and meeting costs incurred in fighting the constituency election campaign.

The finance of British parties has been more tightly regulated in recent years, following the publication of a special report of the Neill Committee on Standards in Public Life (1998). Labour broadly accepted its recommendations and embodied many of them in its Political Parties, Elections and Referendums Act (2000). Among other things, this Act imposed a ceiling on general election expenditure, currently fixed at £20 million.

The three main parties all have financial problems and are prone to heavy indebtedness. In the Blair era, Labour found itself heavily reliant on gifts from corporations and wealthy individuals. The Conservatives have a small number of donors who substantially fund their election campaigns. They all need money from sources that do not undermine the integrity of the political process. Many academics and commentators have pointed to state funding in other developed countries as the way forward for Britain (see Box 7.7). The concept is supported by Labour and the Liberal Democrats, both of whom have most to gain from such an experiment.

In Britain, recent surveys suggest that the vast majority of the public is currently against the funding of political parties by taxpayer's money. An Ipsos MORI poll for The Electoral Commission published in October 2006 found that 13 per cent favoured full state funding, 24 per cent favoured full funding from private donations and 25 per cent preferred parties to be funded equally from public

Table 7.3 Incomes and spending of the three main parties, 2010 (£)

a. Donations received

Party	Donations
Conservative	31,783,476
Labour	19,861,173
Liberal Democrat	4,889,221
Plaid Cymru	142,415
Scottish National Party	353,590

NB These figures do not include all donations accepted by political parties. The law requires political parties only to report donations above £7,500 to the party HQ and above £1,500 to the party's accounting units.

b. Public funds received

Party	Short money (House of Commons)	Cranborne money (House of Lords)	Financial assistance to parties (Scottish Parliament)	Policy development grants (Electoral Commission)	Total
Conservative	1,640,775	253,910	66,003	28,230	1,988,918
Labour	3,685,125	195,140	319,807	155,773	4,355,846
Liberal Democrat	595,976	85,377	105,114	459,371	1,245,837
Plaid Cymru	45,525	0	0	158,722	202,474
Scottish National Party	127,858	0	0	178,386	306,244

c. Total spending in the general election

Party	Spending
Conservative	16,682,874
Labour	8,009,483

Table 7.3 (continued)	
Party	**Spending**
Liberal Democrat	4,787,595
Plaid Cymru	144,933
Scottish National Party	315,776

Source: all figures adapted from those provided by the Electoral Commission.

money and private donations. The belief that parties should stand on their own financial feet is underlined by the third of voters who feel it would not harm the democratic process if political parties were allowed to go bankrupt. On the other hand, there is also strong support for the principle that people should have the right to make donations to parties they support.

Party organisation: general trends

In the last few decades, there have been developments in party organisation. Originally spurred on by the creation of a mass electorate in the days when universal franchise was granted, parties saw the need to create national and local organisations to ensure that they were in a position to maximise their support. They needed to raise funds, organise canvassing and provide opportunities for the new voters to become involved, among other things. Usually the organisation operated on a top down basis, under which national organisations were created and they were given the task of supervising the activities of local branches established throughout the country. Decisions were taken at the centre, and policy statements and lists of likely candidates were handed down to the local associations where much of the day-to-day voluntary work of mobilising the voters was carried out.

This pattern has been less evident in recent years. Older parties have had to adapt to changing conditions, and the arrival of television has, as we have seen, made local organisation less essential; indeed, some party associations have lapsed to such an extent that they have effectively disappeared, only to be briefly resurrected at

Box 7.7 State funding in Britain: for and against

For

- The nub of the case in favour of political funding is concerned with the importance of party activity to the democratic process. Political parties and their competition for political power are essential for sustainable democracy and good governance. Visible party competition requires well-entrenched political parties that need to be encouraged to develop and strengthen. Adequate resources are required for necessary activities.

- It would reduce the excessive dependence of the two main parties on their large institutional backers, companies in the case of the Conservative Party and companies and trade unions in the case of Labour. State funding avoids the perception that wealthy backers are able to buy influence over the operations of a political party.

- Parties of the Centre-Left tend to be at a disadvantage with those of the right, for they do not have the means to compete. Labour still derives much of its strength from the inner cities, where voters tend to be relatively poor. By contrast, many Conservative voters are more affluent and can afford to be more generous in their political giving. They are also more likely to join a political party. Working people do not tend to be 'joiners' of organisations to the same extent. The difficulties of poorly funded parties are compounded when several elections arise together as in 1979 and 1997, making the annual costs of electioneering high.

- The principle of some state assistance to British political parties has already been conceded. Help is given to opposition parties (in the form of 'Short' and 'Cranborne' money) to assist them in the performance of their parliamentary work, and at election time facilities are made available to them at no cost. The amount of money involved in terms of government spending on such assistance is small. By ensuring that payment is dependent on a certain level of success in the last election, the difficulty of the state financing small and extreme parties such as the Communists or the British National Party is removed.

Against

Critics of state funding tend to emphasise these arguments:

- Politics is essentially a voluntary activity. If parties are currently short of funds, then they must either curtail their costs or seek funds in other ways such as more local fund-raising by volunteer workers. With state funding available, there would be little incentive for parties to go out and recruit a mass membership.

- The decline in membership and waning popularity of the two main parties suggests that they are not as popular as they once were. The answer is that they need to pursue policies more in tune with the needs and wishes of the voters. When they are perceived as being 'in touch', they will be more attractive to voters who are potential recruits.

- Taxpayers who are not interested in politics might resent being asked to finance party activity. Cynicism and disillusion with politicians are widely prevalent. They would be increased if the public was expected to spend money on their activities. Sceptics might suspect that any extra money be spent on needless extravagances, such as glossy brochures and advertising material.

- Popular support for state funding has often increased when corruption seems to be all-pervasive, but there is little evidence that state funding ends corruption, and some people even argue that it can increase rather than diminish it. In Italy, assistance was initially introduced in 1974 to reduce the bribery and scandals so endemic in political life; by 1993, as details of illegal payments and the abuse of power were exposed, it was dropped because of its misuse. Other countries that have state aid – France, Germany and Spain among them – have also experienced financial improprieties.

- 'The time is not ripe', in a period of recession. (For many voters it never will be. Subsidising parties seems a low priority in good or bad times.)

election time. In Britain, Labour has been concerned to modernise its image and organisation, and the Conservatives in opposition engaged in an overhaul of their traditional approach, streamlining the party and making it more open in its operations. In both cases there has been a new emphasis on making the party more democratic in the sense that members should have a greater say in how the party functions, whilst also seeking to ensure that the leadership retains key powers to act to keep out dissidents who might bring discredit on the organisation. In Europe and in America too, parties have seen the importance of employing new techniques to galvanise the electorate via mass mailings and other devices. The US parties have been effective in using the modern technology of campaigning and in mastering complicated laws that affect how money is raised and spent. Since the 1980s, they have employed a substantial professional staff to conduct such activities.

Newer parties are wary of formal party organisation, seeing it as a means of stifling dissent or ignoring the views of party supporters. They have been more democratic in their workings from the beginning. Green parties in most countries have tended to shun the central control associated with established parties, and often operate more informally via a network of informal local organisations. In as much as they need leadership, they have sometimes been willing to experiment with new forms, such as having joint leaders or a troika of decision-makers. The emphasis has been on democratic consultation with the membership, rather than on strong leadership that manipulates the rules to keep decision-making effectively in its own hands.

The experience of the new democracies of Central and Eastern Europe has been of interest to those studying political parties. Once the old systems of state control disappeared, the formation of parties was an early priority, a point to bear in mind when considering whether parties are generally losing their importance. In several cases, the pro-democracy movement soon split once freedom was achieved, and several strands of party opinion appeared. They dominated the early elections, but within a few years the discredited communists reappeared and regrouped. They benefited from the fact that they had a long history during which they had a network of branches, members and lists of former members. By contrast, the new 'freedom' parties lacked such organisational assets, and having only a central organisation they failed to mobilise all of their potential support.

The organisation of British political parties

In studying party organisation, the key issue is where power resides. The two parties are organised very differently, reflecting their different origins. The Conservatives developed as a party at Westminster back in the early nineteenth century, before the extension of the vote to working people. Once the franchise was extended, they needed to ensure that their MPs were supported by a network of local associations to organise support within the constituencies. They developed a Central Office to act as the professional headquarters of the party.

Central Office controls the activities of the provincial areas and the constituency agents. But such organisation, local, regional and national, was there to serve the parliamentary party and the leadership. The leader's influence over the machine has always been a strong one, it was his or her personal machine to help the occupant pursue the desired goals and prepare the party for election success.

Labour originated outside Parliament, and developed out of the wish of trade unions, early socialist societies and others to get working people elected into Parliament. Its 1918 Constitution made provision for the control of the party by the extra-parliamentary elements. In other words, the party in Parliament was made responsible to the party outside. Labour was therefore keen to avoid a focus on the figure of the party leader. The affiliated organisations, the constituency Labour parties and the parliamentary party are all important elements in what is a federal structure.

Both parties have several tiers in which people can be active, local, regional and national. They may join the local party organisation as fee-paying members and participate in its political and social activities within the constituency, ranging from fund-raising to canvassing and distributing party literature. Labour associations have affiliated organisations, including trade unions, socialist societies and young socialists. Party members have a voice in the selection of the constituency candidate, when a vacancy occurs. Periodically, they will also have a chance to take part in a leadership election, when there is a contest for the top position. This is the grassroots level of party organisation, the party in the country.

One of the pleasures for grassroots members is the opportunity to attend the annual party conference.

Party conferences in Britain

The party conference is the most important annual gathering of the Conservatives and provides the main forum for the expression of opinion by all sections of the party. It serves as a rally of the faithful who enjoy the opportunity to vent their feelings and urge the party forward. Representatives of the constituency associations have complete freedom to speak and vote as they choose. They are not delegates committed to act in a certain way.

The agenda is carefully controlled and only rarely are formal votes taken at the conclusion of a debate. Revolts can occur over sensitive issues such as Europe, immigration and law and order, on all of which forthright views are held. However, many debates are anodyne and in any case they are only advisory, having no binding effect on the people at the top. However, the conference sets a mood and a wise leadership will take its view into account. Today, there are more revolts than in the past, along with stronger expression of feeling, but this is combined with a strong sense of deference to the leader.

By contrast with the Conservatives, the Labour conference was given the supreme function of directing and controlling the affairs of the party. The 1918 Constitution established that party policy is the responsibility of conference and that decisions taken by a two-thirds majority are supposed to be regarded as sacrosanct and included in the next manifesto. However, although opposition leaders pay greater respect to the sanctity of such decisions, Labour prime ministers have often treated them in a more cavalier manner.

The role and significance of the Labour conference has long been a matter of controversy and academic debate. Strong leaders, even in opposition, can override its decisions if they have the backing of the National Executive Committee, the administrative authority of the party that acts as the guardian of conference decisions. As the unions have lost much of their former status in the party and the Left has been effectively sidelined in recent years, so conference has lost much of its former status. It has a diminished role, for the modernisation of the last decade or more has seen the development of alternative sources of power and influence. In particular, the centralisation of the party structure around the leader, his office and entourage, has concentrated media attention on the person at the helm. Prior to the 1997 election, when there was a scent of victory in the area, delegates were reluctant to rock the party votes in front of the television cameras. From time to time, reassertions of conference's authority may occur, but more generally the tendency is to listen to and applaud appearances by the party luminaries.

In both parties, conferences are now heavily stage-managed. The leaderships are conscious of the television coverage they receive and speeches are seen as a chance to communicate directly with the public as well as a chance to address an audience at Blackpool or Bournemouth.

Party leaders: how the main British parties choose them

There have been changes to the way in which both main parties choose their leader over recent decades. Labour reformed its selection process in 1981 and the Conservatives did the same twenty years later. In both cases, the membership now has a say in the choice and there is provision to rid the party of an unwanted incumbent. Labour's arrangements are more complex because it has the membership of trade unions and its other affiliated bodies to consider. In either party, a leadership contest enables the party to resolve issues of personality, as well as party policy and direction.

The Conservatives
The sitting leader can be challenged if 15 per cent of the MPs in the parliamentary party express their lack of support for the leader. They do so by signing an open letter to the chairman of the backbench 1922 Committee. The leader needs to win 50 per cent plus one in a secret ballot on a motion of confidence in his leadership. Should he or she fail, then he or she is excluded from the contest. At this stage, other candidates step forward. The parliamentary party holds as many rounds as it takes to choose two candidates, with the worst performing MP eliminated from each ballot. Then, the party members vote and the candidate with the greater number of votes wins. If a vacancy occurs because of the resignation or death of the incumbent, then the parliamentary party moves straight into a series of ballots of MPs.

Following the third successive electoral defeat in 2005, some leading Conservatives were keen to downgrade the role of members of the party in the choice of leader. However, there was grass-roots resistance to any change. Accordingly, the election of David Cameron was conducted under the same method as was used to elect Iain Duncan Smith. Party members voted for Cameron by a decisive margin of 134,446 to 64,398 votes.

Table 7.4 The Conservative system in operation: the choice in 2005

Round one: votes of MPs	Round two: votes of MPs
Cameron 56	Cameron 90
Clarke 38	Davis 57
Davis 62	Fox 51
Fox 42	

Round three: votes of party members, November–December 2005

Cameron 67.6%

Davis 32.4%

Labour

Labour uses an Electoral College to choose its leader. It includes a 33 per cent share for each of the Parliamentary Labour Party, the party members and the trade unions, which form an integral part of the party structure.

Those MPs who wish to become leader need 12.5 per cent of Labour MPs to back them if there is a vacancy or 20 per cent if there is a challenge to a sitting leader. To be elected, a candidate needs to receive an absolute majority of the votes cast. If no one achieves this, then further ballots are held on an elimination basis. To avoid repeated balloting, voters are asked to express second and third preferences.

In 1994, the procedure worked relatively smoothly to elect Tony Blair who won a majority in each of the three elements of the party vote. He received 57 per cent of the vote overall, out of 952,109 votes cast. At the time, the election was widely seen as the biggest democratic exercise in European party politics, giving the winner what his admirers called 'a million vote mandate'. Nonetheless, some people within the party were keen to see the College abandoned and a more straightforward system of 'one person, one vote' adopted, in which each vote counted equally.

Table 7.5 The Labour system in operation: the choice in 2010 (%)

Candidate	Round one	Round two	Round three	Round four
Abbott	7.42			
Balls	11.79	13.23	16.02	
Burnham	8.68	10.41		
Miliband D.	37.78	38.89	42.72	49.35
Miliband E.	34.33	37.47	41.26	50.65

NB Ed Miliband's victory in the final round was based on his support in sections two and three of the Electoral College, the party members and the affiliated members, respectively. David Miliband and Ed Miliband received the backing of 140 (17.81%) and 122 (15.52%) MPs/MEPs in section one, respectively.

The same system was, however, used to elect Ed Miliband. In the first three rounds of voting, David Miliband was ahead. It was only when votes were reallocated as the other candidates were knocked out that his younger brother was pushed over the winning line, in round four.

This is probably not the definitive Labour scheme. That would be for all members of the Labour Party, either those who pay the levy-plus through their union or who join the party directly, to have a vote on the choice of leader. There would be no Electoral College, but a large mass party with an increased membership. That would be a genuine 'one man one vote' approach.

The Liberal Democrats
The Liberals were the first party to involve party members in the choice. Under the Constitution of the Liberal Democrats, the candidate for the leadership must be nominated and proposed by two other MPs and supported by at least 200 members in no less than twenty local parties. The leader is elected by a simple 'one person, one vote' method of all members, including of course MPs. The system, used to elect Paddy Ashdown, Charles Kennedy and Nick Clegg, worked smoothly on each occasion.

The powers and security of party leaders

Any leader of a main political party in a two-party system is either an actual or potential prime minister. As such, he or she is bound to have great authority, for either now or in the future, there will be a chance to distribute ministerial offices and make or break the careers of rivals.

The opposition leader is a key figure. Traditionally, he or she has been more powerful in the Conservative Party, although the experience of recent years points the other way: Neil Kinnock and Tony Blair operated a highly centralised system of control and leaders from Hague to Howard had some difficulties in establishing their undisputed authority. More recently, whereas Ed Miliband's early authority and leadership have been questioned, that of David Cameron from 2005–10 was widely seen as generally successful in establishing his personal ascendancy, though on the right of the party there was a dislike of his willingness to abandon traditional party beliefs and impose his own vision of a more modern Conservative party. In the words of ex-Thatcherite minister, Lord Tebbit,[25] he was behaving like Pol Pot (a former Cambodian communist dictator), 'intent on purging even the memory of Thatcherism before building a New Modern Compassionate Green Globally Aware Party'.

If the party leader becomes prime minister, he or she may become so powerful that writers describe Britain as having 'prime ministerial government' or 'government by prime minister' (see pp. 128–34).

The Conservatives

At face value the Conservative leader has enormous power. Many years ago, Robert McKenzie[26] described the incumbent as possessing greater authority and being subject to less restraint than his or her counterpart in any other democratic country. The leadership was once described by the American writer, Austin Ranney,[27] as 'one of autocracy tempered by advice and information'.

In particular, the leader has exclusive responsibility for writing the election manifesto and formulating party policy, does not have to attend meetings of the 1922 Committee of Conservative backbench MPs, has enormous control over the activities of Central Office and the party machine, appoints (and dismisses) the party chairman, vice chairman and treasurer and chooses the Cabinet or shadow Cabinet. This is an important package of powers, recognition of the fact that the party embraces the idea of strong leadership, having grown up as a part within the House of Commons and wanting to see a powerful leader who could espouse the party cause and dominate the chamber.

Yet the position is one of leadership by consent and there is ample precedent for power melting away and that consent being withdrawn. This is particularly the case when the party is in opposition, although the experiences of Margaret Thatcher (challenged in 1989 and 1990 and forced out of office) and John Major (challenged in 1995) suggest that even a Conservative prime minister is not as secure as a formal reading of the leader's powers would suggest.

When the party has been defeated in an election or appears to be making little electoral headway, it can act harshly against its leaders and make them scapegoats for failure. It likes, and has in the past been used to, electoral success. Several leaders have lost the support of MPs and been under pressure to go, including William Hague following the 2001 defeat and Iain Duncan Smith who never even had the opportunity to lead his party into an election. After the defeat in 2005, Michael Howard soon announced that he would be standing down (on grounds of age) once the party had rethought the process for choosing a new leader.

Since 1945, the Conservatives are on their eleventh leader. Recent experience suggests that they have found it difficult to find a strong figure who can unite the party, impart vigour to its performance and achieve electoral success. Generally speaking, parties accept strong leaders when they are delivering the goods (electoral success or the prospect of it). If that strength shows signs of becoming too overbearing and particularly when electoral success is proving elusive, a reaction sets in. The leaders then need to watch their backs. Having led the party out of its electoral wilderness, the present incumbent – whatever criticisms may be voiced about him – is unlikely to face a threat to his leadership in the early years of his premiership.

Labour

Labour originally had a chairman of the Labour MPs in the House of Commons, but no leader. It only appointed a leader when it had become a party large enough to mount a significant electoral challenge to the Conservatives and Liberals. The way the party developed and a bad experience of excessive leadership power in 1931 combined to make party members reluctant to recognise the supremacy of the leader over the Labour movement. They have always wanted to ensure that he or she is accountable.

Accordingly, the 1918 Constitution imposed restrictions on the power of the leader, in order to ensure his subservience to the party in Parliament and to the mass organisation outside. Leaders have to attend backbench meetings of the Parliamentary Labour Party (PLP), (in opposition) work with a shadow Cabinet the membership of which has been elected by MPs, implement policies in line with conference decisions, attend conference and give an annual report of their stewardship. They also lack the control over the affairs of the party organisation that Conservative leaders possess.

Yet in recent years, Labour leaders have become markedly more dominant than this portrayal suggests and the leadership has accumulated ever-greater power. The process gathered pace under Neil Kinnock who did much to weaken internal opposition. In the Blair era, the leadership maintained an iron grip, so that dissident voices were weeded out, the union ties loosened and power concentrated in the leader's hands. Starved of victory for many years, many Labour members were for a long time willing to give Blair a remarkably free hand, although as he became more out of touch with grassroots opinion on issues such as the Iraq War, they lamented the centralisation of power. He strained the bounds of party loyalty by many of the policies that he adopted.

The Labour Party has been less severe on its leaders than the Conservatives, many of them enjoying a lengthy period of service. It shows less brutality to those who lead it, so that although there were often mutterings about the performances of Neil Kinnock in the House and real doubts about whether he was an electoral asset, talk of a replacement was infrequent. He easily survived a challenge to his position in 1988.

In the case of Tony Blair, his success in three general elections cushioned him against any threat to his leadership for several years. He became less of an asset as disillusion with the Iraq War, the 'cash for honours' embarrassment and the party's declining fortunes became more widespread. In September 2006, a letter signed by seventeen Labour MPs called for him to resign. Shortly afterwards, he announced to the annual conference that it would be the last he would attend as leader. He finally stepped down in June 2007, after concerted pressure from several **Brownites** and others for him to relinquish office.

Gordon Brown never experienced electoral success as party leader and by the time he had finally entered Downing Street, the party's fortunes were in decline and many voters felt it was 'time for a change'. Between the end of 2007 and September 2008, his popularity declined significantly and his position came increasingly under threat after the May 2009 expenses scandal and Labour's poor results in the 2009 local and European elections. Brown faced a second assault on his leadership in January 2010, but he survived and later led his party into the election. When the outcome was a hung Parliament, he announced his intention to resign on 10th May 2010 in order to help broker a Labour-Liberal Democrat deal. However, as this became increasingly unlikely, he announced his resignation as Prime Minister and leader of the Labour Party. He never benefited from Labour's traditional indulgence of leaders, even in tough times.

The decline of political parties: do they still matter?

Some writers point to a crisis in party politics, noting the decline in party membership, increasing partisan dealignment and the rise of extremist parties. Parties such as those of the Far Right in many parts of Europe are sometimes labelled 'antiparty parties', in that they aim to subvert traditional party politics, rejecting parliamentary compromise and emphasising popular mobilisation.

Established parties in several countries are finding their task more difficult. They have been the victims of public disillusion, as voters compare the promise and performance of parties in government. They have also lost support because many young people especially feel that they do not speak about issues that matter to them. Their ideas seem less relevant to a post-materialist society. On topics such as animal rights, gender, nuclear power and the environment, pressure groups articulate popular feeling more successfully than parties.

Why have traditional parties lost some of their support?

- *Single issue protest politics seem more relevant and exciting*, particularly to the young. They seem to prefer more loosely organised, less authoritarian and centralised, parties, compared with the oligarchical established parties whose membership is often inactive or engaged in dull, routine tasks.
- *Traditional parties having served in office – and the politicians who represent them – have been tainted by power and lost their freshness and appeal.* They are seen as sleazy, jaded failures, sometimes prone to lapses of financial probity. They have often been unable to make their performances match up to the promises once made and have lost respect.
- *Perhaps countries are today more difficult to govern.* People have high expectations which politicians find it hard to match, because often their capacity to influence events in an age of globalisation is strictly limited.

Blondel[28] finds that the prospects for parties are less bleak in the Scandinavian countries than elsewhere. For the rest of continental Europe, he believes that the loss of support is clearly perceptible, and that 'the representation of interests and views is increasingly provided by groups which are closer to the people than parties'. He distinguishes between the situation in continental Europe and that in the USA, and notes that in the West there are three distinct scenarios:

1. Traditional parties have lost ground to newer parties that seem to be more attuned to the people's interests, resulting in the formation of more significant parties and no one party emerging with 'a true grip on political life'.
2. In Britain and older Commonwealth countries, this outcome has largely been avoided, because of their attachment to the FPTP electoral system.
3. In America, parties have a more symbolic role. They do not

propose programmes; they do not even select candidates, since these are in effect chosen by **primaries** which are outside the control of party leaders.

It is possible to exaggerate the extent of party decline. Party systems have always undergone change, with new ones emerging to replace those that have lost their original justification. In emerging democracies, new parties have been created, and the removal of dictatorships in Greece, Portugal and Spain inspired a growth of new organisations, as did the breakdown of communist rule in Eastern Europe. There have, it is true, been shifts of support in an increasingly volatile age, and inevitably recently established parties in long-standing democracies have had to pick up their support from existing ones.

Party fortunes are generally in a state of flux. Budge et al.[29] make the valid point that electorates in Europe have been broadly stable in the Left-Right allegiance, and that there has been no sign of a dramatic shift from one end of the spectrum to the other side. Rather, it has been a case of 'significantly shifting support' between Left and Right parties as blocks. On the right, for example, there has been an erosion of support for traditional parties balanced by a growth of right-wing, nationalistic ones. Such splintering has been apparent in several internal elections but also in recent European elections.

The case of Italy

In twentieth-century Italian politics, several parties emerged to represent different political traditions and personalities. They benefited from the proportional electoral system that encouraged small party representation in the Chamber of Deputies. In the absence of a few strong parties, coalitions were inevitable, so that for several decades after 1945 Italy was regarded as a byword for governmental instability. This was the period when the centre-right Roman Catholic Christian Democrats dominated the political landscape, serving in every administration. Appealing widely to all anti-communists (the communists were the second largest party), the party retained office via its generous use of patronage.

Italy experienced a massive change in its party system in the early 1990s, with the collapse of its dominant party system. Of the traditional adversaries, the Christian Democrats vanished and the communists reformed as the Democratic Party of the Left (PDS). In their place, two loose 'umbrella' groupings were formed under the influence of high-profile personalities such as Silvio Berlusconi, Prime Minister on three occasions before his downfall in 2011 and replacement by the technocratic Mario Monti.

In the Berlusconi era, power was in effect contested by two broad coalitions of the Centre-Left and Centre-Right, which brought together several – often small – parties. Various factions combined to bring down the long-serving Prime Minister, as he struggled to survive corruption scandals and an economic storm.

Italian parties lack ideological cohesion and a mass membership. They take the form of 'shells for ambitious politicians' and 'parties are more like campaigning institutions before elections than permanent institutions propagating ideology'.[30]

The case of the USA

From a historical and international perspective, American political parties have always seemed weak. They have never had the solid class-based electoral support common in other developed countries. Given the weakness of party discipline in the United States, they have never been sure that they could turn any detailed policy commitments into legislative effect. Maidment and McGrew[31] regard them as 'vast and disparate coalitions with no coherent sets of beliefs'.

Various factors explain the historical weakness of American parties, notably:

- *the federal system of government*, which means that the attitudes adopted in each party vary from state to state
- *the operation of separation of powers*, which encourages members of all parties in Congress to act as a watchdog in the Constitution, even checking the actions of a president with whom they are in nominal political agreement
- *the notion of consensus in American politics*; both Democrats and

Republicans subscribe to the ideals of the 'American Creed', liberty, equality, individualism, democracy and the rule of law
• *the ethos of individualism in American society*, which stresses the role of the individual citizen in shaping his/her own destiny.

For much of the twentieth century, the parties were even weaker, because of: the growing use of primary elections; the development of the mass media, which placed more emphasis on candidate-centred electioneering; the arrival of new issue such as civil rights, feminism and Vietnam on the agenda in the 1960s and 1970s, which cut across the party divide; the increasing importance of pressure groups and Political Action Committees which meant that there were more causes in which Americans could participate and alternative bodies for fund-raising for candidates; and the breakdown of traditional allegiances among sections of the electorate and a growth of volatility in voting behaviour. However, in the closing two decades there were indications of renewal. In particular, party organisation became more effective, as first the Republicans and shortly afterwards the Democrats saw the potential of high-tech fund-raising. Hence Herrnson's[32] observation that: 'The parties' national, congressional and senatorial campaign committees are now wealthier, more stable, better organised and better staffed than ever before.'

Parties have shown a greater ability in recent years to raise money by new techniques of fund-raising and have become more organised at the federal level. Moreover, some of the 'new issues' have lost much of their earlier impact. For all of their alleged weaknesses, parties have not been displaced. They:

• still serve as a reference point for the voters, the bulk of whom still think in terms of Republicans and Democrats
• remain a reference point for presidential candidates and congressmen, almost every one of whom belongs to one of the major parties.

• •

✓ What you should have learnt from reading this chapter

• Most political parties have not been stable over a long period. Stability is associated more with the Atlantic and Commonwealth countries than the rest of the world. The disappearance of Soviet control in Eastern Europe has shown that even strong single-party systems are not endurable.

- Yet for all of the signs of weakness and fragmentation in party systems, parties are unlikely to become extinct. Even if the bonds are somewhat tenuous, they remain the only mechanism which links the voters and those who rule them, and they continue to perform useful tasks, notably recruiting representatives for national legislatures; educating the electorate by developing, elaborating and 'selling' policies; and offering an opportunity for popular participation in the political process.

- In Britain, there has been a regular alternation of Conservative and Labour rule, the two parties traditionally having different approaches, ideas and bases of support; in recent years, pragmatism appears to have replaced ideology. Third parties have gained ground, but the use of FPTP for Westminster elections tends to reinforce the dominance of the two main rivals.

Glossary of key terms

Adversary politics A style of politics in which there is a fundamental ideological disagreement between the main parties. Finer's suggestion was that this meant that a change of government resulted in a sharp change of direction in key areas of policy.

Big Society A flagship policy idea included in the 2010 Conservative manifesto, the term implies: a slimmed-down role for the state; a smaller and streamlined network of public services; decentralisation of power from Whitehall to the people; and a strong emphasis on the role of charitable bodies and volunteering. There is disagreement whether this is really a continuation of the traditional emphasis on the useful role of voluntary endeavour or something fundamentally knew.

Blue Labour An influential tendency within the Labour Party that stresses the need to regain support from working-class and 'squeezed middle' voters, via the adoption of more conservative policies on, especially, crime and immigration. Advocates are critical of the Blair/Brown years, because of their neo-liberal and centralising approach.

Brownites Supporters of the person and ideological thinking of Gordon Brown. Brownites tended to be more committed to the role of the state and the role of the unions within the Labour Party than Blairites, and less enthusiastic about market-driven reforms and the use of media management techniques.

Catch-all parties Umbrella or 'broker' parties that seek to maximise their voter appeal by reaching out to as many groups as possible, rather than representing specific class, regional or partisan interests.

Communitarianism The set of beliefs associated with Etzioni, arguing that both liberal individualism and massive state interventionism have failed and that the best way forward is through individuals recognising the importance of community. As citizens, they have rights but must also be aware of the duties and responsibilities to society.

Compassionate Conservatism Compassionate conservatism is a political philosophy that shows concern for the welfare of society and particularly for those in need, but emphasises the need to employ traditionally conservative solutions – such as support for low taxes, limited government regulation and the free enterprise system – in order to achieve it. Adherents prefer to see social issues tackled via cooperation with charitable bodies, churches and private companies than by government; they also urge personal responsibility and self-reliance.

Consensus politics Consensus implies general agreement. Consensus politics means that there is substantial agreement between politics of all parties and the public over fundamental values and policies, even if there are differences of emphasis and degree. It refers to a style of politics based on compromise and conciliation. In Britain, the era of consensus (usually described as being 1951–79) was associated with widespread acceptance of the need for full employment, a mixed economy and a welfare state.

Europhobic The attitude of those who are hostile to the EU and its workings.

Euroscepticism The term that became fashionable in the 1990s to describe the attitude of those opposed to European integration and sceptical of the EU, its aims, policies and practices.

Maastricht rebel A reference to those members of the Conservative Party who rebelled against the government during the passage of the Maastricht Treaty in the early 1990s.

Marxian socialism A variety of socialist thinking associated with the ideas of the left-wing German political thinker, Karl Marx, which has a strong economic as well as an ethical dimension. It also emphasises the importance of a class analysis to society's problems.

Mixed economy An economy in which there is a significant role for both private and public ownership, as existed in Britain between the late 1940s and the 1980s before Margaret Thatcher embarked upon her programme of privatisation.

New Labour The term applied to the rebranded Labour Party after Tony Blair became its leader. It drew its inspiration from Bill Clinton's New Democrats. It was used in a party manifesto, New Labour, New Life for Britain, which set out a range of attitudes and ideas that represented a 'third way', Centre-Left approach. Subsequently, it came to describe the stance of the party in the Blair/Brown years, but since 2010 it has been shelved.

Partisan dealignment The theory explaining how the public increasingly dissociates itself from both main parties; the erosion of party identification, as reflected in an increase in voter volatility.

Primaries Preliminary elections in the USA, in which the voters of a state choose the candidate who will represent their party in the main or general election.

Pro-European The attitude of those who are sympathetic to the aims, policies and personnel of the EU.

Pro-Life Alliance Founded as a political party with the primary goal of placing the abortion issue back on the political agenda, the Pro-Life Alliance fielded candidates in local, regional, national and European elections. Believing that its original aims have been achieved, it now operates via education and campaigning.

Proportional representation The collective term for electoral systems that award seats in the legislature in proportion to the number of votes cast for each party.

Short Money A grant payable to opposition parties to assist them in their discharge of House of Commons work; named after the Leader of the House who originally introduced it. (In the Lords, the money is sometimes know as 'Cranborne money'.)

Socialism Socialists believe that unrestrained capitalism is responsible for a variety of social evils, including the exploitation of working people, the widespread existence of poverty and unemployment, gross inequality of wealth and the pursuit of greed and selfishness. They are in favour of a social system based on cooperative values; emphasise the values of community rather than of individualism; believe in the need for a more equal and just society, based on brotherhood and a sense of social solidarity; and in the case of Marxian socialists have a clear preference for common ownership (nationalisation) of the commanding heights of the economy.

Thatcherism The creed associated with Margaret Thatcher, involving a market-based economic system and an emphasis on competition, free enterprise, lower taxes and curbs on trade union power.

Third way A middle path between Left and Right, between socialism and capitalism, akin to centrism; essentially, a non-doctrinaire approach, which suggests that 'what matters most is what works'.

Triangulation A reference to the approach of those politicians who present their ideology as being neither Left nor Right, but something above and beyond the traditional positions on the political spectrum. It involves adopting some of the ideas of political opponents, enabling the triangulator to take credit for anything that is popular and protecting him or her from opposition attacks. The term is often used in association with discussion of the pragmatic third way approach.

? Likely examination questions

Why are parties essential to a democracy?

Does the United Kingdom have a two-party system?

Do the terms Left and Right any longer have relevance in describing the British political scene?

Does New Labour still exist?

Can the Cameron-led Conservative Party be described as Thatcherite?

Discuss the choice, power and security of British party leaders.

'Political parties do not matter any more.' Are parties in long-term decline?

 Helpful websites

www.conservative-party.org.uk

www.labour.org.uk

www.libdems.org.uk

 Suggestions for further reading

Useful articles

S. Fielding, 'Whatever Happened to New Labour?', *Politics Review*, 19:1, September 2009.

P. Graham, 'Has UK Conservatism Moved beyond Thatcherism?', *Politics Review*, 19:2, November 2009.

M. Grant, 'Is the Labour Party Still a Socialist Party?', *Politics Review*, 15:1, September 2005.

P. Lynch, 'Britain's Multiparty Systems', *Politics Review*, 18:3, February 2009.

P. Lynch, 'Conservative Party Policy under Cameron', *Politics Review*, 19:3, February 2010.

Useful books

R. Dalton et al., *Political Parties and Democratic Linkage: How Parties Organize Democracy*, Oxford University Press, 2011.

R. Hefferman, 'Political Parties and the Party System', in P. Dunleavy et al. (eds), *Developments in British Politics 7*, Palgrave, 2003.

CHAPTER 8

Pressure Groups

Contents

Introduction	283
Group activity in modern societies: pressure groups and movements	284
Pressure groups and political parties: their differences and similarities	285
Classifying pressure groups	287
The methods employed by pressure groups	291
The European dimension to British pressure-group activity	297
Pressure groups under recent governments	300
The benefits and disadvantages of pressure groups	306
The case of Scotland	308
The case of the USA	309

Overview

Pressure groups are organised associations that aim to influence the policies and actions of those who hold government office. They operate in the space between government and society, consulting with ministers and providing continuous opportunities for citizens to become involved in political life.

In this chapter we survey the range of pressure groups that exist and the nature and extent of group activity, before exploring how organised interests play a part in the government of the country.

Key issues to be covered in this chapter:

- The distinctions between pressure groups, movements and political parties
- The different ways of classifying groups
- The nature and scale of group activity
- How groups operate
- The changing pressure group scene in Britain since 1979
- Factors influencing group success
- The contribution of groups to the workings of democracy
- The characteristics of groups and their operations in Scotland and the United States

Introduction

Pressure groups are voluntary organisations that seek to influence public policy by defending their common interest or promoting a cause. Their nature and degree of influence vary from country to country. Generally speaking, 'big business' is close to government, for what government does affects business just as the decisions of businessmen in areas such as job creation and investment have important repercussions for ministers. However, many other interests in society are also affected by ministerial decisions and wish to make their views known in the appropriate quarters. Employees are organised via the trade union movement, and various other groups represent farmers, churches and a host of civic, environmental and social causes.

There are myriads of British groups, covering the whole spectrum of policy issues. Some 34,000 organisations are recognised by the Directory of British Associations, but there are many more that operate at the local level. In addition to a huge number of defensive and campaigning groups, there are more than half a million voluntary bodies. Groups are as diverse as they are numerous, ranging from the high profile National Farmers Union to the rather more obscure groups that campaign for the provision of better public lavatories.

In particular, there has in recent years been a surge of interest in single-issue campaigning, on subjects from gay rights to the export of live animals to the Continent, from gun control to the siting of a motorway or other public amenity. Over the last two or three decades, the number of these and other pressure groups has soared, and the number of outlets at which they target their propaganda has increased. New techniques of putting across ideas and information have emerged, in particular the growth of professional lobbying.

The behaviour of activists in the campaigning field has raised important questions about the role of pressure groups in modern democracies. Many of the issues are relevant to European and American experience as well as to life in the United Kingdom. In all countries, the increasing trends towards the development of privatised industry and market economies, and the inevitability of

---

Box 8.1 A note on terminology

There is no agreed terminology to cater for pressure group activity across the world. The Americans talk mainly of interest groups and lobbying, whereas in Britain the tendency is to use the term 'pressure groups' and then to classify them into different categories. The word 'pressure' is unfair to the many groups that operate without resorting to any degree of coercion. In this case, pressure usually amounts to influence and persuasion, rather than use or threat of intimidation. It is because of the negative connotation of the term pressure groups that campaigning voluntary groups such as Cafod and Oxfam tend to now describe themselves as non-governmental organisations (NGOs).

The term 'interest groups' is unsuitable as a description of the myriad of promotional or single-issue groups that seek to propagandise on behalf of a cause and have no self-interest in the matter in the issue with which they are involved. For our purposes, 'pressure group' is a convenient general label to cover the range of organisations under discussion.

---

globalisation have had clear repercussions for the way in which groups function and the influence they can wield.

Group activity in modern societies: pressure groups and movements

Pressure groups exist in all societies. Free societies are **pluralist**, in that a variety of organisations are allowed to exist and compete for influence over government. In some pluralist societies, there are strongly antagonistic ethnic, linguistic or religious groups; others may be based more on social class. In Western liberal democracies, thousands of bodies seek to influence the conduct of power and make their views known. In a free country, groups seek to exert influence via many avenues, mostly peaceful, but on occasion they may resort to more violent forms of protest. No single group can exert a monopoly of power and manipulate the system for its own advantage.

Pressure groups differ considerably in their internal operation, some being democratically structured, others led by a powerful elite that dominates proceedings on a regular basis. Some are large, others are small; some operate at a national level, others do so regionally or locally; some are particularly effective and have popular appeal, others cater for minority interests and needs. Some are durable and make a great impact, others are short-lived and make little impression.

Movements and the politics of protest

Since the 1960s there has been what Heywood[1] has referred to as an 'explosion in pressure and protest politics'. In his view, this burst of activity 'may be part of a broader process that has seen the decline of parties and a growing emphasis on organised groups and social movements emerging as agents of mobilisation and representation'. The **new social movements** that have emerged since the 1970s are less structured and cohesive than pressure groups. They tend to have a core group that provides general direction and a network of widespread supporters who are only loosely organised. Often, their activities arise at grass-roots level, before later evolving into national crusades. They are broadly united around a central idea, issue or concern whose goal is to change attitudes or institutions, as well as policies. Characteristic concerns include equality for women and ethnic minorities, the environment and animal rights, globalisation and international peace.

Those who involve themselves in social movements often provide a radical critique of mainstream societies and institutions, and are interested in finding different ways of organising political activity. They want fundamental change to the status quo and the dominant values in society. Members of pressure groups may want to see substantial changes in public policy, but broadly they are more likely to support the existing political and social framework in society, and the dominant values that underpin it.

Pressure groups and political parties: their differences and similarities

Pressure groups differ from political parties, for they do not seek to win elections to gain political office. Indeed, they do not usually contest elections and if they do so, it is mainly to draw attention to some matter of national concern. Their goals are narrower, in that they do not attempt to advance ideas covering the whole range of public policy. Indeed, some of their aspirations are non-political.

Yet there is some overlap between parties and pressure groups. Both types of organisation are vehicles through which opinions can be expressed and outlets for popular participation. Both have a role in the workings of government, in the case of parties by forming or opposing an administration, in the case of groups by providing information and assisting in governmental enquiries. There is also an overlap between their activities. For example:

- There may be a close relationship between pressure groups and political parties. Many trade unions are actually affiliated to the Labour Party and form part of the wider Labour movement in the country. Some staff are active in 'social' pressure groups and in the ranks of the Labour or Liberal Democrat parties.

- Within the parties there are groups that seek to influence party thinking, such as the Tory Reform Club and the Bruges Group in the Conservative Party and the Tribune Group in the Labour Party. These tendencies or factions are effectively pressure groups within a party.

- Some **think tanks** act alongside the political parties. Members share the broad outlook of the party, but act independently and seek to have an impact on the general thrust of public policy. Examples are the Institute for Public Policy Research on the moderate left and the Centre for Policy Studies on the right.

- Some groups actually put up candidates in an election, as have Friends of the Earth (FoE) in the occasional by-election and the Christian Peoples Alliance (CPA) in recent general elections. In these cases, the point is not any desire to attain office, but rather to achieve publicity for a particular cause. In 1997, the Pro-Life Alliance fielded enough candidates (fifty-three) to qualify for a party election broadcast, thus providing a good opportunity to air members' thinking on issue such as abortion, fertilisation and embryology.

Classifying pressure groups

In an early study of pressure groups, Samuel Finer[2] distinguished between groups involved in different areas of activity, such as the 'labour lobby', 'civic' groups, and 'educational, recreational and cultural' ones. There are two more usual ways of classifying them. The first describes them according to what and whom they represent, the second in terms of their relationship with government and the way in which they operate:

Protective and promotional groups

The distinction originally made by Stewart[3] and subsequently employed by many others, divided groups into: (a) those which seek to defend the interests of persons or categories of persons in society (protective, interest or defensive groups), and (b) those which seek to advance particular causes and ideas not of immediate benefit to themselves (promotional, propaganda, cause or ideas groups).

Protective groups are primarily self-interested bodies that seek selective benefits for and offer services to their members. Business interests are among the most powerful players in pluralist societies such as Britain, France, Italy and the United States. They are of strategic importance in the economy, and governmental interests and their own often tend to coincide. Many of them are represented in peak organisations, which bring together within one organisation a whole range of other bodies and coordinate their activity and speak on their behalf. Such umbrella groups may represent the broad interests of capital (the Confederation of British Industry and the Institute of Directors) or the firms belonging to specific industries (Motor Manufacturers Association). They are usually well organised and financed. In addition to their membership of peak business and trade organisations, many large companies have their own public relations departments and engage in their own lobbying of government departments. For example, Tesco has a formidable lobbying team, concerned with issues varying from company law and business taxation to farm policy and land-use planning policy.

Trade unions are probably the best-known protective or interest groups. They exist to represent the interests of organised working people, by defending and improving their wages and working conditions. Individual unions often belong to an umbrella organisation, in Britain fifty-eight being affiliated to the Trades Union Congress (TUC) and in the United States fifty-five belonging to the American Federation of Labour and the Congress of Industrial Organisations (AFL/CIO). In recent decades, unions have lost much of their bargaining power in Britain, Europe and America. The decline of manufacturing industry and high levels of unemployment in the 1980s, the trends to globalisation of national economies and the increase in new and less unionised employment have seriously affected their membership and generally taken a toll of union influence.

Farmers constitute a third important group in many countries. They too are losing some of their former political strength, farming having become less dominant in national economies. Farmers have one advantage over the other two groups, in that whereas employers and workers each have to combat their antagonists on the other side of the industrial fence, farmers do not face a powerful and articulate voice to argue against their influence. Usually, there is little organised opposition to agrarian interests, many people actually being sympathetic to those who are seen as maintaining the countryside and upholding the values associated with the rural way of life. The National Farmers Union has long been considered to be one of the most effective protective groups, representing as it does a clear majority of British farmers. Its views are listened to with respect in Whitehall.

Other highly significant protective groups cover the interests of those engaged in the professions, doctors, lawyers and teachers among them. Because they represent clear occupational interests, protective associations are often well established, well connected and well resourced.

In contrast to protective groups, *promotional groups* seek to advance ideas and causes which are not of benefit to their membership, other than in a most general sense. They are selfless rather than self-interested in their concerns. They are also open to people from all sections of the community who share the same values, whereas members of interest groups have a shared experience. Again, unlike the many interest groups that have been in existence for several decades, many promotional ones have a short span of life, disappearing once their cause has been appropriately tackled.

Promotional groups are defined by the cause or idea they represent. The Electoral Reform Society advocates a change in the electoral system, Help the Aged tackles the needs of the elderly, Greenpeace urges greater environmental awareness, Anti-Slavery International takes up issues of human rights and Amnesty International campaigns on behalf of political prisoners. Many cause groups are today **single issue** ones. In Britain, Snowdrop had a brief existence. It lobbied effectively for a ban on handguns and when the goal was attained, its *raison d'être* was removed. Single-issue groups were first identified in the United States, many being on the left of the political spectrum.

Promotional groups are traditionally weaker than protective ones, less well organised and resourced. Many operate with limited funds and few, if any, full-time staff. They have a tendency to split into rival factions. They also tend to have less access to government.

In addition, there are some **hybrid groups**, such as the Roads Campaign Council. The Royal Association for Disability and Rehabilitation (Radar) defends the interests of its members who are disabled, but works for the general betterment of the lot of disabled people. Of course, many other interest groups also pursue causes as a secondary objective. The British Medical Association (BMA) engages in campaigning on general health issues such as diet and smoking, although it primarily exists to defend the interest of professionals involved in health care.

Insider and outsider groups

Groups may also be classified by an alternative typology developed by Wyn Grant.[4] He finds the *protective versus promotional* distinction unsatisfactory because along with it there tends to be the assumption that protective groups are more influential than cause groups, because they represent powerful interests. Also, it is easy to assume that promotional groups are of greater benefit to society than protective ones, because they are more concerned with the general good rather than personal advantage.

Grant's preferred approach is based on the relationship of groups with the central decision-makers in government. For him, the key

Table 8.1 Examples of British protective (interest) and promotional (cause) groups

Protective	Promotional
Association of British Adoption Agencies	Electoral Reform Society
Confederation of British Industry	League Against Cruel Sports
English Collective of Prostitutes	Shelter
Institute of Directors	United Nations Association
National Farmers Union	World Wide Fund for Nature

issues are whether any particular group wants to gain acceptance by government and – if it does – whether or not it achieves that status. In his words:

> The principle on which such a typology is based is that in order to understand pressure groups, one needs to look not just at the behaviour of the groups but also at the behaviour of government.

Grant divides groups according to whether they are insider or outsider ones. *Insider groups* are regularly consulted by government, having good access to the corridors of power. *Outsider groups* either do not want such access or are unable to attain recognition. Many but not all protective groups are insider ones, and have consultative status. Similarly, in most cases promotional groups are 'outsiders', but there are several exceptions; the Council for the Protection of Rural England and the Royal Society for the Protection of Birds are in frequent touch with representatives of government. The status of others fluctuates over a period.

The Grant typology has itself come under some criticism, because:

- Some groups pursue insider and outsider strategies at the same time, so that the distinction is not clear-cut. Tactics such as peaceful public demonstrations and letter-writing campaigns are compatible with insider status, but more violent direct action is not. In Greenpeace, tensions exist over tactics. Over the years, it has shifted towards more dialogue with government and business,

Table 8.2 British groups: their characteristics summarised

Characteristics	Protective groups	Promotional groups
Aims	Defend interests of membership	Advance an idea or cause
Focus of their attention	Executive (Whitehall) and legislature (House of Commons), and EU institutions	Legislators, public opinion and international bodies such as EU
Membership	Restricted to those in trade or profession	Open to all
Status	Usually insider groups, with a consultative role	Often, but not always, outsider groups; not usually consulted by government

whilst maintaining direct action activities that attract money and popular support.

- More groups have insider status than Grant originally suggested. It is not hard to be consulted – some 200 are on the list for consultation on issues relating to motorcycles, but their influence may be marginal. In other words, consultation is not a special privilege.
- If the *insider versus outsider* distinction was valid several years ago, it is less valid now because new forms of politics have arisen in the 1990s and subsequently. Pressure group politics has changed, with more middle class involvement in animal welfare and anti-roads protests. Also, there are more arenas than before, most obviously the European Union. Some groups concentrate much of the time on Brussels and this gives a new dimension to talk of access to the corridors of power in Whitehall.

The methods employed by pressure groups

In any free society there are **access points**, formal parts of the governmental structure that are accessible to group influence. Where the emphasis is placed will vary from democracy to democracy. In Britain, the most obvious ones are:

The Executive (ministers and civil servants)
The legislature (MPs individually and as members of the party)
Public opinion.

In Britain, the approach adopted depends on the type of group involved. Large, powerful protective groups have close contacts in Whitehall, for in a highly centralised country decision-making is concentrated; key decisions are made in government departments. They may also have contacts in Westminster, and in the case of the unions have close links with several MPs. By contrast, many promotional groups will have very infrequent contact and little influence in Whitehall, unless they are an insider group such as the RSPB. They may have some spasmodic support at Westminster but will try to persuade public opinion in their favour in the hope that the press and MPs will then take up the cause if it proves to be one of much concern. The Campaign for Nuclear Disarmament (CND) has little contact and even less influence in Whitehall, but has a cross-party group of MPs that raises its campaigning priorities. However, it mainly seeks to create a public mood in favour of unilateralism.

Pressure groups and government
In almost all countries, Interest groups target the executive branch of government. Sometimes, they deal with ministers directly, but elected politicians mainly set out what Hague et al.[5] refer to as the 'broad contours' of policy. More often, lobbyists – who are interested in the small print of policy – have contact with senior figures in the various departments of state. Groups require access to the seat of power, and it is in the departments that decisions are made and the details of legislation finalised. Matthews[6] explains why this is so:

the bureaucracy's significance is reinforced by its policy-making and policy-implementing roles. Many routine, technical and 'less important' decisions, which are nonetheless of vital concern to interest groups, are actually made by public servants.

Most British interest groups have close contacts in Whitehall. It is the higher civil service that offers advice to the Secretary of

Box 8.2 The types of relationship between groups and government

In recent years much attention has been paid to the concept of **policy networks**, a term which describes the different kinds of relationships between government and organised interests in any particular sector. Each sector has its own policy network involving decision-makers and group lobbyists working together to do something that may be of benefit to them both or at least prevent them from developing attitudes and adopting policies that damage one side or the other. These relationships may be close and continual **(policy communities)** or loose and wide **(issue networks)**.

When it was first advanced, the idea of policy communities fitted in well with Grant's classification of insider and outsider groups, the former having close involvement in decision-making. Food and drink policy, technical education and water privatisation were examples of areas in which the dialogue was close and regular, both sides (government representatives and groups) attaching importance to mutual and largely secret cooperation.

Since the 1980s, the dominance of those involved in such communities has given way to broader consultation and discussion in issue networks. Other players have become more involved in shaping public policy, including research institutes and the media. Media scrutiny and the attentions of consumer protest groups – for example in the food and drinks sector – have led to a more probing analysis of policymaking processes, so that secret deals and mutual back-scratching are now less frequent and less effective. The impact of any particular group (for instance, academics or the consumers) may vary from time to time or issue to issue, partly depending on the expertise it possesses in any given case.

The players involved in determining agricultural policy
A few decades ago, policy was largely determined in the corridors of Whitehall, between representatives of the NFU and the Ministry of Agriculture. Today, DEFRA (the successor body to the Ministry) will meet with:

- European civil servants
- The NFU
- Other interested pressure groups, such as environment campaigners in Friends of the Earth

- Food manufacturers
- Academic and research specialists
- Consumer organisations.

State, the political head of a government department, and so it is very worthwhile to contact senior civil servants. Civil servants/ ministers find the Lobby (the network of groups with whom they are in dialogue) very useful. They can get technical information and advice, and maybe help in carrying out a policy. In return, the groups learn the department's current thinking and hope to influence its decisions and get bills drawn up in line with their recommendations.

The concentration of power in the British Executive makes it an obvious focus for group activity, contact being arranged via formal and informal links such as in government-established committees and via the circulation of government documents. The NFU and those employed at the lower end of senior policy grades in the Department of Farming and Rural Affairs (DEFRA) are in frequent contact. The NFU values its consultative status in Whitehall and likes to operate in a quiet, behind-the-scenes manner that avoids too much publicity. Only when a row breaks out will it turn to open public methods.

Pressure groups and the legislature

Groups often voice their views via parliaments and assemblies, although whether they place much emphasis at this level depends in part on how much influence the representative body can wield. The US Congress and the French National Assembly are major channels through which groups can communicate, whereas the strong system of party discipline in the UK and Canada means that MPs are likely to respond to group persuasion. Powerful British groups prefer contact with the Executive, although they also lobby MPs, just as promotional groups do. Both types have shown increasing interest in lobbying the European Parliament, its MEPs and committees, the more so as its powers have increased.

British groups lobby Parliament because it can influence public policy. In one study,[7] 75 per cent of them claimed to be in regular or frequent contact with MPs and more than half also maintained contact with the House of Lords. They might rank its influence below that of the executive branch, but the trend since the 1980s has been towards more lobbying of the legislature. This has been in part because of the growth of the select committee system as another target for influence, but also because the Thatcher and Major governments were less receptive to group campaigners, professional lobbying of MPs has increased. In addition, the existence of governments with large majorities means that it is sometimes more productive for groups to work on backbenchers in the hope of persuading them to oppose what ministers are trying to steamroller through the House.

Elected representatives have often worked as businessmen, lawyers, teachers or trade unionists in their earlier life, so that there are likely to be members more than willing to speak up for the interests of various groups in the community. They may be willing to champion individual causes or even put forward a private member's bill. MPs who draw a high position in the annual ballot to introduce such a bill, soon find themselves contacted by campaigners who hope to persuade them to introduce a measure relating to their cause. They may have a draft bill ready or else provide assistance in devising one; for example, pro-life groups are keen to find someone willing to introduce legislation restrictive of the circumstances under which abortions can be carried out.

Influence at the parliamentary level can be channeled through elected representatives, committees or even a particular party. Prominent British pressure groups often claim to be non-political, though some have clear party leanings. CBI attitudes on 'free enterprise' broadly coincide with Conservative ones. The unions have historic links with the Labour Party, many being affiliated to it. The TUC is not formally linked and plays no part in the Labour organisation, though there is regular contact between the two bodies and they share a common desire to change society for the benefit of working people.

In lobbying Parliament, groups hope to:

- amend or sponsor legislation in a direction favourable to them
- influence the climate of discussion on relevant issues of public interest

Box 8.3 British pressure groups and the House of Lords

When Finer wrote *Anonymous Empire* in the early days of research into group activity, he did not mention the House of Lords as an access point. Today, this would be regarded as a serious omission. According to the Study of Parliament Group survey (1990), 70 per cent of group representatives interviewed claimed to have had contact with the House of Lords. Other studies have confirmed that lobbying of the upper house has increased and that on balance groups find it beneficial and effective.

The House has undergone something of a renaissance since the 1980s (see pp. 68–72) and the esteem with which it is regarded has developed considerably. Campaigners have observed its growing spirit of independence and willingness to vote down aspects of government legislation. They have done their best to provide ammunition to peers, in order to fortify them in their opposition on issues such as ID cards and the treatment of asylum seekers. They have also sought to insert technical amendments during discussion of bills, using letter writing and email, as well as personal meetings, to make initial contact and advance their causes.

- gain parliamentary backing for causes they may have first raised outside the chamber.

The appeal to the public

Groups try to influence the public who, after all, are the voters in the next election. American groups have long gone in for this style of pressure, especially via the use of background campaigns, which over a period seek to create a favourable impression for a cause. In Britain, Aims for Freedom and Enterprise, a long-time crusading organisation against nationalisation, keeps up a steady flow of information, and becomes more prominent at election time. A dramatic **fire-brigade** campaign may quickly rally support and get MPs and government ministers to take notice, as happened with the Snowdrop campaign in 1996–7.

Whereas the public level seemed to be the least influential a few years back, in the last couple of decades it has become more common. The coming of television has provided opportunities for publicity and some organisations now campaign via this medium. By persuading voters to take an issue on board, they hope to generate public interest and raise awareness. Environmental groups, which have grown rapidly in the last decade, have consciously sought to mobilise support through the use of television images and discussions.

For those groups that employ **direct action**, television can provide valuable publicity. The campaigning activities of Fathers 4 Justice have attracted much media coverage, as have those of Plane Stupid.

Other outlets

The courts are another focus for the attention of lobbyists. In the USA, litigation is a powerful weapon of campaigners who may bring a class action on behalf of others who share their concern. As yet, British groups have made less use of the legal route, although bodies such as the Equal Opportunities Commission and Greenpeace have won considerable victories in the courts. The Countryside Alliance used the judicial route in an attempt to delay the implementation of the ban on fox hunting, claiming that it was a denial of members' rights under the European Convention.

Other than by direct approaches to the three tiers of government and the public, groups can be effective in other ways, by working with political parties, lobbying other pressure groups and companies, and using the mass media to create a favourable climate of opinion for their action. There are also other layers of government that provide access, at the local, devolved and European levels.

The European dimension to British pressure-group activity

From the time the United Kingdom joined the European Community in 1973, some groups saw the need to lobby its institutions. The larger manufacturing interests and organisations such as the NFU were first off the mark. Since then, many others – including bodies such as Friends of the Earth and Greenpeace in the environmental field, and the British Veterinary Association and the Royal Society for the Prevention of Cruelty to Animals operating in the topical area

Box 8.4 The use of direct action

In the last two or three decades, there has been an upsurge in the growth of forms of direct action by individuals and groups. These range from demonstrations and 'sit-in' protests, to squatting and striking, from interrupting televised events and non-payment of taxation to the invasion of institutions in which the activities conducted cause offence. Groups committed to opposing abortion in the United States and hunting or other forms of alleged mistreatment of animals in the United Kingdom, have often been willing to resort to forms of direct action to voice their protest. On a global scale, the 1990s saw the emergence of a widespread movement of opposition to **globalisation**, in which a wide variety of groups – environmentalists, campaigners for debt relief, human rights activists and so on – took part in a series of demonstrations such as those in 1999 (in London on May Day and in Seattle at the World Trade Organization conference) and in 2001 in Genoa at the time of the G8 summit, where 100,000 demonstrators gathered in protest.

Many local action and promotional groups have used direct action as an additional tool. There are many examples of 'not in my back yard' (**NIMBY**) groups that have used this approach in their bid to block moves to build a housing estate on green belt land, or stop the felling of some ancient tree in the name of progress. NIMBY groups have mushroomed, often using media-oriented tactics in their campaigning, as well as social networking.

The case of Plane Stupid
Plane Stupid is a network of grassroots 'climate groups' that take non-violent direct action in pursuit of its demands for an end to short-haul flights and airport expansion, a ban on aviation advertising and a just transition to sustainable jobs and transport.

In 2010, Plane Stupid activists deposited a large mound of manure outside the south London HQ of soft drink giant *Red Bull*, because they had applied for planning permission to build an aerodrome opposite London City Airport. Three members, dressed as 'avenging air hostesses' in wigs and mini-dresses the same colour as the company's logo, crowned the mound with placards reading: 'Red Bull-sh*t', 'Red Bull gives you (plane) wings' and 'No second runway by stealth'.

Table 8.3 Summary of access points available to British groups

International level	UK national government
United Nations	Executive
UN-related bodies such as the World Bank	Parliament (both chambers)
G8	Courts
Overseas governments	Devolved machinery
	Local authorities

European Union level	Miscellaneous
Council of Ministers	Public
Commission	Other pressure groups
Parliament, via MEPs, their party groupings and the committee network	Private companies
Court of Justice	Public corporations
	Media

of animal welfare – have seen the need to embrace the European dimension. Indeed, in Baggott's 1992 survey[8] of some 100 groups, more than 60 per cent reported an increase in contact with EC institutions over the previous decade.

As a relatively open bureaucracy, the European Commission is keen to hear the views of various 'interests' in the early stages of draft legislation. MEPs, their party groupings and committees of the Strasbourg Parliament are also the focus of attention. The Commission estimates that more than 15,000 people and 2,500 organisations are engaged in lobbying at the European level, with an increase in numbers being matched by a growing professionalism and sophistication in much group activity.

With the passage of the Single European Act and the opening up of the Single Market, more and more decisions are being taken in Brussels. European institutions are an obvious target for British lobbyists. Three avenues are open to groups that wish to lobby the European machinery:

1. *Placing pressure on the national government.* Many groups try to influence the stance adopted by their governments in EU discussions and to influence the implementation of EU decisions. They can do this by entering into discussions with ministers and senior civil servants in the relevant Whitehall ministry. Some groups prefer to operate via the British government rather than make a direct approach to the Union.

2. *Operating through Euro-groups.* Many groups feel that in addition to utilising their contact with their own governments, they wish to exert pressure via a European-level federation of national groups. The TUC is a member of ETUC, a Eurogroup that currently represents seventy-seven national organisations from thirty-five countries. The RSPCA belongs to the Eurogroup for Animals, which represents bodies in twenty-five countries and seeks to present a united voice on behalf of animal welfare concerns in Europe.

3. *Direct lobbying.* Direct contacts with Union institutions are becoming increasingly important for many groups. A few large ones such as the CBI and Law Society have established offices in Brussels, as a means of closely monitoring European legislation and – in the latter case – serving as an outlet that can offer protection for its members working in the EU. More usually, contact takes other forms, such as working via MEPs, approaching formally or informally a Commissioner or writing letters to/phoning Union institutions.

Pressure groups under recent governments

In the 1980s, Tory governments had large majorities and could override most backbench rebellions. Ministers were not well disposed to group activity, Douglas Hurd attacking them as 'strangling serpents' that created unnecessary work for ministers and made it difficult for them to reach decisions in the public interest. He argued that they distorted the proper constitutional relationship between the

Executive, Parliament and the electorate. Along with some other senior Tories, he seemed to be casting doubt on the right of groups to have their say in the formulation of policy. This was particularly the case in relation to the unions, for ministers were wary of **corporatist** arrangements via which unions and big business would develop a close relationship with government. Margaret Thatcher was especially hostile to the idea of negotiating with such groups, which she viewed as essentially self-interested.

Pressure groups under New Labour

By contrast with the Conservatives, the Labour Party has traditionally been committed to changing society, so that often there is an overlap between pressure group activists and Lib-Lab supporters. Some Labour MPs and ministers were once group activists. Patricia Hewitt once worked for the National Council for Civil Liberties (now Liberty) before becoming an MP and then achieving Cabinet status; so too did Harriet Harman. Even if Labour governments very often disappoint them, groups in the social field may often find that their staffs, supporters and objectives sit more easily with a Labour administration that at least shares some of their values and priorities than with a Conservative one.

From the beginning, those involved in the New Labour administrations were willing to listen and consult more widely than their Conservative predecessors. A code of conduct was introduced concerning how departments should operate, a reflection of the leadership's wish to legitimise its initiatives and policies by embracing as many 'stakeholders' as possible within its 'big tent'. In particular, as Tony Blair[9] made clear to a group of financiers shortly after assuming the premiership, he was keen to establish Labour as 'the natural party of business'. In furtherance of this ambition, there was a new emphasis on personal meetings between the Prime Minister and heads of large companies and – at a lower level – between ministers and their officials with bodies such as the British Chamber of Commerce and the CBI. Individual businessmen and women played a prominent role in government, with some actually serving in office at a high level.

This relationship deteriorated over the course of the Blair/Brown years. Consultation continued, but many business organisations complained of increased interference and regulation by ministers – even if a number of the new impositions originated in the European Union rather than party policy. During the Brown years in particular, there was growing unease about the direction of policy and the competence of Labour's handling of taxation issues.

More surprisingly, many initially sympathetic pressure groups also became increasingly disappointed with the performance of New Labour, most notably the trades unions who were especially uneasy about the Blair administration's generally good relationship with business leaders. From the beginning, key spokespersons for the government made it clear that they would do 'no special favours' for the unions. They were willing to meet union officials and discuss issues of concern to them. Indeed, the unions achieved some of the goals that mattered to them, such as action on a minimum wage and youth unemployment, the signing of the Social Chapter and the recognition of unions at GCHQ. But on other policy matters, union leaders were often unable to extract concessions to their viewpoints. They found ministers more inclined to respond to the concerns of business than to those of labour.

For social groups, their enthusiasm for the government was weakened by the adherence of the Chancellor to the strict limits on expenditure in the early years. When the reins were later slackened, with the willingness to spend heavily on the NHS and education, this won ministers more kudos amongst some group activists. However, the 'tough' policies adopted on welfare policy (towards lone parents and the disabled) left many disillusioned. So too groups operating in the area of civil liberties became increasingly disenchanted with the Blair and Brown administrations. Members perceived ministers to be insufficiently responsive to their representations when considering measures that restricted personal liberty in the name of national security.

Generally, the environmental lobby has received greater recognition over the last two decades, a reflection of the increase in public interest and media attention since the late eighties. Margaret Thatcher had an interest in aspects of the environmentalist agenda, a point observed by members of Friends of the Earth and other organisations which found a receptive ear for some of their ideas. Their efforts led to modest 'greening' of the policies of the three main parties, which has existed ever since.

Trends in group activity

There has been a dramatic increase in nationwide popular movements. More single-issue groups have emerged, and via television have achieved enormous publicity, and demonstrated the extent of popular feeling in favour of their campaign. So too have certain causes such as the countryside and environment gained popular backing. The Countryside Alliance has mobilised rural interests and revealed to ministers the scale of unrest in country areas about trends in governmental policy in recent years; it claims 105,000 members.

More typical of the situation in most European countries have been the New Social Movements. New Left politics are characterised by the involvement of younger and better-educated people within society. They take up issues such as minority rights, anti-nuclear protest, international peace, anti-globalisation, Third World concerns and the environment in general. Using tactics ranging from boycotts to passive resistance, and engaging in activities such as protests or more violent demonstrations, these unconventional forms are no longer new, having become an accepted feature of group activity in Western societies.

Other key trends already mentioned have included the growing importance of lobbying the House of Lords (see pp. 295–6), the devolved institutions of Scotland (see pp. 194, 203 and 205), Wales and Northern Ireland, and the European Union (see pp. 297–300) in this age of **multi-level governance**. Another trend has been the growing use of professional lobbyists by some protective groups, to help them defend their interests.

The increasing use of professional lobbyists

In recent years, pressure groups have developed a more sophisticated approach to the ways by which they seek top influence 'pressure points' in the political process. Some have turned to the use of the new commercial 'lobbying industry', an American-style import. Professional lobbyists were defined in a House of Commons report as those who are 'professionally employed to lobby on behalf of clients or who advise clients on how to lobby on their own behalf'.

These agencies trade their political knowledge and expertise to clients in return for considerable financial reward. They are hired for their inside knowledge of the workings of government and their contacts. Some are small specialist bodies, such as political planning services. Others have a much larger client base. Most major pressure groups either have a specialist lobbying department or employ the services of one of the professionals.

Concern has been raised over the activities of these professional groups, especially over their close relationship with certain MPs. Most MPs do not provide very much in return for payment as consultants, mainly reporting back to the group monthly on relevant political developments of interest to the company, and acting as 'eyes and ears'. From the lobbyists' point of view, they are pleased to be able to use the MP's name on the top of their notepaper. It creates the impression that the group has access to and influence in the 'right places'. The fear is that in some cases that connection might be misused, and that companies are buying influence over legislation, influence which is denied to smaller, less-funded groups within the community.

Some MPs have been less than open in disclosing their connections. Disquiet aroused by several cases in the early to mid 1990s led to the establishment of the Nolan Committee, which in 1995 made recommendations regarding payment from outside sources. MPs went further than the Committee suggested, and prohibited the practice of any paid advocacy by MPs. They were no longer able to advocate a particular cause in Parliament in return for payment, and had to disclose money from outside bodies paid to them by virtue of their status as MPs. For instance, income from a company for advice on how to present a case to government now had to be declared.

The relationship of MPs and lobbying companies came under close scrutiny in March 2010. In a Channel Four television programme, three Labour ex-ministers revealed their willingness to take money from a fictitious lobbying firm in return for help in influencing legislation. As a result they were suspended from the parliamentary Labour Party, pending an inquiry by the Parliamentary Standards Commissioner into whether they had broken parliamentary rules on paid advocacy. The then Leader of the Commons, Harriet Harman, argued that lobbying companies should be subject to a strict statutory code. She also suggested a tightening of the rules on former ministers seeking jobs in the private sector.

Box 8.5 Factors influencing the success of different groups

Different pressure groups experience varying degrees of success. For these purposes, success may be interpreted as gaining access to a centre of decision-making and exerting influence over the development of policy. Baggott[9] distinguished three general considerations that determine the effectiveness of all types of group:

1. Their resources
2. Their political contacts
3. The political environments in which they operate.

Traditionally, British protective groups are thought to have possessed more power in Whitehall than promotional ones, but their success varies according to specific factors such as:

- *The degree of government support for the aims and ideas of the group*: e.g. (particularly in the past) unions may benefit more from a Labour administration, business from a Conservative one.
- *The government's need for cooperation and support*: the NFU and BMA – among other organisations – are in a position to provide valuable information and assistance to ministers.
- *The bargaining power of a group within the economy*: some groups have the capacity to withhold their support and thereby cause hardship and inconvenience. The BMA has much power, for ultimately its members could (and have) threatened to withdraw from the operation of the Health Service.
- *Timing is all-important*: if there is general public feeling in their favour, it can work to the advantage of pressure groups. In 1972–4 the miners had widespread public sympathy at a time when their produce was much needed because of the quadrupling of oil prices in the Middle East. Coal was seen as vital to the economy in the 1970s, and expendable or replaceable by other sources of energy in the 1990s; the time for coal had passed, in the eyes of Conservative ministers.
- *The representativeness of the leadership*: any union or organisation that speaks for the vast majority of people in its sector and is perceived as being representative of opinion (as is the NFU) is in a better position to advance its claim. In the early Thatcher years, it was easier to ignore the views of union leaders who were criticised as being unelected or elected for life, and not accountable to those who put them in their position.

Generally, promotional groups are viewed as less powerful than groups that consult with Whitehall, though as we have seen, some such organisations are influential insiders. Lacking such access, most operate more directly with the public. Factors of relevance here include:

- *The attitude of the government*: CND is unlikely to make any significant impact on a Conservative government, Aims for Freedom and Enterprise on a Labour one.
- *Proximity to an election*: ministers might be more susceptible to influence when an election looms.
- *Parliamentary support from all parties*: wide backing may smooth the passage of a bill being promoted in the House, and suggest to the government that there is a wide consensus on the issue.
- *A good case*, well informed, well argued and not too partisan.
- *The climate of opinion*: attitudes may change over a generation; e.g. whereas the Lord's Day Observance Society could wield considerable influence in the early post-war years, its position has been undermined in recent decades by the waning of religious devotion.
- *Media attention*: television exposure offers cheap publicity, and can demonstrate that a group's interest corresponds with public concern; it is then more difficult for ministers to ignore the case presented.

The benefits and disadvantages of pressure groups

In recent years, the tendency of many politicians has been to criticise pressure-group activity as damaging to the democratic process. Groups are seen as essentially self-interested and lacking in concern for the needs of the wider public. Yet this is only part of the picture, for they also raise issues of popular concern and provide a useful channel through which preferences may be expressed. Democracy would be unable to function without them, for they are at the heart of the policymaking process. Given such a position the need is to monitor their activities and ensure that they are efficient, open and representative, rather than to imagine that their contribution can be either ignored or removed.

Among specific arguments advanced in favour of and against their contribution to democracy are the following.

In favour

- In a pluralist society, in which power is dispersed in many different locations, pressure groups are seen as being at the heart of the democratic process. In particular, they perform a valuable function within the political system for they allow participation in decision-making by ordinary individuals. Many people otherwise only participate in political life at election time, but they can indirectly do so by joining groups which can influence the decisions of public bodies.
- They provide valuable information to government departments based upon their specialist knowledge of their field. In some cases, this is backed by cooperation in administering a particular policy and monitoring its effectiveness. They are indispensable to governmental decision-making because they are available for regular consultation. Indeed, this may be on a very frequent basis, there being continuing dialogue between a government department and a key interest group such as the CBI or the BMA. The government knows that a group of this type represents the bulk of people in that particular sector. Most farmers are in the NFU, and therefore its voice is representative.
- They act as a defence for minority interests, especially those connected with parties not in government.
- They counter the monopoly of the political process by political parties, and sometimes they raise items for discussion which fall outside the realm of party ideas and policy, and which do not tend to get in the manifestos. They made the running in the 'green' arena, before the parties took up ecological issues.
- In a democracy such as ours, they are an inevitable feature. The chance to freely voice a viewpoint is basic to a democratic system. The group system has mushroomed in recent years and this growth is unlikely to be reversed.

Against

- A frequent criticism is that not all sections of the community are equally capable of exerting influence, though virtually everyone is free to join a group. There is not a level playing field for influence.

Some, especially ideas groups, are much less likely to be acknowledged. Campaigners can point to the failure of the Child Poverty Action Group and other welfare groups to prevent Labour from cutting benefits to one-parent families and the disabled. Of the interest groups, the voice less frequently heard is that of consumers who are difficult to organise, other than via the ballot box. By contrast, the producer groups, the unions and particularly in the Tory years, the industrialists, have easier access to Whitehall.

- The leadership of some groups is unrepresentative. This was the case with a number of unions before a change in the law forced them to hold elections for the post of General Secretary. It is important that any government knows that people it talks to do genuinely reflect their members' wishes, and that deals made with leaders will stick because they have the backing of group supporters.

- Some people worry about the secrecy under which bargains between interest groups and Whitehall departments are made – hence Finer's[10] plea for 'Light, More Light'. Also, they fear that too many MPs are beholden to outside groups and business commitments.

- A pressure group by definition represents a number of broadly like-minded citizens in society. In other words it is a 'sectional interest', in the way that the NFU represents farmers and the NUM miners. Governments have to govern in the 'national interest', and consider the views/needs of all sections of the community, not the voice of the powerful only.

The case of Scotland

Following the introduction of devolved government in 1999, many UK pressure groups have shifted their focus in response to the new arrangements. This is particularly true north of the border, for the Scottish bodies have greater powers and responsibilities than those created in Wales. Before the creation of the Scottish Parliament, there were exclusively Scottish interest groups. However, since 1999, their range and number have significantly increased and they now concentrate much of their attention on the Scottish Parliament and Executive. Moreover, several UK groups have developed separate Scottish branches in order to lobby more effectively. Those groups that regularly come into contact with the Edinburgh machinery generally appear to have a positive view of the process.

From the beginning, the Executive has encouraged groups and individuals to become involved in the process of consultation; sometimes, ministers and their officials have directly approached a pressure group for advice. The presence of Labour and the Liberal Democrats in office until 2007 may have facilitated a close relationship, for there was some movement of personnel between social group activists and the two broadly progressive parties. So too, MSPs have encouraged campaigners to petition Parliament and liaise with its committees. Committees engage in consultations, in a bid to discover public opinion on a wide range of issues prior to proposed legislation. The Scottish Council for Single Homeless regularly takes part in committee meetings to work towards a long-term policy on homelessness.

The resulting growth in activity has inspired the media to report on group demands, so that journalists have extensively covered some issues. In particular, the **Souter Referendum** and the subsequent repeal of **Section 28** were high profile events that generated much journalistic activity and discussion.

Overall, those groups recently contacted by the author[11] generally had a positive attitude towards devolution. They felt that their input was being taken into consideration as decisions were made. In addition, they found it convenient to be able to lobby in Edinburgh, rather than in London, (the access point in the days before devolution). They felt that they were in close proximity to the key political players and of course also benefited from savings in time and travelling costs. These are still early days in which to assess the efficacy of groups in the consultative process, but there is no doubt that the passage of the Scotland Act created an important new dimension to group activity in the UK.

The case of the USA

American groups vary considerably in size, influence and resources. Among protective groups are large institutional bodies representing businesses across the nation (the US Chamber of Commerce) and the

Table 8.4 The 'top five' lobbying organisations in April 2011, based on total spending

Organisation	Total spending on lobbying ($)
ActBlue	52,443,515
American Fedn of State, County and Municipal Employees	45,237,853
AT&T Inc.	41,197,490
National Assn of Realtors	39,707,910
National Education Assn	36,310,095

Source: The Center for Responsive Politics at www.OpenSecrets.org.

American Medical Association. Among promotional groups, some are based on support or a single issue (the National Abortion and Reproductive Rights Action League), whereas others are concerned to promote a wider range of causes within a given area (Friends of the Earth).

Groups operate at all levels of government, national, state and local, benefiting from the number of access points available in a federal system of government. Congress is a particular focus for lobbyists. Both the Senate and the House of Representatives are powerful bodies with a key legislative role. Many legislators are financed by substantial contributions from **Political Action Committees** (PACs), the political and financial arm of American groups. Elected every two years, representatives are also aware of the need to keep their constituents 'back home' contented. Many of them come from areas where a substantial proportion of the population is engaged in a key interest, such as farming in the Midwest.

Activity at the Congressional level is more overt than that aimed at the Executive, much of which often takes part behind closed doors. Congress is a key part of the policy process, especially its committee system. Indeed, a few decades ago there were particularly close links between interest groups, committee chairpersons and government departments, an arrangement known as **iron triangles**.

US party discipline is much weaker than at Westminster, providing group activists with a real opportunity to influence votes by their campaigning. Weak party discipline and strong pressure-group activity at the legislative level tends to coincide, whereas by contrast – as the experience of Britain and Canada indicates – tighter discipline makes lobbying of elected representatives less worthwhile.

America has the most developed system of group activity of any democracy. Groups benefit from:

- a Constitution that provides protection for freedom of speech and expression
- the participatory tradition of the American people
- an open form of government, with powerful Freedom of Information laws
- a fragmented party system
- issue-based rather than party-based election campaigns.

American groups differ from British groups in several respects:

- There are proportionately more of them, reflecting the participatory tendency of Americans and the greater number of access points for them to lobby
- They exist in an atmosphere conducive to their operations, with constitutional protection and an executive and legislative framework much influenced by federalism and the separation of powers
- They employ a range of different methods, including fund-raising via PACs, paid political advertising and the use of technology
- They make more use of the courts, both federal and state
- They are less likely to target the Executive, for whereas in Britain this is the location of key decision-making, in America Congress is very influential in determining policy.

. . . .

 ## What you should have learnt from reading this chapter

- The importance of the dense network of voluntary organisations to the workings of a liberal democracy.

- Groups flourish where there exists a range of access points to which they can apply pressure. There is a vast number and range of groups, which vary considerably in the institutions they target and the way they operate.

- In many countries, there is a close relationship between business and government, ranging from highly formalised corporatist arrangements to looser consultation with insider groups. The tight policy communities of the past have given way to more open, looser policy networks in decision-making today.

- The influence and effectiveness of pressure groups varies according to the country and its internal circumstances, as well as to the time and the nature of the cause.

- Overall, there has been a change rather than a decline in pressure-group power in Britain in recent years, a situation reflected also in other countries. Traditional groups have in many cases lost some of their former influence, but local action organisations and enthusiasts for new causes publicise their case strongly.

- Although a vibrant pressure-group scene is essential to the workings of a modern pluralist democracy, so too there are dangers that can make group activity a threat to democracy.

Glossary of key terms

Access (or pressure) points Those parts of the governmental structure which are accessible to pressure group influence.

Corporatism Corporatism/'corporatist arrangements' refers to the tendency of governments to incorporate leading peak organisations (such as the CBI) into the process of policy making, thereby institutionalising group consultation. Tripartitism refers to the three sides involved in such consultations, government, business and the unions.

Fire-brigade campaign A dramatic type of group campaign designed to rally support quickly.

Globalisation This refers to the increasing interdependence of people, organisations and states in the modern world and the growing influence of global cultural and economic forces or trends. For many critics, it is the process whereby life is increasingly shaped by decisions or events taken at a distance from them. Anti-globalisation protesters worry especially about the influence of American capitalist values, seeing the United States as the cause of many of the world's difficulties, such as a degraded environment and world poverty and indebtedness.

Hybrid groups Groups that do not neatly fit into the protective versus promotional typology. They exist to protect the interests of their members, but also do a substantial amount of promotional work. In some cases, they are established by interest groups but exist to propagate a cause or idea.

Iron triangles The close, three-sided relationship between government departments, pressure groups and politicians that used to characterise US policy networks.

Issue networks Issue networks are large, flexible and open networks of particular individuals and groups operating in any given policy area. They are wider than policy communities and involve more participants.

Multi-level governance A term to describe the multiple layering of government, which means that several tiers are involved in formulating policy. It is often used in EU countries, for the existence of the Union adds a supranational level to national, regional and local ones.

New Social Movements Organisations that have emerged since the 1960s in order to influence public policy on issues such as the environment, nuclear energy, peace and women's rights. They have wider interests and are more loosely organised than most pressure groups, tend to have supporters rather than members and do not operate via detailed involvement with government. They are concerned to bring about fundamental change in society.

Nimby groups Local action groups whose members wish to protect their own lifestyle; they campaign against developments that impact adversely on the view from and value of their own house or land.

Pluralist Pluralism refers to the belief that power in modern societies is widely distributed between a multiplicity of competing interests. From time to time, new groups emerge, ensuring that there is further competition in the political market place. Pluralist societies are ones in which group activity can flourish, the various organised groups each having the opportunity to articulate their various demands.

Policy communities These are small, stable and consensual groupings of government officials and group leaders involved in decision-making in a particular policy area.

Policy networks This refers to the different kinds of relationships that can apply between government, pressure groups and the range of other players involved in policymaking in a particular sector. Issue networks and policy communities are subsections of policy networks.

Political Action Committees (PACs) US organisations that represent the political wing of pressure groups and engage in raising funds to distribute to candidates and parties. They are the means by which a range of organisations such as large corporations and labour unions can donate money to political campaigns. They developed as a result of the bid to clean up campaign finances in the 1970s. They have to register with the Federal Election Commission and keep within the limits allowable for donations to candidates and political parties.

Section 28 A clause of the Thatcher administration's Local Government Act (1988) that prohibited 'the promotion of homosexuality in schools'. It was offensive to many sections of the community. New Labour acted on its pledge to remove it both in England and Wales, and in Scotland.

Single-issue groups Groups that concentrate their attention on the achievement of one specific objective.

Souter Referendum A privately funded ballot of all Scottish people on repeal of the contentious Section 28. On a 34 per cent turnout 87 percent wished to retain the section, 13 per cent to remove it. The Electoral Reform Society refused to conduct the ballot, as it believed the poll would not be a legitimate democratic exercise, for people were being asked to give an opinion on the Section, without knowing the detail of what would replace it. Many groups hostile to Souter's stance had called for a public boycott of the poll, leading to doubts over the representativeness of the result.

Think tanks Groups formed to research and develop policy proposals, and campaign for their acceptance among opinion formers and policy makers. They are often ideologically based, their ideas sometimes being influential with the parties with which they share a broad affinity – e.g. the Institute of Policy Research and the Labour Party.

? Likely examination questions

Why is the distinction between pressure groups and political parties often unclear?

Why do many leading British interest groups concentrate their attention on Westminster rather than Whitehall?

Discuss the growing impact of the European dimension to British pressure-group activity.

Compare the activities and tactics of environmental groups with those of other types of pressure groups.

Discuss the view that the activities of pressure groups constitute a threat to the operations of liberal democratic systems of government.

🖥 Helpful websites

For basic information on pressure groups, their characteristics and influence, and on pluralism, consult:

www.historylearningsite.co.uk/pressure-groups.htm

Most individual pressure groups have their own sites, covering such aspects as the history, objectives and organisation of organisations, such as:

www.demos.co.uk Demos.

www.cbi.org.uk Confederation of British Industry.

www.etuc.org European Trade Union Confederation.

Suggestions for further reading

Useful articles

A. Batchelor, 'US Pressure Groups: a Blight on Democracy?', *Politics Review*, 19:2, November 2009.

W. Grant, 'Pressure Groups: Good or Bad for Democracy?', *Politics Review,* 19:1, September 2009.

W. Maloney, 'Interest Groups in Britain', *Politics Review*, 16:4, April 2007.

H. Margetts, 'Political Participation and Protest', in P. Dunleavy et al., *Developments in British Politics 7*, Palgrave, 2002.

D. Watts, 'Lobbying Europe: an Update', *Talking Politics*, September 2004.

D. Watts, 'Pressure Group Activity in Post-devolution Scotland', *Talking Politics*, January 2006.

Useful books

A. Cigler and B. Loomis, [US] *Interest Group Politics*, CQ Press, 2011.

W. Grant, *Pressure Groups and British Politics*, Palgrave, 2000.

J. Greenwood, *Interest Representation in the European Union*, Palgrave, 2003.

P. Lynch, *Scottish Government and Politics: An Introduction*, Edinburgh University Press, 2001.

D. Watts, *Pressure Groups*, Edinburgh University Press, 2007.

CHAPTER 9

Voting and Elections

Contents

Introduction   317
Election campaigning   318
British election campaigns and campaigning   321
Electoral systems   328
Types of electoral systems   333
British experience: the operation of FPTP in the general election of 2010   338
Some arguments surrounding the debate over FPTP versus PR   341
Voting behaviour   347
Voting in Britain   352
Turnout in elections   356
Turnout in the United Kingdom   358
Direct democracy: initiatives and referendums   360
The use of referendums in the United Kingdom   366
The case of France: the use of referendums   367
The case of the USA: election campaigning   368

Overview

All Western countries hold regular elections. They are central to any definition of a representative democracy, for the right to vote is the primary symbol of citizenship, allowing citizens to decide who shall govern them. By an election, we mean a competition for office based on a formal expression of preferences by a designated body of people at the ballot box. Such a contest holds those in office to account and if necessary provides a means for their replacement.

In this chapter, we are concerned with: the conduct of elections; the choice of electoral system; the nature of campaigning; the influences upon people when they cast their vote; the reasons for non-voting; and the growing popularity of direct democracy across the world.

Key issues to be covered in this chapter

- General characteristics of elections
- Various types of electoral system and their impact
- Systems currently in use in the United Kingdom
- Trends in election campaigning, particularly the influence of television
- Role and importance of money in modern elections
- Trends in voting behaviour
- Turnouts in recent elections in Britain and elsewhere
- Growing interest in forms of direct democracy
- The cases of France and the United States

Introduction

Elections in established democracies are generally free and fair. In a report for the Commonwealth Parliamentary Association, two Canadian writers, Gould and Jackson,[1] see the key determinant of 'free and fair' as being whether 'the will of the majority of voters is expressed, freely, clearly and knowledgeably, and in secret'. Today, more countries hold elections that meet these criteria than ever before. In the last quarter of the twentieth century, millions of people acquired the right to vote for the first time. In 1994, South Africa held its first free election in which the previously disenfranchised millions gained the **franchise**. On the African continent, elections providing a choice of candidates and multi-partyism are now the norm, even if in some countries rulers attempt to undermine the opposition. In several of the newly emergent Eastern European countries, there is free and open competition. Even countries such as communist North Korea allow for a narrow range of candidates.

Elections can range from being a meaningless exercise in which there is no genuine voter choice to a downright fraud, because of the tampering with votes or the lack of freedom under which polling is carried out. Yet even in countries with dubious democratic credentials, elections are still recognised by the ruling authorities as being useful. They create the illusion of popular participation and endow new office-holders with authority. Hence they are not only a means of filling public offices, but of conferring legitimacy on the government. In Britain, we may only get a vote in a general election every few years, but at least there is a genuine opportunity to express an opinion on those who have presided over our fortunes and to indicate whether it is, in our view, 'time for a change'.

In most countries, the voting age has been lowered, eighteen being the most common age for qualification. Of course, entitlement to vote is not the same as the ability to vote. In a democracy, it is important to ensure that there is an effective procedure by which people can be registered. In several countries there are permanent registers, amended at periodic intervals, as in Britain and most of Europe. Elsewhere, registers have to be created from scratch, so that in most American states it is necessary for the would-be voter to register his or her vote before polling day; this reflects the American emphasis on the mobilising effect of elections. Such an approach tends to be less efficient in ensuring eligibility and is likely to result in low turnouts.

Whatever the system, it is likely that some voters – perhaps 5–10 per cent or more – will not be registered. Of those who are registered, others will be unable to cast their vote because of illness, absence or other pressing circumstances. Some people are just unwilling to make the effort, especially if obtaining a postal vote is a complex process. Hence the remedy introduced in several countries, compulsory voting. Australia, Austria, Belgium and some Latin American states are among those that have resorted to this method, but in most cases its effectiveness is limited by the low level of fines and the difficulties in collecting those that are due.

Election campaigning

Campaigns and campaigning are an integral part of the democratic process. The task of those who run campaigns is to ensure that the electorate is well informed about the personalities and issues involved. In particular, campaign managers wish to reinforce wavering voters, recruit those who are undecided and convert those whose initial preference is for another party. Above all, they need to see that there is a maximum turnout of their own sympathisers on polling day.

British election campaigns are much shorter than American ones. Even though there is much speculation and a pre-election atmosphere in the third or fourth year of the lifetime of a Parliament, the campaign proper lasts only three to four weeks. Campaigns for all elective offices in America are longer, especially for the presidency.

Election campaigns have never been the same since the televising of politics began in the late 1950s. New styles of campaigning have developed, so that in recent years there have been innovative polling techniques, the wider use of **focus groups**, the introduction of professional advisers and an emphasis on the training of candidates. This greater professionalism of campaigns has been fairly general in all political systems, as has the increasing emphasis on the qualities of the candidate rather than the party. In this world of more **candidate-centred campaigning**, professional **political consultants** have acquired a new importance. For years major parties have brought in outside agencies to advise them, but now they maintain a core of their own **spin doctors** and image and marketing specialists who are either employed permanently at headquarters or are easily available.

Skilful use of the media has become something of an art-form in modern elections, and campaigns are often based around opportunities for media coverage, particularly on television. Like the cinema, television is a medium of entertainment so parties, politicians and their advisers have seen the need to attune performances to its demands. The emphasis in political campaigning is now increasingly on broad themes rather than policies, emotion rather than rational debate. **Soundbites** have often been a substitute for genuine discussion.

Media consultants are always on the look out for opportunities to maximise free television coverage. Election advertising is expensive, whether the money is spent on American-style paid advertisements or on poster hoardings. So rallies and speeches addressed to large meetings are often scheduled to ensure that they gain as much exposure as possible on news bulletins.

In presidential countries such as the USA, the marketing of politics has been particularly well developed. Electioneering has always been more candidate-centred, parties having been less entrenched in the political system. The new techniques of electioneering have crossed the Atlantic, leading to accusations about the 'Americanisation of elections'. Britain has in many ways learnt from the American experience, for there has been an increasing emphasis on **walkabouts**, **photo-opportunities** and **pseudo-events** created for the media. As in other countries, parties have adjusted to the changed environment in which they now operate.

In some states such as the Netherlands and the USA, party access to television time is unlimited, but in most countries governments have regulated the situation to ensure that justice is done to all parties. In Ireland, New Zealand and the United Kingdom, time is allocated according to the proportion of support obtained in the last election, whereas in Denmark and France among other examples there is equal access to all parties irrespective of their size.

Box 9.1 The importance of money in campaigning

The issue of funding election campaigns has become highly controversial in recent years. The necessity for heavy party spending has been increased by the trends in modern campaigning, with their emphasis on image and marketing.

Best-financed parties have a clear advantage, being able to commit greater resources to advertising on hoardings or (in the United States) on television. Between a quarter and a third of the total campaign expenses in American congressional elections goes for radio and TV advertising. In all countries, much of the money that does not go on direct advertising is still focused on the media. The work of campaign consultants in developing and testing themes and strategies, targeting audiences, surveying focus groups and conducting polls is done in preparation for taking the party's or candidate's message to the media for transmission to the voters.

In Britain, the Conservatives have traditionally been able to outspend Labour and the Liberal Democrats, although their advantage was markedly curtailed in the 1997, 2001 and 2005 elections, in which Labour was almost able to match their expenditure. The possibility of one party being in a stronger position was much reduced by the passage of the *Political Parties, Elections and Referendums Act (2000)*, which – among other things – imposed a limit on how much any party can spend (currently the ceiling on campaign spending is £20 million).

In 2010, according to the official figures of the Electoral Commission, overall national spending (£m) by the three main parties was:

Conservatives 16.7
Labour 8.0
Liberal Democrats 4.8

Of the total money spent by all parties contesting the election (over £32 million, down more than 11 million on 2005), the five most expensive components were: unsolicited material to electors, 12 million; advertising, 9 million; market research/canvassing, 2 million; rallies and other events, 2 million; and transport, 1.5 million.

British election campaigns and campaigning

In a sense, parties engage in continuous campaigning, but as legally defined the campaign in British elections must cover at least three weeks prior to polling day. Campaigns follow a fairly regular form. At the constituency level, candidates and volunteer helpers continue to canvass, address meetings and deliver election addresses to elector's homes, although the amount of energy devoted to arranging meetings for the candidates and door-stepping has markedly declined.

Constituency campaigning has been transformed in recent years into something much more sophisticated than it was until the 1980s. Party headquarters now plays a significant role in planning and managing local campaigns. Resources are increasingly targeted on **marginal constituencies** (often referred to as 'target seats') and in particular on categories of voters within them such as 'school gate mums'. The use of computers and telephone banks has enabled party campaigners to develop a profile of individual voters and send them an appropriate message.

Party leaders now engage in frantic tours around those constituencies that may change hands. Their itineraries are planned in great detail, as they are whisked from one end of the country to another in a carefully controlled schedule of meetings and events. They address gatherings in the large towns and cities; sometimes attend and make statements at the daily morning press conferences; and prepare for their television broadcasts, interviews with established interrogators and appearances before studio audiences.

During the campaign proper, the amount of political activity intensifies dramatically. Great political expertise and professionalism are employed to get the message across. *But does all of the massive and expensive effort actually make any difference to the outcome of the election?*

The traditional academic view of election campaigns was that they had little impact on the voters. In an age when voting behaviour was more habitual and predictable, then the campaign was less likely to influence the firmly held loyalties of the voters. In this context, party managers saw the purpose of the campaign as being to stimulate interest and maximise their potential turnout on polling day. Particular attention was concentrated on the marginals where the extra effort might affect the outcome. The floating voters – especially those in target seats – were the key target of the party managers; a small shift in opinion or an increase in their turnout could prove decisive.

In recent decades, the combination of **class dealignment** and **partisan dealignment** and the development of television as the main form of mass communication have led to a questioning of these earlier assumptions. It is commonly agreed that the electorate is more volatile, and notions of class and party identification are less deep-seated. In this situation, there are likely to be more people who are undecided before the campaign proper gets underway. According to Heath et al.,[2] the number of voters who only made up their minds during the campaign doubled to 24 per cent between 1970 and 1992.

If voters are more open to persuasion, then it is reasonable to assume that campaigns ought to be more significant. Nonetheless, it remains difficult to prove that the impact of the campaign is very extensive. In 2010, the ratings of the two main parties did not significantly shift in the weeks before polling day, although the experiment with leaders' debates led to some significant fluctuations during the course of the campaign. As often happens, the third party (the Liberal Democrats) benefited from the increased publicity that an election generates; this time, it received an additional lift after the first televised debate.

British electioneering, past and present approaches: marketing the party image

An interest in publicity and marketing is not a novel concern for parties and politicians. Early in the twentieth century, the Conservatives were keen to exploit the opportunities offered by the new forms of media, be they radio or film. Strategists of what was referred to as the 'psychology of the electorate' were keen to promote 'party image' as far back as 1908, when Graham Wallas[3] first coined the term. A few years ago Fletcher[4] could write that:

> So far from political advertisers copying baked beans and detergents, as the oft-repeated cliché has it, baked beans and detergents have been copying political advertisers, for ages. This should not be surprising. Persuasive communication is the essence of politics, and

it has been since the dawn of time. The marketing of branded consumer goods is a relative newcomer to the scene.

Television first played a significant part in British electioneering in 1959. Ever since the election of that year, it has dominated our political life, not just at polling time but throughout the duration of every parliamentary session. However, it is from 1979 onwards that there developed a new professionalism in the arrangements for handling matters of image, propaganda and marketing. In the Thatcher era, it was inspired by the partnership between the Conservative communications director Gordon Reece, Saatchi executive Tim Bell, and the leader herself. Since then, packaging and presentation have been central to the campaign, leading some to observe than the essence of modern politics is style rather than substance.

Much of this concern for party image is reflected in the skilful use of television, the main medium of communication today. Bowler and Farrell[5] refer to the 'increasing importance of television as a tool in election campaigning'. Two writers in their survey of marketing and strategies[6] note how today electoral contests are 'media-driven', and suggest that 'free elections in a modern democracy would easily collapse if the **mass media** . . . were to ignore election campaigning'.

British electioneering in the television age

Election campaigns today are made for television. TV dictates the form and style of electioneering, and in addition it has a significant influence over the agenda for discussion. **Agenda setting** has an important effect on what people learn about the politicians and their beliefs. TV producers have the power to draw attention to issues that they believe to be interesting and/or contentious, and so help to determine the content of election discussion. By stressing some areas and ignoring others, they can assist in shaping the impression the public acquires of particular parties, leaders and policies.

Television producers like a good story (particularly one with pictures), and party media advisers seek to ensure that they are given a plentiful supply of both. In other words, skilful politicians and their consultants themselves help to determine the agenda, by maintaining a regular flow of material 'ready-made for television'. Most leaders have been willing to take advantage of photo-opportunities, carefully stage-managed episodes in which the leading figure is set against a particular background perhaps to demonstrate concern for the area or its industry. The advisers to Margaret Thatcher were aware of the humanising potential of the photo-opportunity. One of their most famous contributions was the incident in 1987, of which Rawnsley[7] has written:

> She inaugurated a new softer image with a charge down a Cornish beach with a borrowed King Charles spaniel: 'I would love a dog', breathed the Prime Minister, 'but my job won't allow it.'

In the campaign, leaders visit local party committee rooms, take part in staged events, visiting places where they can be photographed by television cameramen and doing campaign walkabouts. Just occasionally, for all of the careful pre-planning, something happens to disturb the arrangements. In 2001, an angry Sharron Storer waylaid the Prime Minister as he entered a Birmingham hospital, protesting at delays in the treatment for her partner, a victim of cancer. The scene was much relayed on screen. So too was the famous or infamous Prescott punch when Deputy Prime Minister John Prescott landed a punch on an egg-throwing farmer in Rhyl.

It is quite possible for a party to run an impressively organised and professional campaign and still lose the election. In 1987, Labour was widely credited with winning the campaign but it still contrived to lose by a substantial margin and added only 3.0 per cent to its total vote from the its record low of 1983. In 1992, it added only another 3.6 per cent, again in spite of running what was judged to be a broadly superior campaign. As Kavanagh[8] observes: 'packaging and presentation can only do so much.'

The campaign in 2010

There were several familiar aspects of the 2010 campaign, among them the leaders' tours of the marginal constituencies, the walkabouts, the party election broadcasts and the plethora of opinion polls (see pp. 329–32). The so-called 'new media' became an established part of the campaign, an embarrassing Twitter story putting an end to the candidacy of one Labour hopeful at an early stage. The Internet had a role in making a mass of information and statistics available, to commentators and the public alike. Yet the key moments of the campaign all took place on television and talk of this being the first 'Internet election' was no more accurate than in earlier elections.

In the case of Gordon Brown, his initial tours revolved around him visiting what were meant to be closely controlled groups of party supporters, sometimes in their homes, rather to the neglect of communicating with a wider cross-section of voters. Even these sorties could go wrong, as the case of Gillian Duffy and '**bigotgate**' in Rochdale showed. Later, he took part in more walkabouts and spontaneous visits, when it became clear that the national media were not showing much interest in his low-key events.

The key innovation in the 2010 campaign was the introduction of televised debates (see pp. 326–8) between the party leaders which, whatever the merits of the idea, were likely to shape the character and 'feel' of the campaign. They assumed such an importance that other aspects of the national campaign were modified by the new form of campaigning and lost much of their impact. The national press conferences, so much used in previous elections and initially planned for 2010, almost disappeared; on no single day, did all three parties stage a London-based session and when there was one, it had little impact. In part as a consequence, outgoing ministers and shadow ministers were less deployed in 2010 than five years earlier, because the debates and the frenzy surrounding them tended to dominate everything else.

The debates helped Nick Clegg present himself as a fresh alternative to the two main parties, his well-rehearsed talking-to-camera approach and use of the questioners' names making him seem 'in touch' with the public mood. His performance gave the Liberal Democrats a boost in the polls, inspiring talk of a 'yellow surge' that did not materialise to the extent that at one time seemed likely.

For the Conservatives, this was the first election since 1987 in which they began the campaign with a clear lead in the opinion polls (see pp. 330–1). However, the 8 per cent lead in the YouGov poll in the *Sun* on the day that the election was announced pointed to the possibility of a hung parliament, an outcome that seemed likely throughout the campaign and was eventually to materialise. As with Labour, the party's campaign was tightly managed, although there were more situations in which David Cameron met a wider selection of voters.

Box 9.2 Televised debates in British elections

Several countries hold television debates, the USA since 1960, Germany since 1969 and Australia since 1984, among them. In these and other democracies, they are now an established part of the political process and attract large audiences. In November 2008, the American presidential debates were of a high standard and many enthusiasts for political discussion found them enthralling. They were 'good television' and made for informative political debate. Most of the major issues received an airing and clear differences of character, style and policy emerged between Barack Obama and Senator McCain.

In Britain, the argument for debates has traditionally been made by the Opposition, which have seen them as providing a useful opportunity to attack the Prime Minister. Managers on the government side are wary of allowing their leader to be subjected to them. In 1997, negotiations became embroiled in the detail of whether the Liberal Democrats should take part, and under what terms. As a result, it was only too easy for those who were never convinced that it was a good idea to ensure that the obstacles proved overwhelming and no agreement could be reached.

Those who favoured them argued that a leader's debate, in whatever form, would engage voters and increase public awareness, an important consideration given the low turnouts of recent years. Carefully moderated contests of some ninety minutes or thereabouts, would force the politicians to discuss policy, rather than indulge in yah-boo politics and easy sloganising.

Critics of the idea pointed to the difficulties in staging such contests, not least that:

- British voters are not asked to choose directly between two or three party leaders. Instead, they vote for a party or – more precisely – for a local party candidate, making a debate between leaders in a sense irrelevant.
- whereas American voters choose between two presidential candidates, three at most, British voters might be in practice choosing from among candidates from the main parties, with possibly those of Respect, UKIP and the Greens and others, as well. This made it harder to determine who should be involved in a debate.
- (perhaps more seriously), such a televised debate would tend to encourage presidential-style politics at a time when many people lament the decline of Parliament. Debates would help to

further the political process and therefore reduce the role of the House of Commons as the main political arena.

- finally, it was argued that there was less need for such a televised clash in Britain than in the United States. American presidents are not members of Congress and do not have to attend to account for their actions. Every week, prime ministers face a grilling in the House, not least from their main opponent. On issues such as Iraq or foundation hospitals, Tony Blair had to justify his policy and persuade the House to back him in major debates. George Bush was under no such pressure from members of the legislature. In Britain, we actually fund a Leader of the Opposition to oppose, attack and present an alternative choice to the incumbent of Number Ten and he has many opportunities to question the Prime Minister of the day.

2010

In 2009, Sky News began a campaign for televised debates between the three party leaders. A joint approach was later made by the BBC, ITV and BSkyB to stage three live debates, one for each broadcaster. In March, a set of seventy-six detailed rules were announced, covering issues such as the selection and role of the audience, the structure of the debates, the role of the moderator and the layout of the set.

After a debate between the Chancellor and would-be Chancellors, there were three Leaders' debates:

1. Domestic issues (ITV)
2. International affairs (Sky)
3. Economic policy (BBC)

The average audiences for the three debates were, respectively: 9.4, 4.1 and 8.1 million. They indicated the popularity of the debates, which stimulated discussion well beyond the numbers who had actually seen them. Nick Clegg was widely perceived to have emerged most successfully from the debates, subsequent polls suggesting that he had won the first, was joint-winner with David Cameron of the second and second behind Cameron in the third. Kavanagh and Cowley[9] quote the prevailing view that emerged in a post-mortem of broadcasters and politicians held under the auspices of BAFTA, namely that the debates 'had been a success and that they had come to stay, with only a little tweaking of the rules at the next election'.

Plaid Cymru and the SNP complained about their exclusion. Some broadcasters were disappointed by the 'collateral damage' they caused, particularly the down-playing of other traditional forms of television coverage such as serious political interviews, which had already lost much of their influence and importance in previous general elections. So too news bulletins and other current affairs programmes spent so much of their time preparing the ground for debates, assessing performances and seeking to gauge their impact, that their own distinctive character and approaches tended to be lost.

Electoral systems

Electoral systems and the issue of electoral reform have been on the political agenda in many parts of Europe and beyond in recent decades. In the 1970s, those Mediterranean countries (Greece, Portugal and Spain) that moved away from dictatorship to become fledgling democracies had to decide upon the most desirable method of election. In the early 1990s, the creation of 'new democracies' in Central and Eastern Europe meant that several more countries faced a similar decision. Apart from this interest in electoral systems in countries where the system of government had changed, there has been developing interest in the subject in long established democracies ranging from Italy to Japan, from New Zealand to the United Kingdom. In established democracies, change does not come about easily in peacetime, because the political parties in power have a vested interest in the system that elected them.

The choice of electoral system is important. To a considerable degree, it shapes how the body politic operates. As Farrell points out:[10] '[Elections] are the cogs which keep the wheels of democracy properly functioning'. They are relevant to any discussion of representation, parties and party systems, the formation of governments and the politics of coalition. Indeed, the interim report of Labour's Plant Committee on the subject observed that:[11] 'There can be nothing more fundamental in a democracy than proposals to change an electoral system'.

The choice of system raises issues about the nature of representative government and the purpose of elections. Representative government is based on the idea that the legislature represents the will of the people. For some, it is crucial that the elected chamber should mathematically reflect the voters' wishes and be sensitive to

Box 9.3 Opinion polls: their uses, accuracy and value

Opinion polls are a familiar feature of modern election campaigns. Polling has been carried out in Britain since 1938, but it has been only since the 1950s that it has been done on a regular basis. Two main methods have been tried, random and quota sampling. Random sampling, based on the Electoral Register, has been used in conducting the majority of surveys in the last three elections, only MORI continuing with face-to-face interviewing. As random polling has been refined with the use of more phone contact, it is increasingly favoured by polling companies, because:

- it has a lower probability of error
- it is now possible to get higher response rates.

The record of the pollsters
In the early years of regular polling, in the 1950s and 1960s, the record of the polling companies was very good. They were remarkably successful in pinpointing the actual outcome of elections, often within a small percentage of the result achieved by each party. In 1970, twenty out of twenty-one got things badly wrong, only one poll getting the winner right. Thereafter, fortunes were mixed. In an age of greater voter volatility, as class voting began to break down, it was less easy to gauge the true intentions of the electorate and to be sure that those who inclined to one party would actually turn out and vote for it. The performance in 1992 was particularly poor. Most polls predicted a 'hung Parliament', in which Labour would be the largest party. The error in the predictions of the likely gap between the two parties was greater than it had ever been.

Ever since the failings in 1992, there have been serious doubts about the performance of the opinion polls. In 1997 and 2001, they were accurate in predicting the winning party, although bearing in mind the scale of the two Labour victories this success was unsurprising. However, particularly in 2001, there was a vast variation in the Labour lead, which ranged from 11 per cent (Rasmussen) to 17 per cent (MORI) in the final polls taken.

Between 1992 and 2005, there was a consistent pro-Labour bias in almost all of the surveys. They overstated Labour support and understated the Conservative vote. Each polling company took steps to correct such biases, but their solutions depended on what they saw as the causes of past error. Three explanations were available:

1. *Defective sampling methods*: the polls tracked down too many Labour supporters and too few Conservatives
2. *The spiral of silence*: some shy Tories claimed to be undecided, being unwilling to admit their allegiance to a stranger asking questions. This may be because they thought that they might be perceived as acting selfishly, if they backed a party with a tax-cutting thrust.
3. *Turnout*: in assessing their data, pollsters made insufficient allowance for differential turnout of Labour and Tory supporters. Labour supporters were more likely to stay at home, especially in safe Labour seats.

2010

Prior to the election, opinion polls influenced Gordon Brown's decision not to hold an election soon after assuming the premiership and they helped to shape the Conservatives' political and electoral strategies. In the campaign proper, they performed an even greater role in the 2010 election than they had in previous ones. There were more polls (over ninety) – taken by a wider array of polling organisations (eleven) – than ever before, with new arrivals such as BRMB, OnePoll, Opinium and TNS all publishing occasional findings. For the first time, the bulk of the research work was done online, rather than in telephone and face-to-face interviews.

Allowing for sampling error, in the early stages of the campaign the polls were broadly agreed in their findings and they continued to point to a hung parliament throughout the campaign. However, the impact of the television debates was to produce a remarkable third party surge, a change in standing greater than anything previously seen in a UK poll. Of the last sixty-four polls taken, forty-nine showed the Liberal Democrats in first or second place.

In the event, the polls had a mixed experience. They were very wrong about the popularity of the Liberal Democrats, the nine eve-of-poll results all overestimating support by between 2 and 5 per cent. They all underestimated the Labour performance by between 1 and 6 per cent and seven underestimated and none overestimated Conservative support. The nine final polls were better at anticipating the gap between Labour and the Conservatives than they were in assessing Liberal Democrat strength. Overall, the final ICM poll was the most successful in anticipating the election outcome.

This was the first time that the polls had underestimated Labour strength since 1983. Boon and Curtice[9] point out that the 'shy-Conservative' syndrome gave way to a 'shy-Labour' variation, in which voting Labour was regarded as unfashionable. In 2010 no fewer than one in five of those who actually voted failed to declare their voting intention when interviewed by ICM for its final poll – and they were nearly twice as likely to vote Labour as Liberal Democrat. Although ICM's final poll prediction (unlike many others) included an adjustment that took into account evidence that Labour voters were apparently particularly reluctant to declare their intentions, that adjustment may not have been sufficient to take full account of what actually happened.

The accuracy of the exit poll was something for which the entire research industry could feel grateful. It had the advantage of relieving some of the pressure on the pre-election pollsters, whose own performance is perhaps more deserving of a place in the dock. Using a larger sample and taken over a wider number of sites than previously, it was particularly geared to assessing close Labour-Liberal Democrat contests. Its 10 p.m. finding was astonishingly accurate, having a total average error of just 1.5 seats. It accurately assessed the number of Conservative victories, underestimated by three the number of Labour ones and overestimated the Liberal Democrat performance by two.

Do polls have any influence and importance?
In the early days of polling, the successes of many pollsters led many commentators to accept their findings without question. Problems in some elections since 1970 have led to greater caution in the use of poll findings. However, whatever the reservations, poll results are still viewed with much interest by politicians, the media and many members of the public – especially when an election is looming.

Polls play an important role in the campaign. Parties do their own private polling to find out about which voters they should target. Polls are useful to party leaders and professionals to help them assess their parties standing with the electorate. They may also assist them in devising their policies and strategies, for when there is evidence that a party is failing to appeal to a key group among the voters or that its policies in one area are out of touch, then it may be wise to make an adjustment.

Prime ministers may find polls helpful in determining when to call an election. Some have been skilful at 'playing the polls', in other words timing the election date to coincide with a period when the polls are showing that their party is 'riding high' in public esteem. However, today, in an age of greater electoral volatility, it is less easy to count on people voting as they say they will. They are more likely to change their minds at the last minute. Moreover, the move to fixed-term elections (see pp. 94–5) will make it more difficult in the future for the Prime Minister to time elections to his or her advantage.

Certain academics and journalists have claimed that polls may affect voting behaviour. There is no consistent evidence one way or the other. Some of them have suggested that there is a bandwagon effect in favour of the party in the lead. According to this theory, the polls encourage voters to climb on the winning party's bandwagon, so they end up backing the victorious side. If such an effect operates, then this should lead to an increase in the lead of the winning party throughout the campaign and between the publication of the final pre-election polls and the election itself. The results of several elections disprove this. In 1992, following several poll leads, Labour lost in the only poll that really mattered, the one on election day. In 1997, the margin of victory in percentage terms was smaller than what polls were suggesting.

Others have mentioned a contradictory boomerang effect in favour of the party in second place. Similarly, if there is a boomerang effect in which electors are encouraged to change sides and support the losing party, the underdog, there ought to be a consistent set of results showing that the margin of the leading party should be cut between the final polls and polling day, whereas the performance of the second party should improve. This is not easy to demonstrate. Results in post-war elections do not uniformly show that the trailing second party improved its rating on election day.

Some countries ban publication of polls in the build-up to polling day, lest there is any influence on voting patterns; critics also suggest that they trivialise the campaign, detracting from concentration on major issues. To many commentators, such a measure seems illiberal in a free country, for companies have a right to publicise what people think, just as have the voters the right to know their findings and – if they so wish – to allow them to influence the way they vote. In any case, if we do not know for sure what effect – if any – polls might have, the case for banning seems unproven. Furthermore, if findings are not published, the results can still leak out; it would be hard to stop poll findings from being published abroad.

every shade of opinion, thereby catering for minority views. Out of the resulting chamber, a government will be formed. For others, it is less important to have a system that mathematically reflects the way electors vote. In their view, an election very broadly represents the swing in the public mood, so that in Britain in 1997 few would doubt that the country wanted a change of government, even if the scale of the Labour victory was exaggerated. According to this view, it is more important to find a system that produces strong government, based upon an effective parliamentary majority. This enables those in power to develop coherent and consistent policies, without facing the risk of regular defeats in the legislature.

Types of electoral system

Controversy over electoral systems centres primarily on how votes are converted into seats. Broadly speaking, there are two categories of electoral system, those that are proportional and those that are not. Within both groups there are many potential variations. Moreover, it is possible to combine elements of the two categories.

Non-proportional systems are the simplest to explain and to operate. The key point about them is that voters are not rewarded strictly according to the share of votes they obtain. In proportional systems, the opposite is true. Their guiding principle is straightforward, namely that parties are awarded seats directly according to the number of votes they win. In its most perfect form, this means that a party winning 45 per cent of the voters cast will receive 45 per cent of the seats available. In practice, although the mechanics are designed with that goal in mind, most systems are not exactly proportional and tend to offer some modest bonus to the largest party – although far less than applies in non-proportional systems.

Non-proportional systems: plurality and majoritarian methods of voting

The most straightforward non-proportional system is the British *first past the post (FPTP)* method, under which the successful candidate is the one who receives the most votes in the single-member constituency. In any contest, a simple plurality of votes is necessary for victory, not a majority. Nationally, FPTP normally leaves one party with a parliamentary majority. The largest party – and sometimes the second party – gains a substantial bonus in seats. Because of this, one party will usually win an outright majority in the legislature.

Other non-proportional methods are majoritarian ones, in which the candidate needs a majority of the votes cast to win the election. This requires a run-off election between the top candidates in a second ballot. The case for such a system is that it ensures that no candidate represents only a minority of the voters. In this category are the French *Double Ballot*, the *Supplementary Vote (SV)* used to elect the London Mayor and the Australian *Alternative Vote (AV)*. The Jenkins enquiry, a commission into possible reform of the UK electoral system established by Tony Blair in December 1997, recommended the AV for the geographical aspect of its proposal for a mixed-member system known as *AV-plus*.

Proportional systems

There are many different forms of proportional representation (PR), all of which are designed to ensure that the number of seats allocated in the legislature is broadly in line with the number of votes won by each party in the election. Unlike the plurality and majoritarian systems above, they operate in multi-member constituencies. Two main sub-divisions are:

1. *The list method*, the most widely used form in which the elector votes for a list of party candidates rather just for a single person. The number of votes won by a party determines how many of its candidates are elected from the party list. List may be closed or open. Under the closed lists used in countries ranging from Portugal to South Africa, voters have no choice over candidates and simply cast a party vote. At the other extreme, are open lists of the sort that enable Swiss voters to vote for individual candidates. Most list systems allow for some element of voter choice.

2. *The Single Transferable Vote (STV)* is used for local and European elections in Northern Ireland. It is the option favoured by the Electoral Reform Society. Voters list candidates in order of preference, and can if they so wish choose contenders from more than one party. To get elected, a candidate needs to obtain a quota determined by a mathematical formula. The candidates with the least votes are eliminated and have their votes transferred to the remaining candidates on the basis of the second preferences, a process that continues until all seats are filled.

There are also *hybrid systems* such as the *Additional Member System (AMS)*. These have developed in the post-war era, in a bid to obtain something of the best of both worlds. They have become popular in the new democracies of Central and Eastern Europe. They

Table 9.1 International voting systems

	FPTP	AV	SV	AV-Plus	List PR	STV PR	AMS
Where used	UK, US, Canada, India	Australia (Lower House)	London Mayoralty	Urged by Jenkins	Israel, most of Europe, Latin America	Irish Republic, Malta	Germany, Hungary, Japan, UK devolved elections
How it works	Leading candidate elected in first and only ballot.	Voters rank candidates in order of preference, 1, 2, 3, 4, etc. Candidates eliminated from bottom up, votes allocated to others until someone gets 50%.	Variation of AV. Voter ranks only 1, 2. All but top two candidates eliminated, their votes allocated to those remaining.	Mixed system in which up to half the seats are elected by AV, the rest distributed to candidates on a party list.	Electors vote for a party's list of candidates. Parties win seats according to votes they obtain. Successful candidates taken from list.	Voters list candidates in order of preference. Candidates need to obtain quota to get elected. Their surplus votes are redistributed according to second preferences shown on their ballot papers. Then, step-by-step elimination of candidates from bottom, until all seats are filled.	Some seats allocated on a plurality basis (FPTP), others on a party basis using PR. The latter acts as a 'top-up' to secure an overall proportional outcome.

	FPTP	AV	SV	AV-Plus	List PR	STV PR	AMS
Merits	Simple, easy to operate. Normally produces clear outcome, makes one-party government likely. Retains MP–constituency link.	Fairly simple to graft on to present system. Keeps MP–constituency link, ensures winning candidates have majority support at local level. More fair to smaller parties, but single-party government possible.	Fairly simple to graft on to present system. Keeps MP–constituency link, ensures winning candidates have majority support at local level. More fair to smaller parties, but single-party government possible.	Limited, not radical change. Depending on exact division of constituency and top-up seats, can produce a fairly proportional result, yet still make single-party government possible. A compromise between stability and fairness.	Usually a strong connection between votes won and seats obtained. Fairer to small parties, good where there are minorities in population. Open lists allow for voter choice. Likely to produce coalitions, which have their advantages. Good at securing election of more women and other minorities to legislature.	Good connection of votes and seats. Fairer to small parties, good where there are minorities in population. Also allows voter to choose between candidates of same party. Likely to produce coalitions, which have their advantages. Good at securing election of more women and other minorities to legislature	Produces effective proportional results. Fairer to small parties. Keeps MP–constituency link. Makes coalitions – with their possible advantages – more likely. Good at securing election of more women and other minorities to legislature

Table 9.1 (continued)

De-merits						
Produces distorted results, greatly favouring governing party. Some areas of country are dominated by MPs of one party – e.g. Wales. Leads to election of 'minority' MPs. Harsh on third and small parties, poor for election of women and minority candidates. Limits voter choice.	Can produce very distorted results, as it would have in 1997, 2001 because of tactical voting. Poor for election of women and minority candidates. Makes some votes more valuable than others, as preferences count.	Can produce very distorted results, as it would have in 1997, 2001 because of tactical voting. In some parts of country, one main party can gain few or no MPs. Not fully just to third and small parties. Poor for election of women and minority candidates. Makes some votes more valuable than others, as preferences count.	Can be unfair on third and small parties, much depending on division of seats. Role of 'top-up' MPs unclear – who do they represent? Might they be seen as second-class members? Could lead to coalitions, which have some disadvantages.	Closed lists place power in the hands of the party managers who can position 'troublesome' candidates near the bottom. They deny voter choice. PR makes coalitions more likely, with all their alleged disadvantages. No link of MP and constituency.	A more complex system than the others, although the difficulty is for the Returning Officers rather than the voters: slower results etc. PR makes coalitions more likely, with all their alleged disadvantages. No link of MP and constituency.	Doubts re status of 'top-up' MPs, as to who they represent and whether they are seen as second class. Makes coalitions more likely, with all their alleged disadvantages.

Abbreviations: FPTP, First Past The Post; AV, Alternative Vote; SV, Supplementary Vote; AV-Plus, Alternative Vote Plus; List PR, List Proportional Representation; STV PR, Single Transferable Vote Proportional Representation; AMS, Additional Member System.

combine the geographical representation of the plurality method with the party representation of the proportional schemes and do so in a way that also delivers a broadly proportional outcome. Again, schemes vary significantly in detail, but in Germany half of the seats in the Bundestag are filled by plurality voting in single-member seats (thus ensuring a geographical link of an elected member and his constituency), whilst the other half are allocated to parties, with the aim of achieving a proportional result overall. The victorious candidates under the proportional element are taken from the party's lists.

Variants of proportional representation might well produce a more representative parliament whose composition fairly reflects all or most shades of popular opinion. They are less likely to yield a 'strong' government.

British experience: the operation of FPTP in the general election of 2010

It is often observed by critics of FPTP that it is has ceased to be relevant to UK politics over recent decades. The system works best when there are just two main parties and the minor parties secure only a very small proportion of the vote. During the 1950s, the Conservatives and Labour always won at least 94 per cent of the vote, the Liberals never getting more than 6 per cent. However, in times of greater political pluralism, British politics may no longer be well served by a voting system designed for such a two-party era. According to its critics, FPTP not only fails the 'fairness test' by generating major discrepancies between the number of votes secured and the proportion of seats won in the House of Commons. As the outcome of the 2010 general election illustrates, it can no longer guarantee single-party government.

Many of the anomalies that can arise under the British FPTP system (see p. 333) were again in evidence in 2010. Among the foremost of them:

- There was a clear discrepancy between the proportion of total votes gained by the parties and the seats they won. The largest party benefited from the system, the Conservatives winning

Table 9.2 The outcome in 2010

Party	% votes obtained	No. of seats obtained	% of seats obtained
Conservatives	36.1	307	47.2
Labour	29.0	258	39.7
Liberal Democrats	23.0	57	8.8
Others	11.9	28	4.3

more than 47 per cent of the seats, yet only 36.1 per cent of those who voted, a mere 23.5 per cent of the 45.6 million electorate supported them. Labour also won a much larger share of the seats than its share of the popular vote merited. Third parties suffered, the Liberal Democrats winning more than 850,000 votes more than in 2005 yet losing five seats. Other small parties fared badly. With 1 per cent of the national vote, the Greens won their first seat, but Respect lost its single MP. UKIP and the BNP failed to win any seats in spite of securing 3.5 per cent and 3.8 per cent of the vote, respectively, in the seats where they stood (3.2 per cent and 1.9 per cent, nationally). Overall, it took only 33,350 votes to elect a Labour MP, 34,989 to elect a Conservative MP, 119,788 to elect a Liberal Democrat and 285,616 to elect a Green.

- There was still a bias that operated against the Conservatives in the electoral system, brought about by a combination of factors: Labour's vote is more efficiently distributed than that of the Conservatives, Labour representing many sparsely populated inner-city seats; the fact that English constituencies are historically larger than those in Scotland and Wales, where Labour does better (over Great Britain as a whole, in spite of a modification of electoral boundaries prior to this election, the average electorate in those seats won by the Conservatives was 3,811 higher than the equivalent figure for those seats won by Labour); and the effects of some anti-Conservative **tactical voting** (less of a factor than in 1997 and 2005, in part because the Conservatives were

less unpopular and Labour less popular than on those occasions).
Curtice et al.[13] calculate that such is the anti-Conservative bias
that it still remains the case that if the two main parties were to
secure the same overall share of the vote, 'Labour would have as
many as 51 more seats than the Conservatives'.

- The **'electoral deserts'** highlighted by the Jenkins enquiry[12]
  were once more in evidence. Conservative voters were effectively
  disfranchised in much of Scotland (16.7 per cent of the votes, one
  seat), and still lacked significant representation in several large
  conurbations; on Merseyside, they won 21.1 per cent of the vote
  and won one out of fifteen seats. Labour supporters across whole
  swathes of the South were left unrepresented. Although in combination the Liberal Democrats and Labour won on average 38.3
  per cent of the votes cast in Surrey, the Conservatives control
  each of the county's eleven constituencies.
- More MPs than ever before (433, 66.7 per cent) were minority
  ones, in that they did not receive the support of 50 per cent of
  their local electorate. The smallest winning percentage of votes
  was that of the Liberal Democrat in Norwich South who won
  with just 29.4 per cent of the votes.
- Women and members of ethnic minorities were underrepre-
  sented. Only 22 per cent of the successful candidates were female
  and only 4.2 per cent belonged to ethnic minority groups.

As a result of such anomalies and distortions, the issue of electoral
reform again came up for reconsideration. Some commentators
(e.g. Bogdanor[13]) pointed out that in a three-party situation FPTP
has become a particularly blunt instrument whose bizarre outcomes
are a travesty of democracy. However, whereas in the past attention was often drawn to the unfavourable treatment received by the
Liberal Democrats, on this occasion their reduced number of MPs
was sufficient to make them eligible as coalition partners for the
Conservatives. Moreover, even before the election took place, there
was more sympathy for electoral reform, Labour having pledged to
support the Alternative Vote in a referendum, in spite of the hostility of many of its own MPs. Once the election was over, part of the
Coalition Agreement was to hold such a referendum, eventually held
in May 2011.

Some arguments surrounding the debate over FPTP versus PR

For FPTP and against PR

Farrell[14] has neatly summarised the three main themes in any defence of the British system, as 'simplicity, stability and constituency representation'. These points are worthy of further consideration:

- *The FPTP system is easy to understand* especially for the voter who marks an X on the ballot paper. It has the alleged merits of simplicity and familiarity, and as such, is widely accepted.

- *It usually produces clear and unambiguous outcomes, leading to the formation of strong, stable, single-party governments with an overall majority* (see Table 9.3); coalition government other than in times of emergency is virtually unknown. Single-party governments pinpoint political responsibility. The voters know who to praise or blame when things go right or wrong. Such administrations are also said to be capable of providing effective leadership for the nation. This is viewed as more important than achieving a proportional result. In Britain, we know who is to form the government immediately after the election is over. There is no need for private deals to be done by politicians who bargain in smoke-filled rooms, away from the public gaze; it is the voters directly who choose which party is in office.

- *Because we have single-member constituencies, there is a close relationship between the MP and his or her constituency.* The one member alone has responsibility for that area which he or she can get to know well.

Table 9.3 Party majorities in recent elections

Year	Majority
1987	101
1992	21
1997	178
2001	146
2005	67
2010	78 Coalition majority in hung parliament

Once elected, the MP represents all who live in the area, not just those who voted for one particular party; all citizens know who to approach if they have a problem or grievance needing resolution. This is very different from what happens under some more proportional systems in which several elected members represent a broad geographical area.

In his enquiry, Lord Jenkins[15] himself recognised that FPTP is not without benefits, referring to the 'by no means negligible' merits of the present system. In addition to the points above, the Commissioners made the point that it ensures that governments and MPs are accountable. It enables the electorate sharply and cleanly to rid itself of an unwanted government; in other words, it is easy to punish those directly responsible for their errors, to 'throw the rascals out'.

Apart from the positive case for FPTP, there are disadvantages associated with proportional representation. Among specific criticisms often made, it is suggested that:

- PR encourages minor parties to stand for election and makes it more difficult for any one party to emerge victorious. Duverger's[16] observation is often quoted, namely that: 'The simple-majority, single-ballot system favours the two party system; the simple-majority system with second ballot and proportional representation favour multi-partyism.'
- The primary anxiety of those opposed to an abandonment of FPTP is that it would greatly increase the likelihood of perpetual coalition government. As neither main party has ever secured a majority of the votes cast in any election post-war, it is unlikely that single-party government would result from any election held under a more proportional system.

For PR

The case for the use of a proportional scheme of voting in Britain has much to do with the allegedly adverse effects of FPTP. Among its anticipated benefits, a proportional electoral system:

- *would not exaggerate movements of opinion within the electorate* and – as in 1997 and 2001 – produce landslide majorities that are often based on an ever-diminishing proportion of the national vote.

- *would not allow a government to exercise power on the basis of minority popular support*; e.g. Labour obtained power in 2005 with the support of only 35.2 per cent of those who voted and 22.8 per cent of the backing of the whole electorate.
- *would provide greater justice to third and small parties.* Traditionally, it has been the Liberals in their various guises who have suffered from FPTP, although in 1997 the Conservatives lost all representation in Scotland in spite of gaining 17 per cent of the vote.
- *would yield governments which have the backing of the majority of the electorate,* and therefore could claim legitimacy; they may be coalition governments, but the parties which voted for them would *in toto* have a broader appeal than is the case at present.
- *would avoid the geographical divisions brought about by FPTP.* In 1997 the Conservatives were wiped out in Scotland, Wales and the large English provincial cities, just as Labour had suffered badly in the southern half of England back in the 1980s.
- *would overcome the problem of 'electoral deserts' identified in the Jenkins enquiry,* in which the opposition can make little impact and get even less reward. Many seats in the House of Commons rarely change hands, so that supporters of the minority parties (e.g. Conservatives in Glasgow) have little likelihood of ever securing the election of a representative who supports his or her views. Significant sections of the population are condemned to almost permanent minority status.
- *would, unlike FPTP, be better at producing parliamentary representation for women and ethnic minorities.* For instance, since the introduction of a more proportional system in New Zealand, there has been a marked in crease in the percentage of women elected.

In addition, of course, there is a positive case for proportional representation and coalitions. Proportional representation:

- *is fair* because it produces a close relationship between votes and seats
- *gives minority parties more representation* and encourages voters to back them in the knowledge that they will not be wasting their vote
- *makes coalitions more likely.* Coalitions can provide government that is stable (because it rests on broad backing), legitimate (because it has wide popular support) and with a propensity towards

moderation (because it encourages the politics of consensus and cooperation).

Some general points about coalitions to bear in mind

The primary anxiety of those who oppose any abandonment of FPTP for Westminster elections is that it would greatly increase the likelihood of perpetual coalition government. In that a 'third force' (probably the Liberal Democrats) would gain a greater share of influence, this would be at the expense of the two main parties. Because of its implications, the pros and cons of coalition government are highly relevant in any discussion of electoral systems.

Inevitably, on either side of the argument, examples are used selectively and the case tends to be overstated or oversimplified. Coalitions can be strong or weak, successful and unsuccessful. Much depends on the nature of the country involved and its political system. Some points are, however, worth stressing, notably that:

- In Europe, where proportional electoral systems are used, coalition governments are common.
- Coalitions and PR may be associated with greater instability of government but not all countries experience this. Under the Weimar Republic, before Hitler's take-over in 1933, Germany did, but the country was then facing acute problems; post-Nazi Germany has had coalitions and stable government. Much depends on the social and political system, on whether or not there is a tradition of stable politics and whether there are many parties, reflecting the existence of many groups within society or acute regional differences. Modern Germany is often cited as producing strong, effective coalitions that have ruled well. Is it this that has produced the economic policies that have given her prosperity, or is it because of these economic successes that governments have been long-lasting? Of course, we have the experience of Scotland's devolved government to draw upon. The Executive has been governed by coalitions or a minority administration since its creation in 1999. The arrangement has proved a stable one, with ministers capable of implementing a programme agreed with their partner, or (in the case of the SNP 2007–11) one that had the tacit support of the Green contingent at Holyrood.

- Where coalitions have not lasted nearly as well, as in France's Fourth Republic to 1958, one can overstate the instability involved. Coalitions including Socialists, Radicals, MRP and Independents frequently broke up because of disagreements on colonial and foreign issues, and stalemate could result. Italy still has such disagreements, but though – as in the Fourth Republic – ministries often collapse and a game of 'musical chairs' is played over government positions, there has often been much continuity of policy and considerable economic achievement in both countries.

- Sometimes these coalitions have taken a few days to form, often longer. Back in pre-1958 France, one took a month and Belgium (2010–11) set a world record of 538 days of very prolonged bargaining. If stable administrations result (that can last a few years), then the wait may seem worthwhile. At least, the changes made by such a government will be agreed ones, backed by a group of parties who have more electoral support than a British government normally has.

- Germany has been quoted as having stable and generally effective governments. Stability implies continuity, a lack of conflict, and for Germany the system seems to have worked well. To be effective, government doesn't always have to be so stable and governments that are stable don't always produce effective policies.

- In many of these countries, there is no tradition of a two-party system where voters know that the party they vote for will be able to put their programme into effect. At best, their party will be part of a governing coalition, able only to carry out the parts of its policy that its partners agree upon. By contrast, under the British FPTP system, the voter knows that the winning party (yes, because of a distorted electoral system!) will be largely able to carry out its programme, and thus an election is a choice of a party and set of policies to govern. The idea of coalition arrangements (with bargains and deals over policy after the election) is alien to our tradition. This may not matter, but has to be appreciated.

- In spite of the preceding point, the experience of the period since May 2010 has shown that – contrary to some expectations – coalition government can work in the UK. How well it can deliver its policies is too early to assess and involves personal judgement. However, it has survived its first year and under the terms of its own legislation on fixed-term parliaments should be secure until 2015.

No best electoral system

There are different views of the criteria necessary for a good electoral system. The then Home Secretary, Jack Straw, set out four for the Jenkins enquiry into the most appropriate way of electing our MPs. Its brief was to

> observe the requirement for broad proportionality, the need for stable government, an extension of voter choice and the maintenance of a link between honourable members and geographical constituencies.

There are inevitably trade-offs that have to be made between these criteria. Much depends on the view taken of the primary function of an election. There are two schools of thought. The first argues that elections are about choosing a legislature that represents the popular will, an outcome likely to be brought about by some form of proportional representation. The second argues that they are primarily concerned with choosing a government, an outcome more usually associated with use of the FPTP system. Broadly speaking, on the Continent the emphasis is upon choosing a representative assembly. From its midst, a government can be constructed which commands sufficient support – usually, a coalition. In Britain, the emphasis has traditionally been upon choosing a government that is likely to be stable and strong, allowing ministers to get on with the job, but ultimately accountable to the electorate.

Of course, governments can still be effective if they are coalitions and the virtues of strong administrations can be overplayed. Different writers reach different conclusions about what constitutes strength. Norton,[17] as a defender of the first past the post method used in British elections, sees strong government as a situation in which one party dominates the House of Commons. In contrast, Bogdanor[18] argues that a government cannot be strong unless it represents the majority of the voters. By this definition, no post-war British government would have passed the test.

Table 9.4 UK electoral systems currently in use: a summary

General and local elections	First past the post
European elections	Closed list PR
Scottish and Welsh devolved elections	AMS
Scottish local elections	STV
London Mayoralty	SV
London Assembly	AMS
NI local/assembly/European elections	STV PR

There is no perfect system that is necessarily best in all circumstances, ideal for all countries at every period of time. In countries with acute social or political divisions (Israel and Northern Ireland among them), a proportional method is appropriate in that it ensures some representation for minority groups and reduces the danger of tyrannical majority rule. In stable countries in which government changes hands at fairly regular intervals, there is arguably not the same need to show concern for opposing and minority viewpoints.

Indeed, it is quite possible to have different types of election within a particular country, as Britain currently experiences (see below). All of them have their merits and demerits.

Voting behaviour

In all developed countries, social changes have occurred that mean that old nostrums have had to be reconsidered in the light of experience. This applies to Britain and America, as well as on the Continent.

The trend in most countries is now for voters to be less committed to their long-term allegiances. Stability rather than change was once the established pattern in voting behaviour, and many voters were reluctant or unwilling to deviate from their regular habits. In recent years, partisan dealignment has occurred, and this means that there has been a weakening of the old loyalties, and a new volatility among the electorate.

Table 9.5 The relative importance of class voting: some examples

Importance	Examples
Low	USA, 'new' democracies – e.g. Hungary, Poland
Relatively low, little evidence of decline	Ireland, Netherlands, Spain
More significant, but in decline	Austria, Belgium, Germany
Relatively high, but in decline	Denmark, Sweden, UK

Based on data provided in T. Bale, *European Politics: A Comparative Introduction*, Palgrave, 2005.

Social class was once a key determinant of voting, with the working classes tending to vote for the more progressive party and the better-off inclining to the political Right. It was still important in the 1980s and 1990s. For instance, Ball[19] shows how in the French presidential contest of 1988 more than two thirds of the business, agrarian and professional classes voted for the conservative candidate, Chirac, whereas an even higher percentage of working people voted for the socialist, Mitterrand. In the same way, Labour in its bleak years in the 1980s continued to find its core support from the least well-off in the inner cities, and in regions such as Scotland and Wales.

Class voting varies considerably between countries, relatively significant in some, much less so in others, as Table 9.5 indicates. However, the hold of class is not what it was. Whilst there were always many voters in Britain and the rest of Western Europe who deviated from class voting, that number substantially increased in the 1980s as right-wing administrations managed to increase their appeal among the more skilled working people who had aspirations to upgrade their lifestyles and prospects. Old class structures have broken down as many sections of the population have become better off and the manual working class has diminished in size.

The personality of the candidate has assumed greater importance, the more so as party leanings have become less firm and voters are able to learn and see so much more about those who would lead them via the mass media. The importance of issues and of the election campaign have also become more significant as there are more votes 'up for grabs' today.

Determinants of voting behaviour

Long-term influences include:

- *Party identification and loyalty.* Electors identify with a particular party and loyalties are forced, so that a strong long-term alignment exists (partisanship). Family influences are often reinforced by the membership of particular groups and later social experiences.
- *Social class.* Whereas in the United States, the deep-seated association with a party was often stressed, in Britain and on the Continent more attention was paid to membership of some social grouping. As Hague and Harrop[20] put it: 'Their social identity anchored their party choice.'
- *Other factors relating to the social structure, such as age, gender, occupation, race and religion.*

Short-term influences include:

- *The economy.* This covers indicators of inflation, unemployment and disposable income and in particular how voters view their future prospects (whether or not they 'feel good'). Governments like to 'go to the country' at a time when people will feel good about their material circumstances and their future prospects.
- *The personal qualities and appeal of the party leaders.* These are more important today given the media's infatuation with personalities.
- *The style and effectiveness of party campaigning.* This has already been explored in some depth on pp. 318–33.
- *The impact of the mass media.* As we have seen in the above, the media now play an important part. They may or may not have a direct influence on how voters vote (see pp. 350–1), but they help to determine what the election is about and the issues that are important. They provide information and – in the case of the press – dramatic headlines which can damage the standing of leaders (e.g. the damaging portrayal of Neil Kinnock in 1987 and 1992, in the *Sun*).

Box 9.4 The impact of the mass media on voting: conflicting theories

Extensive research has been done into the effects of the mass media – in particular, television – on public attitudes and voting behaviour. None of it has been conclusive. Nor can it be so, not least because the influence of television is difficult to distinguish from the impact of other long- and short-term factors.

Between the wars, in an era when dictators were aware of the power of propaganda, it was common to believe that the organs of communication must have a significant impact in moulding people's outlooks. Studies often used *the hypodermic model*, by which a passive and gullible public was seen as highly vulnerable to a syringe injection of indoctrinated material. It was assumed that the electorate would be unable to withstand the malign influences of those who sought to manipulate them.

This 'manipulative theory' was soon challenged for American researchers were unable to find any evidence to substantiate it in a democratic country. They developed a *minimum effects model* that suggested that voters used the media to reinforce their own outlook. They know what they need from the media and take that and that alone. In other words, as free agents rather than mindless victims, they filter information which substantiates their own predetermined beliefs. Hence the name sometimes employed for this theory, *the uses and gratifications model*, a term used by Blumler and McQuail[21] in their 1968 study.

The reinforcement theory held sway for many years, but as television became more pervasive and played such a key part in people's daily lives, its adequacy was called into question. It gave way in the 1970s to the theories advanced by the Glasgow University Media Group. Its members emphasised the importance of *agenda setting*, stressing that by deciding on the issues that are granted coverage, television and papers help to determine what the public is thinking about, if not actually what they think. As Walter Lippman[22] put it many years ago, in speaking about press influence: 'It is like a beam of a searchlight that moves restlessly about, bringing one episode and then another out of the darkness and into vision'.

In an election campaign, the media directs our attention to the candidates and the issues, determining what will be discussed on a particular day. If the manner in which stories are presented tends to reinforce consensual values and portray 'extremists' in an unflattering light, then this might be an important influence.

The most recent studies often refer to *the independent effects model*. This recognises that the impact of media messages will vary according to the person or group that receives the message. Indeed, they may have different effects on different people, and at different times, but that it is common-sense to assume that as voters nowadays spend so much time viewing TV programmes they are likely to be influenced by them in some degree – the more so in an age when traditional allegiances have substantially been eroded.

The suspicion nowadays is that the media have a greater importance than that accorded to them in reinforcement theory. At the very least they provide plenty of information, so that people should know more than did those who lived in previous generations. Particularly in areas of policy on which they are ignorant or lacking much knowledge, it is reasonable to assume a greater degree of influence, the more so as many of them confess that they get most of their information from television.

The difficulty is to measure the extent of any media influence on voters. It is hard enough to do this over a short period, but to do so over the long term is almost impossible. The cost of establishing research over many years and the complexity of the task of interviewing the same people, are enormous barriers to investigation, so that analysts are bound to rely on reasonable speculation in this area. However, we do have some research from studies of cultural effects of television and the printed word.

Controversy continues to surround the issue of media influence. Cultural attitudes, social values and political opinions are all liable to media influence, but the extent and nature of that influence is difficult to ascertain and continues to be a matter of academic contention.

- *The events leading up to the election.* The 'Winter of Discontent' wrecked Labour's chances in 1979, in the same way that the humiliating circumstances of British withdrawal from the ERM (1992) and the connection in the public mind of the Major government with sleaze (1997) seriously undermined faith in the Conservatives. More recently, the handling of the war with Iraq seriously damaged the reputation of the Labour administration, and in particular made many voters question the veracity of Tony Blair. In contrast, the successful outcome of the Falklands War boosted the prospects of Margaret Thatcher in 1983.

Broadly, the long-term factors have declined in their importance in British politics and the short-term ones have assumed an increased significance. The breakdown of these traditional associations has been of considerable importance for the parties that can no longer count on the support they once took for granted.

Voting in Britain

Post-war patterns

The features most noted in the post-war years up to 1970 were:

- the stability of voting patterns, as people stayed loyal to the party they had always supported. As Punnett[23] put it in 1971: 'For most people, voting behaviour is habitual and ingrained'.
- that elections were determined by a body of floating voters in key marginal constituencies, whose votes needed to be targeted by the parties if they were to have a chance of success.
- the uniform nature of the swing across the United Kingdom, which showed that voters in one area tended to behave in much the same way as those elsewhere.
- the domination of the two main parties which between them could count on the support of the majority of the electorate. This reached a high point in 1951 when the Conservatives and Labour between them gained 96.8 per cent of the vote, but in 1966 they still obtained 89.8 per cent.

In the past thirty years many of those assumptions have proved to be no longer valid. The parties can no longer anticipate the degree of support they once enjoyed. Since the 1970s, the rise of third parties has made inroads into the share of the vote the two parties can command, as the figures indicate:

Table 9.6 Average share of the vote for each party in post-war elections			
	Conservative	**Labour**	**Liberal/Liberal Democrat**
1945–1970	45.3	46.0	7.1
1974–2010	37.9	36.3	9.4

Voting behaviour in recent years

In 1994, Madgwick[24] concluded that: 'Voting is still related to social class, but the relationship is complex, and there is less confidence about the significance of the term'. His conclusion was heavily influenced by the work of Ivor Crewe whose researches in the 1970s and subsequently showed that not only was class identification weakening, but so was party identification generally.

Crewe's publication of *Decade of De-alignment*[25] was a psephological milestone. Using data from Essex University's *British Election Study*, Bo Sarlvik and Crewe analysed elections in the 1970s, culminating in the Conservative victory in 1979. They showed the extent to which the two parties had steadily lost their once reliable supporters, people who voted for the same party in successive elections. In particular, the writers discovered that demographic changes were taking their toll of Labour, for the old working-class communities were being destroyed by redevelopment schemes and inner cities were emptying. Workers moving to new towns and expanding small towns around London were less likely to vote Labour. Areas of population decline – like the North and South Wales – were traditionally Labour, while growth areas – mainly in the South East – were strongly Conservative, a point emphasised by constituency boundary changes. Labour's electoral base was being eroded, a point which led Kellner[26] to write that the 'sense of class solidarity which propelled Labour to power in 1945 has all but evaporated'.

The Crewe study was particularly famed for its distinction between the old and the new working class. He wrote of 'the traditional working class of the council estates, the public sector, industrial Scotland and the North, and the old industrial unions . . . the affluent and expanding working class of the new estates and new service economy of the South' [the new working class]. By the 1980s, it seemed that **embourgeoisement** was a significant factor favouring the Conservatives, for in 1979 members of the skilled 'new' working class were seduced by Thatcherite support for tax cuts, and shared certain Conservative attitudes on race, unions, nationalisation and crime.

Labour's claim to be the party of the working class took a strong blow in the 1980s. It may be true that the Labour vote remained largely working class, but the working class was no longer largely Labour. To be successful again, Labour had to succeed in attracting

Category	Current % of population	Groups included
Table 9.7 Social class categorisations in common use by polling companies		
A/B	28	Higher/lower managerial, professional and administrative
C1	29	White collar, skilled, supervisory or lower non-manual
C2	19	Skilled manual
D/E	23	Semi-skilled and unskilled manual/residual, casual workers, long-term unemployed and very poor

more skilled workers back into the fold. Under the Blair leadership, the position dramatically improved. In 1997 and 2001, New Labour did well in all social categories (as listed in Table 9.7), and only among the AB voters did the Conservatives retain a lead. In 2010, the Conservatives outperformed Labour in all sections of the community, other than classes DE.

What influences British voters today?

We have noted the broad trend in all democracies away from group or party voting. This is not to say that there has been a complete dealignment, but rather a weakening of existing patterns and attachments. But the consequences of this dealignment have been profoundly important for voting behaviour. In particular, there is now a more volatile and sceptical electorate whose votes are 'up for grabs', liable to be influenced by a range of factors. These include the short-term factors to which we have already referred:

- Political issues
- The economy
- Party leaders
- Party image
- The effectiveness of party campaigning.

Table 9.8 Voting behaviour in the 2010 general election

Category	Conservative	Labour	Lib Dem	Other
Social class				
AB	39	26	22	12
C1	39	28	24	9
C2	37	29	22	12
DE	32	35	13	20
Gender				
Men	38	28	22	10
Women	36	31	26	8
Age				
18–24	30	31	30	9
25–34	35	30	29	7
35–44	34	31	26	9
45–54	34	28	26	12
55–64	38	28	23	12
65+	44	31	16	9

Source: Ipsos MORI, 'How Britain Voted in 2010', 21 May 2010.

In more pragmatic times, voters come to a general assessment of the parties, based on what they have done and what they propose to do. They look for competence and the skill of consultants and other marketing men is to generate an impression of confidence and trust in the abilities of ministers and would-be ministers. They are much influenced by prevailing economic conditions, particularly their disposable income, and levels of inflation and unemployment, rewarding success and punishing poor performance. In 1997, the perception that the Conservatives were no longer competent in economic management was a devastating blow to party prospects.

Voting is now much influenced by the opinions and judgements of the voters, what Denver[27] calls 'judgemental voting'. As he concludes:

People will disagree over what exactly the judgements are about – issues, ideologies, images, personal economic prospects, party leaders – and this may vary from election to election: but it is the transition from an aligned and socialised electorate to a dealigned and judgemental electorate that has underpinned electoral developments in Britain over the past half-century.

Turnout in elections

Voting is the most usual form of political participation. Voter turnout refers to the percentage of the voting-age population that actually turns out on election day. A good turnout of voters is often considered to be a healthy sign in any democracy, as this appears to indicate vitality and interest.

Many advanced countries have turnouts consistently above 75 per cent, some over 90 per cent, but those with exceptionally high figures (Australia, Belgium and Italy) have compulsory voting laws. Among European countries that do not compel people to vote, Austria, Denmark, Germany, Norway and Sweden have had impressive turnouts in recent elections. All of them have arrangements which facilitate easy registration.

Britain has usually fared less well than the established European democracies over the last few decades, its 59.4 per cent figure in 2001 being dramatically down on its traditional 70–75 per cent turnout. Turnouts for local, devolved and European elections have usually been abysmally low.

Turnout is lower in the United States than almost any other advanced industrial democracy in the world. Many analysts would say that the way in which American states organise and administer voter registration explains its lower voter turnout, to a significant degree. Piven and Cloward[28] have shown that of the Americans who do register, more than 85 per cent turn out on election day. This places them much further up the turnout league for the world's democracies than the percentage who actually voted in the 2008 election (itself the best figure since 1960) would suggest.

Most democracies have found that the figures for turnout have declined in the last few elections and this has led to alarm about the degree of apathy about or even alienation from the political system

Box 9.5 Turnout: some international comparisons

Turnout in the post-war era appears to be relatively high in the established democracies of Western Europe and low in countries which have gained their freedom more recently. Yet in South Africa, the excitement produced by the first democratic elections has inspired many people to vote. In the United States, where elections of various types are so often held, there is no such enthusiasm.

The figures for turnout in the most recently held election to mid 2009 in an assortment of countries were as follows (in %):

Australia (2007)[a]	95.2
Austria (2008)	81.7
Belgium (2007)[a]	91.1
Brazil (2006)	83.3
Denmark (2007)	86.6
Finland (2007)	65.0
India (2004)	57.8
New Zealand (2008)	79.5
Portugal (2009)	59.7
South Africa (2009)	77.3
United Kingdom (2010)	65.1
United States (2008)[b]	56.9

Figures taken from IDEA
[a] Country with compulsory voting.
[b] Presidential, rather than parliamentary, election.

that many voters now experience. Many voters across Europe and America seem increasingly disillusioned with the performance of parties in office and with the politicians who represent them. Promise has not always been matched by outcome and, in the eyes of many voters, the parties and politicians all seem as bad as each other. Moreover, party differences have narrowed as some of the big issues of capitalism versus communism, and peace and warfare, in the Cold War have ceased to be so relevant. The distinctions between party programmes are not often fundamental ones.

It may be the case that the descendants of the committed voters of yesteryear are perhaps today's pressure-group campaigners who see involvement in environmental and community issues as more worthwhile. Perhaps in a post-materialist age in which the majority of people live a much better life than their predecessors, what matters more are quality of life issue such as ecology and minority rights issues. Pressure groups arguably represent these causes more effectively than do the parties that contest elections.

Some writers would suggest that rather than lower turnouts being a sign of apathy and resentment, they may reflect broad contentment. Non-voting may amount to general satisfaction with the conduct of affairs, so that voters do not feel stirred to express their feelings at the ballot box. According to this theory, they are more likely to vote when there is a sense of anxiety or even crisis, as in the UK in February 1974 during the miners' strike and three-day week.

Of course, the motives of voters may vary among different groups, some feeling that they don't need to go out and vote because all seems to be going along satisfactorily whilst others – often the young, the poor and members of ethnic minorities among them – may feel that there is nothing in the choice of party or candidate relevant for them.

Turnout in the United Kingdom

Turnout in general elections has varied considerably in the post-war era. The variation from constituency to constituency is also very large, often ranging from well in excess of 80 per cent to just over 50 per cent. The trend in national turnout has been broadly downward, interrupted by occasional better results.

Turnout in the twenty-first century

The average turnout in post-war British elections up to and including 2001 was 75.2 per cent, but in the election of that year there was a sharp decline in participation, the worst in living memory. Many voters may have felt alienated from the political world, including many young people who saw the party battle as increasingly irrelevant, sterile and out of date. Older people who did not turn out may have failed to do so either because:

- (as Labour supporters), they felt disappointed or disillusioned with a government that had let them down.

Table 9.9 Turnout in post-1945 general and European elections

General elections		European elections	
1945	73.3		
1950	84.0		
1951	82.5		
1955	76.8		
1959	78.7		
1964	77.1		
1966	75.8		
1970	72.0		
1974 Feb.	78.1		
1974 Oct.	72.8		
1979	76.0	1979	31.6
1983	72.7	1984	32.6
1987	75.3	1989	36.2
1992	77.7	1994	36.5
1997	71.5	1999	23.6
2001	59.4	2004	38.8
2005	61.2	2009	34.7
2010	65.1		

- in the absence of any credible alternative, they were content to let Labour get on with the job that it had undertaken of improving the public services; it seemed to be on the right lines, but there was much to be done.

In 2005, there was a modest increase in turnout on the very low base of four years earlier. In 2010, the figure was again up, though still lower than in any election held between 1922 and 1997. The increase may have resulted from the uncertainty of the outcome, for polls pointed a close result and the likelihood of a hung parliament and the possibility that the Liberal Democrats might overtake Labour in the share of the popular vote. For the first time for several years, there was in 2010 the realistic prospect of a change of party control at Westminster.

Nearly 29.7 million voted, but voter interest varied substantially from the relatively high of Renfrewshire East (77.3 per cent) to the low of Manchester Central (44.3 per cent). Generally speaking, turnout increased most where it had in 2005 been very low, although in areas with high levels of social deprivation the increase was less evident and in areas with a higher percentage of university graduates it was greater.

Many voters clearly remain unimpressed by the choice on offer and do not feel inclined to vote. They feel disengaged from the political process and feel that party politics has limited relevance to their lives. In 2010, such feelings may have been intensified in the wake of the expenses scandal, although overall the result provided no evidence that the disconnection between the electorate and the political process has grown stronger.

Direct democracy: initiatives and referendums

Elections are a feature of representative democracies. They give the people a chance to choose who will decide issues on their behalf. By contrast, referendums and similar devices such as the initiative and the recall are forms of direct democracy, in which the voters give their own verdict on the issues under consideration. They are designed to ensure that those in power are aware of and act in accordance with the express wishes of the electorate.

Whereas a general election provides an opportunity for the electorate to offer a broad judgement on the overall performance of the government of the day and of the suitability of the opposition parties as an alternative, a referendum and associated devices is a vote on a single issue. Such a vote gives the electorate a chance to answer a simple 'yes' or 'no' to whatever question is asked of it.

The increasing popularity of direct democracy worldwide

Direct democracy was employed in the early years of the twentieth century in some American states. In most cases, they opted for the

Box 9.6 Direct democracy: some definitions

The referendum: Magleby[29] defines the referendum as a 'vote of the people on a proposed law, policy or public expenditure'. In other words, it is a vote on a single issue of public policy, such as a constitutional amendment (e.g. the British devolution referendums, 1979 and 1997; see p. 367).

The initiative is a procedure through which an individual or group may propose legislation by securing the signatures of a required number of qualified voters. In several countries and American states that have referendums, there is also provision for the right of popular initiative as well (e.g. in November 2010, voters in Washington rejected two initiatives that would have privatised its state-run retail liquor stores.)

The recall is a much less frequently used device that enables a certain number of voters to demand a vote on whether an elected official should be removed from office (e.g. the Californian recall 2003, which enabled state voters to reject Gray Davis as Governor; as a result, Arnold Schwarzenegger was elected to the office).

initiative and referendum. However, for several years it went out of fashion in the United States. Nor was it widely popular elsewhere, although in the Nazi and other dictatorships of the interwar era it was not unusual for the leadership to seek popular approval from the people directly. This is why referendums (or plebiscites as they were often called in a non-democratic context) incurred odium in free countries. The British Prime Minister Clement Attlee (1945–51) described them as 'devices alien to our traditions' and saw them as instruments of 'demagogues and dictators'. He pointed to their often suspiciously high turnouts.

More recently, referendums were used by the notorious Chilean dictator, General Pinochet. His use of them showed how the wording of the question could be so framed as to get the answer required. He gained 75 per cent acquiescence for the proposition: 'In the face of international aggression unleashed against the government of the fatherland, I support President Pinochet in his defence of the dignity of Chile.' In the referendums held by French President, Charles de Gaulle (1958–69), there was again suspicion that the wording was designed to secure the desired response. There was also strong pressure on the media to publicise the presidential case.

It is the memory of such past experience that troubles some democrats who fear the purpose and management of such means of consultation with the public. However, the undemocratic overtones have largely disappeared from the debate about the merits of direct democracy. Initiatives and referendums are now used with increasing regularity in countries and states with impeccable democratic credentials.

Referendums and initiatives have been used more widely in recent decades. Since the 1970s, a growing number of American states have used them to decide on contentious moral issues from the use of cannabis for treatment of the sick to the right to 'death with dignity' via euthanasia, on social issues such as the rights of minorities to health reform, and on constitutional issues such as term limits for those who serve in positions of political power. Some member states of the European Union have used them to confirm their membership or to ratify some important constitutional development. In Switzerland, the heaviest user of referendums among European countries, they are built into the regular machinery of government, and are held on a three-monthly basis. The new democracies of Central and Eastern Europe, particularly the fifteen republics of the former USSR, have used them to decide a range of issues relating to the form of their new governments. Among highly significant ones in the last decade were those that enabled white South Africans to reject the prevailing system of apartheid (separate development of the races) and East Timorians to vote for their independence from Indonesia.

Most of the world's national referendums have taken place in the last thirty three years.[30] The issues broadly covered three main areas:

1. *Constitutional matters* – e.g. the ratification of treaties and change to the electoral system in Italy and New Zealand.
2. *Territorial matters* – e.g. the decision of a country as to whether it should join a larger unit such as the European Union and issues relating to devolving power to regions or provinces.
3. *Moral/social matters* – e.g. whether to allow abortion, gambling or the legalisation of soft drugs.

In Britain, Labour was converted to the value of referendums for deciding contentious issues that posed problems for political leaders, whether they were thorny constitutional issues or local controversies such as the fate of grammar schools. It portrayed such consultation as an extension of democracy and voter empowerment, which gave people a direct say in decision-making and ensured that any decision taken had legitimacy. The Conservatives and Liberal Democrats also increasingly recognised the popularity of the genre. Governments of both parties have found referendums helpful in resolving controversial issues that cut across the party divide, such as Europe, devolution and electoral reform.

The timing and status of referendums
We have mentioned above how questions can be worded to achieve the desired outcome. In other ways, it is possible to limit the impact of what the voters decide. There are controversies relating to the timing and status of referendums. Even in democratic countries, they are normally held at the most propitious moment for the government. In 1997, Labour was careful to hold its vote on devolution in Wales after the similar one on Scotland. The Welsh were known to be lukewarm over the proposals, whereas the Scots were enthusiastic about gaining greater autonomy.

Referendums may be binding or advisory. In Britain, with its commitment to the idea of parliamentary sovereignty, only Parliament can cast a decisive vote on any issue, but it is unlikely that a majority of legislators would make a habit of casting their parliamentary vote in defiance of the popular will as expressed in a referendum. In 1975, Prime Minister Wilson accepted that a majority of even a single vote against so doing would be enough to take Britain out of the European Community. Both ministers and MPs accept that they should treat the popular verdict as mandatory, in the sense that it was morally and politically binding. The Swedish government had no such qualms in 1955, when the people voted to continue to drive on the left and it chose to ignore their decision. Swedish ministers showed a similar reluctance when in 1980 the voters opted for the decommissioning of nuclear power stations; it took almost twenty years before the first reactor was taken out of action. Most governments have accepted that to consult and then to ignore the people's verdict is worse than never to have sought their opinion.

The merits and demerits of direct democracy

In favour of votes on single issues, perhaps the strongest argument is that they give people a chance to take decisions that affect their lives, whereas in a general election they can only offer a general verdict. If democracy is supposed to be based upon the people's will, surely a referendum is the most direct and accurate way of getting their verdict. Such an exercise in direct democracy has an intrinsic appeal, for the idea of 'letting the people have their say' appears to gel with the usual understanding of what democratic government involves. A *Guardian* editorial[31] recognised the strength of this case, when it discussed the idea of a vote on electoral reform. It noted that Britain suffered from 'an enormous and increasing democratic deficit' and saw a need to encourage politicians to go out and persuade people of the merits of their standpoint: 'imaginative means have to be sought to redress the imbalance . . . [a referendum] would generate an urgent civic discussion which will never take place with such purpose in any other way'.

Otherwise, it can be pointed out that:

- They encourage participation, stimulating interest and involvement in public policy and – via the campaigns fought on either side of the issue – provide a forum for information and education of the citizen.
- They allow governments to put difficult issues to the people that they would rather not take themselves, perhaps because they are internally divided or because the issue is a major and controversial one that has to be decided but on which support and opposition cut across the party divide. A 'yes' vote can strengthen the ministerial hand, as they seek to resolve an impasse. As Hague and Harrop[32] vividly put it: 'Like a plumber's drainrods, referendums resolve blockages'.
- They resolve questions in such a way that there is a final solution to an issue which will not go away. The 1979 referendum resolved the devolution issue for several years, as did the European vote in 1975, even if that particular matter has returned to haunt

some politicians. Critics of a particular policy are more likely to accept the result if they know that it is the public view, which is why Labour held its referendums on devolution in 1997, before the House of Commons began the legislative process, rather than after.

- They ensure that there is interaction between politicians and the public, forcing the former to engage with the voters and the public mood, and not live in splendid isolation at Westminster.

Against votes on single issues, the key point is that they fit uneasily into representative democracies. These are based upon the idea that people do not have to decide specific issues for themselves, but rather elect MPs or Deputies to act on their behalf. Being close to the centre of the argument, these representatives are able to inform themselves fully on an issue, then vote accordingly. If we do not like how they exercise that choice, we can deny them our vote at the next election. If government and parliament pass the question back to voters for their determination, then they shirk the responsibility which representative government clearly places upon them. Other arguments are that:

- Campaigns can be expensive and therefore to the advantage of well-funded groups. Money is too dominant in the process. Business interests have scope to influence the outcome to their own economic interests.
- Many issues are too complex for voters to handle. Their resolution requires a degree of knowledge and understanding that makes it difficult for the average voter to deliver a specific judgement, e.g. perhaps relating to the case for using the euro as a single currency.
- The result of a referendum can get muddled up with other issues. In 1979 opinion polls suggested that the majority of Scots favoured devolution, but there was a background of governmental unpopularity. It is significant that the Conservatives campaigned for a 'no' vote and argued that this was a vote against the Labour government's plans and not against the principle of devolution; indeed, they promised to bring forward proposals of their own!
- The referendum only illustrates what the public are thinking at a particular time, on a particular day. Logically, further votes are

necessary to ensure that ministers are acting in line with the public mood. On Europe, in particular, another vote is arguably necessary to give people a chance to express their viewpoint, bearing in mind how the original European Economic Community has been transformed into a Union.

• Votes on constitutional issues may be a good idea, but there are dangers in allowing popular opinion to determine issues such as abortion, capital punishment and gay sex. The fear is that these contentious topics generate much passion and that voters may be swayed by emotion rather than reason, particularly after seeing images of unborn foetuses or in the aftermath of a brutal killing.

The use of referendums in the United Kingdom

Britain has had little experience of voting on a single issue, even though the case has often been canvassed in the twentieth century. A Conservative leader and former prime minister, Arthur Balfour, told the House of Commons back in 1911 that 'so far from corrupting the sources of democratic life [they] would only be a great education for political people'.

There is no procedure for the use of initiatives in Britain. The only UK-wide referendum was when in 1975 voters were asked whether or not they wished the country to remain in the European Economic Community. Before 1997, there were also local votes on the future status of schools and the ownership of council estates, and in Wales the issue of 'local option' on the Sunday opening of pubs was decided in this way.

After May 1997 referendums were used to resolve the issue of devolution and the future shape of London's government. Also, in concurrent votes, popular approval of the Good Friday Agreement was given by electors on both sides of the border in Ireland. When New Labour took office, it was committed to a vote on electoral reform at some time in the future, but this did not take place. Neither was the promised vote on a new constitution for the European Parliament ever held. However, the Coalition government did submit the issue of using the Alternative Vote in general elections to the electorate, in May 2011.

Table 9.10 UK experience of national referendums

Year	Topic	Turnout	Outcome
1973	Border poll in N Ireland: voters asked if they wished to remain a part of the UK or join the Republic of Ireland.	61%	Massive majority to remain in UK
1975	UK's membership of EEC: voters asked if they wished to stay in the Community or withdraw from it.	64%	2/3 majority to stay in (43% of whole electorate)
1979	Devolution to Scotland and Wales: each electorate was asked if it wanted a devolved assembly.	62.8% 58.3%	Scotland: narrow majority in favour Wales: majority against
1997	Devolution to Scotland and Wales: each electorate was asked if it wanted a devolved assembly.	60.1% 50.1%	Strong majority for Very narrow majority for
1998	Good Friday Agreement on Northern Ireland: voters north (and south) of border asked to endorse the vpackage.	81.0%	Overwhelming majority in favour
2011	Use of the Alternative Vote in UK general elections	42.3%	Strongly against

The case of France: the use of referendums

France has used referendums more than most European countries. The 1958 constitution made provision for such direct consultation with the voters. Nine had been held by the year 2000, all on constitutional issues. However, a constitutional amendment passed in 1995 allows for the use of direct democracy on economic and social policy, and the services that implement these.

Constitutional topics tackled include self-determination and later independence for Algeria (1961–2), enlargement of the European

Community (1972), ratification of the Maastricht Treaty (1992) and the introduction of a five-year presidency (2000), all of which issues were approved. Only once has the ministerial recommendation been defeated, in 1969 when the failure to achieve support for reform of the Senate and the creation of regions led to the downfall of Charles de Gaulle. He had tended to regard referendums as 'plebiscitary confirmation of his own standing'.[33]

Of the votes held since 1960, that on the Maastricht Treaty attracted a turnout of around 60 per cent. Most recently, the vote on the quinquennat, the five-yearly presidential election, failed to inspire public enthusiasm and resulted in the lowest turnout yet recorded in a French referendum. President Chirac was unenthusiastic about putting the issue of the European Constitution up for popular approval, perhaps recognising that it might be a difficult cause on which to campaign. He reluctantly agreed to do so, but the plan backfired. In May 2005, voters rejected the document by 55 per cent to 45 per cent.

The case of the USA: election campaigning

American elections start anywhere from several months to two or three years before election day. They are far more focused on candidates and their personal qualities and/or failings than on their party label or particular issues. With the backing of Political Action Committees, they run much of their own campaigning, parties assisting them in a supportive capacity. Candidates seek to put together a winning coalition of support. They do this by making sure that there are sufficient funds to allow them to get the message across as widely as possible, so that everyone knows who they are and what they stand for.

Campaigning has always demanded certain qualities from the person chosen, a pleasing voice, a gift for public speaking, the ability to sell one's personality and to persuade people of the merits of a particular case. A half century ago, such assets were deployed 'on the stump', as speakers addressed a gathering in the local market place or school hall. John F. Kennedy conducted very active speech-making tours and sometimes spoke from the rear of a railway carriage as he campaigned across the country. However, nowadays any deficiencies are a serious liability exposed before the whole nation, whereas previously many voters did not know of them. Personal failings are also highlighted in the blaze of publicity surrounding a modern election campaign.

Whether the election is for Congress, for the Presidency or for some other position, the trend has been towards far greater professionalism than ever before. Some argue that elections today are increasingly about presentation and style rather than substance, in that television simplifies and trivialises issues, and the political message is sold like soap-powder or cosmetics. Too often, the point has to be conveyed in visual terms, and rather than analysis and depth of discussion, the trend is increasingly for candidates and their backers to buy fifteen- or thirty-second slots of prime advertising time which are often devoted to creating a negative impression of one's opponent.

Expensive television, radio, and direct mail campaigns aimed at persuading voters to support the candidate are launched once the candidates have been chosen in the primary elections. Campaigners will also intensify their grassroots campaigns, coordinating their volunteers in a full court effort to win votes.

There is some evidence of a change in the nature of campaigning, in response to the perceived decline in effectiveness of television advertising and increased dependence on the Internet, which is now a valuable fundraising tool. However, in the foreseeable future, Internet campaigning will not serve as a complete replacement for traditional political campaigning for it does not cater for entire sections of the population. For example, during Obama's 2008 presidential campaign, the Internet was useful in reaching the younger population, many of whom were much engaged with social websites and new media. However, the approach was unsuitable for communicatiung with many members of the older generations and those lacking on-line access.

• •

✔ What you should have learnt from reading this chapter

- Elections and election campaigns are the process by which democracies choose the path they will take in the future. Everyone has a chance to affect that crucial decision, but many voters fail to take the opportunity to do so.

- Those who do vote do so in the light of many influences, party identification and social class being declining factors. In highly visible campaigns in which information is readily available, candidate attributes and policy positions are more important than in the past and can lead voters to abandon their long-term allegiances.

- Campaigns are increasingly candidate-centred, media-driven and increasingly negative. These features have probably contributed to the decline in turnout.

- Voters in the United Kingdom now have a range of elections in which they can vote, such as European, devolved and Mayoral contests. A variety of different voting systems are employed. The outcomes illustrate that proportional systems encourage the success of smaller parties and make coalitions administrations more likely.

Glossary of key terms

Agenda setting The media's function of directing people's attention to particular issues for their consideration; giving some issues special – some would say, disproportionate – coverage; the way in which the media influence not only what we think, but what we think about.

Bigotgate The gaffe and subsequent scandal surrounding Gordon Brown's comments about a voter (Gillian Duffy), accidentally broadcast when he forgot his microphone was still switched on.

Candidate-centred campaigning A campaign in which the emphasis is on the role and activity of the individual candidate, rather than on the party he or she represents. Consultants and volunteers coordinate campaign activities, develop strategies and raise funds, although parties are likely to be involved.

Class dealignment The weakening of the traditional links between voting and the social class to which a person belongs – e.g. the majority of working-class people are now less solidly supportive of Labour as once they were.

Electoral deserts Cities or regions more or less permanently committed to representation by one party, such as Labour in Glasgow.

Embourgoisement The theory that as working-class people became more affluent and acquired more material possessions, they increasingly behaved more like middle-class people in their voting habits.

Focus groups Small groups of people who participate in a moderated discussion in which their views are probed on a range of questions; the intention is to ascertain their thinking and the emotions lying behind their attitudes.

Franchise The right to vote.

Marginal constituencies Constituencies in which the distribution of party support is relatively evenly balanced, the incumbent parties having such a narrow majority that a small net movement of voters will lead to them changing hands. Because the outcomes of elections are decided in the 'marginals' where there are genuine prospects of political change, they are important target seats for the main parties.

Mass media Those means of communication which permit messages to be conveyed to the public, such as broadcasting by radio and television, the press, books, cinema and, more recently, videos and computers. They reach a large and potentially unlimited number of people at the same time.

Partisan dealignment The weakening of the traditional bonds between voters and the parties with whom they once identified.

Photo-opportunity Carefully stage-managed events in which the leading figure is set against a particular background, perhaps to demonstrate concern for the location. Such occasions have a humanising effect, suggesting that the candidate is a 'regular guy'.

Political consultants Used increasingly in recent decades, most of them specialise in some aspect of campaigning, such as fund-raising, personal image and presentation, polling, speech writing, spin-doctoring and staging media-covered events. First coming to notice in the United States and then spreading to other democracies, all are in the business of 'selling' politicians. They tend to associate themselves with the party with whom they have some affinity.

Pseudo events Events that are staged primarily so that they can be reported in the media and create public interest.

Soundbites A short, pithy statement, extracted from a longer political speech, taken from an audiotape or videotape and broadcast especially during a news report on radio or television.

Spin doctor Spin refers to the attempt to change the way the public perceives what is happening, by putting a gloss on events and information to make them appear in a better light; it is a recent name for an old practice, public relations management. Spin doctors are those in the media team whose skill is to 'spin' stories, to make them more flattering to the candidate or party. The term has become pejorative of late, Labour's use of it said to have encouraged disbelief about what ministers were really about.

Tactical voting The practice of voting for a candidate other than the first preference, in order to keep out another candidate of whom the voter particularly disapproves.

Walkabouts Informal public strolls taken by members of the royal family or by political figures in election campaigns for the purpose of greeting and being seen by the public.

? Likely examination questions

'Theoretically admirable, but in practice unworkable.' Discuss this verdict on the differing varieties of proportional representation.

Does the use of First Past The Post for Westminster elections mean that Britain will always have a two party system?

'UK experience of PR has so far failed to establish a convincing case for its use in Westminster elections.' Discuss.

'Turnout in British elections has long been unimpressive by European standards and appears to be in long-term decline.' Does it matter?

'Modern elections are more about personalities than issues.' Discuss.

How important are election campaigns in determining the outcome of elections?

Discuss the view that the media tend to reinforce the existing views of the votes rather than fundamentally alter them.

Do the links between social class and voting matter any more?

Should referendums be held more often in the UK?

 ## Helpful websites

www.charter88.org Charter 88 Information on use of different electoral systems.

www.electoral-reform.org.uk Electoral Reform Society. Useful source of ideas and statistics concerned with alternative voting systems, particularly its favoured STV.

 ## Suggestions for further reading

Useful articles

N. Callop, 'Focus on . . . UK Electoral Systems', *Politics Review*, 19:1, September 2009.

P. Donleavy, 'How Proportional are the British AMS Systems?', *Representation*, 40:4, 2004.

R. Gibson et al., 'The Internet and Political Campaigning: The New Media Comes of Age', *Representation*, 39:3, 2003.

R. Johnston and C. Pattie, 'The Growing Problem of Electoral Turnout in Britain', *Representation*, 40:1, 2003.

P. Norris, 'Does Proportional Representation Promote Political Extremism?', *Representation*, 40:3, 2004.

T. Lundburg, 'A Decade of Electoral Reform in the UK', *Politics Review*, 18:1, September 2008.

Useful books

M. Qvortrup, *A Comparative Study of Referendums: Government by the People*, Manchester University Press, 2005.

C. Robinson, *Electoral Systems and Voting in the United Kingdom*, Edinburgh University Press, 2010.

CHAPTER 10

Britain and the European Union

Contents

Introduction	375
The development and character of the EU	375
Democracy and the Union: the 'democratic deficit' in its workings	383
Britain and the EU: the intergovernmentalist approach in action	386
The impact of the EU on government and politics in the UK	388
Europe: a problem area in British politics	391
Britain, Europe and the future of the EU	397

Overview

The development of the European Union (EU) from a regional economic agreement among six neighbouring states in 1951 into today's twenty-seven country-strong hybrid intergovernmental and supranational organisation represents an unprecedented phenomenon in world history. Although not a federation in the strict sense of the term, the EU is today far more than a free-trade association, having certain attributes associated with independent nations such as its own flag, currency (for some members) and law-making abilities, as well as diplomatic representation and a common foreign and security policy in its dealings with external partners.

In this chapter, we explore the history, membership and institutions of the Union, noting its distinctive character and the difficulties associated with ensuring that it works as democratically as possible. We also explore the impact of the EU on government and politics in the UK and the reasons why Europe has proved a difficult issue for British politicians to handle.

Key issues to be covered in this chapter

- The evolution and character of the EU
- The concepts of intergovernmentalism and supranationalism
- Britain's role in the EU and its impact on the British political scene
- Attitudes to membership in EU countries, particularly the UK
- Britain as a 'reluctant partner' in the Union

Introduction

In the post-1945 era, many international bodies have been formed that enable the nations of the world to cooperate with each other, some on a global scale, some more regional in character. Of the European groupings, the European Union has been by far the most significant. The very fact that so many **new democracies** in Eastern Europe have been attracted to the idea of membership in recent years shows that they recognise that the Union is now an important player not just on the European stage, but on the wider international scene as well.

The EU has a number of distinguishing features, including a very complete set of institutions and a wide range of policy responsibilities. However, what makes it especially distinctive is the fact that members have been willing to hand over powers to some **supranational authority** and be bound by its decisions and policies. Its aim is also grander than that of most other bodies: an ever-closer union of European peoples. As Nugent[1] remarks: 'These characteristics do not make the EU a state, but they do make it a highly developed political system.'

In all the debate in Britain and other member countries about the European Community (now Union), the central issues have in recent years been less about the actual fact of membership than about the sort of cooperation they wish to have with their partners and the nature of the Europe to which they wish to belong. In Britain, there has been some reluctance to embrace the idea of ever-closer union, leaving the country on the periphery of the broad thrust to European **integration**.

The development and character of the EU

In the early years after 1945, there was an unusual willingness among the politicians and writers in Europe to think in European rather than in national terms. Whether they were idealists or pragmatists, they saw the advantages of a peaceful continent in which countries could work towards the achievement of economic, political and military union. One of the most prominent pioneers of the '**European idea**' was Jean Monnet, later to become regarded as the 'father of modern Europe'. He took the view that the sovereign states of the past could no longer solve the problems of the post-war situation. He and others wished to see definite movement towards their grand design, complete political unification as implied by the term a '**United States of Europe**'. Some of these supranationalists wanted to see the speedy establishment of a federal Europe. Others saw federalism as the ultimate goal, but were prepared to work to achieve it over a longer period, via **functional cooperation** in particular policy areas.

Monnet was the architect of the *Schuman Declaration* (1950). This was such a step forward in one sector, for it set out a plan for a new supranational body to manage all coal and steel production in Germany and France, an organisation open to all other countries. The short-term aim was economic, to create a tariff-free market in which there would be no customs barriers to restrict trade in coal and steel across Western Europe, but the pioneers of what became the *European Coal and Steel Community* (ECSC) had in mind a greater goal, political union.

France, Germany, Italy and the **Benelux countries** were members of the ECSC. The success of the enterprise inspired the same six nations to take a further step along the road to greater unity. They agreed to develop the peaceful use of atomic energy via a new body, EURATOM. At the same time, in March 1957 they signed the *Treaty of Rome*, which established the *European Economic Community* (EEC). The Treaty still forms the basis of the European Union today. Beyond its immediate goals (a customs union, in which all internal barriers to trade would be removed), it aimed for 'a harmonious development of economic activities, a continuous and balanced expansion, an increased stability, an accelerated raising of the standard of living, and closer relations between its member states' (Article 2). The 'Common Market' (as the EEC was widely known) was a means to an end, not the end in itself. In 1967, the three communities (the ECSC, EURATOM and the EEC) merged into a single *European Community* (EC). The next major change came in 1986 when all member states (by then, including the UK) signed the *Single European Act* (SEA). According to the terms of the SEA:

• trade barriers and customs duties between members of the enlarged Community were removed, thereby creating a single market

- there would be 'free movement of goods, persons, services and capital
- the powers of the European Parliament would be increased
- the principle of **Qualified Majority Voting (QMV)** would be introduced in EC decision-making.

The twelve states that signed the SEA agreed in its Preamble that it marked another step towards 'ever-closer union' of the European peoples. In 1992, member states went further and signed the *Maastricht Treaty*, which created the European Union (EU), as we know it today. They planned for the creation of a single currency (what was to become today's **eurozone**), promised social legislation via a new **Social Chapter**, extended cooperation into the areas of defence and foreign affairs (the 'Second Pillar') and justice and internal security (the 'Third Pillar'), and introduced the concept of citizenship of the EU. All of us who are citizens of a member state are also citizens of the European Union.

Since then, the EU has continued to develop and expand. Further treaties signed at Amsterdam (1997) and Nice (2000) developed the Union by, among other things:

- extending the powers of the Parliament and the use of QMV
- introducing new and more transparent decision-making procedures
- planning for enlargement
- assuming greater powers over a number of policy areas such as justice and home affairs and the environment.

In 2007, member states agreed the *Reform (Lisbon) Treaty*, intended to streamline the workings methods of what had become a much-enlarged Union. The stated aim of the treaty was 'to complete the process started by the treaties of Amsterdam and Nice, with a view to enhancing the efficiency and democratic legitimacy of the Union and to improving the coherence of its action'. Prominent changes included the move from required unanimity to double majority voting (see QMV, pp. 403–4) in a range of policy areas in the Council of Ministers (for example asylum, immigration and withdrawal of a member state), a more powerful European Parliament, a consolidated legal personality for the EU and the creation of a long-term

Box 10.1 The institutions of the European Union

There are five main institutions in the European Union. Three are *supranational*, involving a transfer of some national sovereignty to an organisation that acts on behalf of all the countries involved. Members are supposed to forget their national allegiances and see issues from a European perspective. The other two are *intergovernmental*, providing opportunities for national governments to cooperate over a range of issues without surrendering national sovereignty.

The three supranational bodies are:

1. *The European Commission* is the executive of the EU. It not only acts as a civil service, carrying out particular policies such as the running of the **Common Agricultural Policy (CAP)**, but also makes some policy decisions. It is based largely in Brussels and is organised in thirty-three directorates-general (departments), each within the responsibility of a European commissioner. There are twenty-seven commissioners in all, each representing one of the member countries and an EU civil service of under 25,000 officials. The British tabloid press regularly attacks the Commission as 'a Brussels monster'.

2. *The European Parliament* meets in Strasbourg. It receives reports from commissioners and holds debates and a question time. Much of its important work is done in committees that meet in Brussels. Parliament's legislative role was initially only advisory, but in every major EU treaty (e.g. the SEA, Maastricht, Amsterdam, Nice and Lisbon) its powers have been increased; the Lisbon Treaty makes Parliament a co-legislator with the Council in a series of new fields (some previously dealt with only by the Council now being handled under the **co-decision procedure**, others being completely new policy areas for the EU). On key areas such as the CAP and taxation, Parliament only gives an opinion, but under the co-decision procedure it can veto Union legislation in some important areas such as the single market and consumer protection. It has the power to dismiss the entire Commission and accept or reject a new President of the Commission. The 785 members are elected five yearly, 1999, 2004, 2009, . . .

3. *The Court of Justice* is based in Luxembourg. The twenty-seven judges rule on matters of Union law, of which there are two categories:

Primary legislation refers to the body of law established by the founding treaties of the EC, together with all later amendments and protocols attached to those treaties.

Secondary legislation refers to all laws passed by EC/EU institutions. The main forms are regulations and directives.

The Court can arbitrate in disputes between major states, having the ability to levy fines on states that do not carry out treaty obligations.

The two intergovernmental bodies are:

4. *The Council of Ministers (officially now the Council of the European Union)*, which makes all policy decisions and issues directives like a government of the EU. One minister represents each of the twenty-seven countries, usually the Foreign Minister though it can be the Minister of Agriculture if agricultural affairs are being discussed or the Secretary of State for the Environment, if appropriate. Preparations for its meetings are handled by *COREPER*, the Council of Permanent Representatives of Member States, which comprises national ambassadors who speak and act on behalf of their member countries on lesser issues. Council decisions are taken on the basis of unanimity or QMV.

5. *The European Council* meets every six months at 'summit meetings'. It includes the twenty-seven prime ministers or their equivalents from each country, who give a push on various issues, to ensure that the Union resolves and progresses difficult policy matters.

Finally, there are three other bodies of note:

- *The Court of Auditors*, which audits all EU revenue and expenditure.
- *The Economic and Social Committee*, which has an advisory role and gives opinions on various proposals to the Council of Ministers. It includes representatives from groups such as employers and trades unions.
- *The Committee of the Regions*, which includes people from each area of the member countries. It must be consulted by the Council to represent regional concerns.

President of the European Council and a High Representative of the Union for Foreign Affairs and Security Policy. The treaty also made the **Charter of Fundamental Rights** (the Union's bill of rights) legally binding.

Table 10.1 An enlarging Union of twenty-seven states

Enlargement (date)	Countries joining (number of members)
First (1973)	Britain, Denmark, Ireland (9)
Second (1981)	Greece (10)
Third (1986)	Portugal, Spain (12)
Fourth (1995)	Austria, Finland, Sweden (15)
Fifth: Part One (2004)	Cyprus, Czech Republic, Estonia, Hungary, Latvia, Lithuania, Malta, Poland, Slovakia, Slovenia (25)
Fifth: Part Two (2007)	Bulgaria, Romania (27)

NB Croatia applied for membership in 2003, the European Commission recommending it as an official candidate for entry in early 2004; its accession is strongly supported by current EU member states. Negotiations were completed in mid-2011; signing of the Accession treaty and a Croatian referendum may both take place by early 2012 and the country should proceed to full membership in mid-2013.

What then is the European Union?

The EU is a supranational and **intergovernmental union** of twenty-seven states, an economic and a political organisation. Established in 1993 by the implementation of the Treaty on European Union (Maastricht Treaty), it is one of the largest economic and political entities in the world, having a total population of more than 500 million. Since its formation, new accessions have greatly increased its membership and its competences (areas of policy responsibility) have considerably expanded.

The EU is *supranational* in that decisions taken at European level have the force of law in member countries, European law being superior to domestic law. The European Commission has the power to take decisions and particularly to issue regulations and **directives** that are binding on member countries. Moreover, the growth of majority voting and the increasing powers of the European Parliament suggest that the element of supranationalism is on the increase. The more integrationist nations (the original six) have strongly backed such developments, seeing the supranational approach as the way forward.

The EU is *intergovernmental* in that in many key areas of policy today, decisions are still taken at the national level (see Box 10.2). Decisions on the broad direction and priorities of the EU are taken by the Council of Ministers (officially entitled the Council of the European Union), which is made up of national ministers. Even where QMV is employed, there has always been an attempt to achieve consensus. This is an approach that suits British politicians well. Within the EU, they have always been keen to retain certain sensitive EU policy areas such as immigration and national security firmly under the control of the Council, where they can employ their **right of veto**. Moreover, in preparation for major treaty revisions member states send national representatives to participate in **Intergovernmental Conferences (IGCs)** in which all member states need to be in agreement with the final treaty or communiqué. Individual national leaders bargain amongst themselves on many of their negotiating positions, making compromises in one place in order to secure concessions in another.

A unique institution

The European Union is a distinctive creation. There have been several examples of countries that have joined with one another in ventures of mutual benefit, but in aim, method and achievement this one has gone much further than the others. From the signing of the Treaty of Rome, the Community always aspired to be more than just a customs union. It aimed for an ever-closer union of its peoples and developed supranational institutions with powers binding upon member states.

Today, the European Union is difficult to characterise. It is neither a state nor just another international organisation, but has elements of both. EU members have transferred considerable sovereignty to it, more than to any other non-sovereign regional organisation. But in legal terms, the states remain the masters, in as much as the Union does not have the power to transfer additional powers from states to itself without their agreement through further international treaties. Indeed in some key areas, member states have given up little national sovereignty, particularly in the matters of foreign

Box 10.2 Policies and policymaking in the EU

The European Union does not determine the outcome of all areas of national policy. However, it has evolved over time from being a primarily economic community to an increasingly political one. A growing number of policy areas now fall within its competence, as is recognised in the official guidance provided by the European Secretariat of the Cabinet Office to senior officials across the range of government departments:[2] 'There are very few areas of policymaking that no longer have a European dimension of any kind. From areas of exclusive Community competence such as international trade to those where the Community involvement is more one of promotion of common interests and information-sharing such as culture or sport, we need to be aware of how our decisions fit in to this context.'

Just as the range of policies undertaken by the Union is a wide one, so is the degree to which the EU becomes involved in their management. In some areas, such as agriculture, industry and trade, many important decisions are now taken at European level, which is why national pressure groups spend so much of their time on European policy. In others, including some of those dealt with in the **Second and Third (intergovernmental) Pillars** of the Maastricht Treaty, EU involvement is increasing. This is also the case with many aspects of social policy, particularly those relating to labour relations, working conditions and employment practices more generally. In a few areas, there is little or no Union involvement in national policy. This is true of issues relating to policy on education, health, pension and social welfare, as well as to some matters affecting the personal and moral outlook of Europe's citizens, such as policy on abortion and alcohol consumption.

The level of EU involvement in a range of key policy areas are as follows:

Policy area	Strong	Joint	Little/none
Agriculture	*		
Fishing	*		
Trade	*		
Drugs		*	
Environment		*	

Regions	*	
Working conditions	*	
Foreign affairs and security	*	
Education		*
Health		*
Housing		*
Welfare		*

NB Defence policy was not on the agenda a generation ago, but today there is limited involvement. In the whole area of foreign and security policy, the trend is towards greater EU interest.

relations and defence. Because of this unique structure, writers tend to simply classify the European Union as a *sui generis* (a unique body, *of its own kind*).

Democracy and the Union: the 'democratic deficit' in its workings

A democratic deficit is a situation in which there is a deficiency in the democratic process, usually where a governing body is insufficiently accountable to an elected institution. The term often refers to the lack of accountability in the decision-making processes of the European Union. Three specific issues have been singled out:

1. the feeling that Brussels interferes where it should not do so
2. the absence of knowledge about what is going on in the central decision-making bodies
3. the belief that Brussels lacks sufficient democratic legitimacy.

The Union has taken some action to overcome the first two deficiencies via:

• *the doctrine of subsidiarity*, which says that the functions of government should be carried out at the lowest appropriate level for efficient administration – i.e. at the closest level possible to the people affected by the decision. From a British perspective, it is usually interpreted as meaning the decentralisation of power

from Brussels back to national governments, wherever this is appropriate.
- *simpler legislation and better public information* and by allowing organisations representing citizens a greater say in policymaking.

The third deficiency is more difficult to address. Those who point to the democratic deficit make several points:

- *The way the pioneers of closer cooperation worked in the early years was to impose their vision on the peoples of Europe.* Monnet and his co-founders were not primarily concerned with the democratic legitimacy of the institutions created.
- *The five-yearly elections to the Parliament have many weaknesses.* People vote primarily on national issues rather than European ones; they are 'second order' elections, with voters sometimes opting for smaller, even sometimes extremist parties to register a protest; turnouts are low; and there are no effective transnational parties, so that fighting the campaigns is left to national parties some of which are not really committed to the cause.
- (More seriously) *The way in which institutions operate and the lack of democratic control over those who have the power to make decisions.* As the EU has assumed more responsibilities, the power of its decision-making institutions has been increased and there has been a shift away from issues being examined in national parliaments. But the Council of Ministers is not elected, nor is the Commission. The Strasbourg Parliament is elected, but it has traditionally lacked teeth. The result is that there is still no very credible system of democratic control within the Union. There is no effective accountability of the Council or Commission to either the national parliaments, or to the European one.

How could the democratic deficit be tackled?

- *The Commission could be democratised.* The elected European Parliament could be responsible for the initial choice of the Commission, instead of national governments nominating their commissioner. Or the European public could be allowed to vote for the Union's commissioners, perhaps on the same day as the European elections. A variation would be to allow Parliament to choose the Commission, but for the public to vote for its President.

- *The powers of Parliament could be further increased.* Parliament's powers have been gradually increased since the late 1970s and with the passage of the Lisbon Treaty it acquired wide powers over the EU budget, equal legislative powers with the Council in many policy areas and a key role in the appointment of the Commission President. The problem with any further increase is that those who strongly criticise the democratic deficit are often the very same people who are most reluctant to make Parliament a more effective watchdog. British governments have been particularly keen to ensure that control is firmly maintained in Westminster hands.

- *The role of national parliaments could be strengthened.* Most national parliaments do not have adequate opportunities to influence the decisions at community level. (The Danish chamber, the Folketing, is better placed than others in this respect. It has the reputation of keeping a watchful eye over any European initiatives.) In Britain, apart from the committees which have been established in the two chambers of Parliament (e.g. the House of Lords European Union Committee – see p. 69), there are rare occasions when MEPs are invited to meet with their national colleagues in party committee meetings and informally. Yet keeping up with the burden of work coming from Brussels and providing effective and thorough scrutiny is a difficult task for the British Parliament.

- *Europe-wide referendums could be introduced.* These have been employed in some countries as a means of claiming popular backing for treaty developments. As some countries make little use of the device or have no provision for them, it is unlikely that we shall see anything like a Europe-wide referendum as a means of finding out what the public thinks about European developments.

Some observers are not unduly concerned about the alleged democratic deficit. They argue that: the Union is as democratic as it can or should be; given the nature of its functions, there is no reason to force further democratic mechanisms upon it; and when judged against the practices of existing nation states, there is little evidence that the EU suffers from a lack of democracy in its workings.

Britain and the EU: the intergovernmentalist approach in action

In Britain, from the earliest days of post-war cooperation, there were doubts about the wisdom or desirability of the closer union that Monnet favoured. British ministers of either main party preferred the idea of cooperation between countries in appropriate areas, where they found working together to be to their mutual benefit.

Britain within the Community

Britain stood aside from the early European developments. It had worldwide interests, there being what Churchill[3] termed 'three circles' in our foreign policy: the relationships with the United States, the Commonwealth and – less importantly – Europe. In addition, there was the fact that Britain was – and remains – separated from the Continent by geography, language and culture.

Yet by the early 1960s, a growing number of British politicians began to reconsider Britain's aloof position, seeing dangers in isolating ourselves from events on the European mainland. They came to believe that there were good economic reasons for Britain to seek membership of the EC. Many of them also concluded that Britain would have more chance of influencing world events from inside the Community. After General de Gaulle had twice blocked British moves to join, the government of *Edward Heath* was successful at the third attempt and joined in 1973. In a referendum held to confirm British membership in 1975, there was a majority of two to one in favour of continued membership on renegotiated terms. Many people believed that Britain had a better future inside the Community than outside. However, there was little evidence of widespread popular enthusiasm for working in partnership with other member states.

Developing unease in the 1980s and 1990s

The broad sympathy for British involvement was already beginning to change in the Thatcher years of the 1980s, but it gained momentum after the Maastricht agreement had been signed. There was a widespread popular feeling – fed by elements of the tabloid press – that after several years in the EC membership was bringing difficulties rather than benefits. Moreover, Brussels seemed to be too fond of interfering in our national life.

In office (and subsequently), Margaret Thatcher was a strong supporter of intergovernmentalism. She disliked the integrationist tendencies within the EC, her preference being for an enlarged Community, one that was broader and looser. She always remained a firm **Atlanticist**, seeing merit in the **special relationship** that her government developed with US President Ronald Reagan during the 1980s. Subsequent Conservative leaders have shared her broad outlook.

New Labour: the Blair approach
In opposition and office, New Labour was broadly supportive of the European Union. As Prime Minister, Tony Blair employed pro-European rhetoric and argued for 'constructive engagement' in the Union, a position which was at first well-received by Continental leaders. Yet the language used in the 1997 election was not markedly different from that of the Conservatives, the stated preference being for 'an alliance of independent nations choosing to cooperate to achieve the goals they cannot achieve alone'. Within a few years, several issues arose on which he found himself firmly defending national interests and in opposition to our European partners.

Looking back over the Blair era, two strands remain significant, namely the emphasis on intergovernmentalism and the value attached to the 'special relationship'. The preference for cooperation between nation states for their mutual benefit was reinforced by the Fifth Enlargement, which offered the prospect of support from new entrants for the British outlook in a wider and looser Union. As for the relationship with the White House, it was evident from the early days of the Blair premiership that Bill Clinton and the Prime Minister were personal as well as political friends. The relationship survived the change of personnel in the Oval Office, with George Bush and Tony Blair working together over many areas of policy. A series of events brought the two countries into active cooperation. Over the terrorist attacks on the World Trade Center of 11 September, the formation of the 'coalition of the willing' to fight Al-Qaeda-type terrorism and the decision to invade Iraq, Tony Blair publicly backed the American position.

Tony Blair liked to use the 'bridge' metaphor to describe the British position in foreign policy, portraying Britain as being the pivot at the axis of a range of international relationships. According to this view, Britain has a unique position, one for which the country is well qualified by past history and circumstance. The thinking is that in this role Britain never has to make a choice between the USA and Europe; it is linked to, yet similarly distant from, both continents. But over Iraq, a serious rift began to develop and widen between Europe and the USA. Britain was unable to reconcile the two sides and had to make a choice. The divide could not be bridged by the Prime Minister's determined efforts to bring about agreement. Britain ultimately proved itself to be more Atlanticist than European.

The Blair era illustrated the difficulty of trying to be a key player in Union affairs whilst at the same time firmly standing up for British interests on matters such as tax harmonisation, the euro and common policies on security and foreign affairs. Tony Blair recognised that he was operating in a country where enthusiasm for the Union was limited and sometimes grudging, and in which membership was often seen as a necessity rather than a cause for celebration.

The impact of the EU on government and politics in the UK

Membership of the EU has had an important impact on the British Constitution and on political life over the last thirty-five years. With the passing of the SEA and the signing of subsequent treaties, the trend towards more decision-making in Brussels has accelerated. In the process, many of our constitutional and political arrangements have been modified. Some of the most important effects have been those concerning the Constitution and Parliament.

The impact on the Constitution

Membership has had an important impact on the British Constitution and on British law. By joining the European Community, the UK agreed to accept a body of constitutional law that had already been passed since the creation of the EC. It continues to be bound by European law. This includes primary legislation (as found in the Treaty of Rome and the other treaties) and secondary law (as found in EU regulations and directives). European law takes precedence over UK law, is binding on the UK and applicable by UK courts. In several areas of policy, pieces of European economic and social legislation have conferred important rights on British workers, as in the area of equal pay.

On joining, the UK accepted forty-three volumes of existing legislation that had never been passed by the House of Commons. Since then, most obviously in the *Factortame* case, several judgements have illustrated how the courts can overrule parliamentary legislation which conflicts with Community law. European law trumps national law. Such rulings have undermined the doctrine of parliamentary sovereignty. A sovereign Parliament acknowledges no restraint on its powers and can pass legislation without fear of being overridden. British law can now be changed by EU regulations and directives, even though the British government might oppose them. This is because the use of QMV in many areas of policy means that British ministers have no veto over what is decided in Brussels.

The impact on the Executive and legislature
At the highest level, the Prime Minister and members of the Cabinet regularly have dealings with the EU. Some government departments are particularly involved in EU policy, so that the relevant secretaries of state will from time to time attend or even chair meetings of the Council of Ministers. The Prime Minister has a key role in the European Council. At home, in Cabinet and Cabinet committee meetings, European developments and issues often require discussion. Officials working in government departments are also much involved in European work. Within departments ranging from the Treasury to the Department of the Environment, Farming and Rural Affairs, there are European sections.

The workload of both chambers of Parliament has also been greatly affected by our European involvement. They tackle European issues in debates and at Question Time, and try to scrutinise the proposals initiated by the European Commission. The House of Lords has its highly rated Select Committee on the European Communities (see p. 69). In the House of Commons, the Select Committee on European Legislation similarly acts as a filter for the Commission's proposals. The government of the day makes time available to consider reports of the Select Committee, though there have been criticisms that debates often get a low priority in the timetable and are relegated to late evening when the House may be poorly attended. In Parliament as in other legislatures of member states, the task of coping with the immense volume of European business poses serious problems. MPs often complain about the inadequate opportunities to examine European legislation.

The impact on the four 'Ps': parties, politicians, pressure groups and the public

The original issue of European membership and more recently that of the extent of British involvement in and commitment to the European Union has been a difficult one for the two main parties. Labour suffered internal divisions over its attitude to the European Community in the 1960s and 1970s. The Conservatives found the issue highly divisive in the late 1980s and 1990s, less so subsequently. In the early years of the twenty-first century, Labour found the issue of the Reform Treaty a cause of schism. At times, the divisions have been between the Conservative and Labour parties. Sometimes, the intensity of the splits within the parties has been remarkable.

European issues have also influenced the fate of individual politicians. They caused enormous difficulties for John Major as prime minister, for he led a Conservative party in which there were a few committed pro-Europeans, several strong Eurosceptics or even Europhobes and many more MPs in between who disliked the trend of events within the Union and the way in which their party was being damaged by the friction they aroused. Major found himself trying to strike a middle way between two irreconcilable sides. His task was the more difficult because his predecessor – by then Lady Thatcher – on occasion used the European issue to undermine his leadership.

Whether or not they are pro-European in their approaches, individuals and groups have had to adjust to a world in which many of the policies that concern them are decided not in Whitehall/ Westminster, but in Brussels. Most pressure groups have long recognised that in order to influence policy on issues such as agricultural and the environment, there is now more point in lobbying the Commission or MEPs, rather than British ministers or MPs (see pp. 299–300).

The public has often seemed ill-informed and confused about the European Union. Its views have been sensitive to the attitudes adopted by political leaders and the media. When the voters were directly consulted on continued membership of the EC in the 1975 referendum, they gave an overwhelming (2:1) response in favour. On that occasion – and rarely since – the case for Europe was set out clearly by pro-European politicians. Since the late 1980s, when there has been a developing momentum within the Union to drive the process of integration forward, the mood has changed. The position revealed in several polls has been that the majority of people broadly support staying in the EU, but lack any enthusiasm for closer integration and are sceptical about the attitudes and motives of Continental leaders within the organisation. Most voters still do not feel truly European, in the way that some Continentals do. Many French people feel both French and European, as do the Dutch feel Dutch and European. This is not true of the British population. (See also Box 10.3 for more on British attitudes to the Union.)

Europe: a problem area in British politics

Europe has been a problem area of policy for British politicians for many years. Sometimes, it has become a political football in the party battle, with those who exhibit signs of pro-European attitudes and policies facing a barrage of adverse media criticism in the tabloid press at home. Butler and Westlake[6] make the point that Euroscepticism has a long history: 'If there is a European "problem", it is not restricted to one British political party, but more generally diffused throughout the British political and administrative establishment . . . In truth, virtually every postwar British prime minister has been in a similar position and played a similar role, from Attlee to Churchill and Eden, from Macmillan to Wilson, and from Callaghan to Major and Thatcher.'

Leaders from Attlee to Brown have to a greater or lesser extent been tested by European 'problems'. Their difficulties relate to the problem of leading parties whose composition reflects the ambivalent attitudes of many British people to the post-war position. Britons are caught between the desire to hold on to the country's past greatness and traditions (what one-time Conservative Foreign Secretary

Box 10.3 Political and popular reactions to Europe in Britain and other EU member states

The member states of the EU differ considerably in their approaches to the Union, its institutions, policies, treaties and end-destination. Some are intergovernmentalist, some are federalist; some want a looser Union, others one in which the bonds are firmly cast; some are strongly committed and some are more lukewarm in their enthusiasm.

Several factors determine the attitudes of individual countries towards membership of the Union, how they behave as EU members and the stances they take in Brussels negotiations and over proposed new initiatives. Foremost amongst them are:

- The timing of their entry and the circumstances of their joining
- Their location and size
- Their level of prosperity
- Their political and social characteristics
- Their commitment to the causes of either integrationism or intergovernmentalism.

British attitudes to the EU
Eurobarometer, the EU's polling section, found the following reactions, when surveying popular attitudes to the EU in mid-2008:[4]

- 83 per cent of UK respondents claimed to know little or nothing about it. More than half of the British public (54 per cent) indicated that they did not want to receive more information about the EU.
- 37 per cent of the respondents who expressed a view had a rather positive image of the EU, while just over half took the opposite view (40 per cent).
- 37 per cent of respondents felt the economic benefits of the UK being a member of the EU outweighed the costs and 40 per cent took an opposite viewpoint.
- 44 per cent felt that the UK had a *lot* or *a fair amount* of influence on the way EU laws are made; half (51 per cent), on the other hand, felt that the UK had *little* or *very little* influence.
- Presented with areas where EU membership could be beneficial, a convincing majority agreed on these benefits: the single market (67 per cent), a cleaner environment (58 per cent), more weight in trade negotiations (58 per cent). They were least convinced about improved working conditions (49 per cent).

A *positive* perception of the EU was well above average among the 15-24 age group (47 per cent), those with the highest level of education (55 per cent) and city dwellers (47 per cent). Manual workers were also more positive than the average as far as the EU's image was concerned (45 per cent). On the other hand, British citizens aged fifty-five or over (54 per cent), rural citizens (46 per cent) and those with the lowest level of education (60 per cent) tended to have a *rather negative* image of the European Union. Men also had a more negative image of the EU than women (44 per cent/37 per cent).

The case of Italy
Post-1945 Italy had no reason to look back on the history of the nation state with particular pride. In the years before Mussolini's rule, the country had been torn apart by internal schism. When he was in power, the Italian attachment to democratic government was abandoned and for several years he was an ally of Hitler. After the hostilities ended, many Italians wanted to demonstrate their respectability by showing themselves to be loyal to other West European nations. In so doing, they hoped to buttress their new democracy at home. Membership of the Six might prove economically and politically beneficial, as well as desirable for other reasons.

Today, the Italians do not carry a heavy punch in Union affairs. Partly, this may be because of their failure to show themselves as 'good Europeans' when it comes to carrying out EU policies. It also reflects the post-war weakness and instability of Italian politics and of the national economy. This means that although they do not wish to be in the slow lane when new schemes are planned, they are not always ready to join them. However, they have traditionally been very concerned that the EU should not develop into a two-tier, two-speed Europe and have tended to look with disfavour on opt-outs and exceptions.

Until the last few years, Italians tended to be strongly pro-European. Perhaps because they were critical of their national political leadership, they were more willing to embrace a European identity and support institutions such as Parliament, by voting in good numbers for its elected representatives. Whilst not opposed to enlargement, they were wary of supporting moves that might threaten the solidity of the core.

In the last decade or so, Italians have generally become rather more disaffected and lost much of their idealism about the Union. Public support for European integration has diminished, in part a reflection of a general scepticism vis-à-vis politics and politicians, particularly at the domestic level and also because of the influence of vocal anti-Europeans within the Centre-Right ruling coalition.

> 'This is not to say that Italy's love affair with Europe has come to a bitter end. Italians continue to trust European institutions significantly more than national ones and would like the EU to acquire more competences . . . Tellingly, the Treaty of Lisbon was speedily ratified by the Italian parliament by unanimous vote – something unthinkable in most EU countries.'[5]
> See Postscript on p. 401 for an update.

Douglas Hurd has called 'punching above its weight') and yet also to keep apace with the modern world. Although most MPs and many British people recognise that the country has a European future, a number of them do not enthuse about the prospect. Other countries, lacking the same traditions and attachments as Britain, do not experience the same feelings, or at least not to the same extent. As one former Conservative MP, Sir Anthony Meyer,[7] put it: 'For France, Europe offers a chance to extend its influence; for Britain, Europe is a damage-limitation exercise.'

Most Britons recognise that the country cannot separate itself from the European fold, but within it ministers seem to find it difficult to find ways of making the Union work to the national advantage. By seeming to resist the initiatives that other nations want in so many areas, it then becomes harder to achieve those goals that really matter to Britain. Yet by going along with them, ministers risk having their actions savaged in the Eurosceptic tabloid press. It is difficult for even a pro-European administration to be a constructive, if distinctive, actor on the Continental stage.

Britain's reduced circumstances in the world

Some of the difficulties relate to Britain's reduced circumstances in the post-1945 world. In 1945, Britain was still a 'great power', although its strength even then can be overstressed. As a result of this status, change seemed unnecessary. For a long while the British allowed their awareness of the historical and cultural differences between Britain and Europe to predominate over their political judgement. Hugo Young[8] has written perceptively about popular attitudes at the time:

> The island people were not only different but, mercifully separate, housed behind their moat . . . They were also inestimably superior,

as was shown by history both ancient and modern: by the resonance of the Empire on which the sun never set, but equally by the immediate circumstances out of which the new Europe was born, the war itself. Her sense of national independence, enhanced by her unique empire, absorbed by all creeds and classes and spoke for by virtually every analyst, could not be fractured . . .

Since 1945, Britain's declining economic fortunes have meant that it has not been able to sustain the position it once held. It has been hard to come to terms with that situation. Managing national decline is not a glorious role for politicians, and it is one that arouses little popular enthusiasm. Some people still hanker after the world leadership that was possible in their parents' generation. Many more concede that Britain's capacity to influence events has been much weakened, but are unconvinced that the logic of events should drive the country more closely into the embrace of our Continental partners.

For years, Britain still attempted to preserve its global role. Churchill[9] expressed his view of the competing claims on British foreign policy, in a speech he made in May 1951:

Where do we stand? [Of early European organisations seeking greater European unity] We feel we have a special relation . . . expressed by the preposition 'with' but not 'of' – we are with them, but not of them. We have our own Commonwealth and Empire.

Not surprisingly, the country that 'won the war' felt that with such a worldwide role and importance it could win the peace. It did not need to tie itself in to any commitments with the countries it had defeated or which had been overrun in the hostilities of the Second World War. Britain felt that it could afford to remain aloof from Europe. It was not ready to recognise or admit its increasing weakness.

Such an attitude had deep roots in the British psyche, and it may be considered understandable in the circumstances of the time. However, it was combined with an inability to appreciate the enthusiasm and dedication of other nations to closer integration in pursuit of 'the European idea'. Consistently, British politicians then and in more recent years have underestimated the strength of this determination, and have assumed that carefully constructed measures of intergovernmental cooperation would be a substitute for their more visionary approach.

In 1963, Dean Acheson,[10] a former American Secretary of State, observed that: 'Britain has lost an empire, but not yet found a role'. The comment wounded British pride, but some politicians recognised that it contained more than a little truth. Among them, there was a growing belief that Europe might provide the theatre in which Britain would have the best chance of influencing events and opinions in the world at large.

As it became clear that Britain's capacity to influence the outcome of events had become much curtailed, Conservative Prime Minister Macmillan found it expedient to apply for Britain to join the EEC in 1961. Neither the Commonwealth nor the American connection seemed any longer to count for as much as had been assumed a decade or so before. Eventually, Britain joined the EEC in 1973, fifteen years after it began its operations, twenty years after 'the six' had pioneered the path to unity. However, there never was popular excitement in Britain about belonging to the Community. It was appreciated that it was probably wise and necessary for Britain to work with our new partners, for the alternatives did not look very promising. The point was well made by Northedge:[11]

> [The] important thing about British entry into Europe was that it had almost every appearance of being a policy of last resort, adopted, one might almost say, when all other expedients had failed. There was no suggestion of it being hailed as a brilliant success . . . the impression remained that it was brought about in humiliating circumstances, and when other options in foreign policy had lost their convincingness.

Whereas most of the other late entrants seem to have made the adjustments in attitude required to make a success of membership, this has not been the case for many British people and some of their elected representatives. The British have found it hard to adapt, hence their reputation on the Continent as 'reluctant Europeans'. Perhaps this reflects a long-lasting national difficulty in coming to terms with Britain's reduced circumstances in the world. Young[12] has written similarly of the British entry as being inspired by a mood of failure:

> For the makers of the original 'Europe', beginning to fulfil Victor Hugo's dream, their creation was a triumph. Out of defeat, they pro-

duced a new kind of victory. For Britain, by contrast, the entry into Europe was a defeat: a fate she had resisted, a necessity reluctantly accepted, the last resort of a once great power, never for one moment a climactic or triumphant engagement with the construction of Europe. This has been integral to the national psyche, perhaps only half articulated, since 1973. The sense of the Community as a place of British failure – proof of Britain's failed independence, site of her failed domination – is deep in the undertow of the tides and whirlpools [of Britain's relations with the other European countries].

The story of British relations with the Continent is necessarily unfinished. The process of European integration is ongoing and Britain's long-term approach over the coming years is difficult to foresee. On past performance, it has been resolutely pragmatic, the emphasis being on the search for national advantage. This has inevitably involved ministers in 'a more or less confrontational stance within a Community to which, it was often asserted, nothing significant had been surrendered'.[13]

Britain, Europe and the future of the EU

In the late twentieth century, there were two schools of thought within the Union about how the EU should move forward, by deepening or widening. Some states wanted to cement the bonds between existing states as a top priority. Others were more interested in extending the EU into Central and Eastern Europe. France was traditionally less enthusiastic about widening, fearing a setback to the progress strengthening the links between existing members; it was also uneasy about the prospect of having first- and second-class applicants. Germany believed in enlargement, but was more committed to the accession of economically advanced countries such as the Czech Republic and Slovenia, than to the admission of countries whose economies might be a burden on the EU budget.

The British have long been supporters of enlargement. Under the Thatcher and Major governments, they liked the idea of extending deregulated trading areas and welcomed the fact that the new democracies saw free market solutions as being British-driven. The Blair governments continued with the same policy. Above all, perhaps, the British have been attracted to the idea of enlargement to the East because ministers have felt that it might help to slow down the pace of integration in the West. Being more committed to closer economic rather than political union, the policy of enlargement made sense. It catered for the first, whilst making the second less certain.

The widening or deepening controversy became largely irrelevant in the early twenty-first century, with the admission of ten and eventually twelve new member states. In the eyes of its supporters, the expansion of the EU has had considerable benefits. It has strengthened the Union by increasing its attraction as an export market for non-EU countries; enabled the organisation to speak with a larger voice in world affairs; and helped to increase stability on the Continent, by promoting prosperity among the new states.

A more federal Europe

One of the most contentious issues concerning the future of the Union is the extent to which it moves in a federal direction. Lady Thatcher expressed the fear that a creeping federal system was being achieved, without it being fully appreciated. She urged the need to halt this 'conveyor-belt to federalism'. In the eyes of many right-wing British politicians the word 'federal' remains deeply worrying, for they see ideas of federalism and national sovereignty as fundamentally incompatible. Labour, too, has shunned federal rhetoric and remained committed to the intergovernmentalism that has enabled it to defend British national interests and draw '**red lines**' over which it was not prepared to cross. Tony Blair was no federalist, preferring an enlarged and looser EU to the organisation envisaged by those who dreamed of European integration after the Second World War. That preference for cooperation between nation states cooperating for their mutual benefit has been reinforced by the latest EU enlargement.

The *Oxford English Dictionary* describes the meaning of 'federal' as 'an association of units that are largely independent' and 'a system of government in which several states unite under a central authority but remain independent in internal affairs'. As such, federalism is designed to allow the maximum devolution of decision-making possible consistent with the needs of a workable union. However, the media in Britain, especially the popular press, have often used the term in the way that some Conservatives do, as if it implied the removal of power from the nation state to some **super-state**. It is seen as implying a move to centralisation and deeper integration. Some British MPs pounce on any proposal from the Commission suspecting that it brings the dreaded 'f' word ever nearer. On the Continent, 'federal' arouses no such anxieties, for it implies quite the opposite. To a German, subsidiarity is the very essence of federalism. It is a key element in the division of power between the different layers of government, European, national and regional.

'Federal' has become a slogan for all those who fear the drift of events in the Union. In denying its use, British opponents are not only rejecting the formal structure of a fully fledged federal European state, but all the moves such as the single currency, the stronger European institutions and the increasing search for a common approach to many matters of policy.

Is the EU a giant super-state?

Several British Conservatives have expressed the fear that Britain is in danger of being dragged into some European monstrosity, a form of super-state. In the Labour Party, such a view surfaces less frequently, although it was evident in the discussions over the introduction of the Lisbon Treaty.

William Hague vividly described these feelings when he outlined his 'elephant test'. Simplistically expressed, his view was that if it looks, smells and sounds like an elephant, then it probably is an elephant you're dealing with. Applied to the emerging shape of the European Union, he detected the characteristics of a future super-state, among them a proposed president, a parliament, a court and a single currency. Recognising the possibility of such a state being created without remedial action, a *Mail on Sunday* writer[14] expressed the more extravagant view that this outcome would 'be worse than Stalin's Soviet Union'.

Elements of doubt

Academics, constitutional experts, diplomats and European officials are divided in their views about what form the EU will eventually take, but the general view is that the Union will fall far short of being a super-state. We live in a world where more and more states are banding together – whether in Europe, the Americas or Asia – to make policies that benefit the member states. That does not mean new super-states are being created, rather that we are living in a world where layers of governance overlap in many different ways.

Historian Norman Davies[15] points out that what is evolving is something of an in-between situation, rather than one of either of the extremes sometimes presented. On the one hand, Europe is not going to be just the Common Market created by the Treaty of Rome, a free trading area designed to maximise economic advantage. Neither is it going to be a classic super-state 'which would have a head of state, an executive in permanent session, a legislative assembly to whom it is answerable and its own individual judiciary'. In his view, we are seeing a new kind of organisation emerge, but still one in which the intergovernmental Council of Ministers, rather than the supra-national European Commission, has the final say: 'those ministers represent their national interests, not the interests of a super-state'.

Finally, the point has been made by Larry Siedentop[16] that it is hard to imagine any super-state in which the size of the budget was limited by treaty to 1.27 per cent of the member states' GDP: 'No large state uses less than 30%'.

A more flexible approach to integration?

In order to overcome the many problems associated with progress for the European Union, the idea of **variable geometry** has re-emerged in recent years as a desirable possibility. Sometimes today, it is known by an alternative name of 'enhanced cooperation' (*coopéra-tion renforcée* or flexible integration). This is seen as a way of catering for the economic weakness of some new members and the reluctance of larger states such as Britain to surrender part of their sovereignty, as represented by the national veto.

The Major government took the view that member states should be allowed to adopt differentiated approaches to the wide range of EU policies, just as Denmark and the UK had adopted a different approach to monetary union. The key word was flexibility, enabling the creation of a Europe 'à la carte' in which countries could participate in the policies that suited their national needs. The difficulty was that when so many items on the agenda were unacceptable to London, then leaders in other capitals were likely to hesitate before agreeing to such an approach. They feared that if one or more countries such as Britain opted out of nearly all initiatives, the result would be a 'two-speed' or 'two-tier Europe' in which some countries moved ahead to integration at a rapid pace, whilst others that did not wish to go so far or so quickly trailed behind.

In its early years, the Blair government, not wishing to see Britain left behind, showed little enthusiasm for any variant of variable geometry. Its rhetoric implied that the intention was to join the euro 'when the time was right' and that it would seek to cooperate in other fields unless essential interests were at stake. Yet, in spite of its having two massive majorities and one comfortable one in the House of Commons, 'the time was not ripe'. Moreover, Britain found itself resisting the thrust of integration in other areas favoured by the powerful Franco-German alliance that is usually in the vanguard of further progress.

After the talks on a proposed EU constitution, the terms of which were eventually modified in favour of the Lisbon Treaty, Tony Blair conceded that in order to preserve the red lines that he felt were important to safeguard Britain's interest, it was necessary to agree that other states could be allowed to forge ahead with integration, including a common tax policy. Some states, particularly from the former Soviet block, shared his approach, indicating that what was beginning to emerge was a complex patchwork of alliances that formed and reformed over different issues, and came and went with changing governments.

The outcome for the future may be a looser Union, in which the integrationists form a core group who will drive things forward, with other nations choosing how and when they will participate, as national interests and pressures permit.

Box 10.4 Postscript: the crisis within the eurozone (2009–11) and its implications

In late 2009, as investors became increasingly alarmed by the rising levels of indebtedness in some European states (particularly Greece, Ireland and Portugal) their governments found it increasingly difficult to re-finance their debts. In Greece, there was a serious possibility of default. In May 2010, eurozone leaders agreed to provisions for loans to member states that could not raise funds, via the European

Financial Stability Facility (EFSF). In October, a further package of measures was necessary to prevent the collapse of member economies, including: provision to write off a percentage of Greek debt; an increase in the EFSF; and a strengthening of the finances of European banks. Those member states afflicted with problems of heavy indebtedness were expected to introduce a range of cuts in order to bring their spending under control.

With Greece struggling to restore its finances and other member states also at risk, there was increasing alarm within the EU about the repercussions that their problems would have on the rest of the eurozone. In mid-2011, the problems deepened, as Italy, the country with the Union's third largest economy, found itself in acute difficulties. EU leaders were alarmed at Italy's position. Given the size of the country and its economy, its historical role as a founding member of the ECSC and the danger of any default having repercussions for the rest of the eurozone, they had to act. They faced a dilemma: Italy was too large and too important in the eurozone to be allowed to fail, yet very costly to support financially. They urged the need for drastic measures to be taken by the Rome government to tackle the country's problems. A new government, led by Mario Monti, was formed to introduce austerity measures and work towards structural reform.

For political reasons, countries such as Greece had been allowed to enter the eurozone even though they did not strictly meet the **convergence criteria** agreed at Maastricht. Present EU leaders have had to 'pick up the pieces' and take action to deal with the consequences of those earlier decisions. They recognised that the eurozone was in serious danger of collapse and that its failure would have consequences for the Union as a whole.

Towards fiscal union?
From its earliest days, one of the criticisms of the whole concept of the euro currency system was that it ceded national monetary and economic sovereignty, but lacked a central fiscal authority to issue regulations and enforce the rules. Throughout 2011 there was much discussion among politicians and technocrats, and in the media, of initiatives that might strengthen the role of the Central Bank and move towards the common fiscal policy that many observers thought necessary for the successful operation of a single currency.

France and Germany were inevitably key players in looking for a solution. In early December 2011, President Sarkozy of France and the German Chancellor, Angela Merkel, met at a time when the credit ratings of other eurozone countries were under threat of being downgraded. They agreed a fiscal compact involving strict budgetary discipline, automatic sanctions against countries running excessive deficits, a revamped stability and a key role for the European institutions in monitoring and enforcing the measures proposed. The pact was considered at a meeting of the European Council in Brussels a few days later – the fifth summit to save the euro. EU leaders agreed to the proposals to harden the single currency's budget rules and bolster its crisis-fighting resources, and to use the Court to assess budgetary laws and impose quasi-automatic fines on countries not meeting the 3% of GDP deficit limit. Such measures, involving EU-wide machinery, required new treaty arrangements (in effect, a revision of the Lisbon Treaty) in order to make the single currency work effectively.

What was being proposed did not amount to a full fiscal union, but represented a move to towards greater integration of the finances of countries within euroland. A full fiscal union implies a central finance ministry, harmonised tax-and-spend policies and initiatives such as mutualisation of debts via eurobonds to pool risks and a transfer of funds from stable to vulnerable economies. The package was not as tough as the Germans wanted, for a qualified majority would be allowed to veto fines.

The British government decided to use its first-ever veto to block the deal, because David Cameron and his team did not believe that it protected vital British interests, notably the financial markets. This veto prevented eurozone members from using EU institutions to oversee their plans. This in effect left a 'euro-plus' group of seventen members, six would-be members and possibly three others who might back the proposals, but they would have to go ahead without the backing of the whole Union. In other words, on a key aspect of EU policy there would be a large inner core of committed present/likely future members, with the UK (and maybe the Czech Republic, Hungary and Sweden) on the outside. The prospect of a two-speed Europe was therefore back on the agenda, with a core of countries moving towards ever-closer union, with others remaining in the slow lane. The future of the euro is uncertain, as is the direction of the Union itself.

Britain on the sidelines
As the problems of the eurozone unfolded in 2010–11, the British Coalition government found itself in a frustrating situation. Although most of its Conservative members had been strongly opposed to Britain adopting the euro and some were wary of the whole concept of a single currency, few wanted to see the currency fail, for they understood how much British exporters benefited from the vast market introduced by the Single European Act.

The Cameron-led government wanted to see stability in the eurozone and effective measures to tackle the debt crisis that endangered its future. For some eurosceptics, this was not enough. They saw an opportunity for any revision of the Lisbon Treaty to be accompanied by measures to repatriate social and employment powers ceded by Britain to the Union over recent years. In their view, the crisis in the eurozone gave Britain the chance to refashion the EU as a looser union of independent states.

Most Conservatives were delighted to see the British veto used, though many wanted to go further and use the crisis to regain lost powers or work towards disengagement from the Union. By contrast, their Liberal Democrat partners, traditionally pro-European, viewed events with alarm. In December 2011, it remains unclear how events will unfold. However, use of the veto would appear to have irrevocably changed the tortuous relationship between the UK and the European Union, placed Britain on the margins of Europe and inflicted serious damage upon the Coalition.

• •

 What you should have learned from reading this chapter

- The EEC, a free trade area, has been transformed into the European Union. Political power has tended to shift upwards from the member states to the EU, the Union's role in policymaking being significantly increased.

- Britain was not on the bandwagon of the process of EU integration and since entry into the Community has often been seen as a 'reluctant European'.

- As EU powers have expanded via successive treaties, many British politicians and members of the public have been troubled by the powers ceded by successive British governments.

- Membership of the EU has had a significant impact on the British Constitution and the workings of the political system. Those who work in or with government, be they politicians, officials or pressure group activists, have had to take on board the extent of this 'Europeanisation' and become familiar with the way in which EU institutions function.

- The debate in the UK about the extent of British commitment to the Union is unfinished. The evolution of the EU is a process that moves in 'fits and starts'; each time there is talk of a new initiative, it provokes a backlash amongst Eurosceptics and Europhobes in Parliament and the press who wish to 'rein in' Union powers.

 Glossary of key terms

Atlanticist Someone in the UK who is sympathetic to the United States and favours a strong, positive relationship with it.

Benelux countries The collective name for Belgium, Luxembourg and the Netherlands, which together formed a customs union in 1948 and have remained closely identified ever since.

Charter of Fundamental Rights A charter that brings together in a single document a range of personal, civil, political, economic and social rights previously found in a variety of legislative instruments such as national and EU laws, as well as in international conventions, and enshrines them into EU law. Formally proclaimed at Nice (2000), the Charter was given binding legal effect in the Lisbon Treaty.

Co-decision procedure The main legislative procedure by which law is adopted in the EU. It gives the European Parliament the power to adopt legislation jointly with the Council of Ministers, requiring the two bodies to agree on an identical text before any proposal can become law.

Common Agricultural Policy (CAP) A system of subsidies paid to EU farmers. Its main purposes are to guarantee minimum levels of production (so that Europeans have enough food to eat) and to ensure a fair standard of living for those dependent on agriculture.

Convergence criteria The principles agreed at Maastricht to determine whether the economic performance of individual member states was sufficiently strong to enable them to qualify for membership of the single currency.

European Idea The idea of a Continent united by peaceful means, free, prosperous and untainted by the enmities and rivalries of the past – the dream of post-war pioneers of European unity.

Eurozone The name for the area covered by the seventeen states that have adopted the euro as their single currency system.

Functional cooperation The theory/method of integration by which cooperation is conducted on a sectoral basis, with nations working together in a limited area (e.g. agriculture, coal and steel), with decisions taken by supranational high authorities under the direction of technocrats. As the habit of cooperation develops, so nations may begin to cooperate more closely in further areas.

Integration The process of making a community into a whole, by strengthening the bonds between its component parts. In this case, building unity between nations on the basis that they pool their resources and take many decisions jointly, thereby leading to a deepening of the ties that bind the EU.

Intergovernmental A method of reaching decisions by cooperation between or among governments, on the basis of consensus wherever possible. National sovereignty is not undermined by any surrender of the right to make decisions in the national interest.

Intergovernmental Conferences (IGCs) Gatherings that bring together representatives of EU member states in order to hammer out the details of amendments to the treaties or other history-making initiatives on issues such as enlargement.

Intergovernmental Union A union in which decisions are reached through cooperation between or among governments, by bargaining and often on the basis of consensus. Often contrasted with supranationalism.

New democracies Those countries formerly controlled by the Soviet Union. After the fall of the Berlin Wall, most became democracies and in several cases were keen to join the EU and benefit from its large market. Examples include Hungary and Poland, both now member states.

Qualified Majority Voting (QMV) The most widely adopted method of voting in the Council of Ministers, involving a 'weighting' accorded to each member state very broadly reflecting its population. Large states have more votes than small ones and specified numbers of votes constitute 'qualified majorities'. For instance, France, Germany, Italy and the UK all have twenty-nine votes, Romania fourteen, Cyprus four and Malta three. Since the 2007 enlargement, a QMV decision must have 74.8 per cent of the votes (258/345) and be supported by a majority of the member states. By 2014, under the Lisbon Treaty, decisions will need to be supported by at least 55% of the member states and 65% of the EU population (calculated on a country-by-country basis); no combination of fewer than four states – whatever their size – will be able to block any change desired by the rest. This new method is known as *double majority voting*.

Red lines Points in bargaining discussions that are not negotiable, because the issues involved are regarded as fundamental to the protection of national interests and/or national sovereignty.

Right of veto The right of any country to block a proposed initiative or law in the Council of Ministers. The Lisbon Treaty removed the national veto from a further sixty-one policy areas, covering issues such as energy, health and foreign policy.

Second and Third Pillars of the Maastricht Treaty The parts of the Maastricht Treaty dealing with foreign and security, and justice and home affairs policy, respectively. (The First Pillar was concerned with developing the pre-existing European Community, for example by the adoption of a single currency.)

Social Chapter A protocol of the Maastricht Treaty (subsequently incorporated into the Treaty of Rome, at the Amsterdam summit), committing member states to a range of measures concerned with the social protection of employees. Britain originally had an opt-out; however, the Blair government quickly signed the Chapter.

Special relationship The term used to describe the warm political and diplomatic relations between the United States and some Western nations, particularly Great Britain. The relationship has been the centrepiece of British foreign policy in the post-1945 era.

Super-state The idea of a centralised European state that is considerably more powerful than individual nation states. It represents the fear of those who detect the creation of a United States of Europe, which some see as the inevitable outcome of the integrationist trends of recent years – e.g. the creation of a single currency.

Supranationalist A method of decision-making by processes or institutions that are 'above nations or states' and largely independent of them.

Supranational authority A body that is 'above nations and states' and exercises power beyond their borders, being largely independent of them. Supranationalism is therefore a system of decision-making by an institution or processes that go beyond the authority or jurisdiction of any one national government.

Treaty of Rome The treaty establishing the European Economic Community, signed in March 1957.

Two speed Europe An approach that would allow a core group of EU countries to move faster than the others towards European integration. As such, it is one of the forms of flexibility designed to ensure that the process of integration can move forward, even if not all states feel ready to participate.

United States of Europe The Churchillian vision of a recreation of the 'European family', which would unify the Continent. Churchill's was a more cautious approach to European integration than that commonly advanced on the Continent, which favoured full integration based on a 'federalist' outcome and full constitution. Churchill stressed a unity of Europe based on close cooperation, rather than such a fully fledged federal system.

Variable geometry A model of integration in which not every member state takes part in every EU policy area. Members can decide whether or not they wish to participate in any particular policy, subject to them taking part in a basic core of activities.

? Likely examination questions

To what extent has the EU become a 'supranational' body and to what extent is it still intergovernmental?

'The Council of Ministers is the real decision-making body of the EU.' Discuss.

Should we be worried about any lack of democracy in the EU's governing arrangements?

Are the British right to fear the creation of a federal Europe?

Is the EU destined to become a giant super-state?

What have been the main effects of membership of the European Union on the UK political system?

Why are the British sometimes described as 'reluctant Europeans'?

Helpful websites

www.europa.eu The European Union.

www.ec.europa.eu The European Commission.

www.cec.org.uk The UK office of the European Commission.

www.europarl.europa.eu The European Parliament.

www.europarl.org.uk The UK office of the European Parliament.

Suggestions for further reading

A. Blair, *Companion to the European Union*, Routledge, 2006.

E. Bomberg and A. Stubb, *The European Union: How Does it Work?*, Oxford University Press, 2006.

A. Jones, *Britain in the European Union*, Edinburgh University Press, 2007.

N. McNaughton, *British and European Political Issues*, Manchester University Press, 2010.

N. Nugent, *The Government and Politics of the European Union*, Palgrave, 2006.

D. Watts, *The European Union*, Edinburgh University Press, 2008.

CHAPTER 11

Democracy in theory and practice

Contents

Introduction   410
The development of democracy   411
Democracy: its main forms   412
The characteristics of representative and liberal democracies   413
British democracy in practice   415

Overview

Democracy is the most stable and enduring governing idea in modern politics. It arouses widespread approval, even in states that may seem undemocratic.

In this chapter, we trace the development of ideas about democracy, from the time of the Greeks to the present day. We then examine the characteristics of modern liberal, representative democracies, before assessing how democratic the British system is in practice and noting possible areas where action may be required.

Key issues to be covered in this chapter

- How and why the term 'democracy' has been extensively used
- Direct democracy in Ancient Greece
- The development of modern ideas on democracy
- The nature of indirect and liberal democracy
- British democracy, its virtues and blemishes

Introduction

According to Abraham Lincoln, democracy is 'a system where no man is good enough to govern another man without that other's consent'. More famously, on another occasion, he described it as 'government of the people, by the people and for the people'.

Democracy in vogue

Today, almost all of us describe ourselves as democrats and more people than ever across the world live under conditions of democratic rule. According to the **World Forum on Democracy**, democracies now exist in 120 of the 192 existing countries and constitute 58.2 per cent of the world's population; in 2007, **Freedom House**, put the figure at 123 (up from forty in 1972). This is not to be complacent about the nature of some regimes and the brutalities and breaches of human rights that they practise. Rather, it is a statement of the fact that tolerable levels of democracy prevail more widely and over more people than ever in the past.

Doctrines such as capitalism and socialism are called into question, but democracy is an abiding principle to which most of us feel attached. Hardly any group would disown the label, even though they might think very differently about what it entails. Communists and Conservatives, Liberals and Socialists, Anarchists and Fascists often try to hijack the word, as though they have a particular understanding of its meaning. In fact, very few groups would like to be described as undemocratic and the same is true of countries, as well. North Korea calls itself the Democratic People's Republic. Sri Lanka sees itself as a Democratic Socialist Republic.

The nature of the world's 'democracies' varies spectacularly. In many cases, they are far removed from those that operate in Western Europe and the United States, with their emphasis on representative and limited government. Perhaps unsurprisingly, Bernard Crick[1] felt impelled to refer to democracy as 'the most promiscuous word in the world of public affairs . . . she is everybody's mistress and yet somehow retains her magic even when a lover sees her favours being illicitly shared by another.'

Whatever the definition of democracy employed, democracy is in practice a model form of government to which it is easy to aspire but difficult to achieve. Even those states commonly regarded as among the most democratic often have blemishes upon their record in particular areas.

The development of democracy

The city-states of Ancient Athens provide the first great experiment in democracy. Essentially it was a form of government based on mass meetings, with major decisions being made by the Assembly to which every citizen belonged. Pericles described the experience as a system in which government was the concern of the many rather than the few. From our point of view, however, there were obvious flaws in the Athenian model, in that the right to vote was limited to free citizens, men of Athenian ancestry. Foreigners, slaves and women were denied the chance to participate in decision-making.

From the collapse of the Roman republic in the second century BC until the eighteenth century, **autocracy** was the usual form of government, although in Britain from the seventeenth century a concept of parliamentary control over the arbitrary actions of the monarch began to emerge. The *American Declaration of Independence*, chiefly written by Thomas Jefferson and based on the ideas of the English philosopher John Locke, marked an important development. It contained references that today sound profoundly democratic. It spoke of 'inalienable rights' and proclaimed that 'all men are created equal' and that 'governments derive their just powers from the consent of the governed'.

In the *Federalist Papers* which followed the drafting of the American Constitution, the protagonists wrestled with key issues of government, such as how to make it strong enough to keep order and protect men's liberties and basic rights, yet ensure that it was not so all-pervasive that it limited their freedoms. The answer was indirect, representative democracy, with certain checks and balances to ensure the protection of minority rights.

The American experiment influenced early leaders of the French Revolution. The *Declaration of the Rights of Man* (1789) described men as being 'free and equal in rights' and proclaimed ideas such as 'popular sovereignty' and 'equality before the law'. For many years, the Declaration was the watchword of European reformers who were stirred by its battle cry of 'liberty, equality, **fraternity**'.

Modern democracies developed in three main phases or waves:

1. The 'first long **wave of democratisation**'[2] occurred between 1828 and 1926, during which nearly thirty countries – ranging from Britain and the United States to France and the Scandinavian countries – established at least minimally democratic national institutions. In some cases, the process was in part reversed as a result of a move to dictatorship in fledgling democracies, such as Austria, Germany and Italy.

2. The second wave began in wartime, lasting from 1943 to 1962. It included countries ranging from Austria and West Germany to India and Israel, often countries that had become brutal dictatorships. Again, there were reversals in some countries, particularly in much of Latin America and post-colonial Africa.

3. The third wave, from 1974 to 1991, comprised three highly diverse elements: the ending of fascist dictatorship in three Mediterranean countries, Greece, Portugal and Spain; the fall of several military regimes in Latin America; and finally, the collapse of communism in the USSR and Eastern Europe following the dismantling of the Berlin Wall in 1989.

Democracy: its main forms

The word 'democracy' derives from two Greek terms, *'demos'* meaning people and *'kratia'*, signifying rule of or by. Democracy is commonly described as meaning 'people power', with government resting on the consent of the governed. There are two main types of democracy:

1. *Direct or classical democracy*, the situation in which it is possible for all the citizens to come together in one place to make decisions as to how the state should be run.

2. *Indirect or representative democracy*, the form of democracy which emerged to replace the direct form, in which the voters choose representatives who will govern on their behalf and according to the wishes of the majority.

In modern states, the growth in population and the size of the area to be governed meant that the old Athenian form of direct democracy was no longer viable, other than in very small communities. It went out of fashion. In the nineteenth century, representative democracy developed in Britain, with the extension of the right to vote and the evolution of a constitutional monarchy.

The characteristics of representative and liberal democracies

Representative democracies

Key elements of a modern representative democracy include:

- *Popular control of policymakers.* Government must be subject to control exercised through elected representatives, popularly chosen.
- *The existence of opposition.* Without a right to oppose, there can be no democracy.
- *Political equality.* Every adult must have the right to vote, each having only one vote.
- *Political freedoms.* There must be a free choice of candidates and a range of basic liberties and rights – free speech, assembly and organisation among them.
- *Majority rule.* The right of the majority to have their way may seem just, but it needs to be accompanied by toleration of and respect for any minority.

From this listing of criteria, we can piece together the following definition: a democratic political system is one in which public policies are made, on a majority basis, by representatives subject to effective popular control at periodic elections which are conducted on the principle of political equality and under conditions of political freedom.

Liberal democracies

Democracy involves more than people having voting rights. It is essential that there are opportunities for citizens and the media to exercise freedom of speech, assembly and political opposition. There are checks on the power of government to protect citizens from arbitrary or unfair action, so that a liberal democratic regime is characterised by:

- *pluralism* – the existence of diverse centres of economic and political power
- *limited government* – constraints on the power of government
- *open government* – non-secretive government which can be seen to be fair and accountable
- *an independent judiciary* – a just, impartial legal system.

Box 11.1 Semi or façade democracies

The versions of democracy outlined in the text are based primarily on the experience of Western Europe and North America. In other parts of the world, newer forms of democracy have been developed which cannot be included within the orbit of liberal democracy. Hague and Harrop[3] referred to them as semi-democracies in 2004, but by 2007 they used the arguably more appropriate term '**illiberal democracies**' to describe regimes that blended features of a Western-style representative democracy with more authoritarian impulses, the 'democracy not extending far beyond the election itself'. They have been developed in countries whose conditions are very different to our own and are an attempt to graft on the familiar democratic features of elections to regimes whose tone has in the past often been severely repressive. Finer[4] dismissed them as 'façade democracies', but less unflattering terms include 'limited democracies' and 'authoritarian democracies'.

Good examples are provided by some of the Asian states such as Malaysia and Singapore, in both of which effective, stable government has been provided by regimes that are 'repressive-responsive'. Again, particularly in some countries of the old Soviet Empire, there is little attention to individual rights and the media is used to convey the government message. There may be 'roughing up' of opponents and harassing of dissidents, as in the Ukranian elections of 2004. Among other abuses in the Ukraine, supporters of the Prime Minister were bussed from place to place, so that they could vote again; people were brought in from Russia to vote for him; and likely voters for opposition candidates were given pens to mark the ballot paper from which the ink disappeared shortly afterwards.

In liberal democracies, the power of government is limited by the recognition of free play between autonomous voluntary associations within society. There are several checks and balances. Important foci of power include trades unions, professional associations and private companies. The task of government is to reconcile and coordinate these various interests, only imposing coercion when other methods of harmonisation fail to operate effectively.

Liberal democracies are characterised by a spirit of tolerance towards competing groups and particularly towards the views of minorities. There is due recognition of everybody's interests, but it is understood that government should be concerned with the good of the whole community. According to Freedom House (2010), liberal democracy prevails in eighty-nine countries, all of which can be regarded as free, respectful of basic human rights and the rule of law.

British democracy in practice

Is Britain a working democracy? For most people, the answer is a resounding 'yes', in that it has the usual characteristics of liberal, representative democracy. Indeed, Hacker[5] felt inspired to describe Britain and the United States as 'the world's two leading democracies'. Today, the USA provides 'the clearest picture of a liberal democracy in which the liberal dimension is entrenched by design'. As Lyon[6] elaborates: 'Only in periods of external threat, including post-9/11, do individual liberties come under threat.'

In Britain, by contrast, the rights of the citizen have never been so explicitly stated as they are in the American Constitution; the widening of the franchise was a much slower process, brought about in stages in some of which the propertied classes needed to have their fears of further reform massaged; and the concept of democracy more closely follows the 'Schumpeter model'[7] of being 'electoral competition between organised parties'. In British democracy, such has been the extent of Executive power that the winning party is rewarded with an exceptionally free hand.

Traditional features of the democratic way of life have long existed in both countries, including:

- ample opportunities for the free expression of opinions
- elections by secret ballot from a choice of candidates
- government resting on consent and being accountable to the people
- opportunities for people to influence government
- a spirit of tolerance prevailing between the majority and the minority
- a reluctance to coerce recalcitrant minorities, and via free elections the means by which a legitimate and peaceful minority may seek to transform itself into a majority
- the provision for power to change hands peacefully
- limited government and the protection of individual rights
- an independent judiciary
- a free media.

Doubts about British democracy

The ending of the Cold War in the late twentieth century gave rise to widespread euphoria about democracy and the democratic process. Yet, even as democracy celebrated its triumph over communism, there were signs of public unease about the vitality of the democratic process. Joseph Nye[8] and his colleagues demonstrated how low levels of political trust among the American public continued into the 1990s. Several subsequent cross-national analyses suggested this was not a distinctly American phenomenon. Indeed, some writers went further and suggested that there was a 'crisis of democracy'. Fuchs and Klingemann[9] claimed that the public in several democracies had become increasingly alienated from the democratic system, as a result of

- greater centralisation
- its failure to deliver what citizens want
- lower opportunities for participation.

Democracy is more than observance of a particular form of government, based on the existence of free institutions. The framework may exist, but it needs to be maintained in a constant state of good repair. As in other democracies, there are blemishes within the British system, many of which have been considered elsewhere in this book, among them:

- lack of knowledge, interest and belief in politicians on the part of the electorate
- low levels of political participation and of turnout in elections
- the electoral system, as used at Westminster
- ownership and control of, and trivial content in, the news media
- the denial or erosion of civil liberties
- the growing importance of money in politics, in particular reliance on large donations – be they from unions, business or affluent individuals
- the existence of quangos
- allegations that we have an 'elective dictatorship', in which governments armed with a Commons majority can drive their programme onto the statute book
- the relative lack of openness in government and the slowness to develop strong freedom of information legislation
- the limited use of direct democracy, as a means of engaging people's interest
- the lack of popular control over institutions of the European Union, the so-called 'democratic deficit'.

Some would question whether these are blemishes upon the British record. Not everyone is convinced that proportional electoral systems are more democratic, or that regular (or any) referendums are a good thing. Others listed, such as the allegedly inadequate protection of rights or the lack of freedom of information, have recently been addressed to some extent. The elective dictatorship theory is open to challenge and – in the light of the outcome of the 2005 election and the ending of the Blair premiership – we may no longer be in an era of 'prime ministerial' or 'presidential' government.

Comparing the state of democracy under the Conservatives to May 1997 and Labour to 2002, the researchers of the 2003 *Democrat Audit*[10] suggested that in every area other than voter turnout, democracy under the Blair government fared better than its predecessors. However, they also noted that on issues such as accountability to Parliament, devolution (England being described as 'a hole in the heart of devolution'), open and responsive government, and women in public life, their findings were generally damning.

A few years later, a dossier compiled by the **Convention on Modern Liberty**[11] outlined a devastating analysis of the erosion of civil liberties in Britain since 1997. It claimed that almost sixty new powers contained in more than twenty-five statutes had whittled away at freedoms and broken pledges set out in the Human Rights Act and Magna Carta. Among other things, it criticised police powers of detention, new stop-and-search powers handed to police (allowing them to stop people without reason at airports and other designated areas), the restrictions on the right of peaceful protest and the rise of the 'surveillance state'. The critique appeared to be devastating, although its critics might portray many of the policies as being a necessary part of the threat to national security in the twenty-first century.

Few countries can legitimately claim to have a near-perfect democracy. If in Britain, the reality has sometimes fallen short of the democratic ideal, the commitment to democracy has long been apparent and there are always people ready and free to highlight any lapses from that ideal. There is a strong tradition of freedom and people have the benefit of living in a country that develops via peaceful change rather than through violent upheaval. The attitudes and way of life of British citizens provide a setting in which democratic principles and practices have generally flourished.

As society evolves, so too must our democracy. New situations create a need for new remedies. As more power becomes centralised in the hands of the Executive, so new checks and balances become necessary. Successful adaptation requires that our politicians, media and people have a critical appreciation of our institutions and are vigilant against any abuses of the best democratic practice.

· ·

✔ What you should have learnt from reading this chapter

- Democracy is a term of widespread approval and in some form or other it is widely practised around the world.

- Britain is widely seen as being one of the foremost representative and liberal democracies.

- Some people have doubts about the effectiveness of British democracy in Britain and feel that it has serious limitations.

- Democracy is an ideal to which many countries may aspire, but several fall seriously short in practice.

Glossary of key terms

Autocracy Government by an individual with unrestricted authority.

Convention on Modern Liberty A one day gathering held in February 2009 to discuss fundamental freedoms and rights.

Fraternity Bonds of comradeship and sympathy between people who are united in their aims and interests: brotherhood.

Freedom House Freedom House is an independent watchdog body that supports the expansion of freedom. It supports democratic change, monitors freedom and speaks up for human rights around the world.

Illiberal democracies Electoral democracies in which leaders are elected without undue falsification of the count, but do their best to ensure that there is no level playing field for other candidates, by interfering with the rule of law, the media and the market. Individual rights are not respected, nor are they protected by a weak judicial system.

Wave of democratisation Huntington's theory of how democracy emerged in a series of waves, 'a group of transitions from non-democratic to democratic regimes that occur within a specified period of time and that significantly outnumber transitions in the opposite direction during that period.'

World Forum on Democracy A gathering of academics, civic and religious leaders and former government officials that took place in Warsaw (2000). It urged the importance of elections and traditional democratic values such as free speech, freedom of expression and freedom of association.

Likely examination questions

Are modern forms of democracy truly democratic?

Winston Churchill described democracy as 'the worst form of government except all the others that have been tried from time to time'. How can democracy be defended against this charge?

How well does democracy work in Britain at the present time?

In what ways could British government be made more democratic?

Helpful websites

www.ucl.ac.uk/constitution-unit The Constitution Unit.

www.democraticaudit.com Democratic Audit: produces briefing papers on such topics as electoral fraud and the finality or otherwise of referendum verdicts. See the findings of its 2011 Audit.

 Suggestions for further reading

C. Bromley et al., 'Is Britain Facing a Crisis of Democracy?', Constitution Unit, 2004.

B. Crick, *Democracy: A Very Short Introduction*, Oxford University Press, 2002.

R. Dahl, *Democracy and its Critics*, Yale University Press, 1989.

S. Huntington, *The Third Wave: Democratization in the Late Twentieth Century*, University of Oklahoma Press, 1991.

References

Chapter 1

1. A. Hanson and M. Walles, *Governing Britain*, Fontana, 1977.
2. A. Birch, *The British System of Government*, Allen & Unwin, 1975.
3. J. Blondel, *Comparative Government: An Introduction*, Prentice Hall, 1995.
4. CRE research conducted for *Connections*, Commission for Racial Equality, Winter 2004–5.
5. L. Pye, 'Political Culture', in S. Lipset (ed.), *The Encyclopaedia of Democracy*, CQ Press, 1995.
6. A. Heywood, *Politics*, Macmillan, 1997.
7. H. Cantril, *The Pattern of Human Concerns*, Rutgers University Press, 1965.
8. I. Inglehart, *Culture Shifts in Advanced Industrial Society*, Princeton University Press, 1990.
9. R. Dalton, *Citizen Politics in Western Democracies*, Seen Bridges Press, 2001.
10. G. Almond and S. Verba, *The Civic Culture*, Princeton University Press, 1963.
11. G. Almond and S. Verba, *The Civic Culture Revisited*, Princeton University Press, 1980.
12. J. Curtice and R. Jowell, 'Trust in the Political System', in R. Jowell et al. (eds), *British Social Attitudes: the 14th Report*, Ashgate, 1997.
13. 26th British Social Attitudes Survey, National Centre for Social Research, 2010.
14. J. Blondel, *Comparative Government: An Introduction*, Prentice Hall, 1995, and R. Punnett, *British Government and Politics*, Gower, 1971.
15. R. Punnett, *British Government and Politics*, Gower, 1971.

Chapter 2

1. J. Marais, as quoted in J. Danziger, *Understanding the Political World*, Addison Wesley Longman, 2001.
2. A. Heywood, *Politics*, Macmillan, 1997.

3. J. Derbyshire and L. Derbyshire, *Political Systems of the World*, Helicon, 1999.

4. A. Heywood, *Politics*, Macmillan, 1997.

5. K. Wheare, *Federal Government*, Oxford University Press, 1963.

6. A. Dicey, *Introduction to the Study of the Law and the Constitution*, Macmillan, 1885.

7. E. Wade and G. Philips, *Constitutional Law*, Longman, reissued 1998.

8. A. Hanson and M. Walles, *Governing Britain*, Fontana, 1997.

9. H. Elcock, 'The British Constitution: Broke, but Who will Fix It?', *Talking Politics*, 9:2, Autumn 1996.

10. A. Adonis, *Parliament Today*, Manchester University Press, 1993.

11. P. Norton, 'Constitutional Change: A Response to Elcock', *Talking Politics*, 9:2, Autumn 1996.

12. P. Hennessy, *The Hidden Wiring: Unearthing the British Constitution*, Gollancz, 1995.

13. T. Blair, *The Guardian*, 10 September 1995.

14. T. Blair, as quoted in R. Hazell, *Constitutional Futures: A History of the Next Ten Years*, Oxford University Press, 1999.

15. D. Irvine, as quoted in R. Hazell, *Constitutional Futures: A History of the Next Ten Years*, Oxford University Press, 1999.

16. T. Blair, as quoted in *The Guardian*, 10 September 1995.

17. G. Peele, 'Introduction', in P. Dunleavy et al. (eds), *Developments in British Politics 7*, Palgrave, 2003.

18. Governance of Britain, Green Paper CM 7170, HMSO, 2007.

19. R. Hague and M. Harrop, *Comparative Government and Politics: An Introduction*, Palgrave, 2004.

20. A. Dicey, *Introduction to the Study of the Law and the Constitution*, Macmillan, 1885.

21. F. Klug et al., *The Three Pillars of Liberty*, Routledge, 1996.

22. K. Starmer, 'Two Years of the Human Rights Act', *European Human Rights Law Review*, 1, 2003.

23. V. Bogdanor, *The British Constitution in the Twentieth Century*, Clarendon Press, 2003.

24. G. Morris, 'The European Convention on Human Rights and Employment: to Which Acts does it Apply?', *European Human Rights Law Review*, 1, 1999.

25. M. Howard, 'Judges must bow to the will of Parliament', *Daily Telegraph*, 10 August 2005.
26. L. Hartz, *The Liberal Tradition in America*, Harcourt Brace, 1955.

Chapter 3

1. R. Hague and M. Harrop, *Comparative Government and Politics: An Introduction*, Palgrave, 2007.
2. J. Bryce, *Modern Democracy*, Macmillan, 1921.
3. V. Bogdanor, 'Reform of the House of Lords: a Sceptical View', *Political Quarterly*, 1999.
4. M. Bragg, as quoted in F. Cooney and P. Fotheringham, *UK Politics Today*, Pulse Publications, 2002.
5. P. Norton, 'Adding Value? The Role of Second Chambers', *Asia Pacific Law Review*, 15:1, 2007.
6. K. Bartlett, *Citizenship PA*, January 2004.
7. Charter 88, Response to the Government White Paper on reform of the House of Lords – Completing the Reform, 1 September 2003.
8. M. Russell, 'House Full: Time to Get A Grip on Lords Appointments', press release by UCL Constitution Unit, 20 April 2011.
9. P. Norton, 'Foreword', to A. Taggart and S. Emery, *Towards an Effective House of Lords*, www.bowgroup.org
10. R. Hague and M. Harrop, *Comparative Government and Politics: An Introduction*, Palgrave, 2007.
11. House of Commons Liaison Committee, *Shifting the Balance: Select Committees and the Executive*, HMSO, 2000.
12. G. Thomas, *Parliament in an Age of Reform*, Politics Association/SHU Press, 2000.
13. A. Mitchell, as quoted in G. Thomas, *Parliament in an Age of Reform*, Politics Association/SHU Press, 2000.
14. Hours survey, as quoted in G. Thomas, *Parliament in an Age of Reform*, Politics Association/SHU Press, 2000.
15. M. Foot, as quoted in A. Heywood, *Politics*, Macmillan, 1997.
16. Hansard Society, *7th Annual Audit of Political Engagement*, www.hansardsociety.org.uk, 2010.
17. P. Richards, *Parliament and Conscience*, Faber & Faber, 1970.
18. P. Norton, 'The House of Commons: the Half-empty Bottle of Reform',

in B. Jones (ed.) *Political Issues in Britain Today*, Manchester University Press, 1999.

19. H. Berrington, 'Political Ethics: The Nolan Report', *Government and Opposition*, 30, 1995.
20. I. Budge et al., *The Politics of the New Europe*, Longman, 1997.
21. W. Wilson, *Congressional Government*, Meridian Books, revised edition 1956.
22. J. Blondel, *Comparative Government: An Introduction*, Prentice Hall, 1995.
23. P. Norton, *Does Parliament Matter?*, Harvester Wheatsheaf, 1993.
24. R. Hague and M. Harrop, *Comparative Government and Politics: An Introduction*, Palgrave, 2007.

Chapter 4

1. 'To call Attention to the Constitutional and Parliamentary Effect of Coalition Government', Background note for debate on subject (20 January 2011), House of Lords Library Group, January 2011.
2. W. Bagehot, *The English Constitution*, reissued by Fontana, 1963.
3. A. Heywood, *Politics*, Macmillan, 1997.
4. Lord Hailsham, *'Elective Dictatorship'*, *The Richard Dimbleby Lecture*, BBC Publications, 1976.
5. A. Heywood, *Politics*, Macmillan, 1997.
6. A. Heywood, *Politics*, Macmillan, 1997.
7. I. Jennings, *Cabinet Government*, Cambridge University Press, 1959.
8. P. Walker, *The Cabinet*, Cape, 1970.
9. A. Hanson and M. Walles, *Governing Britain*, Fontana, 1997.
10. P. Madgwick, *Introduction to British Politics*, Hutchinson, 1984.
11. P. Norton, *The British Polity*, Longman, 2001.
12. R. Crossman, *The Diaries of a Cabinet Minister* vol. 2, Hamish Hamilton/Jonathan Cape, 1976.
13. N. Lawson, *The View From No. 11*, Bantam, 1992.
14. M. Burch and I. Holliday, *The British Cabinet System*, Harvester Wheatsheaf, 1996.
15. P. Hennessy, *The Prime Minister: The Office and its Holders Since 1945*, Allen Lane, 2000.
16. L. Butler et al., *Review of Intelligence on Weapons of Mass Destruction*, HMSO, 2004.

17. G. Jones, as quoted in D. Barrett, 'Cabinet "too big to make decisions"', *Daily Telegraph*, 20 June 2009.
18. D. Butler, as quoted in D. Barrett, 'Cabinet "too big to make decisions"', *Daily Telegraph*, 20 June 2009.
19. M. Heseltine, *The Observer*, 12 January 1986.
20. T. Blair, as quoted in P. Hennessy, *The Prime Minister: The Office and its Holders Since 1945*, Allen Lane, 2000; P. Madgwick, *Introduction to British Politics*, Hutchinson, 1984.
21. P. Madgwick, *Introduction to British Politics*, Hutchinson, 1984.
22. R. Crossman, in an introduction to a reissue of W. Bagehot, *The English Constitution*, Fontana, 1963.
23. J. Mackintosh, *The British Cabinet*, Stevens, 1977.
24. T. Benn, 'The Case for a Constitutional Premiership', in A. King, *The British Prime Minister*, Macmillan, 1985.
25. P. Mandelson, *The Third Man: Life at the Heart of New Labour*, Harper Press, 2010.
26. Lord Oxford and Asquith, *Fifty Years of Parliament*, Cassell, 1926.
27. M. Foley, 'Presidential Politics in the UK: the Blair Inheritance', *e-pol*, 3:3, September 2010.
28. M. Foley, *The Rise of the British Presidency*, Manchester University Press, 1993.
29. M. Foley, *The Rise of the British Presidency*, Manchester University Press, 1993.
30. D. Mayhew, *Divided We Govern*, Yale University Press, 1991.
31. Sir Gilbert Fleming, as quoted by D. Bell, *Guardian Professional*, 20 January 2010.
32. Lord Salisbury, House of Lords debate, 8 April 1878.
33. R. Hague and M. Harrop, *Comparative Government and Politics: An Introduction*, Palgrave, 2007.
34. G. Wasserman, *The Basics of American Politics*, Longman, 1996.
35. R. Neustadt, *Presidential Power: The Politics of Leadership*, Wiley & Sons, 1960.

Chapter 5

1. Lord Denning, *What next in the Law?*, Butterworths, 1982.
2. Lord Hailsham, House of Lords judgement, 1997.

3. C. Falconer, as quoted in *Monitor* (The Constitution Unit Bulletin), 27, July 2004.
4. A. Sampson, *Who Runs This Place? The Anatomy of Britain in the 21st Century*, John Murray, 2004.
5. A. Sampson, *Who Runs This Place? The Anatomy of Britain in the 21st Century*, John Murray, 2004.
6. J. Griffiths, *The Politics of the Judiciary*, Fontana, 1997.
7. G. Drewry, 'Judges and Politics in Britain', in *Social Studies Review*, November 1986.
8. S. Lee, 'The Law and the Constitution', in A. Seldon and D. Kavanagh (eds), *The Major Effect*, Macmillan, 1994.
9. I. Budge et al., *The Politics of the New Europe*, Longman, 1997.
10. L. Taylor, 'The Judiciary in the Nineties', The Dimbleby Lecture, 1992.
11. H. Woolf, *The Guardian*, 18 December 2002.
12. J. Jowell (ed.), *Lord Denning the Judge and the Law*, Sweet & Maxwell, 1984.
13. H. Woolf, *The Guardian*, 18 December 2002.
14. P. Boateng, as quoted in G. Peele, *Governing the UK*, Blackwell, 2004.
15. R. Hague and M. Harrop, *Comparative Government and Politics: An Introduction*, Palgrave, 2007.
16. K. Ewing and C. Gearty, *Freedom under Thatcher*, Clarendon Press, 1990.
17. C. Hughes, speech at Elmira, 3 May 1907, quoted in *Addresses and Papers of Charles Evans Hughes, Governor of New York, 1906–1908*, Putnams & Sons, 1908.
18. J. Biskupic, 'Justices want to be known as Jurists, not Activists', *Washington Post*, 9 January 2000.
19. T. Yarborrough, 'The Supreme Court and the Constitution', in G. Peele et al., *Developments in American Politics* 4, Palgrave, 2002.
20. J. Blondel, *Comparative Government: An Introduction*, Prentice Hall, 1995.
21. T. Bingham, as quoted in K. Ewing and C. Gearty, *Freedom under Thatcher*, Clarendon Press, 1990.
22. L. Lloyd, as quoted in P. Norton, 'A Bill of Rights: the Case Against', *Talking Politics*, Summer 1993.

20. C. Hamilton, 'The Third Way and the End of Politics', *The Australian Institute*, www.australianreview.net/journal/v2/n2/hamilton.pdf
21. E. Miliband, 'I'll make capitalism work for the people', *The Observer*, 29 August 2010.
22. J. Macintyre, 'D. Miliband declares the end of "New Labour"', *New Statesman*, 16 May 2010.
23. C. Pattie, P. Seyd and P. Whiteley, 'Citizenship and Civic Engagement: Attitudes and Behaviour in Britain', *Political Studies*, October 2003.
24. T. Laiprakobsup, 'Economy and Political Parties: the Impact of the Economic Conditions on the Party Membership Trend in England and Germany, 1950–1994', paper presented to MPSA Annual National Conference in Chicago, 3 April 2008.
25. Lord Tebbit, 'The end of Thatcherism?', *The Economist*, 4 February 2006.
26. R. McKenzie, *British Political Parties*, Heinemann, 1963.
27. A. Ranney, as quoted in R. McKenzie, *British Political Parties*, Heinemann, 1963.
28. J. Blondel, *Comparative Government: An Introduction*, Prentice Hall, 1995.
29. I. Budge et al., *The Politics of the New Europe*, Longman, 1997.
30. R. Hague and M. Harrop, *Comparative Government and Politics*, Palgrave, 2004.
31. D. Maidment and D. McGrew, *The American Political Process*, Sage, 1992.
32. P. Herrnson, *Party Campaigning in the 1980s*, Harvard University Press, 1998.

Chapter 8

1. A. Heywood, *Politics*, Macmillan, 1997.
2. S. Finer, *Anonymous Empire*, Pall Mall, 1967.
3. J. Stewart, *British Pressure Groups*, Oxford University Press, 1958.
4. W. Grant, *Pressure Groups and British Politics*, Palgrave, 2000.
5. R. Hague and M. Harrop, *Comparative Government and Politics: An Introduction*, Palgrave, 2004.
6. T. Matthews, 'Interest Groups', in R. Smith and L. Watson (eds), *Politics in Australia*, Allen & Unwin, 1989.
7. M. Rush, *Parliament and Pressure Groups*, Clarendon, 1990.

8. R. Baggott, 'The Measurement of Change in Pressure Group Politics', *Talking Politics*, Autumn 1992.
9. R. Baggott, *Pressure Groups and the Policy Process*, Politics Association/ SHU Press, 2000.
10. S. Finer, *Anonymous Empire*, Pall Mall, 1967.
11. D. Watts, questionnaire to fifteen groups, 2005.

Chapter 9

1. R. Gould and C. Jackson, *A Guide for Election Observers*, Commonwealth Parliamentary Association, 1995.
2. A. Heath, R. Jowell and J. Curtice, *Labour's Last Chance*, Dartmouth, 1994.
3. G. Wallas, *Human Nature in Politics*, Constable, 1908: reissued 1948.
4. W. Fletcher, as quoted in P. Norris et al., *On Message: Communicating the Campaign*, Sage, 1999.
5. L. Bille, in S. Bowler and D. Farrell (eds), *Electoral Strategies and Political Marketing*, Macmillan, 1992.
6. D. Farrell and R. Schmitt-Beck (eds), *Do Political Campaigns Matter?*, Routledge, 2002.
7. A. Rawnsley, 'Box of Political Tricks', *The Guardian*, 9 September 1988.
8. D. Kavanagh, *Election Campaigning: The New Marketing of Politics*, Blackwell, 1993.
9. M. Boon and J. Curtice, 'General Election 2010: Did the Opinion Polls Flatter to Deceive?', *Research Magazine*, 6 July 2010.
10. D. Farrell, *Comparing Electoral Systems*, Harvester Wheatsheaf, 1997.
11. Report of the Plant Committee, 'A Working Party on Electoral Reform: Interim Findings', 1991.
12. *Voting Systems: The Jenkins Report*, House of Commons Library Research Paper 98/112, 1998.
13. V. Bogdanor, 'General Election 2010: is first-past-the-post on its last legs?', *Daily Telegraph*, 21 April 2010.
14. D. Farrell, *Comparing Electoral Systems*, Harvester Wheatsheaf, 1997.
15. *Voting Systems: The Jenkins Report*, House of Commons Library Research Paper 98/112, 1998.
16. M. Duverger, *Political Parties*, Methuen, 1962.
17. P. Norton, *The Constitution in Flux*, Blackwell, 1982.
18. V. Bogdanor, *The Observer*, 4 April 1992.

19. A. Ball, *Modern Government and Politics*, Macmillan, 1993.
20. R. Hague and M. Harrop, *Comparative Government and Politics: An Introduction*, Palgrave, 2004.
21. J. Blumler and D. McQuail, *Television in Politics*, Faber & Faber, 1967.
22. W. Lippman, *Public Opinion*, Macmillan, 1938.
23. R. Punnett, *British Government and Politics*, Gower, 1971.
24. P. Madgwick, *A New Introduction to British Politics*, Thornes, 1994.
25. B. Sarlvik and I. Crewe, *Decade of Dealignment*, Cambridge University Press, 1983.
26. P. Kellner, *The New Society*, 2 June 1983.
27. D. Denver, *Elections and Voters in Britain*, Palgrave, 2003.
28. F. Piven and R. Cloward, *Why Americans Don't Vote*, Pantheon Books, 1998.
29. D. Magleby, 'Direct Legislation in the United States', in D. Butler, *Referendums Around the World*, Macmillan, 1994.
30. R. Hague and M. Harrop, *Comparative Government and Politics: An Introduction*, Palgrave, 2004.
31. Editorial in *The Guardian*, 4 March 1993.
32. R. Hague and M. Harrop, *Comparative Government and Politics: An Introduction*, Palgrave, 2004.
33. A. Stevens, *Government and Politics of France*, Palgrave, 2003.

Chapter 10

1. N. Nugent, *The Government and Politics of the European Union*, Palgrave, 2006.
2. S. Bulmer and M. Burch, 'Coming to Terms with Europe: Europeanisation, Whitehall and the Challenge of Devolution', *Queen's Papers on Europeanisation*, 9, 2000.
3. W. Churchill, speech to Conservative Party Annual Conference, 1948.
4. Eurobarometer 70, Public Opinion in the European Union, June 2010.
5. M. Comelli, 'Italy's Love Affair with the EU: Between Continuity and Change', *IAI Documents and Working Papers*, 11:8, April 2011.
6. D. Butler and M. Westlake, *British Politics and the European Elections 1994*, Macmillan, 1995.
7. Sir A. Meyer, as quoted in H. Young, *This Blessed Plot*, Macmillan, 1998.

8. H. Young, *This Blessed Plot*, Macmillan, 1998.
9. W. Churchill, speech in House of Commons, May 1951.
10. D. Acheson, speech to Military Academy, West Point, 5 December 1962.
11. F. Northedge, *Descent from Power: British Foreign Policy 1945–1973*, Allen & Unwin, 1974.
12. H. Young, *This Blessed Plot*, Macmillan, 1998.
13. A. Geddes, *The European Union and British Politics*, Palgrave, 2004.
14. *Mail on Sunday*, as quoted in a special report for *The Observer*, 10 December 2000.
15. N. Davies, as quoted in a special report for *The Observer*, 10 December 2000.
16. L. Siedentop, as quoted in a special report for *The Observer*, 10 December 2000.

Chapter 11

1. B. Crick, *In Defence of Politics*, Penguin, 1982.
2. S. Huntington, *The Third Wave: Democratization in the late Twentieth Century*, University of Oklahoma Press, 1991.
3. R. Hague and M. Harrop, *Comparative Government and Politics: An Introduction*, Palgrave, 2004.
4. S. Finer, *The History of Government from the Earliest Times*, Oxford University Press, 1997.
5. A. Hacker, 'Britain's Political Style Is Not Like Ours', *New York Times Magazine*, September 1964.
6. D. Lyon, *Surveillance after September 11*, Polity, 2003.
7. J. Schumpeter, *Capitalism, Socialism and Democracy*, Allen & Unwin, 1943.
8. J. Nye et al. (eds), *Why People Don't Trust Government*, Harvard University Press, 1997.
9. D. Fuchs and H.-D. Klingemann, *Citizen and the State: a Relationship Transformed*, Oxford University Press, 1995.
10. D. Bleetham et al., *Democracy under Blair: A Democratic Audit of the UK*, Politico's Publishing, 2003.
11. *Audit on Labour's record in office*, programme released by the Convention of Modern Liberty, for its gathering on 28 February 2009.

Index

Bold indicates that the term is defined

access points (for pressure groups), 291–2, 299; *see also* devolved and EU institutions
accession countries, 7, **21**
Additional Member System (AMS), 334–7
adjournment debate, 82, **108**
administrative devolution, 193, **222**
adversary politics, 231, 233, 235, **278**
affirmative action (USA), 185, **186**
agenda setting, 323, **370**
Alternative Vote (AV), **56**, 334–7, 340
   UK referendum, 42, 340, 366, 367
Alternative Vote 'top-up' (AV-plus), 334, 335–7
apartheid, 53, **56**
Ashdown Paddy, 253
asylum seekers, 6, 7, **21**
Atlanticist, 387, 388, **405**
attack on World Trade Center (9/11) *see* September 11th 2001 attack on Twin Towers (New York)
Attlee, Clement, 361, 391
autocracy, 411, **419**
autonomy, 190, 222

Bar, 167, **186**
Belfast 'Good Friday' Agreement 1998, 3, **21**, 37, 200, 205, 366, 367
Benelux countries, 376, **405**
bicameralism, 62–4, 68–9, 75, **108**; *see also* House of Lords
bigotgate, 325, **370**
Big Society, 243, **278**

bill of rights, **56**
   case for and against a UK bill of rights, 46, 53
   European Convention on Human Rights, 30, 35, 37, 44, 46, 47, 48, 49, 51, **56–7, 177–8**, 179
   Human Rights Act 1998, 37, 46–52, 418
Blair, Tony; *see also* Cabinet/Prime Minister, New Labour and War against Iraq
   attitude to and measures of constitutional/parliamentary reform, 35–43, 65–6, 70, 73, 79, 191–2, 217–18, 334
   attitude to EU, 387–8, 397, 398, 401
   attitude to lobbying/lobbyists and pressure groups, 301–2
   devolution, 196, 200
   election as leader, 268
   ideas, role and power as Labour leader and Prime Minister, 245–50, 272–3, 351, 417
   judges/judiciary under, 160, 163–4, 172–3, 174–5, 178, 180, 181, 182
   local government, 217–18
   party divisions/loyalty, 85, 87, 133, 147, 150, 272–3
   presidential figure? 135, 136–8
   role in Northern Irish settlement, 40
   use of, attitude to, Cabinet, 120–1, 124–7, 132
   use/organisation of the Centre, 125, 126
Blairites, 251

Blue Labour, 251, **278**
Britain
Act of Union 1707, 2
British society/recent decades, 4–14
Constitution, ch. 2
democracy, 415–18; *see also* EU:
    democratic deficit
historical background, 2–4, 17, 19
ideas/values and political culture,
    14–20, **22**
impact of EU: a problem area for
    British politicians, 388–91, 391–7;
    see also EC/EU Postscript 402–4
joins EU, 386, 396
political change in recent decades,
    13–14
public feeling towards EU, 386, 392–3
racial and religious diversity, 4–13
red lines re. EU, 398
relationship with EC/EU, 13–14, 19,
    ch. 10 esp. 386–405
setting of British politics, ch. 1
special; relationship (with US), 387
British National Party (BNP), 254
'Britishness', 14, 19
Brown Gordon, 95, 133, 138, 273,
    301–2, 325, 391
attitude to and measures of
    constitutional reform, 41, 73
bigotgate, 325
election 2010, 325, 330
New Labour/Third Way, 248, 250
party divisions/loyalty/and removal,
    84, 85, 273
use of Cabinet, 120, 124–5
use/organisation of the Centre, 126
Brownites, 251, 273, **278**
Butler Report, 124

Cabinet, 118–27
    Cabinet Government, 118, 124, **154**

Cabinet Government v. Prime
    Ministerial Government in UK,
    128–34
Cabinet Office and Secretariat,
    125–7
committees, 122–3
inner/kitchen, 123, **154**
membership, 119, 129–30
operation, 120–7
role, 119–20
Callaghan, James, 35, 86, 115, 391
Calman Commission, 198–9, 222
Cameron, David, 128
as Conservative leader/prime minister,
    242–3, 270, 325, 327
attitude to and measures of
    constitutional reform, 40, 42, 50,
    73
Cabinet, 120–1, 130
choice of, as leader, 267–8
judges and judiciary under, 183
candidate-centred electioneering, 318,
    370
career politicians, 92, 103, **108**
'catch-all' parties, 238, **278**
centralisation of government, 191–2,
    196, **222**
Charter 88, 40, 73
Charter of Fundamental Rights, 379,
    405
Churchill Winston, 386, 391, 395
civil liberties, 2B esp. 44–54
civil rights, 2B esp. 44–54
civil service, 139–46
    background of higher civil servants,
        143–4
    creation of Next Steps agencies,
        144–6
    role of higher civil servants, 141–6
civil society, 13
class *see* social class

class dealignment, 328, **370**

Clause Four of Labour Party, 244–6, 247

Clegg Nick, 253, 325, 327

coalition government, 342, 343–6

UK Coalition government 2010– , 42, 50, 53, 55, 74, 85, 87, 94–5, 119–20, 122, 132, 134, 193, 201, 208–9, 213–14, 340, 345–6; *see also* EC/EU Postscript

co-decision procedure, 378, **405**

collective responsibility, 146–8

Common Agricultural Policy, **405**

Commonwealth Immigrants Act 1968, **56**

communitarianism, 246, **279**

compassionate conservative, 242, **279**

confederalism, 191

consensus, **21**
   as characteristic of UK political culture, 20

consensus politics, 232, 233–4, **279**

Conservative party, ch. 6; *see also* election campaign 2010, individual leaders and House of Commons/ House of Lords:social composition
   attitude to devolution, 196, 198, 199, 201–2, 208–9
   attitude to EC/EU, 78, 86, 234, 240–1, 242, 386–7, 390, 398–9; *see also* EC/EU Postscript
   attitude to Human Rights Act, 50, 53; *see also* judges: political influence and involvement in political controversy and The Case of the European Court of Human Rights
   attitudes to lobbying/lobbyists/ pressure groups, 300–1
   attitudes and ideas, 239–43
   conference, 265–7

Constitution and constitutional change, 36, 39–40, 70, 74, 94–5
   divisions/loyalty, 78, 85, 86, 87
   electoral success in C19 and C20, 238–9
   electoral setbacks 1997–2005, 240–2
   election 2010, 322, 324–38, 329–32, 338–40
   finance, 257–61, 320
   history, 232–6, 238–43
   leadership: election of leader, 267–8
   leadership: powers of leader, 270–1
   One Nation, 239
   prospects, 243–4
   Thatcherism, 233, 239–40, 242
   1922 Committee, 86

Constitutional Reform Act 2005, 37, 160

constitutions, ch. 2 esp. 25–43
   Blair government and reform, 35–43
   Brown government and reform, 41
   Cameron government and reform, 40, 42
   Major government and reform, 40
   characteristics, 27–9
   codified v. uncodified (written/ unwritten), 27–8
   constitutionalism/constitutional regime, 25
   constitutional reform in UK, 33–43, *see also topics relating to individual changes – e.g.* Human Rights Act, House of Lords
   conventions, 31, 33
   definition/purpose
   flexibility v. inflexibility, 28
   growing interest in constitutional revision, 26–7
   impact of EU membership, 388–9
   parliamentary and presidential constitutions, 29

constitutions (*cont.*)
  perspectives, 34
  protection or rights, 31, 44–55
  separation of powers, 29, **58**, 104
  sources of UK constitution, 31–3
  unitary v. federal, 28–9
  South Africa, 44, 53–4
  UK, 27, 29, 31–43
  US, 24, 25, 28, 54–5, 104
Convention on Modern Liberty, 416,
  419
convergence criteria, 402, **405**
core executive, 112, **154**
COREPER, 379
corporatism, 301, **312**
Council of Europe, 56, 179, **186**
Court of Auditors, 378–9
Court of Justice, 378–9
Council of Ministers (EU), 379, 381,
  384
Countryside Alliance, 297, 303
'Cranborne' money, 262
Criminal Justice and Public Order Act
  1994, **56**

deference (as characteristic of UK
  political culture), 17, 20, **21**
de Gaulle Charles, 386
democracy, ch. 11; *see also* EC/EU
  democracy/democratic deficit
  across world, 410–11
  characteristics/meaning, 410, 413
  democratic deficit, 383–5, 416
  development, 411–12
  direct democracy, 360–8, 412–13
  doubts about British democracy,
    416–18
  illiberal (semi, façade) democracies,
    414, **419**
  indirect, 'representative' democracy,
    412–15

liberal democracy, 158, **187**,
  413–15
  popularity of, 410
  UK, 19, 415–18
  wave of democratisation, 412, **419**
democratic deficit, 383–5, 417
devolution, 13, **21**; *see also ch. 6*
  administrative, 193
  Calman Commission, 198–9
  Conservatives, 196, 198, 199, 201–2,
    208–9
  English Question, 200–2, 417
  Labour, 191–2, 195–6, 197, 200,
    203, 207–8
  legislative, 195, **223**
  meaning/distinction with federalism,
    192
  Northern Ireland, 205–6
  referendum in Northeast 2004, 206,
    207–8
  referendums: (1979), 192, 193, 202,
    365, 366, 367
  referendums: (1997), 192, 193, 196,
    202–3
  regions in England, 207–9
  Scotland, 33, 35, 37, 192–202
  Spain, 219–20
  UK, 191–211
  Wales, 33, 35, 37, 202–4
devolution-plus, 199, **222**
devolutionary federalism (US), 29, **56**,
  220
direct action, 19, 20, **21**
direct democracy, 360–8
  increasing popularity worldwide/
    UK, 360–3
directives, 33, **56,** 379, 380, 389
direct rule (Northern Ireland), **223**
double majority voting, 406
Duncan Smith, Iain, 241, 243, 267,
  271

economic migrants, 6, 7, **21**

elected mayors, 37, 40, 206–9

election campaigns/campaigning, 318–28

  candidate-centred, 318, **370**

  electioneering: past and present, 318–19, 322–3

  money in, 320

  political consultants/advisers, 318, **371**

  television, 319, 320, 322, 323–8, 369

  UK, 321–8

  US, 368–9

elections and voting; *see also* election campaigns, electoral systems and voting behaviour

  (1950), 242

  (1951), 229, 352

  (1966), 352

  (1970), 242

  (1979), 234, 242, 323, 351

  (1983), 324

  (1987), 324, 349

  (1992), 324, 329, 349

  (1997), 36, 86, 240, 320, 329, 332, 354, 355, 359

  (2001), 241, 320, 324, 329, 354, 356, 358

  (2005), 242, 248, 253, 320, 329–32, 359

  (2010), 229–32, 243, 248, 253, 273, 320, 322, 324–8, 330–2, 338–40, 354–5, 359, 360

  importance, procedures and role, 317–18

  new media, 324

  televised debates, 325–8

  UK, 321–8, 329–32, 335–7, 338–40

  USA, 319

elective dictatorship, 115, **154**

Electoral Commission, 37, 259–61, 320, 378

electoral deserts, 340, **370**

electoral systems, 328–47

  criteria of a reformed system, 346

  debate over PR v. FPTP, 341–7

  significance of choice/effects, 328–33, 338

  types, 42, 323–38

  UK, 37, 38, 230, 335–7, 338–40, 346–7

embourgeoisement, 353, **370**

ethnicity, 4, **21**

ethnic diversity/minorities in UK, 4–13, 19, **21**

  representation of ethnic minorities in parliaments, 93–5, 96–7

Etzioni, Amitei, 246

EURATOM, 376

European Coal and Steel Community (ECSC), 376

European Commission, 299, 378, 380, 384–5

European Community/Union, ch. 10; *see also* Postscript *402–4 for discussion of the crisis in the eurozone, 2009–11*

  British attitudes, 234, ch. 10 esp. 386–405 *and* Postscript

  co-decision procedure, 378, **405**

  Committee of the Regions, 379

  Common Agricultural policy (CAP), 378, **405**

  convergence criteria re. single currency, 402, **405**

  creation, 376

  democracy/democratic deficit, 383–5

  development and character, 375–83, 386–8

  double majority voting, 406

  Economic and Social Committee, 379

European Community/Union (*cont.*)
  elections to European Parliament, 37
  enlargement, 377, 380, 393
  eurogroups, 300
  eurozone, 377, **401–5**; *see also*
    Postscript
  federalism, 211, 398–9
  functional cooperation, 376, **405**
  future, 397–401
  Idea, 375, **405**
  impact on English local government,
    218–19
  impact on Parliamentary Sovereignty,
    30–1, 35
  institutions, 378–89; *see also* EC/EU:
    democracy
  integration, 375, 393, 400–1, **405**
  intergovernmentalism, 381, 386–8
  law (primary/secondary and
    directives/regulations), 33, 67, 69,
    379, 380, 388–9
  new democracies, 375, **406**
  policies and policy-making, 382–3
  popular opinion re EU in member
    states, 392–3
  Postscript, 401–5
  pressure groups and, 297–300
  proposed constitution, 401
  protection of rights, 52
  qualified majority voting, 377, **406**
  right of veto, 381, **406**
  Single European Act, 52, 299–300,
    376–7, 378
  Social Chapter, 52, 302, 377, **406–7**
  subsidiarity, 211, 383–4, 399
  super-state, 399, **407**
  supranational authority, 375, **407**
  Treaty of Amsterdam 1997, 377,
    378
  Treaty of Lisbon/Reform Treaty
    2007, 52, 377–9, 399, 401, **403**
  Treaty of Maastricht 1992, 13, **21–2**,
    211, 219, 241, 368, 378, 382,
    386
  Treaty of Nice 2000, 377, 378
  Treaty of Rome 1957, 52, 376, 381,
    389, **407**
  two-speed Europe, 393, 401, **407**
  United States of Europe, 376, **407**
  variable geometry, 400, **406**
  Italy, 275–6, 393–4, 402
  UK attitudes/referendums, 366, 367,
    386, 388–91, 391–7
European Convention on Human
  Rights, 30, 35, 37, 44, 46, 47, 48,
  49, 51, **56–7**, 177–8, 179; *see also*
  Human Rights Act
European Council, 379
European Court of Human Rights
  (Strasbourg court), 35, 46, 56, 87,
  179–84
European Idea, 375, **405**
European Parliament, 99, 299, 377,
  378, 384–5
Europhobic, 240, **279**
eurosceptics/euroscepticism, 87, 240,
  279
Eurozone, 377, **401–5**; *see also* EC/EU
  Postscript
Executive Agencies, 212
executives, ch. 4
  distinction of political and official,
    111
  distribution of power within and
    increase in power of, 90, 116–18,
    133
  meaning, 29, **57, 112**
  parliamentary and presidential
    systems, 114–16
  Holland, 150–2
  UK, 112, 113–14
  USA, 115, 152–3

Factortame case 1991, 31
Far Right, 8, **21**
federalism/federation and federal
    constitutions, 28, **57**, 63, 190, 191
    European Union, 398–9
    UK, 204–11
    US, 220–1
fire brigade campaign, 296, **312**
first ministers and their increasing
    power, 116–18; *see also* Prime
    Minister *and the Dutch case study*
first past the post/simple majority
    system (FPTP), 230, 231, 235, 333,
    335–7, 345, 346; *see also* adversary
    politics
fixed-term Parliaments, 42
focus groups, 318, **370**
Founding Fathers, 44, **57, 104**
franchise, 317, **370**
Fraternity, 412, **419**
Freedom House, 410, **419**
free votes, 87, 92
Freedom of Information Act 2000, 37,
    39
Fulton Report 1968, 143
functional cooperation, 376, **405**

Gaitskell, Hugh, 244–5, 247
globalisation/anti-globalisation protest,
    298, 303, **312**
government beyond the centre, ch. 6
    European dimension, 211, 218–19
    Spain, 219–20
    UK, ch. 6
    US, 220–1
Greens/Green Party, 252, 254, 264,
    344
guillotine, 93, **108**

Hague, William, 201–2, 240–1, 271,
    399

head of state, 113–14
Heath, Edward, 386
homogeneity as characteristic of UK
    political culture, 4, 5, 20,
    21
House of Commons, 74–93; *see also*
    Members of Parliament (MPs)
    functions, 74–81
    legislative role, 74–7, 93
    lobbying of, 294–6
    HM Opposition party, 77–9
    hours, 92–3
    Question Time, 79–80, 127–8, 137,
        140
    reputation/public confidence, 18, 19,
        89–90, 105
    select committees, 76, 80–1, 91
    social composition, 96–102; *see also*
        ethnicity and women
    standing committees, 74, **109**
    target for lobbyists, 294–6
    voting, 84–7, 88, 92
    watchdog role, 77–81
    reform, 90–5
    women *see* women: House of
        Commons
House of Lords, 64–74
    arguments for and against, 68–74
    Conservative and reform, 64–5
    debate, 67, 68, 70, 71
    European legislation, 67, 69, 389
    functions, 66–73
    growing independence/reputation,
        70, 71–2
    judicial work, 37, 65, 66, 67
    Labour and reform, 65–6, 72, 74
    membership, 64–6
    powers, 32, 64–5, 67, 87, 94
    reform, 37, 43, 64–6, 74, 75
    social composition, 71, 73, 96
    target for lobbyists, 295–6

Howard, Michael, 50, 149, 241, 271
Human Rights Act 1998, 37, 46–52,
    418
  anti-terrorist legislation, 51–2
  protection of privacy, 50
hung Parliament, 36, **57**
Hutton, Lord/Hutton Inquiry, 81, **109,
    166**
hybrid groups, 289, **312**

illiberal (semi, façade) democracies,
    414, **419**
immigration, 5–13
  asylum seekers, 6, 7, 8, **21**
  economic migrants, 6, 7, **21**
  EU, 7, 8
  New Commonwealth, 5, 8, **22**
  refugees, 6, **22**
  tensions surrounding, 8–13, 19
independence, 195, **223**
individual ministerial responsibility,
    146, 148–50
initiative, 361
Inner/Kitchen Cabinets, 123, **154**
integration (EU), 375, 400–1, **405**
International Covenant on Civil and
    Political Rights (ICCPR), 44, **57**
intergovernmental (EU) 381, 386–8, **406**
Intergovernmental Conferences (IGCs),
    381, **406**
Intergovernmental Union, 380, **406**
Internet, 324, 369
Iraq *see* War against Iraq
iron triangles, 310, **312**
issue networks, 293, **313**
Italy, 275–6, 393–4, 402

Jenkins Commission on electoral
    system, 37, 334, 340, 342, 343, 346
judges, ch. 5
  appointment, 160–2

as protectors of liberties in UK,
    180–1; *see also* background,
    political influence, below
  background, 167–73
  interpretation of Human Rights Act,
    47, 49
  political influence and involvement in
    political controversy, 177–9
  security of tenure, 162
  European Court on Human Rights,
    179–84
  UK, 159–84
  US, 166–7, 168, 184–5
judicial activism, 167, 175–7, 184, **186,**
    187
Judicial Appointments Commission,
    160, **186**
judicial independence, 158–62, **186**
  in Britain, 159–62
judicial neutrality, 162
judicial restraint, 176, **186**
judicial review, 51–2, **57**, 158, 173–5,
    186–7
judiciaries, ch. 5
  administration of justice in UK: key
    roles, 163–4
  functions, 158
  meaning, **57**
July 7th 2005 and subsequent bomb
    explosions, 13

Kennedy, Charles, 253
Kilmuir Guidelines 1955, 165
Kinnock, Neil, 35, 80, 349

Labour party, ch. 6; *see also* election
    campaign 2010, House of Lords:
    composition, individual leaders; *and
    see also* judges: political influence
    and involvement in political
    controversy

and voting behaviour, 352–6
attitude to EU, 387–8, 399
attitude to House of devolution,
    191–2, 195–6, 197, 200, 203,
    207–8
attitude to judiciary
attitudes to rights, 45, 46–52, 56
attitudes and ideas, 244–51
Blairism, 245–50
Clause Four, 244–6, 247
conference, 266–7
constitutional reform programme of
    Blair government, 35–43
divisions/loyalty, 84, 85, 86, 87
election 2010, 322, 324–8, 329–32,
    338–40
Electoral College, 268–9
finance, 257–61, 320
history, 232–6
leadership: election of leader,
    268–9
leadership: powers and security of
    leader, 272–3
New Labour, 238, 245–51, 255–6
Parliamentary Labour Party (PLP),
    86, 98
Scotland, 190–7
socialism, 236, 244–7, 251
Third Way, 246, 249–50
Leader of HM Opposition, 64
legislative devolution, 195, **223**
legislature, ch. 3; *see also* MPs, House of
    Commons and House of Lords
bicameral/unicameral, 62–4
decline?, 105–7
meaning, 29, **57**, 61
pay and conditions, 102–3
social composition, 93–102
Denmark, 103
UK, 64–74, 96–102
US, 61, 63, 102, 104–7

Liberal Democrats; *see also* Clegg Nick,
    election campaign 2010
attitude to constitutional reform, 36,
    50, 74, 94
centrist attitudes, 238
election 2010, 322, 324–8, 329–32,
    338–40
electoral performance/success of
    recent years, 232, 238, 253, 325,
    326, 352–6
entry into Coalition, 253
finance, 257–61, 320
in/and devolved legislatures, 195,
    197, 199
leadership, 269
television debates 2010, 322, 326–8
Life Peerages Act 1958/Life Peers, 64,
    66, 70, 73
list PR systems, 334–7
local government, 211–19; *see also*
    London government
relations with central government,
    215–18
structure, 217
London government, 37, 206, 366
elected Mayor/Assembly, 37, 40, 206
Lord Chancellor, 37, 38, 160, 162, 163,
    165, 166
Lord Chief Justice, 162, 163–4

Maastricht rebel, 241, **279**
Maastricht treaty 1992, 241, 368, 386
Macmillan, Harold, 64, 79, 133, 391
Major, John
    as party leader and prime minister,
        40, 70, 76, 86, 87, 124, 138, 147,
        150, 159, 174, 178, 211, 234, 271,
        351, 390, 391, 397
marginal constituencies, 321, 352,
    370–1
Marx Karl/Marxian socialism, 236, **279**

mass media, 293, 297, **371**
  and elections, 321–8, 349, 350–1, 369
  televised debates, 325–8
Members of Parliament, 81–90
  background, 96–102
  conditions and pay, 83, 84, 91–3,
    102–3
  duties/loyalties/role, 81–3, 84, 85
  full- and part-timers/career
    politicians, 90, 92, 102–3
  party loyalty and issues of discipline,
    82–3, 84, 85, 92
  relations with lobbyists, 294–6, 303–4
  reputation/public confidence, 18, 19,
    22, 89–90
  significance/effectiveness, 84–93
Miliband David, 251, 269
Miliband Ed, 248–51, 269, 270
ministerial resignations, 151
ministerial responsibility 146–51;
    see also individual and collective
    responsibility
ministers, 139–46
minister–civil servant relationship,
    144–6
mixed economy, 232, **279**
monarchies, 29
  British monarchy, 113–14
Monnet, Jean, 375–6, 384, 386
Muslims and Muslim attitudes in UK,
    10–13, 14
multiculturalism, 8, **22**
multi-level governance, 303, **313**
multiethnicity, 8, **22**

nationalism/national consciousness,
    13–14, 19, 35, 192–3, **223**
New Commonwealth immigration, **22**
new democracies, 375, **406**
New Labour, 238, 245–51, 255–6, **279**,
    354

EU, 387–8
  pressure groups under, 301–3
new social movements, 285, **313**
Next Steps programme, 142, **154**
Nimby groups, 298
Nolan Committee, 304
Northern Ireland, 2–3, 4, 205–6
  Belfast 'Good Friday' Agreement
    1998, 3, 37, 200, 205
  devolved government post-1998, 37,
    205–6
  devolved government pre-1969, 200,
    205
  direct rule, 200
  establishment and history, 2–3, 205
  peace process/power sharing, 37
  troubles, 19, 35

One Nation policies, 239, 247
opinion polls and polling, 325, 329–32
  influence, 331–2
Opposition party/parties 77–9, 228

Parliament *see* House of Commons and
    House of Lords
  parliamentary reform, 41, 90–3
Parliament Acts 1911 and 1949, 32,
    64–5, 67, 87
parliamentary and presidential systems,
    114–16
parliamentary expenses scandal, 18, **22**,
    41, 89
parliamentary privilege, 33
parliamentary sovereignty, 29–31, 35,
    57
Parliamentary Standards Act 2009,
    41, **57**
Parliamentary Voting System and
    Constituencies Act 2011, 42, 94
partisan de-alignment, 226, **280**, 328,
    347, 353–4, **371**

party list electoral system *see* list PR
    systems
photo-opportunities, 319, 323–4, **371**
Plaid Cymru, 254–5, 327
pluralism and pluralist societies, 284,
    287, 307, **313**
policy communities, 293, **313**
policy networks, 293, **313**
political action committees (US), 310,
    313, 368
political consultants/advisers, 318, **371**
political culture, 15–20, **22**
political freedom *see* ch. 2 esp. 44–53
    alleged recent inroads into, 17, 45–6
political parties
    British parties and Europe, 390–401
    adversarial politics in two-party
        system, 231, 233, 235
    comparison with pressure groups, 225
    conferences in Britain, 265–7
    consensus politics/years, 232, 233–4,
        279
    Conservative Party, 238–44
    decline of traditional parties, 226,
        229, 253, 255–7, 273–5
    definition/comparison with pressure
        groups, 225, 226
    finance, 257–63
    functions, 227–8
    Labour Party, 244–51
    leadership in Britain, 267–73
    Left and Right, 236–8
    membership, 252–7
    organisation, 261–73
    party systems, 228–9, 276
    state funding of, 259, 260, 262–3; *see
        also* 'Short' *and* 'Cranborne' money
    support, 226
    third and minor parties, 232, 251–5
    two-party system (England), 228,
        229–35, 253

Italy, 275–6
UK, 229–35, 238–75
US, 228, 230–2, 247, 263–4, 276–7
Political Parties, Elections and
    Referendums Act 2000, 37, 259,
    320
post-materialism, 16–17, **22**
Prescott punch, 324
pressure groups, ch. 8
    access points, 291–2, 299, **312**
    corporatism, 301, **312**
    definition and classifications, 283–91
    direct action, 297, 298
    effectiveness of groups/factors in
        success, 305–6
    eurogroups, 300
    European dimension to group
        activity, 297–300
    fire brigade and background
        campaigns, 296, **312**
    hybrid, 289, **312**
    insider and outsider, 289–91
    iron triangles, 310
    methods/operation, 291–7
    movements, including New Social
        Movements, 285, **313**
    NIMBY groups, 298, **313**
    political parties: comparison, 225,
        226, 285–6, 357–8
    professional lobbyists, use of, 303–4
    protective v. promotional, 287–9,
        290, 291
    single-issue, 283, 289
    think tanks, 286, **314**
    trends/developments under recent
        governments, 283–4, 300–4
    value/contribution to democracy,
        306–8
    Scotland, 308–9
    UK, 283–309
    US, 309–11

primaries (US), 275, 280
prime minister, 127–39
    appointment, 113–14
    appointment of Cabinet, 119, 127,
        129–30
    calling an election, 94–5, 128
    constraints upon, 127, 132–3,
        134
    duties, 127–8
    presidential figure?, 134–9
    prime ministerial v. cabinet
        government, 128–34, **154**
    spatial leadership, 136, **154–5**
    US president comparison, 137–8
pro-European, 240, **279**, 390
Pro-Life Alliance in Britain, 251–2,
    280, 286
proportional representation, 38, 229,
    275, **280**
    arguments surrounding, 341–7
    effects, 96, 275, 335–7, 338, 341–7
    types, 333–8
    use in UK, 37, 38
pseudo-events, 319, **371**
public opinion, 15, **22**

Qualified Majority Voting (QMV), 377,
    406
quangocracy, 203, **223**
quangos, 35, **57**, 212–14, 203
Coalition approach to, 213–14
Executive Agencies, 212
Question Time, 127–8, 137, 140

recall (UK), 42, **58**
recall (US), **58, 161,** 361
red lines (EU), 398, 401, **406**
referendums, 360–8
    arguments surrounding, 364–6
    growing use, 360–3
    timing and status, 363–4

France, 367–8
UK, 37, 42, 192, 193, 196, 202–3,
    206, 363, 366–7, 386
refugees, 6, **22**
regional government, 207–9; *see also*
    devolution and federalism
    UK, 207–9
regulations (EU), 33, **58**, 379, 380, 389
religion, 10–13
republics, 29
right of veto (EU), 381, **406**
rights and their protection, ch. 2 esp.
    44–55
    bills of rights, 44
    definitions 45
    South Africa, 53–4
    UK, 31, 44–53
    US, 44, 54–5
Roma peoples, 52, **58**
Royal Prerogative/prerogative powers
    of the Crown, 32–3, 41
Rousseau, Jean-Jacques, 29, **58**
rule of law, 17, 19, **22**

Salmond Alex, 195, 197, 198
Schuman Declaration, 376
Scotland, 2, 4, 192–202; *see also*
    devolution: referendums
    Act 1998, 37, 192, 194
    Act of Union 1707, 2, 195
    Calman Commission, 198–9
    devolved government and its merits/
        demerits, 37, 194–202
    electoral systems, 37, 195–6
    Executive/Scottish Government/
        First Minister, 194, 196–200
    growing national consciousness, 35,
        192–5, 196
    history, 2, 192–5
    independence, 195
    Parliament, 2, 13, 194–5

Scottish National Party (SNP), 4, 195, 196–8, 254–5, 327
Second and Third Pillars of the Maastricht Treaty, 382, **406**
second chambers, 75; *see also* bicameralism 62–4 and House of Lords
Section 28, 309, **313**
segregation (US), 184, **187**
separation of powers, 29, **58,** 104
September 11th 2001 attack on Twin Towers (New York), 12, 387, **415**
sequestration, 170, **187**
'Short' money, 77, **109,** 262, **280**
Single European Act 1986, 376–7
single-issue groups, 283, 289, **313**
Single Transferable Vote (STV), 334–7
Sinn Fein, 205
Smith, John, 35
Social Chapter, 302, 377, **406–7**
social class, 4, **22–3**
   voting, 348, 349, 352–6, 370
socialism, 236, 244–7, 251, **280**
Socialist Labour Party, 254
soundbites, 319, **371**
Souter referendum, 309, **314**
sovereignty, 190, **223**
   Parliamentary, 29, 30–1
   popular/of the people, 29
spatial leadership, 136, **154–5**
special relationship, 387, **407**
spin and spin doctors, 319, **371**
stakeholder society, 246, 301
statutory instruments, 68, **109**
subsidiarity (EU), 211, **223**, 383–4, 399
super-state (EU), 399, **407**
Supplementary Vote (SV), 334–7
Supreme Court (UK) 37, **58**, 160, 162
Supreme Court (US), 184–5, 187
supranational authority (EU), 375, **407**

tactical voting, 339–40, **371**
target seats *see* marginal constituencies
terrorism/combating terrorism, 13, 17
   anti-terrorist legislation, 51–2, 76
Thatcher, Margaret and Thatcher years, 159, 191, 215–17, 302, 323, 324, 390
   as prime minister, 80, 131, 136, 137, 138, 145, 234, 271, 301, 351, 386–7, 391, 397
   use of Cabinet, 121
Thatcherism, 233, **280**
think tanks, 286, **314**
third and minor parties, 251–5, 352
Third Way, 246, 249–50, **280**
trades unions/Trades Union Congress (TUC), 247, 287–8, 302, 305, 312
Treaty of Rome 1957, 52, 376, 381, 389, **407**
triangulation, 250, **280**
trust in government and politicians, 18–19, 22
turnout in elections, 356–60
   explanations and theories, 356–9
   international comparisons, 356–8
   UK, 358–60
two-party system (England), 228, 229–35, 253
two-speed Europe, 393, 400–1, **407**

ultra vires, 175, **187**
unicameralism, 62, 68–9, **109**
unitary systems, 190, 191
United Kingdom Independence Party (UKIP), 254
United States of Europe, 376, **405**
usual channels, 79, **109**

variable geometry, 400, **407**
vote of confidence, 115, **155**

voting behaviour, 347–56; *see also*
    embourgeoisement
  compulsory voting, 318, 356
  determinants, 347–52
  impact of campaign, 321–2, 349
  impact of media, 350–1
  social class, 348, 349, 352–6, 370
  trends, 347–52
  turnout, 356–60
  UK, 352–6

Wales, 2, 4, 202–4; *see also* devolution:
    referendums
  Act 1998, 37, 192, 203
  Act of Union 1535, 2
  devolved government, 39, 203–4
  Government of Wales Act 2006, 203
  growing national consciousness, 35,
    202–4
  National Assembly, 13, 40
  Plaid Cymru, 4

Welsh Assembly Government,
    203–4
walkabouts, 319, 324, **371**
war against Iraq 2003, 85, 87, 112,
    132, 133, 135, 137, 248, 253, 272,
    351, 387, 388
War Powers Act 1973 (US), 107, **109**
Warren Earl, 184, **187**
wave of democratisation, 412, **419**
Westland Affair 1986, 125, **155**
West Lothian (English) question, 43,
    200–2
whipping/whips, 86–92, **109**
  Chief Whip, 119
Wilson, Harold, 147, 391
women
  House of Commons, 98–102, 340
  national parliaments worldwide,
    93–102
  Scottish Parliament, 196
World Forum on Democracy, 410, **419**